CONQUEST and REDEMPTION

A History of Jewish Assets from the Holocaust

CONQUEST and REDEMPTION

Gregg J. Rickman

Transaction Publishers
New Brunswick (U.S.A.) and London (U.K.)

This book is printed on acid-free paper that meets the American National Standard for Permanence of Paper for Printed Library Materials.

Library of Congress Catalog Number: 2006040468
ISBN: 0-7658-0346-1
978-0-7658-0346-7
Printed in the United States of America

Library of Congress Cataloging-in-Publication Data

Rickman, Gregg J.
Conquest and redemption : a history of Jewish assets from the Holocaust / by Gregg Rickman.
p. cm.
Includes bibliographical references and index.
ISBN 0-7658-0346-1 (alk. paper)
1. Holocaust, Jewish (1939-1945)—Economic aspects. 2. Jewish property—Europe—History—20th century. 3. Jews—Europe—Claims—History—20th century. 4. World War, 1939-1945—Claims—Europe. 5. World War, 1939-1945—Confiscations and contributions—Europe. I. Title.

D804.7.E26R53 2006
940.53'18144—dc22 2006040468

To Estelle Sapir.
Her sacrifice and endurance trumped evil
and indifference and ensured justice.

Contents

Acknowledgments

I would like to begin by thanking Professor Haim Shaked of the University of Miami for his gracious help and deep interest in helping me pursue this topic as a book. From his material to personal and professional support and advice throughout the process, I owe a great debt of which I could never repay. I want to thank Professor Vendulka Kubalkova for her intellectual advice and support, throughout the time of this effort, which included illness as well as demanding professional duties. I also want to thank Professor Jaime Suchliki for his advice and support in serving as an advisor on my dissertation. I cannot forget to thank Mitch Dabach, Professor Shaked's assistant at the Sue and Leonard Miller Center for Judaic Studies for working diligently to keep tabs on my photocopied chapters as they were mailed down, and for making sure they made their way to the appropriate Professor for review. Finally, I cannot leave out a thanks to all above for their help in navigating my way through the procedures necessary to restart my quest for the Ph.D. after so many years out of the program at the University of Miami. It has all been well worth the effort and I thank them with all my heart.

If it were not for Phil Bechtel, a colleague and friend from the office of former Senator Alfonse M. D'Amato, I would not have made the decision to restart my pursuit of my Ph.D. Seeking Phil's advice on whether to go to law school or not, he strongly advised me to finish my degree and forget about law school. It was not worth my effort, he counseled. I am grateful for his wise instruction.

With regard to sources, above all, I must thank Abby L. Gilbert of the United States Treasury Department for her deep and abiding interest in helping me gain access to numerous documents from the bowels of the Treasury Department vaults. She was an invaluable resource and I cannot thank her enough.

There were others who provided invaluable resources, advice, and to them I am equally grateful. Among these great resources in the Washington, DC area were: Miriam Kleinman, a former colleague and good friend; Greg Bradsher, a dedicated historian and friend who is the Chief Archivist at the National Archives in Holocaust-era records; Willi Korte, the world-renown looted art provenance investigator who directed me to a number of issues of which I had not been aware; Michael Hausfeld, the attorney who both understood and practiced justice on a grand scale; Barbara Pratt, Mike's assistant who graciously helped me with access to survivors and their claims files in a number of legal cases; Michael H. Gray, of the Voice of America Library who helped me obtain much needed and difficult to find resources; Doug Bloomfield, who helped me understand a number of issues better and has fought, and continues to do so, the good fight to ensure survivors receive justice; Michael Bradfield, Paul Volcker's long-time aide, who continues to advocate so strongly on their behalf and who also provided much needed information; Martin Mendelsohn, a friend who continues to push for the truth for survivors, who provided deeper insight into the complicated negotiations surrounding the various efforts; Maureen Walsh, of the Commission on Security and Cooperation in Europe, a U.S. Congressionally sponsored Commission dedicated to secure human rights for all, including survivors; and Stuart Eizenstat, with whom I am proud to have worked on this issue since its inception in the mid-1990s and who dedicated himself for the long-term and has been as strong a leader on restitution as any other.

In New York as well, there were so many to thank, including: Elan Steinberg, formerly of the World Jewish Congress, who fought long and hard, and with whom, I might have shared differences as to approach, but certainly not questions as to his dedication to the plight of survivors and of the establishment of justice; Irwin Nack, who served as an important member of the Office of Holocaust Claims in the New York State Banking Department and provided me with advice and resources on a variety of issues; Ted Poretz, of the Judah Gribetz's Special Master's Office for the Swiss Banks' Settlement for resources; David Javdan, now the General Counsel of the Small Business Administration and former attorney in the law firm of, Strook, Strook, & Lavan, who along with James Shiffrin supplied me with vital resources on the Austrian banks case; and Harriet Tamen, an attorney who provided me with much needed resources on the French Railways case.

In Ohio, I cannot forget the help of Professor Gary Zola and Ina Remus, Director and Project Historian respectively, of the Jacob Rader Center of the American Jewish Archives, Cincinnati, for help as well with much needed resources.

In Israel, I must thank Bobby Brown, of the World Jewish Congress in Jerusalem, and David Akov, of the Israeli Foreign Ministry, for their help while in Israel finding important documents and setting up meetings with experts and practitioners in the restitution field.

From Austria, Hannah M. Lessing, Secretary General, National Fund of the Republic of Austria for Victims of National Socialism was very helpful in gaining further understanding a number of Austrian restitution issues.

There were a number of Professors from all over the United States and Europe that helped with resources and advice. Among them were: Professor Nicholas Onuf, Florida International University, Miami, Florida; Professor Karl Martin Born of the University of Plymouth, United Kingdom; Professor Laurent Leduc, of the University of Toronto, Canada; Professor John Torpey, of the University of British Columbia, Canada; Professor Samantha Power of Harvard University, Massachusetts; Professor Bruce Green of Cardozo Law School, in New York; Michael Bazyler of Whittier Law School, Costa Mesa, California; and Professor Gerald Feldman, of The University of California at Berkeley.

Finally, there were so many Holocaust survivors and claimants that I interviewed. Some had played vital roles in restitution, lending their names and surviving strength to ensuring that those who did not have, received their just compensation. Among those with whom I spoke, and I might add, some of whom did not survive this work, were the following: Marta Druckerova Cornell, New York, New York; Susana David, Buenos Aires, Argentina; Licco Max Haim, Sao Paulo, Brazil; Sybilla Katz-Goldstein, New York, New York; Judith T. Karmi, Buffalo, New York; Dr. Thomas Lys, Chicago, Illinois; Mina Parsant, Rockville, Maryland; Grace Graupe Pillard, New York, New York; Estelle Sapir, New York, New York; Marie Von Saher, Connecticut; Zikmund Schmerler, Montreal, Canada; Martha Saraffian, New York, New York; Martin Stern, London, UK/Tel Aviv, Israel; John C.L. Szekeres, New York, New York; Susan Unger, New York, New York; Dr. Jacqueline Waldman, Baltimore, Maryland; Lilian Politzer-Weingast, New York, New York; and Helen Weiss, New York, New York. Their help and contribution to this work was invaluable and it was an honor to have helped tell their stories.

Introduction

George Melloan, writing in the *Wall Street Journal* explained that "Have-nots for centuries have assaulted the haves. The Assyrians conquered Israel; Alexander, Persia; the barbarian Visigoths, Rome, etc. At a basic level, most military aggression has been organized theft."[1] While the root of the Holocaust is the wholesale slaughter of the Jews of Europe by the Nazi have-nots, the institutionalized robbery of their perceived targets, the Jewish haves, foretold the slaughter and the Second World War itself. For what was the war about if not the aggrandizement of Germany at the expense of all of its victims?

The Nazis not only sought to murder the Jews but they sought take everything from them, their families, their possessions, and even their names. They sought to replace the Jews and erase their very existence. Like their murder then, the robbery of the Jews was an organized, institutionalized effort that produced the largest robbery in history.

The key to understanding the Holocaust in this sense lies in this structural composition and motivation. How did the German people come to believe that it was permissible to isolate, outlaw, rob and then murder the Jews? While ideology was the guiding principle, how that ideology was formed is important to understand. *How*, not *why,* the elimination of the Jews came to be an ideological concept and *how* that concept was used to such violent ends is an important concept to understand in order to gain further insight into the Holocaust.

The organized robbery of the Jews created the system facilitating their slaughter. Jews were isolated, robbed, and left homeless, fittingly viewed as parasites in the Nazis' eyes. Once destitute, what else could the Nazis do but murder them? The robbery was part of the plan, this much is clear.

How this robbery was carried out can be explained through an exploration of the Nazis' creation of a new religion of which the suppression of Judaism and the Jews was the goal. In doing so, the Nazis deligitimized the Jews as a people, placing themselves as superior to them, collectively more deserving of history, recognition, and lasting acceptance. The Nazis created a "holy" and religious cause to achieve this supremacy which was expressed through a complex structure of religious rules, practices, and institutions.

It was because, as Hitler explained, the Jews were part of a religion that included the notion of "chosenness," that he felt the Nazis were deprived—as being the have-nots. As such, Judaism stood apart from the others, by their own scriptures, as they were singled out by God. In this sense, the Nazis sought to supplant the Jews, seeking that mantle of chosenness for themselves, again expressing jealousy over being the have-nots.

Furthering this concept, the Nazis too, in their propaganda, were victimized, always held as separate from the Jews who were viciously hovering and subjugating the Germans—even as the Jews were being annihilated in death camps across Europe, the Nazis spread this belief. The Nazis, then, were to have no equal, no superior.

Moreover, the Germans' destiny was preordained. They would now be the inheritors of the "new covenant." Under their supreme leader, they were now "chosen" to replace the Jews. In replacing the Jews then, the Nazis felt justified, and even worthy, of all that the Jews possessed. Once perceiving themselves to be emasculated, in the Nazis' way of thinking, killing the Jews was only natural and proper.

With the robbery and the murder of the Jews underway, the Nazis pursued a war they ultimately could not win, entangling themselves in a struggle of overwhelming proportion. Upon the loss of the war and the eventual Allied occupation of Germany, an effort was undertaken to return that which was taken from the Jews.

The exigencies of a post-World War II world took precedence over restitution. Rebuilding Germany and creating a bulwark against a triumphant Soviet Union, sitting astride its conquest of Eastern Europe, posed problems far greater for the now divided Allies and pushed the idea of returning pilfered material and property to the back burner. If true restitution was made, the Allies feared, Germany would never be able to reemerge from the ashes of the Second World War.

Because of the emergence of the Cold War, mirroring the chilly relations between the former Allies, the status of restitution to ransacked people was likewise cold and unmoving. For the next half-century, survivors dependent upon the meager returns of their families were denied justice by both circumstance and willful obfuscation by those holding their assets.

With the emergence of Mikhail Gorbachev as the leader of the Soviet Union in 1985, the chill began to lift. By 1990, he was gone and so was the Soviet empire. With the end of the Cold War came the reemergence of the unfinished business of the Second World War, restitution to its victims. As the old structures of the past fell, survivors who had long written off their lost world and all that was taken from them, were at last presented with a second chance. The World Jewish Congress and a legion of politicians, other Jewish organizations, researchers, and lawyers pursued a world-wide program for restitution that changed the dynamics of this struggle. Where once survivors of the Holocaust were obliged to prove what was taken from them, now those that took it from them were forced to prove that they had, in fact, not kept this stolen property from others. The tables were turned. Now banks, insurance companies, art museums, and entire countries were put on notice that the onus was on them to return the assets that they had held for so long.

This is a story about conquest and redemption. It explains *how* the Nazis stole the possessions of the Jews, obtained the cooperation of cooperative institutions across Europe, which participated in these crimes of convenience, taking and keeping these possessions, and *how* those institutions were brought to justice over fifty years later for their continued retention of their ill-gotten gains from the Holocaust and its true victims.

This history will explain *how* the robbery was accomplished, tracked, stalled, and then finally reversed. It also explains clearly *how* the robbery was inextricably connected to the murder of the Jews. The robbery was an essential piece of the story of the Holocaust, and a clear warning of worse to come. This is a vast and complicated story involving billions of dollars in property and lost wealth. The Holocaust is a memory of unequalled pain and suffering, but the story of the return of stolen goods to the survivors is ultimately one of a partial victory for the long-aggrieved.

This story then is called of *Conquest and Redemption: A History of Jewish Assets from the Holocaust.*

Note

1. George Melloan, "Global View: There Are Always Barbarians at the Gates," *Wall Street Journal*, December 13, 2005.

1

Patterns of Plunder

"It is not easy to discover how it concerns him that gathers the produce, or receives the rent of an estate, to know through what families the land has passed, who is registered in the Conqueror's survey as its possessor, how often it has been forfeited by treason, or how often sold by prodigality. The power or wealth of the present inhabitants of a country cannot be much increased by an inquiry after the names of those barbarians who destroyed one another twenty centuries ago, in contests for the shelter of woods or convenience of pasturage. Yet we see no man can be at rest in the enjoyment of a new purchase till he has learned the history of his grounds from the ancient inhabitants of the parish, and that no nation omits to record the actions of their ancestors, however bloody, savage, and rapacious."[1]—Samuel Johnson

"In 1941," explained Sybilla Katz-Goldstein of New York, "members of the Einsatzstab Reichsleiter Rosenberg (ERR) along with officers of the Weirmarcht [sic] marched into our home." Mrs. Katz continued, "My family stood frozen as we watched Nazi officers acquire our property by pointing to their selections. Art objects, furnishings, and jewelry were subsequently removed from our home."[2] In an operation that was repeated thousands of times throughout the Holocaust, Europe's Jews, like the Katzes, were plundered. In a robbery of unimagined proportions, Nazi officers, their political leaders, allies, simple bystanders, and even the Western Allies, wittingly or unwittingly, participated in the plunder and despoilment of an entire people. On a continent scattered with resplendent riches, open to their whim, the Nazis took what they wanted through legal falsehoods, threats, and outright seizure.

The explanation of *how* the Jews came to be plundered in the context of the Holocaust is a subject that concerns itself as much with the motivations of the war as it does human nature itself. It is therefore important to understand that the plunder of the Jews was the beginning of the Holocaust. It is for this reason that an examination of the plunder of Europe's Jews, and the patterns in which this was done, is a necessity in understanding the complexities, depth, and breadth of the problems behind the restitution of Jewish property.

* * *

While hatred of Jews is by no means a new phenomenon, the campaign of thievery carried out upon them in such an organized and determined fashion, by such an implacable enemy, is something wholly different. Hannah Arendt, in her seminal work *Antisemitism*, explained the Jews' plight on the eve of the Holocaust this way. "Antisemitism reached its climax when Jews had similarly lost their public function and their influence, and were left with nothing but their wealth."[3] With only their wealth remaining then, the Nazis took that too, thus leaving the Jews with nothing. With no role to play in Germany or in Europe, the Jews were, according to Nazi rules, parasites that should be, and later would be, eliminated. Additionally, as the true story has emerged over the last decade, the Jews were robbed in a systematic and programmed manner. The Nazis then, acted not only out of hatred for Jews, but out of jealousy as well. As an outcome of the rules the Nazis first established, if not also being the ultimate immoral agents of Germany, they first created the conditions for the robbery, then the murder of the Jews of Europe.

A Prime Target for Conquest

While nothing in this work shall imply or suggest that economic factors were the leading or sole cause for the Holocaust, it is impossible to consider the Holocaust in any context as a singularly critical event of the twentieth century and of history itself, without examining how economic motivations went hand-in-hand with genocide. Through an examination of the patterns, procedures, and practices of the Nazis' and their accomplices' employed in their drive for, and expropriation of, Jewish wealth, a better understanding of this phenomenon can be gained.

While today the world is better educated as to the more commonly known statistics of the Holocaust, six million Jews dead, five million non-Jews also exterminated, the vast numbers and types of assets taken from the Jewish people in thousands of raids on homes like the Katzes above, as well as the surrender, abandonment, and outright confiscation of the assets of the Jewish people during the Holocaust, is less well-known or, for that matter, understood.

Over the past several decades, historians have differed over the importance the wealth of the Jews played in the motivation for the Nazis' drive for the extermination of this group. Many have argued back and forth, and vehemently, over the exact motivation of the Nazis. Many feel that it is wrong to merely attribute economic motivations to this, or any other, genocidal act; for this model then, they argue, fails to hold up to scrutiny when other acts of genocide are considered. Yet, the genocide perpetrated upon the Jews of Europe by the Nazis, it can be argued, was motivated by several factors, economics among them.

Arthur Ruppin, a professor of Jewish Sociology at Hebrew University in Jerusalem, writing in 1939, suggested that "[t]he Jews who had settled in France, Belgium, and England before 1880, descendants of Sephardic or German Jews, were almost exclusively occupied in banking, wholesale trade, or the independent professions, and belonged to the upper social strata of the population."[4] This concentration of occupational specificity was also highlighted during the war by intelligence analysts observing the Jews' plight in Europe. Analysts from Office of Strategic Services wrote of the role of Jews in Austria, describing them as "significant participants in the establishment and development of many industries ... [having] some connection with about 25 percent of the total industrial production of the country."[5] Ruppin asserted that Jews represented 67.6 percent of the furriers there, 39.8 percent of the jewelers, 31 percent of the watchmakers, 31.1 percent of the dentists, and 21.5 percent of the opticians.[6] In Poland in 1931, 36.6 percent of those in the trade and insurance businesses and 42.2 percent of those in the industry and handicrafts businesses, were Jews, according to Ruppin. In Germany, 52.5 percent of the population occupied in the communications and transport fields were Jewish.[7]

These numbers, as well as recent work by economic historians, point to, at the very least, to the Jews' clear societal association with several specific trades across Europe. Their disproportional representation within those trades provides some suggestion as to their collective vulnerabilities, especially due to their more well-off economic positions within the pervasive anti-Semitic atmosphere of the time. If this over-representation points to anything, it is that Jews were terribly exposed, both economically and by connection, socially. While the truism remains that "the only thing necessary for anti-Semitism to flourish, is anti-Semites," these facts cannot be overlooked.

"The demonstrable over-representation of Jews in the economic elites of many continental European countries," wrote W.D. Rubinstein, "was itself a potent force for creating and engendering anti-Semitism, arguably the most important single force which persisted over the generations."[8] Rubinstein's work strongly suggests the idea that Jews, in concentrating so heavily and disproportionately in certain commercial/financial sectors of their countries, drew attention to themselves, and did so to their clear disadvantage. The evidence is obvious that the presence of Jews in Europe in the upper-class trades, professions, and services, did, in fact, contribute to their social position within their countries of residence and, by association, their political and social exclusivity. As such, Jewish populations in the countries occupied by the Nazis, and administered either directly or indirectly by proxy forces, were a prime and unavoidable target for robbery for more than simply ideological or racial reasons. The mere presence of Jews within the upper economic strata of nearly every nation of their habitation provided them wealth, but also vulnerability.

How Much Was Lost

This wealth, in economic terms, has been hard to quantify, but attempts have been made to do so. In 1944, Siegfried Moses, a member of the Association of Central European Immigrants in Palestine, did not provide a clear number, but suggested that "any restitution which assumes the form of money can satisfy only a minute fraction of the misfortune and unhappiness brought upon the Jewish people by Nazi Germany.... For the Jewish people needs reparations because a very large part of the economic assets of the Jews have been destroyed..."[9] Moses was already writing in 1943 of the international legal bases upon which the Jewish people could eventually make claims against a defeated Germany.[10]

Nehemiah Robinson, of the World Jewish Congress writing a year after this, put a number to the amount of the robbery. He suggested a sum of $8.2 to $8.6 billion for losses of the Jewish people during the Holocaust.[11] In 1962, Robinson revised his estimate, raising the amount of Jewish material losses to $12 billion.[12]

In 1945, the American Federation of Jews from Central Europe, in New York, tabulated some of these losses in Germany alone. For 420 Jewish congregations in Germany alone. Nathan Stein, the group's Chairman, surmised the loss of slightly over $70 million in communal assets, as opposed to individual assets, covering the assets of some 70 percent of the total Jewish population in Germany in 1933.[13]

Louis Lipsky, Chairman of the Executive Committee of the American Jewish Conference, writing to Secretary of State James F. Byrnes two years later in February 1946, suggested a number similar to Robinson's:

> Germany and her associates murdered some six million Jews, destroyed all Jewish communal institutions wherever their authority extended, stole all the treasures of Jewish art and learning and seized all Jewish property, public and private, on which they could lay their hands. It has been estimated that the monetary value of the material losses thus inflicted upon the Jewish people may amount to over eight billion. The mass murders, the human suffering, the annihilations of spiritual, intellectual and creative forces are probably without parallel in the history of mankind.[14]

In 1998, following the conclusion of the lawsuits against the Swiss banks, and after three years' of archival study worldwide, possibly due to increased interest and academic access, more precise and detailed studies were produced. Once again, the World Jewish Congress produced a study, this one by Sidney Jay Zabludoff, a former CIA and FinCen intelligence analyst, claiming Jewish losses amounted to between $9 to $14 billion in twenty countries the Nazis occupied in Europe.[15]

Finally, in a methodical, internationally researched study for the Independent Committee of Eminent Persons (hereafter known as the Volcker Commission) by former Federal Reserve economist Helen Junz, a total of $12.9 billion in Jewish material losses was concluded for only six target countries.[16] This study was based on newly accessed tax, probate, property, and other records in Europe was undertaken to aid the Volcker Commission as it searched for Jewish assets in Swiss banks.[17]

What Was Lost

Louis Lipsky provided an apt description of what the Jewish community in Europe lost during the Holocaust. From communal to personal property, the Nazis left little to chance. The historian Jeanette Greenfield, while mitigating Nazi plunder in light of other historical plunders, nevertheless depicted the program as "only exceptional in its scale, its ruthlessness, its planning, and even its recording."[18] Yet, there was much more to the Nazi plunder than Greenfield's summary. The Nazis undertook a methodical effort to eradicate the Jewish presence completely, having accomplished it to such a great extent that by October 1943, Heinrich Himmler, speaking to SS officers in Posen could declare plainly, "We have taken away the riches that they had...."[19]

Adolf Hitler had first expressed the idea of robbing the Jews as a socio-economic "necessity," in his terminology, in a letter described as that which launched his political career in 1919. Replying to Adolf Gemlich, a German constituent writing to the Reichswehr News and Enlightenment Department in Munich, Hitler wrote, "Everything men strive after as a higher goal, be it religion, socialism, democracy, is to the Jew only means to an end, the way to satisfy his lust for gold and domination." The logical conclusion of this Hitler wrote, "an antisemitism [sic] based on purely emotional grounds will find its ultimate expression in the form of the pogrom. An antisemitism based on reason, however, must lead to systematic legal combating and elimination of the privileges of the Jews, that which distinguishes the Jews from the other aliens who live among us (an Aliens Law). The ultimate objective must, however, be the irrevocable removal of the Jews in general."[20] From this sentiment came the very laws enforced by Nazi officials like Himmler that led to both the robbery and murder of the Jews of Europe.

When it came to robbing the Jews, very little was missed. Jewish bank accounts,[21] insurance policies, securities, jewelry,[22] property—personal and landed, businesses, pensions, pensions, art, wine, book, manuscript, and stamp collections, were all catalogued,[23] accounted for, and redistributed. Clothes, shoes, hats, household and business goods, were even utilized for resale, state use, or simply collected for museum exhibits, all dedicated to an extinct culture according to Nazi assertive belief.[24] Even dental gold from concentration camp inmates was smelted and reused for the SS Medical Service. So much was delivered, that there was a five-year back-up supply and an order by SS Brigadier General Frank put a halt to the deliveries and a redirection of the gold flow in October 1942.[25] In short, all that was once Jewish was to become German. In Nazi idealist assertions, Jewish property, like the people themselves were to be, was to be superseded—taken over by the Germans.

Property as a Rule

Kurt Burch has written on the concept of property as a form of rule. As such, it had become commonly agreed on historically that property, as such, was an individual "sovereign" right based on an individual's assertion—those such as "I am entitled to own," or "I own," a particular piece of property.[26] For the Nazis, as the Jews were inherently not due the rights entitled to them as human beings, therefore the loss of the right to hold property was a natural outgrowth of this assertion and by further extension, it was the Nazis' "sovereign" right to restrict the Jews from holding property.[27]

Furthermore, Burch argues, property itself is a necessity for freedom and survival.[28] With the Nazis taking all that was Jewish, with the goal of total dehumanization and eventual elimination in mind, it was only natural that their property would go the way of their names, as was the case in their being reduced to mere numbers in the concentration camps.

To understand the extent of the plunder, an explanation of the six types of plunder and the methods by which it was done must be explained.

Plunder by Decree

In the first of six patterns of the Nazi plunder of the Jewish people, *Plunder by Decree* was the most effective and was issued on a wide expanse, first in Germany and then across Europe by Germans and their proxies in all places; and was done in order to direct the de-emancipation of the Jews, separate them from the Aryan people, and eliminate them as a race. The Nazis first robbed, then killed, six million European Jews. In this manner, Hitler ensured the fulfillment of his promise and prophesies toward the elimination of the Jews.

It was in this setting then, that Hitler sat atop the Nazi government and religion, issuing decrees—assuming a false legality, as he so stressed in his letter to Gemlich, that would first limit, then isolate, then eliminate the Jews as an obstacle to German salvation that he and the Nazis had so stridently advocated.

Equally important was the fact that Nazi ideology was aided by simple greed, for as Christopher Simpson wrote, "Among the Nazis' first acts in power...were the introduction of incentives to encourage persecution of Jews. New Aryanization laws created a profitable business for banks, corporations, and merchants willing to enforce Nazi racial preferences."[29] At first the necessity was lacking. But as Ian Kershaw has written regarding the practice, "Under the growing pressure of the armaments economy, however, 'big business' had a direct interest in the acquisition of Jewish capital and keenly promoted the 'aryanization' of Jewish concerns in late 1937 and 1938."[30] The leading agents of big business, it will be shown below, abused Jews not only through the misappropriation of their property, but also by use of their forced labor. These industries helped bring about Hitler's promise of the "irrevocable removal of the Jews." Accomplished first through a series of decrees in Germany, and later in Europe as a whole, Hitler's war against the Jews began.

These decrees centered on the gradual disenfranchisement of the Jewish people so that certain sectors of the economy would not be damaged, at so early a time in the world-wide Depression. As Hjalmar Schacht, Nazi Economics Minister, declared in 1935, "...the solutions to these problems must be brought about under State leadership, and cannot be left to unregulated individual actions, which mean a disturbing influence on the rational economy..."[31]

At first though, only Jewish professionals, not industrialists, were banned. Beginning with a series of decrees solidifying his rule after the Reichstag fire, the Nazis issued the *Law Regarding the Admission to the Bar* of April 7, 1933, barring Jewish attorneys from practicing law.[32] Four days later, Jewish employment in the Civil Service was banned with the *First Regulation for Administration for the Law for the Restoration of the Professional Civil Service* of April 11, 1933. "If a civil servant was not already a civil servant on August 1, 1914, he must prove that he is of Aryan descent ... " read the decree. Aryan descent, was described as:

> A person is to be regarded as non-Aryan, who is descended from non-Aryans, especially Jewish parents or grandparents. This holds true even if only one parent or grandparent is of non-Aryan descent. This premise especially obtains if one parent or grandparent was of Jewish faith.[33]

Non-Aryans, then, were excluded from the Civil Service. On June 30, 1933, Jews, as non-Aryans, were excluded from serving as Reich officials.[34]

Exclusionary decrees such as the *Law Against Overcrowding of German Schools and Higher Institutions* showed that the decrees were not limited to the professions. On April 25, Jewish Students were limited proportionately to the number of Aryan students in German schools.[35]

Exclusionary decrees excluding Jews form the public life of the Third Reich were based on blood or ancestry. At this point in the formative evolution of Nazi policy, a regulative standard was not yet arranged, but the genesis of such a policy is seen in *The Homestead Law*, of September 29, 1933. Trying to ensure the "well-spring of the German people by securing the German tradition of ancestral rights," the decree was issued banning Jews from the peasantry. This restriction was based on the possession of "German blood," meaning ancestry, dating back to January 1800.[36]

What eluded Nazi theorists during the course of these early decrees was the precise definition of "Jewishness." That definition, for the purposes of the

Nazis, had to move beyond the vague and unquantifiable idea of blood. On September 15, 1935, in the beginning volleys of the Nuremberg Laws, the concept of Reich citizenship became defined as a citizen is only that "person who belongs to the protective union of the German Reich ... "[37]

On the same day, the decree, *Concerning the Protection of Blood and Honor* was issued prohibiting the marriage of Germans and non-Aryans, as well as sexual relations between the two.[38] The status of German Jews became ever more precarious as the demarcation between Jews and "Aryans" became further refined legally.

The uniform definition of "Jewishness," was finally decreed in the *First Regulation Under the Reich Citizenship Law* of November 14, 1935. In this decree, the definition of being a Jew was clearly delineated for the first time, as a "A Jew is anyone who is descended from at least three grandparents who were racially full Jews," or "A Jew is also one who is descended from two full-Jewish grandparents..."[39]

As such, Jews were stripped of their citizenship. They now could not vote or occupy public office. Jewish officials were to be retired as of December 31, 1935. Two years before, as a foreshadowing of the fate of German Jews, on July 14, 1933, German Jews who emigrated from Germany before that date, were stripped of their citizenship for "having so conducted themselves that German interest have been injured and have broken faith with the German people..."[40] In essence, they insulted Germany by leaving before they could be robbed and forced out of the country.

With the *Anschluss*, or reunion of Austria and Germany, whereby Austria became a province of the German Reich on March 13, 1938, a new class of decrees was issued against the Jews of Austria. Additionally, the decrees issued previously against German Jews now applied to Austrian Jews, and retroactively so. Finally, new decrees were issued against the Jews of the larger Reich, applying jointly to Austrian and German Jews equally. For Austrian Jews, the decrees depriving them of their rights came much faster. For example, soon after the *Anschluss*, with the stroke of a pen, a decree mandated the confiscation of close to 6,000 Jewish apartments in Vienna.[41]

It was one thing for German Jews to have experienced the tightening of the noose piecemeal and unknowingly, by the Nazi decrees, but it was a wholly other experience for Austrian Jews to face the same all at once. The decrees, largely retroactive, fell down upon Austrian Jews like a ton of bricks, leaving them with few options. This much can be seen by the emotional postwar testimonies provided to U.S. military authorities by Austrian Jews seeking restitution for their property. Their stories speak of a curtain of unduly harsh persecution falling on top of them. They were suddenly and swiftly robbed of their possessions, blackmailed, threatened, and forced out of Austria or simply put into concentration camps. In the short time between March and November 1938, some 50,000 Austrian Jews had left the country, compared with only 10,000 German Jews during the same timeframe.[42] Nazi officials had expressed dismay over their success in forcing the emigration of so many Austrian Jews, yet so few German ones.[43]

In the first anti-Jewish decree issued for application in the Austrian province, only two days after the *Anschluss*, the decree on the *Swearing in of Officials in Austria* declared that all public officials in Austria must be sworn in, pledging their allegiance to Adolf Hitler. According to Article 3 of the decree, however, "Jewish officials are not to be sworn in."[44] Following this decree, of March 15, on the same day, the Nuremberg laws were applied to Austria, defining the racial qualifications of a Jew only, not conferring immediate citizenship on non-Jewish Austrians.

Austrian Jews faced an ever more difficult existence when the Nazis decreed that the Reich Emigrant Tax would be applicable to them. While in existence in Germany since 1931, and amended each year until 1941 with ever harsher consequences,[45] the tax was originally intended to restrict the flight of German currency out of Germany during the Depression, and the subsequent precipitous drop in the value of German currency. With the Nazi party' accession to power, it soon became a popular legislative tool or "power relationship between the State and the people," for the confiscation of Jewish property.[46]

The Reich Flight Tax became abusive and discriminatory in nature and intent. As a study by the United States Federal Reserve Bank noted in 1943, "While the Government of the Weimar Republic was anxious to protect the taxpayer by law against arbitrariness of the tax administering authorities, the Nazi government was responsible for a systematic deterioration in the position of the taxpayer in relation to the government."[47]

According to Avraham Barkai, the tax at its inception, was only applicable to assets totaling more than RM 200,000. In May 1934, the amount and purpose was changed. From then on, the tax was levied on all assets of RM 50,000 or more. Moreover, the sum was based upon the estimated tax value of the asset, not the amount received for sale of that property.[48] This change meant a huge difference. When Jews, were forced to sell properties whose assessed value was high, they received little in return. The flight tax compounded their loss.

The discriminatory and retributive nature of the flight tax was explained by Leonhard Hildebrand, formerly of Vienna, who made claims following the war through the U.S. State Department. Hildebrand explained that payments from pharmaceutical products he "licensed" [more than likely under duress] to Dr. Alfred von Siebenrock and his wife, one day before the *Anschluss*, were owed to him, yet diverted to the German government for payment of the Flight Tax.

> Apotheke C. Haubner did submit such monthly statements for the period March 21, 1938 to December 31, 1938 inclusive, indicating the monthly profits credited to my

> account but allegedly paid to the German Treasury (Steuerbehoerde) for assessment of "Reichsfluchtsteur."[49]

Hildebrand had claimed a loss of $33,857 from the time. While a lot of money then, the equivalent value today would be over $277,000, and this was only for a nine-month period.[50]

As the decrees increasingly isolated, disenfranchised, and impoverished German Jews like the attorney David Detmar Loewenstern who was barred from practice by way of the *Fifth Decree Concerning Reich Citizenship* of September 27, 1938,[51] the Flight Tax allowed for the near total confiscation, through taxation, of Jewish assets as was the case with Mr. Hildebrand and so many others. In 1932, the Flight Tax brought in 900,000 Reichsmarks in revenue; six years later, that number had risen to 342.6 million Reichsmarks, or a 379.6 percent increase. Soon, all exemptions for the assessments of taxes imposed upon Jews were excluded as well.[52]

Decrees also centered on the mandate of a variety of census takings in order to initially classify people according to their genetic differences. In 1934, Protestant churches in Berlin began collecting genealogical data for this purpose. From this came census calculations of "genetically diseased" persons. In 1936, foreign-born Jews were forced to register,[53] and as stated below, in 1938, Jews were forced to register their assets.

Of the 1939 census, as David Luebke and Sybil Milton wrote,

> Comparative machine analysis of census data enabled Reich statisticians to determine the exact geographic, demographic, and professional composition of Nazi Germany's largest victim group.[54]

The supplier of the technology to enable that analysis was IBM. As Edwin Black wrote concerning the Nazis' use of these machines,

> When Germany wanted to identify the Jews by name, IBM showed them how. When Germany wanted to use that information to launch programs of social expulsion and expropriation, IBM provided the technologic wherewithal.[55]

Christopher Simpson declared that the SS used IBM Hollerith machines "to register and keep track of their liquidations."[56] This helps to explain the speed of Nazi operations in their new province and *how* they were able to achieve the high level of Austrian Jewish emigration.

In this regard, the Jews' lot in Germany worsened in January 1938, and later in Austria as well, when they were banned from adopting all but specifically sanctioned given names. If they already had given names, they were to add the name Israel or Sara to that name.[57]

In April 1938, Jews in both German and Austria were legally bound to declare their property. On April 26, 1938, Elisabeth Grünbaum, like all other Austrian Jews, rich and poor, was forced to declare her property. Among her holdings was a bank account at the Kreditanstalt in Vienna, holding 3,706.91 Reichsmarks; graphics and prints worth 5,791 Reichsmarks; jewelry worth 750 Reichsmarks; 720 Reichsmarks in books; life insurance policies taken out with Riunione Adriatica di Sicurta in Vienna, worth 21,835.50 Reichsmarks, one with Generali worth 30 Reichsmarks, and one with Phönix worth 5,600 Reichsmarks; gold, and a three-page, single-spaced inventory of artwork and sculptures and a great deal more.[58] These forms would, in addition to exposing Jews as to the amount and variety of their wealth, allowed for a more orderly classification and identification of them as individuals and as a community, exposing them to even greater isolation and persecution. As would prove to be the case, this declaration would prove a valuable tool to the Nazis in whatever land they occupied. This requirement would also be levied against Jews in German-occupied territory from the Channel Islands to Macedonia.[59]

In July came decrees requiring identity cards, the legal requirement for Jews to identify themselves in all written or oral applications. All Jewish physicians were also barred from practicing medicine.[60]

On October 4, all Jews were required to have their passports marked with a "J," for "Jude." [61] For Max Israel Chowdowski, of Berlin, the omnipresent red "J" on the first page of his passport properly identified him according to Nazi regulations, but was actually stipulated, however, by Swiss requests, fearing an influx of Jews from neighboring Austria flooding their country at the instigation of the Nazis.[62] Chowdowski's added name of "Israel" in his passport, reflected the name change law introduced in Austria in January 1938, and more specific to him being a Jew from Berlin, in Germany in August 18, 1938.[63] This requirement would resurface for Jews in Romania in March 1941.[64]

Because of this "mark of Cain," the red "J" in their passports, Belgian Jews Nissen and Estera Schachne were caught at the border of Switzerland, at Chancy, having escaped from a roundup of Jews in Nice, France. Initially accepted, then refused entrance into Switzerland, they were cast back into France, where they miraculously survived the war, while fifty-six other members of their family did not.[65] Over 24,000 refugees fleeing the Nazis like the Schachnes were also refused entry by the Swiss government or forcibly turned back by Swiss police because of the presence of this mark on their passports or simply because they were Jews.[66] Swiss police, under the leadership of Heinrich Rothmund, insisted on these procedures because of "the passive attitude by German officials toward Jewish refugees."[67]

Following these decrees, *Kristallnacht*, the "Night of Broken Glass," so-named in Nazi terminology purposely to lessen the extent of damage to Jews physically, and to redirect the destruction only to their property only. This Nazi-directed assault was the product of the Nazi leadership itself acting through secret, yet directive, orders to "let loose the people's rage" on the Jews. Rampant murder and destruction was carried out upon the Jews of Germany and Austria from the largest to the smallest of villages.

Following this rampage, the Nazis imposed a collective fine of one billion Reichsmarks upon the German Jewish community. This sum amounted to roughly $400 million and was imposed through decree.[68] The basis for this decree, however, lay deeper in Nazi sentiments expressed by Hitler, who wrote in a memorandum of August 1936 and given to Albert Speer, on his belief that the Reichstag should pass a law "making the whole of Jewry liable for all damage inflicted by individual specimens of this community of criminals upon the German economy, and thus upon the German people."[69]

The size of the fine was based on the amount of damage the Nazis wreaked upon the Jewish community in the *Regulation for Administration of the Decree Imposing an Atonement Fine on Jewish Subjects* of November 12, 1938.[70] The amount of the assessment was calculated from the results of these property declarations forced upon the Jews in April. The fine, however, would be far greater than the actual damages. According to figures assembled by the Jewish Agency for Israel from newly acquired documents in captured German archives found in Moscow, the damages amounted to 22,660,126 RM, or a little less then $10 million.[71]

The concept of a collective fine would later be passed on to other conquered or allied territories as well. In Bulgaria,[72] Romania,[73] and France,[74] punitive fines were imposed upon the Jewish community collectively, either through official decrees or private, arbitrary demands. These fines posed severe threats to the communities already under the strain of ever-tightening persecution and economic hardship.

Yet, while the community as a whole was to pay a collective fine, according to the Fire Insurance Branch of the German Association of Property Insurers writing to the State Ministry for Economic Affairs, in December 1938, "damages concerning demonstrations against Jews...[were] not part of fire insurance and even less so relating to burglary and theft insurance. Therefore any redress regarding a comprehensive claim is impossible."[75] Hermann Göring shared the belief that redress to the Jews would be impossible, asserting that it was "insane to clean out and burn a Jewish warehouse then have a German insurance company make good the loss."[76] To avoid this, Goering declared:

> I am not going to tolerate a situation in which the Insurance Companies are the ones who suffer. Under the authority invested in me, I shall issue a decree, and I am, of course requesting the support of the competent Government Agencies, so that everything shall be processed through the right channels, and the Insurance Companies will not be the ones who suffer.[77]

With this declaration, the Jews of Germany would pay the cost of the damages of the violence directed against them. "With an effrontery calculated to reduce the Jews of Germany to helpless rage," Peter Gay wrote, "the Nazis first committed the atrocities of Kristallnacht and then promptly blamed the victims."[78]

On the same day, in the *Decree Ousting Jews from German Economic Life*, Jews were forbidden to manage a firm or be a member of a cooperative society. It also became legally permissible, from then on, to oust a Jew as a leading employee in a business.[79] It was from this decree that the vast program of Aryanizations began providing for the removal of Jews from their businesses and the wholesale transfer of these Jewish businesses to the Germans, including the companies' buildings, assets, products, stock, patents, trademarks, and even its business contacts, contributing to what Gerald Feldman described as "a distinctive politics which imperialist and national ambitions were of great moment as well as an economic logic."[80] The process began slowly, based at first upon coercion or duress, described below, and increased pressures directed against leading companies to turn their businesses over to "Aryan" owners. The economy, though, dictated the speed with which the pace of the Aryanizations proceeded.

By 1937, however, with the economy improving due to rearmament and increased employment, the Nazis felt more comfortable to speed up and expand the process.[81] By this time, some German Jews had even begun to prosper, despite boycotts and other social and economic acts of persecution directed against their businesses. With this improved economic position, Jews left running some aspects of Germany's industry began to gather wealth at the same time the Nazis began to gather greater self-assurance. Soon the practice of Aryanization increased, evolving into an institution whereby outright confiscation became the practice. "Violent anti-Semitism," wrote Christopher Simpson citing economic historian Arthur Schweitzer, "became accepted by various segments of the middle class as a means of economic reform."[82]

The ends to which the Nazis would go to achieve Aryanization were extraordinary. This much was shown by Cornelia V. Paur, of Munich, who wrote a letter directed to President Truman following the war, detailing the particularly cruel experience of Aryanization she and her husband encountered:

> Under the nazi government I was with my family subject of heavy persecutions. In the course of these persecutions on racial grounds, my husband Dr. Rolf v. Paur was removed from his office as chairman of the board of directors of the Freundlich Brothers Ltd. by a Gestapo agent, the Captain (Hauptsturmführer of the SS & SD Fritz Schlamp[)]. Prominent members of the nazi Party tried to get hold of the shares of our company. In order to achieve this goal, my husband was thrown into prison and was as stated in his KZ Pass Nr. 1552 proves, for over one year and four months deprived of his liberty. Myself was imprisoned too and later was forced to work in a factory at the age of fifty-seven, where I developed a serious heart trouble. My son, Claus V. Paur, in a mine, as his KZ Pass Nr. 1170 proves [sic].[83]

Schlamp, following the Aryanization of the Paur's company, would divide their assets, transferring some to other companies, wiping away all that they possessed. There are countless stories of Aryanization that are equally heart-wrenching. What was also true of these efforts against the Jews was the audacity of the methods involved and the lengths to which the Nazis would go to take a company away from someone who had put his dreams and life's toil into it.

Aryanization would prove to be a valuable tool, like the Flight Tax, to complete the separation of Germany and Austria's Jews from their assets and identification as a people in the Third Reich. As Barkai wrote regarding the Flight Tax, "it functioned as an important factor in the decisions of affluent Jews about whether to emigrate."[84] Soon any action was permissible, and in fact even encouraged, toward this end. As the authors of a U.S. Foreign Economic Administration report on looted assets wrote, "This pillage of the anti-Nazi and non-Nazi population took place on a gigantic scale. Not only were those groups robbed which subsequently were ostracized by law, but also large groups which were never singled out by law..."[85]

After the war, in denying the return of the Aryanized shoe store of Frederick B. Weissmann of Berlin, M. Bally of the Bally Shoe Concern feigned ignorance when he replied to his entreaties for restitution of his store, "I was, until now, under the impression, that apart from your motives in selling the business, the contract was completely voluntary and that the sales price was based on the balance as shown in the books of your concern at that time."[86] While Weissman's store was clearly sold under duress, which will be dealt with more extensively below, what is also clear is the purposeful undervaluing of Weissman's property. Clearly Bally was being disingenuous, for as Frank Bajhor wrote regarding the Aryanizations taking place in Hamburg before the war, and repeated thousands of times throughout the Reich and the occupied lands after, "there were specific instructions to underestimate the value of the stocks, inventory, and net book amount in assessments conducted by estimators from the chambers of industry and commerce," those aiding the ongoing Aryanization drives.[87]

These decrees were established in Germany and Austria and with that, the Nazis' policies evolved as they fulfilled the promises they made to the German people. As the Nazis moved first into the Sudetenland, then into Czechoslovakia, creating the *Reichsprotectorate* in Bohemia and Moravia, and the puppet state of Slovakia, the same decrees were introduced banning Jews from economic life in conquered territories. This same process was repeated in Holland, Belgium, France, and to a lesser extent in Slovakia, Romania, and in Hungary as well. As Dr. Vitka Toshkova, of the Institute of History of the Bulgarian Academy of Sciences wrote, "The Germans were anxious to see their potential allies accepting anti-Jewish legislation tailored on the German pattern."[88]

In general, when the Nazi administration began, the first acts after imposing the oath of allegiance on the civil and municipal administrations, was the introduction of the Nuremberg decrees and definitions throughout the land. Then, on different time schedules, the laws were speedily introduced, choking off the Jews. With Germany as the original testing ground for these practices, the pace and speed of the introduction of discriminatory decrees was further refined in Austria. This pattern set the template for the Nazis' wholesale export of the economic spoils of Jewish wealth to conquered territories. In some form, within certain Nazi-occupied countries, the issuance of certain decrees was left to the Nazi puppet, or newly allied regime. This was considered acceptable to the Nazis because of the political reliability and national circumstance as much as anything else, but was always done with an eye toward abiding by Nazi rule.

In Slovakia, thirty-eight decrees were passed as part of an anti-Semitic system of rules that was called "the most elaborate in all of Axis Europe."[89] There were differences in composition in Slovakia's case, as well as in France which issued a number of discriminatory decrees patterned after the Nazis. Slovakia's circumstances differed with respect to agricultural lands, and also as to that government's more narrowed definition of Jews as being simply those who adhered to the "Israelite faith."[90] Other changes to the general pattern of decrees came through evolution. As new and more intricate forms of decrees were issued in one country, their re-issuance in a later occupied country was the result of emulation and thus became the template and evolutionary model for Nazi decrees elsewhere. The Nazis and their allies learned from this basic model. As the model was changed, even slightly, that innovation could resurface in rules issued against the Jews in another country.

Illustrative of this was the case of Holland, where there was a larger pool of wealthy Jews forced by the decree of August 8, 1941, to deposit their cash, checks, securities, and bank accounts wherever located—even overseas through the forced request for the transfer of accounts and securities back to Holland from abroad—into the Aryanized Jewish banking firm of Lippmann, Rosenthal & Co. in Amsterdam, controlled by the Nazi occupation authorities.[91] The Nazis would later decree the surrender of assets to specified institutions in other occupied countries, including Czechoslovakia[92] and France, where the appointed banking administrator, H.J. Caesar, oversaw the liquidation of French-Jewish and Allied-owned banks, bank accounts, stocks, bonds, and securities.[93]

Jews there suffered even more. Like in Austria, the Jewish presence was deeper and more ingrained and, therefore, the depth of the laws and decrees was likewise deeper. Moreover, the depth of the anti-Semitic idealist commitment and allegiance of the Vichy regime with the Nazis, like that of the regimes in Romania, was very strong. From October 1940 until December 1941,

109 anti-Semitic laws and decrees were promulgated in Vichy France.[94] A February 1942 decree imposed a curfew on Jews, forbidding them to travel outdoors between 8 P.M. to 6 A.M. Then, beginning on June 7, 1942, Jews over six years of age were required to wear Stars of David.

For Mina Parsont, the humiliation, however, turned to horror when nine days after the Star of David requirement took effect, Nazi agents leading one of numerous roundups of Jews in Paris and elsewhere, arrested her parents at work and took them away. Their apartment, one of thousands taken like those in Vienna shortly before, was stripped bare of furniture and all their other possessions were also taken, including their car. Mina, only five at the time, tearfully recalled salvaging only a teddy bear from all of her toys and possessions taken.[95]

In Romania, wrote Jean Ancel, anti-Semitic measures were passed by the Goga-Cuza and later National Legionary regimes, "under the 'new atmosphere created by the Nazis in Europe."[96] Decrees spanned the realm of anti-Semitic legislation from definitions of Jewry to restrictions on professions. Confiscations of factories, mills, farms, apartments, and other enterprises was also carried out.[97] In Constanta, a twenty-room villa at 43 Mircea Street, owned by Leon Vlodinger, was confiscated on orders from the local Council of Ministers on July 7, 1941. The villa was converted into a cultural hall and museum, including a library. There was no compensation provided or even offered.[98]

In Belgium, there were nineteen specific laws and decrees explicitly directed against the Jews, mirroring the German Nuremberg laws.[99] The decrees were issued by General Baron Alexander von Falkenhausen, the German military commander for Belgium. The Gestapo section for Jewish Affairs enforced and carried then out.[100]

In general though, the patterns established first in Germany and then in Austria held sway. First came the discriminatory decrees; the imposition of a flight tax, as well as other punitive taxes including immigration taxes; the forced declaration of property; and the forced confiscation and Aryanization of Jewish property; and finally the deportation of the Jews.[101]

Plunder by Abandonment

On September 5, 1938, Johannes Rohony, of Budapest, opened a safety deposit box, No. 137, at Schweizerische Hypothekenbank or HypoSwiss Bank in Zurich, listing his wife Anna Rohony on the box with him. Rohony never returned to Zurich, dying in January 1945 at Ohrdruf concentration camp in Germany. Three years later, in November 1948, HypoSwiss Bank attempted to notify Mr. Rohony, at an address in Amsterdam to inform him that they had not heard from him since he had opened the account ten years earlier. The bank notified him that he would be charged 100 sfr. for this long period of inactivity. Of course no answer was possible or forthcoming.

When in December 1963, HypoSwiss Bank forcibly opened Mr. Rohony's box, bank officials found six bank account books, from different Swiss banks, worth 13,600 francs, 300 sfr., and 150 French francs, as well as two safety deposit box keys. Five of the bank account books were registered in the name of Joseph Rotter, the other in the name of Victor Müller. Also included in the box, were legal Powers of Attorney from Rotter for Anna Rohony (Mr. Rohony's widow, including her maiden name, Gereben) for two of the accounts.[102]

What is inherent in the example above, is the length and ingenuity to which, and with which, one man went to conceal wealth from what he correctly saw as the coming deluge—the Nazis. In contradiction to most who believed that it was difficult to recognize, or act on, Nazi persecution as it was developing, especially while one was in the midst of it, Johannes Rohony apparently did.[103] He hid access to numerous bank accounts and two additional safe deposit box keys in another safe deposit box in a Swiss bank in Zurich in 1938. This is intriguing because these bank accounts held money, along with powers of attorney. Yet, the existence of keys to two additional boxes suggest strongly that his was an active attempt to place further funds out of reach of the Nazis.

Heinrich Stern of Stuttgart also placed assets in safe deposit box #710 in the Bar Bank in Zurich. While Mr. Stern's granddaughter Susana David, was told that only papers were found in the box in 1996, she was also told that the box was in fact opened earlier in 1952. Ms. David has proof that her grandfather had bonds and perhaps accounts as well in a Zurich branch of Credit Suisse as well, suggesting that there might well have been more than paper in box# 710 than was reported.[104] These cases beg the questions, where did the contents of Mr. Rohonny's boxes and the others go, and were there others still? Moreover, how many others took this avenue to conceal their wealth?

As Tom Bower discovered concerning the boxes, "mysteriously, their contents—jewels, cash, paintings and gold—had been stored for 'administrative reasons' elsewhere in the bank and had disappeared. Bank employees later spoke of a 'sudden huge inheritance,' from a distant relative."[105] What was lost from each of these boxes in this manner leaves one wondering.

Johannes Rohony was one man among so many of these unfortunate victims of the Nazis. Yet, he is a prime example of how the Jews of Europe did in fact place funds in numerous places that were simply "abandoned" and many times later confiscated. Efforts to conceal wealth, disguise it, and otherwise seek to protect it, rose due to the belief that all might not go well for those doing this hiding. They saw the threat posed by the Nazis and took great pains, at times paying with their lives, to hide their wealth from them. Many instructed their children that while they believed all would be alright, were it not to be so, they should make every effort to go back to where that money was hidden and retrieve it for their use. For these reasons, this second category is called *Plunder by Abandonment* as assets or property for the most part, were "abandoned" not by choice, but due to circumstances beyond people's control, and left either with those entrusted with them, or left dormant, at times for decades.

Johannes Rohony was joined by thousands of others who left equally as many assets or perhaps more behind. According to the Treasury Department's *Census of American-Owned Assets in Foreign Countries*, it was suggested that over $1.6 million was left in Europe alone by refugees.[106] These assets were left in banks across Europe, in Switzerland,[107] France, England, Holland, and America. In South America there is evidence to suggest that assets in the form of "flight capital" survived Nazi seizure to reach institutions in Uruguay,[108] perhaps in Brazil,[109] and Argentina.[110] The only problem was that banks were then, and well toward the end of the last century, unwilling to admit it. In 1957, one such admission came when a Swiss diplomat, Walter Stucki, pointedly declared:

> From rather reliable French and Swiss sources I believe that I must accept that very significant 'valuables' are located in the safes of West [sic] Swiss banks which had been deposited by private French citizens shortly before the last war. It is quite possible that the depositors died during the war without their families and heirs being informed about the deposits and that since then in some cases nothing more has been prescribed in any way.[111]

Transfers to Swiss banks were done secretly to counter laws forbidding the transfer of wealth. Many Swiss banks had correspondent branches in Eastern Europe and assets were transferred from there. The sister and brother-in-law of Yaakov Altman performed this service for Jews in Kovno, Lithuania.[112]

In New York City, banks holding accounts for European institutions lacking American branches, as well as Swiss banks' branches themselves, also held flight capital. "It is a fact," wrote Maurice Golay, the General Manager of the Swiss Bank Corporation in Basel:

> that just before the outbreak of war a strong tendency in Europe existed to transfer to America all the wealth possible because the public at large had lost their confidence in European affairs and wanted to put aside in America the largest portion possible of their assets.[113]

"Institutions in European financial centers, particularly in Switzerland," wrote W.H. Rozell of the Federal Reserve Bank of New York, in June 1940 "have for some time been engaging in an active and probably lucrative business of transferring European refugee funds to New York in accordance with a system devised by Swiss capitalists."[114] Evidence of these accounts was found following the freeze of Swiss bank accounts in the United States by President Franklin Delano Roosevelt on June 14, 1941. Among the thousands of accounts found by Treasury Department investigators were largely foreign accounts totaling, at that time, over $14 million.[115] Because of the lack of immediately available identification for these accounts, the accounts were frozen en bloc.[116]

In many cases, flight capital came to the U.S. and Swiss banks' American branches and were commingled into an omnibus or "rubrique" account, therefore disguising the ownership of the accounts.[117] The deposits, Rozell wrote, were "no longer reported to us as foreign deposits, despite the instructions on our report forms to that effect."[118]

The use of numbered accounts or middlemen were other means of disguising the ownership of accounts.[119] According to the U.S. Federal Reserve:

> through agreement with the New York correspondents [banks] these Swiss companies are said to have provided for the protection of their European clients, by means of a provision for the immediate transfer of the ownership of these funds to third parties under certain conditions, such as invasion or threat of invasion.[120]

Hiding assets under false or anonymous names happened in Europe as well as in the U.S.

In Switzerland, was one place, this occurred. Golay explained,

> Let us suppose—although I am convinced that this cannot be the case to any considerable extent—that such deposits have been opened under cover and in the name of Swiss citizens who lent their assistance for this purpose. First of all you may well realize that the owner of any property does not let easily this property pass into another name, which implies a confidence in the new owner that is rarely found. But let us suppose again that this is the case and that there are in Switzerland large size assets actually owned by Germans but deposited under Swiss names. In that case it is quite clear that the German beneficial owner of such property can do absolutely nothing with it and still less make it serve German purposes, because his aim has been precisely to escape German control. On his side, the Swiss owner of such property would make himself liable to all heavy Swiss taxes [sic].[121]

Golay believed that the use of middlemen was more common than American officials belied, or so he let on. When the Swiss Bankers Association published its series list of account holders, however, one list it published in November 1997, contained 140 names of people holding powers of attorney for accounts.[122] These accounts were only the dormant accounts—ones that those holding the powers of attorney did not claim following the end of World War II. During the war, there were numerous OSS, State, and Treasury Department investigations undertaken to locate and list Swiss lawyers holding assets of Germans and perhaps others.[123] How many holding powers of attorney for Holocaust victims, took advantage of this opportunity to claim the account for themselves? How many were family members hiding money—looted money—for Nazis?[124]

Golay concluded his explanation of the reasoning for the transfer of accounts to American banks by explaining:

> The present situation of Switzerland from an economic and materialistic point of view, is not the result of hazard, but is due to the foresight of its Government, and particularly of the late Federal Councillor Obrecht, who had already taken economic measures of protection as far back as 1936. It is also due to the hard work of its people and to their understanding of real democracy.[125]

As time would show, Golay would be proven right in one respect: Switzerland's actions to protect itself were due to government foresight. That foresight, however, turned out to be of dubious design and fifty years later would test its "real democracy" as well as the mythical version of its own history.

While bank accounts and small, movable property stored in safety deposit boxes were the most common type of asset involuntarily abandoned by European Jews, these assets were by no means the only forms abandoned. An art dealer, the biggest in Amsterdam, Jacques Goudstikker, was forced to abandon his gallery and an immense collection of his own paintings as well as those of others fleeing Europe. Collector Wilhelm Kleemann, for one, left thirty paintings with him for safekeeping.[126] Goudstikker, had transformed the small family gallery in 1919 and turned it into an international enterprise with customers such as William Randolph Hearst.[127] When he left for London in 1939, he entrusted the gallery to his lawyer who subsequently died in a freak accident the day before the German invasion of Holland.

Goudstikker fared little better. When traveling on a transport ship crossing the channel fleeing Holland from the Nazis in May 1940, Goudstikker was walking at night out on the deck and fell into the uncovered hole, falling to his death. Leaving a widow and young son of three, now exiled from Holland, and coupled with the death of his attorney, there was no one to watch over the collection and gallery of over 1,000 paintings. Soon the gallery was pillaged by Nazi officials, including Goering, through the services of the infamous art agent Alois Miedl, who assumed control of the gallery in July 1940 with the aid of J. Dik, the Goudstikker-appointed manager. Dik, along his son and another Dutch citizen, Miss Denijs, sold off numerous paintings to dealers.[128]

Lilian Politzer-Weingast, who left Vienna with her divorced father in August 1938 with "a sheet and a pillowcase," left behind nearly as much.[129] As the sole survivor of a wealthy family, she has laid claim to a rich collection of paintings spread over all the largest museums in Europe, including works by Matisse, Monet, Da Vinci, Rubens, and Renoir.[130] Ms. Weingast wrote:

> The night before we left, both my father's and mother's families came to our house and said au revoir. I had several uncles who were bachelors and they told me that night that I will be their heiress. I was the only girl in the family. Of course we all thought that this

> horrible time would pass and we would be reunited.... As far as I know, they all perished when Hitler marched into France. I tried to find them after the war but was not successful in locating them.[131]

Isabella Rottenstreich, writing from Roxbury, Massachusetts to the State Department Office for Claims Against Germany and Austria in August 1946, pled for compensation for a different lost asset—lost rent from a building she owned, but entrusted to a friend in Vienna.

> Already before my emigration from Vienna, Austria, I had appointed Mrs. Carl Guber Widow, Vienna XXI, Am Spitz 4, as my administrator for my real estate aforesaid. She had to collect all the rents from the tenants in said building, and has done so up to date as she still is the administrator of my real estate. At the end of 1938, the monthly rent income was 510.-Austrian shillings, but later the rents were increased and the monthly rent income, therefore, must have become larger. Since January 1, 1939, I have not received any money from rents, collected by Mrs. Guber; she had to pay or deposit all rents collected with the "Ober-Finanz-Praesiadministrator of my real estate in Vienna XX Brigttenau, Hannovergasse 10, Mrs. Carl Guber widow, has to lay account on her administration for the period from January 1, 1939 up to date, and on all rents collected from all tenants in said real estate during the same period...[132]

Like Mrs. Rottenstreich, Frederick William Koerner, also was forced to leave property in Austriaollowing the Anschluss. Koerner wrote the City of New York in December 1946 seeking relief for his lumber business in Vienna. Koerner wrote that he had:

> been a partner of the above named firm, which was founded in 1896 and was one of the leading lumber exporters in Austria with lumber yards in Vienna, St. Johann in the Salsburg province of Austria and in Steinhaus and Spital, in the Styria province of Austria. There were agencies of the firm in Italy, France, Switzerland, Germany, and Hungary.[133]

Others like Hugo Mayer, formerly of Sofia, Bulgaria, shipped priceless antique rugs through Trieste. After the war, he tried to claim what was then worth $50,000.[134] William Herzog, formerly the editor-in-chief of the Berlin newspaper *The Republic*, was forced to hurriedly leave Berlin, leaving behind his library filling seventy-six cases totaling 8,000 books.[135] Margit Freud of the famous Freud family, claimed compensation for the contents of their flat in Berlin, as well as the income from the translation royalties they had due to them from their work translating some of Jack London's books into German.[136]

What all these people had in common was that they left property in Europe, at times with institutions they assumed were reliable, and at others with acquaintances and friends they trusted. In far too many cases, that trust was betrayed.

Plunder by Duress

"By virtue of the measures taken in Germany to eliminate Jewish influence from the German economic life," wrote Frederick B. Weissmann after the war, "I was forced to sell my firm in 1938 at a ridiculous price."[137] He was not alone.

While some Jews did escape from Europe, even while abandoning their assets, their departure was less complicated. For others, however, this was not to be the case. Many who were fortunate enough to get out, were forced to sell their assets under duress. Germans from all walks of life found the opportunity to profit from the hardship of the Jews. With full knowledge of the Jews' impending departure, at times even acknowledged by the Jews themselves, people of all kinds took advantage of them. As such, their assets were "sold" by contract at bargain level prices abiding by the legal fiction concocted by the Nazis to assume the appearance of a voluntary act. In this way, the Nazis made use of their own laws telling the Jews it would be in their own best interests to accept their fate, surrender their property, and salvage whatever they could in return for their properties. The threat of immediate harm to themselves and their families, though, was designed to lessen the threat of future danger in return for assets. This was the third form of plunder—*Plunder by Duress.*

Mrs. Wera Elfriede Klipstein, her lawyer wrote to the U.S. Occupation authority in Germany following the war, "had to liquidate her German property as otherwise no permission would have been granted to her to emigrate. The mortgager," Ignatz I. Rosenak wrote:

> whose name and address are not available to my clients at this time, thereupon state that he was only willing to pay to the mortgagee the sum of about RM 8,000, i.e. half the amount of the mortgage provided the mortgagee would execute satisfaction piece in respect thereto. Mortgagee, as a Jew being subject to the well known Nazi persecution had no choice but to accept the said RM 8,000 and to execute satisfaction piece with respect to the said mortgage. All the above took place after the year 1933 and, in the circumstances above described, must be considered as a transaction entered into under duress.[138]

Obtaining only a fraction of the true value of their property, Jews were put in a difficult position. Having the foresight to leave, they were being given the chance to do so, but of course unable to take unmovable property with them, which they lost due to the connivance of the Nazi authorities and the German people.

Ordinary Germans, as well as Austrians and native non-Jewish inhabitants from other occupied countries, suddenly had opportunities they never could have imagined in the nation-wide "evacuation sales" of property from the departing Jews from their nations.[139] Herbert Schaefer, the son of a chauffeur, in 1937 was in Law School in Berlin. While working as a legal intern, he was earning the amount most other Germans were earning annually, less than 1,000

RM. Yet, according to Schaffer, he was quite well-off by that time, enabling him to buy "Le Grand Pont," a landscape by Gustave Courbet at an auction. Two years before, the Corbet, sold at a previous auction for 17,000 RM.[140] According to the art provenance researcher Willi Korte, who did much of the research involved with the provenance of this painting, it was auctioned a second time from a collector, Max Silberberg, who sold the painting under duress for the original price of 17,000 RM.[141] The painting was then auctioned off by a German art dealer, Paul Graupe, to a wealthy Czech Jew from the Weinmann family who had no knowledge of the painting's provenance. [142] Mrs. Weinmann herself had to later flee Germany and abandoned the painting in Berlin. At this point Schaeffer stepped in and bought the painting, later buying others and profiting handsomely from the bargains.[143] Schaeffer went on to become quite wealthy off the backs of desperate people hoping to salvage even a fraction of their assets in order to leave Europe for exile elsewhere.

Other Germans also took advantage of the growing climate of laws initiated against the Jews. Tenants in some cases refused to pay their rents, preferring instead to seek relief from German courts and civil authorities who most times were all too willing to take their side in disputes with Jews, who were viewed as gouging and duplicitous toward their German tenants. Others simply extended the concept of the boycott, used with such devastating effect against Jewish businesses, to choose not to live in Jewish-owned buildings. Lacking rental income, Jewish owners suffered. Credit institutions routinely called in loans, refused additional credit, or demanded to exorbitant credit terms.

At times, tenants even made claims on the confiscated or abandoned property of Jews. To this, the State Secretary of the Reich Ministry of Finance declared on December 3, 1938:

> Petitions have been submitted to me by various individuals, who, claiming to have once been damaged by Jews, now request to let them have an indemnity from the yield of the Jewish property contribution. I wish to point that the decree on the payment of atonement of the Jews of 12 Nov 1938 imposes on the Jews the payment of a contribution to the German Reich. The German Reich as the trustee of the whole German people derives exclusively the yield of the Jewish property contribution.[144]

German Jews were thus faced with great difficulties in making mortgage payments. When financial institutions refused credit or improved the terms of the mortgage, default was usually the only option remaining. Forced auctions were common and "Aryan" purchasers, individuals and commercial, were then able to pick up the property under conditions favoring them.[145] Following their purchases, improved credit and advantageous tax situations, such as reductions in land taxes, suddenly became available for those purchasing the properties.[146] These tax breaks, however, were not passed on to German Jews.[147]

In Austria, some 5,000 less wealthy Jews had their apartment leases canceled on short notice. Their properties left behind were sold at duress prices.[148] Needless to say, Austrians were not the only ones to benefit by this process.

While subject to private profiteers, Jews faced very public ones as well. German authorities required the payment of the above-mentioned Reichsfluchtsteur, or "Flight Tax," which seemed to rise and fall with the amount of assets departing Jews had available to them following the forced liquidation of their property under duress. The primary motivation for Nazi officials being that "every emigrant is a potential smuggler of capital."[149]

For the Nazis, this institutionalized robbery was practiced with a cynical exactitude. "Through the intervention of the new Nazi house administrator, an SS man in uniform," wrote Hugo Lowenfeld on behalf of Mrs. Gisela Lowenfeld, "the house [in Vienna] was 'sold' to Mr. And Mrs. Karl and Barbara Krodlinger, residing in Vienna III, Salmgasse 15." Mr. Lowenfeld continued:

> From the purchase price of RM 105,000.00 or about $42,000 the amount of RM 102,000 was magically deducted and taxed away, the real value of the house being much higher. The remaining RM 3,000 have been paid out to my sister in monthly installments until her deportation to a concentration camp in 1942 whence she was never heard from. And for my jewels, I just got a receipt.[150]

Furthermore, Mrs. Lowenfeld attested, remaining funds, if there were any, were to be paid into blocked accounts in German banks under the supervision of the *Devisenstellen,* nominally under the control of the Finance Ministry.[151] These funds were permitted to be exploited in any of three ways: 1) to grant credit to a German, 2) to make insurance payments, and 3) to acquire real estate. All three were intended solely to help Germans, not Jews.[152] These accounts were ostensibly held in the name of the departing emigrant, but in reality were subjected to taxes themselves, as well as confiscation following the Jews' departure.

Each emigre, in order to leave, was required to register with a variety of government agencies to obtain passports, visas, certificates attesting to their criminal record, and statements that they had fulfilled all their tax obligations, however onerous they might have been. When leaving Germany, it was obligatory to use German travel agencies to plan their emigration, and with these reservations came even more fees for arranging the trip.[153] Emigres were also required to fill out a detailed form explaining their assets, and then were subjected to an examination of their declaration to ensure that nothing of consequence or importance was owed to or would escape the reach of the Reich.[154] Items of value were assessed a triple tax based on purchase price.[155] Finally, prior to departure, bags were checked ahead of time and sequestered to insure that no smuggling occurred depriving the Reich of further revenue.

For Fred and Herta Rosendorff of New Jersey, their accounting of the sting of their departure at the hands of the German tax authorities amounted to $7,200 for the "Jews levy," $5,796.40 tax for leaving Germany, $500 tax on commodities, and a loss of $7,438 from selling blocked accounts to the Deutsche Golddiskontbank in Berlin.[156] The practice of forced emigration was clearly and completely rigged against the Jews in order to fully rob them and do so under duress.

Historian Martin Dean explained that the steadily growing and "complex network of currency restrictions and extortionate taxes applied especially against Jews seeking to emigrate, also made it increasingly difficult for them to leave the country."[157] For those who did manage to emigrate, they would, as so planned, leave largely destitute. As Eric Johnson wrote, quoting a German Foreign Office circular in 1939, "it is in the German interest to force the Jews over the border as beggars, because the poorer the immigrants, the greater the burden that the host country faces."[158] This, in itself, would make destination countries less likely or willing to accept fleeing Jews.

Duress, while unpleasant from the start, became quite a bit more unpleasant and anguishing when it involved hostage-taking and ransoming in return for assets. Sometimes, these cases appeared as a result of more extreme or desperate maneuvers to obtain assets. In some respects, as well, these cases arose out of more personal or pecuniary reasons as well. The plight of the Bernheimer family of Munich is one such case.

In return for the forced sale of their coffee plantation in Venezuela, the Bernheimers were allowed to emigrate from Germany to Venezuela, but not before Otto Bernheimer was imprisoned for five weeks in Dachau and forced to denounce his and his family's German citizenship, surrender the family wealth, and leave the country. He was taken from his home at 3 A.M. in the morning on November 9, 1938, the night of *Kristallnacht*, when as Susie Bernheimer wrote, "the house-bell rang and five men, clothed in the uniform of Hitler-Youth-Leaders, forced my husband to hand over to them Mk. 50,000 in cash—in addition to that a 'gift certificate' which was dictated to him, that he voluntarily had given the amount for the purpose to build new dwellings for the youth." Otto Bernheimer was arrested and taken to Dachau as were some 10,000 of his fellow Jews.[159] According to Mrs. Bernheimer, the plantation they were trying to buy was that of the niece of Hermann Goering, Mrs. Erika Rode. Apparently, the imprisonment and harassment was designed to influence them to forego their purchase. It worked.

Others, such as Martin Aufhauser,were imprisoned in Dachau as an "incentive," in this case for surrendering a Rembrandt, "Portrait of the Artist's Sister."[160] Bernard Rosenthal, spent four days in the municipal prison at Neustadt in order to convince him to surrender his dry goods store in Nordheim.[161]

As these practices increased in Germany itself, the Nazi authorities learned from their deeds, and the practice of ransoming on an individual scale, evolving this into an institution unto itself. What began with individual cases of ransom, soon became collective on a family level, and then evolved to the practice of ransoming entire groups.

From mere threats securing the surrender of assets for the purpose of emigration from Germany, the Nazis developed this into a rule and used the same practices in the occupied countries. According to the American Legation in Bern in 1942:

> How the National Socialist Government of Germany extorts ransom monies from or on behalf of persons desirous of emigrating from Germany or from European territory under German control has recently been the subject of an inquiry by this Legation and the several American consular establishments in Switzerland. ... The ransom system as practiced at present seems to be an extension of the practice instituted by the Nazi Government where under emigrants were permitted to leave Germany if the state were compensated on their departure by all of their visible wealth, with the exception of a small percentage, usually reduced in effect to about ten or twelve and one-half percent, which the emigrant was permitted to retain and to export abroad. It is very apparently designed to provide foreign exchange for the furtherance of the German war effort (though there may be reason for suspicion that individual members of the Nazi Party may personally profit by it).[162]

As the practice spread to occupied lands, the Germans preyed upon wealthy Jews wherever they could, including in South America and even in the United States, to exact further foreign exchange.[163] The evolution of this institution started in Germany took new shapes first in Austria, with a captive and wealthy community of Jews, and then in Holland with an even larger and wealthier community.

"The Nazis," wrote Justice Department investigators, "threaten Dutch Jews residing in the Netherlands with deportation or concentration camp [sic] unless large sums are deposited abroad in favor of the Germans. Fifteen thousand Swiss francs per head is not an unusual price."[164] As would be the case later, this price would soon rise, as the desperation increased, to as high as 100,000 Sfr.. The locations for money deposited abroad suggested banks in Germany, Holland, France, and even in Latin and South America, including Cuba, Chile, and Argentina.[165]

In the days following angst-ridden cables back to Washington, DC by U.S. personnel in late October and early November 1942, U.S. and British officials searched for ways to prevent the practice in ways that did not harm the particular families in question, but would deprive the Reich of the much-needed foreign exchange it was accumulating from the growing ransom trade. Describing Nazi ransom schemes as "an important as well as sinister development," Winant concluded that the growing practice should be given "wide publicity" and that the Allies should move against the middlemen allowing this practice to proceed.[166] Winant and others suggested placing those middlemen arranging ransom payments to be referred the Black List Committee[167] for inclusion on the Proclaimed List, an assertive expression assuming the force of rule of a directive concerning those persons and companies known to, or quiet possibly only suspected to have, economic relations with the Nazis and Axis powers. Those included on the list were in violation of the *Trading with the Enemy Act* and subjected to sanctions.

The use of the Proclaimed List, however, was not universally accepted as a panacea for the problem. On November 16, Winant argued that:

> [q]uite apart from the detriment to the blockade which would be involved by any condonation of this traffic, His Majesty's Government feel that to acquiesce in it would, in the long run, prove the worst service that could be rendered to potential victims in Occupied territories. It is the universal experience that surrender to blackmail merely increases the appetite of the blackmailer. There are still many persons in occupied Europe with wealthy friends, relatives or business associates abroad, and to permit this situation to be exploited will merely add to the sum of human misery among the peoples now under German domination.[168]

Winant concluded that the only option was to officially blacklist and declare all brokers and intermediaries enemies regardless of their location. The Proclaimed List had the force of law in inter-Allied dealings, yet had not been so promulgated. This was due, in many cases, to the simple belief of an existing relationship on the part of the violator. Thus, on November 24, 1942, the governments of the United States, Great Britain, and the Netherlands Government-in-Exile, formally announced a warning but this time with a consequence concerning what would happen to those individuals participating in and encouraging "this barbaric and inhumane practice":

> Warning is hereby given that any person in a country to which the Proclaimed List of Certain Blocked Nationals applies who acts as a broker or agent in this traffic will immediately be included in that list and thereby be publicly designated as an enemy. Furthermore, persons in such countries who pay ransom are warned that they are assisting the enemy in his war effort and are rendering themselves liable to treatment as enemies.[169]

With this action, ransoming became an act of warfare. Immediately, the Allies placed two Swiss nationals on the Proclaimed List: Dr. Arthur Wiederkehr and Anna Hochberg, who were said to have worked in tandem on ransom cases.[170] Wiederkehr was said to be a frequent visitor to Holland and was well-known throughout Europe, South America, and even in the United States for acting in the role of intermediary between the Nazis and the Jews.[171]

According to the American Legation in Bern, he was said to have demanded money up front for a visa for a Dutch Jew who fled to Holland and who had actually been referred to Wiederkehr by German authorities there. Once the money, in this case, was given directly to Wiederkehr, the escapee was free to make his way to the French border with Belgium, only to be quickly discovered there by the Gestapo who sent him back to Amsterdam.[172]

Wiederkehr was also said to be in close contact with German officials as well as German and Dutch banks. As per this practice, money, sometimes as high as $30,000 per person, was to be transferred to the bank in question, a cut kicked back to him, and then he would verify the delivery of the funds to the German authorities, who would then release the person in question. Wiederkehr's associate, Anna Hochberg, was said by intelligence reports to regularly "canvass Dutch Jews in Switzerland about the possibility of getting relatives and friends out of Occupied Territory [sic]."[173] In addition to these two, there were other middlemen such as Bernard Gaesche, J.B.de Haay, Pierre Atteslander, Moritz Bing, Walter Buchi, and Dr. René Niederer, all of Switzerland.[174]

Those Jews getting into Switzerland took many paths—forging work permits, bribing border guards, paying Swiss citizens to smuggle them, or fulfilling ransom demands of the Germans. "People just suddenly got wealthy," explained Dr. John Graz, whose grandfather in France was executed for helping Jews get across the Swiss border.[175] Regardless of their method of entry, these refugees were, nevertheless, targets for opportunistic middlemen.

From this point on, the American and British Embassies began to search in earnest for those thought to be arranging for the emigration of Jews in distress. What became confusing for embassy officials was the motive of the intermediaries. Were they mercenaries, as Wiederkehr was said to have been, or were they merely people with numerous connections, unaffiliated with the Nazis in a nefarious way and who simply were trying to help friends and colleagues to get out of Europe? After all, Anna Hochberg, Wiederkehr's associate, was described as a "Jewess."[176] Why would a Jew do this to another Jew? Where were Allied investigators to draw the line between criminality and life threatening acts of kindness?

Of the multitude of interlopers, mercenaries, and entrepreneurs investigators had to separate into good and bad, one such figure was Jacques Salmanovitz. U.S. intelligence had conflicting views about this wealthy Swiss businessman. "One report indicates," an OSS analyst wrote to the State Department after the war:

> that during the war the subject's firm, Societe Generale de Surveillance, furnished information to the Germans and Allies at the same time. However, another report indicates that subject had a large transport insurance business with subsidiaries all over southeastern Europe...from which he was in a position to gather considerable information relating to economic warfare for the British Intelligence Service ... he was strongly anti-German and was regarded by Berlin as dangerous.[177]

Yet, only two months before this report was written, the American Consulate in Geneva referred to Salmanowitz as "our great friend."[178] Despite these differing opinions of Salmanovitz, he came to be known for his "extraordinary humanitarian efforts and personal generosity on behalf of persecuted Jews."[179]

Salmanowitz indeed acted as an intermediary, but on less onerous, indeed purely selfless grounds.[180] As an owner of a company that inspected, tested, and verified cargo for shipment in seaports, his company SGS, did business all over Europe as well as in the United States. With business accounts spread across the world, his generosity was such that his customers needing help came to him, desperately seeking shelter for either themselves or their assets. "Due to the exigencies of the war and the extreme danger faced by many of SGS's Jewish customers and associates," wrote Jonathan Greenblatt, attorney for SGS in 1996:

> SGS maintained account balances in favor of some of them as an accommodation to their concerns about the security of their assets in their home countries. SGS did not profit from these arrangements, nor were they part of the company's ordinary course of business. Rather, they were unusual arrangements undertaken for humanitarian reasons to help Jews transfer their assets out of Nazi-dominated countries.[181]

Following the war, Salmanowitz also sought the release of blocked funds of friends and employees of formerly ex-enemy countries, writing numerous letters to the Allies on their behalf seeking the assets' unblocking.[182]

The role of SGS as a shipping inspection firm itself aroused the suspicions of Allied intelligence. If SGS could certify shipments, and the Nazis were eager to get shipments in and out of ports, reasoned Allied investigators, what would prevent them from bribing SGS inspectors? Investigators looked at other shipping firms, such as the German firm of Shenker, which they believed, "did most of the packing and shipping of loot for the Germans."[183]

Yet, what confused the Allies, was Salmanowitz' more material help to the Nazis' intended victims through his intermediary work handling ransom payments. Gardiner S. Platt of the OSS inquired after the war of Salmanowitz' efforts regarding the ransoming of the family of Oscar Perlberger, the former head of the coffee importing firm N.V. Hergoma in Amsterdam.[184]

Perlberger, writing to Salmanowitz on September 18, 1942 from New York City explained in desperation, "As you know, I am working without stop in order to do everything I can from here to help the departure of my family."[185] Perlberger had made numerous inquiries to the American Legations in Geneva and Bern seeking a visa for his wife and three children, who were under thirteen.

He had also sought and obtained the help of Congressman Samuel Dickstein of New York, the Chairman of the House Committee on Immigration and Naturalization.[186] Through Dickstein's help, an American visa was arranged for the

Perlbergers. However, they needed to obtain a Swiss visa and post a $35,000 bond at a bank in Lugano against their becoming a public charge in Switzerland.[187] The price of their exit amounted to 300,000 Sfr. or almost $72,000. Finally, after an excruciating two-year wait, the Perlbergers were given approval at the end of October 1942 to assume temporary residence in Tessin, Switzerland.[188] Salmanowitz also obtained the permission for Claire Perlberger's father Henri Untermanns, their family, as well as Fritz Geyerhahn, Oscar Perlberger's business partner, and his family, to leave Holland.[189]

While the Perlbergers were successful in their quest to get out of Holland, Allied determination to prevent the Reich from obtaining hard currency prevented numerous other Jews from successful emigration. According to the British Embassy in Washington, DC by April 1943, twenty-three families in the United States had been prevented from ransoming out relatives. Once warned by missions in the field, seventy-eight more refused to negotiate for ransom demands, others were warned either by Dutch or British authorities.[190] Banks too, feared participating in ransom efforts for fear of their placement on the Proclaimed List. Indeed, by July 1943, as David L. Barrett of the U.S. Treasury Department wrote to the Head of the Remittance & Personal Accounts Unit in Foreign Funds Control, Charles H. de Zevallos, "[t]he ransom traffic had diminished greatly in the last six months." Barrett detailed how the British had perfected a system to check all middlemen operating ransom schemes. Leaders of communal organizations were also advised to heed warnings against acquiescing to ransom requests. Finally, Swiss civilians and corporations had vowed, he understood, not to engage in ransom schemes in the future.[191]

While correct in assuming that the traffic in ransom cases had greatly subsided, Barrett had been hampered in his analysis by the lack of knowledge of Nazi intentions in Hungary, where as in Holland, a wealthy class of Jews would soon fall prey to the Nazi onslaught. Moreover, he could not have known then that within a year, the Nazi economic position would worsen all the more in direct proportion to the decline of its military position.

With the outright invasion and occupation of Hungary by the Nazis on March 19, 1944, the Jewish community came under the direct administrative control of "Kommando Eichmann." Now, in conjunction with the persecution of Hungarian Jews, the ransoming practice began anew. Wealthy Hungarian Jews were subjected to the same procedures under Eichmann as were the Jews of Austria and Holland under him and his deputies a few years earlier. Members of the prominent Hungarian Weiss and Chorin families, related through marriage to one of Baron Manfred Weiss' daughters, paid a steep price for their freedom. In return for the emigration of ten members of the combined families to Switzerland in June 1944, they agreed in an exchange with Heinrich Himmler himself, to a twenty-five-year lease of Weiss Industries to Goering Werke, again in a mocking legality. Weiss Industries focused on steel production, an ever more important aspect of the Reich's war plans.[192] Moreover, as the American Legation in Bern observed, there may have also been a cash payment of several million Swiss francs and a number of valuable paintings involved as well.[193] It was also stipulated that up to ten members of the joint family were to remain in Vienna as hostage of the Gestapo to insure final payment.[194]

As the war worsened for the Nazis, their urgent need for supplies increased and they again resorted to ransoming but this time on a much grander scale. Soon, instead of simple ransom payments in return for the freedom of whole families, the practice of group ransoming began. Now, mass efforts were undertaken not only for money, but for supplies and equipment as well.

Between August and December 1944, a series of negotiations between the Germans and the U.S. War Refugee Board, through former Swiss Federal Councillor Jean-Marie Musy, were concluded whereby over 1,200 Jewish refugees would be released in return for 5.5 million Sfrs. The deal, negotiated with Himmler, allowed for the Jews to make it safely to Switzerland. The money was paid through Saly Mayer, the European representative of the American Jewish Joint Distribution Committee with contributions from abroad as well as from the refugees themselves.

In August 1944, as well, with Slovakian Jews under threat of deportation, the community suggested a ransom plan to the Nazis. Leaders in Bratislava proposed funds from Jews in Switzerland could be used to buy them out of harm's way.[195] While $400,000 was raised and deposited in an account in Switzerland, nothing more came of the effort.[196]

A more ambitious effort, to be called "Goods for Blood," was undertaken whereby Adolph Eichmann proposed to trade the freedom of up to one million Jews in return for military trucks; one truck for every 100 Jews, as well as 800 tons of coffee, 800 tons of tea, 200 tons of cocoa, two million bars of soap, and $1 million U.S. dollars, Swiss francs, and a variety of South American currencies.[197] This proposal was made in April 1944 to Joel Brand, a representative of the Jewish Rescue Committee in Hungary, led by Dr. Rudolf Kastner. Trying to drive a wedge between the Allies, Eichmann promised to only use the trucks on the Eastern Front, against the Russians.

The Allies, suspicious of the proposal, denied any chance for it to succeed, and it did not. Brand's detainment in Cairo by the British, in transit from negotiations, only reinforced the fate of this proposal.[198] There were questions whether it could have succeeded at any rate. The attempt to split the British and Americans off from the Russians was all too implicit, yet the deal was pursued because to have done nothing or to have refused it, David Ben-Gurion, then of the Jewish Agency, reasoned would have been acquiescence to a million deaths.[199]

There were other deals that did reach fruition, such as the transfer of close to 400 Jews to Switzerland through the intervention of Kastner in the spring of

1944.[200] For the Nazis, these were deals first of economic opportunism, and later of economic desperation.

Of even greater concern to the Allies at the time was the continuation of Swiss banks in facilitating the institution of Nazi ransoming practices.[201] With the Allies, already greatly concerned with the Swiss material and financial activity on behalf of the Nazis, this cooperation only made matters worse.

The Bergier Commission, formed at the instigation of the Swiss Government in 1996, following disclosures of great historical improprieties by the United States Senate Banking Committee and the World Jewish Congress, committed to a six-year, in-depth study of banking and other financial issues relating to Switzerland. The commission found that of some 400 individual cases of ransoming out of Holland alone, half involved a connection through Swiss banks resulting in freedom for 154 people.[202]

Plunder by duress was an insidious form of extortion, taking advantage of people at the height of their fears—fears over life and death for themselves and their family. With full knowledge, the Nazis took advantage of the Jews of Europe for their own and the Reich's enrichment. While the preceding forms of plunder involved a process designed to 'legally' deprive the Jews of their assets, or to influence them to simply leave the assets or surrender them under threat, the next pattern of plunder was a more simple one: outright seizure.

Plunder by Seizure

"The complete stock of the jewelry store," plead Siegfried Politzer, "consisting of 1,206 pieces of merchandise at a cost value of at least 200,000 schillings was taken away by order of the government.... I could not even dare to protest against this as protesting would be for me identical with being killed or sent to a concentration camp."[203]

In Western Europe, most of the property taken from Jews was done in a more formal, more ordered manner. Initially, Nazi plunder was done through the processes of decree, abandonment, and duress. They utilized the assets gained largely for state purposes, with the exception of artwork collected by Nazi leaders, on a grand scale with many German businesses, their owners, and none too few lesser businessmen and attorneys enriching themselves in ways they could never have imagined, expanding business opportunities through the acquisition of formerly Jewish properties and businesses.[204] In essence, the taking of assets in the early years of the Nazi era was the result of a loose plan which later evolved into practices and eventually, with time and the attendant benefits which the Nazis and the German people came to appreciate, an institution that slowly arose and gained coherence and legitimacy. As Gerald Feldman explained, " ... the unusual business of looting became business as usual."[205]

As the Nazis moved east, however, the patterns of plunder changed, in part because of the speed with which they had to react to, rather than merely accommodate, the newly incorporated local population and governments. With some types of assets, particularly gold from national treasuries, which came to be known as "monetary gold," and gold from the personal possessions of Nazi victims, known as "non-monetary gold," the Nazis came to rely on seizure, rather than the more complicated "legal" constructs they had previously devised, to plunder other assets. The process of seizure was based then on the principle of directive orders to German troops or specialized units to take whatever they were directed to bring back to the Reich, and deny to the Jewish people, both publicly and privately. Seizure was a concept mandated in secret, and became a product of deception in Nazi-occupied lands. This fear was most clearly expressed in the need to confiscate assets, yet to do so quietly, necessitating the need to mask the multi-part mission (to rob and later destroy) of its perpetrators. The source for the aid and cover the Nazis required was in Switzerland. The same cover Switzerland offered and provided to Jews hiding their assets, would now be extended to the Nazis as well.

"From today's vantage point," wrote Robert Vogler the former Archivist for the Swiss National Bank, "...the SNB appears not to have considered the possibility of the then German government recasting foreign ingots, marking them with Reichsbank stamps and providing fresh papers."[206] Whether they considered the possibility or not, the Swiss National Bank (SNB), as well as the Bank of International Settlements (BIS) (the Central Bank of all Central Banks), located in Basle, to a lesser extent, were the central depositories for gold looted by the Nazis.[207] Both banks laundered the looted Nazi gold, and asked precious few questions as to its origins, accepting the legitimacy of the Nazis' stories. That gold, taken from the central banks of the conquered nations of Europe, had co-mingled in it as well, gold from concentration camp victims. This fact, now proven, has caused great consternation in Switzerland, but has become one of the most sordid aspects of the Nazi seizure of Jewish assets during the Holocaust.

In an undated (probably 1945-1946) draft memo from the American Embassy in London, officials laid out the destination of all the looted gold in Europe.

a) that the German Reichsbank maintained an important depot of gold in the Swiss National Bank throughout the war;
b) that two-thirds of all German gold shipments abroad during the war were destined for the Swiss National Bank;
c) that more than half of the Belgian gold stolen by the Germans in France was, after resmelting, sent to the Swiss National Bank; and
d) that part of the gold looted by Germany during the war was sent to the Bank for International Settlements.[208]

In 1953, State Department analysts concluded that "it is obvious that the tremendous amount of gold transferred by banks, firms,and individuals to

Switzerland, could only result from looting."[209] The Nazis, it became clear, had to have a central location for the disposition of their looted gold. Switzerland afforded them that haven. The gold, confiscated from all over Europe, before being deposited in Switzerland, was processed in Berlin. Karl Graupner, the head of the Goldgeschäfte Branch in the Foreign Exchange Department of the Reichsbank in Berlin, explained during his interrogation by Army investigators in 1945, regarding deposits of gold from foreign countries, that the:

> Asservat 'Der was formed around 1937/1938, and in this account were booked all gold amounts placed at the disposal of the Four Year Plan (Hermann Goering). It consisted of gold, delivered according to the order to turn in all gold in Germany, further of gold from Danzig (1939), Sudentenland, and later of gold from territories occupied by German troops for example in Belgium the entire amount of gold at the Belgian National Bank including some 12 Mill. RM. Gold of the Bank of Luxemburg).[210]

Once smelted and stamped with the Reichsmark emblem, the gold was then sent to Switzerland, largely to the SNB for the Reichsbank account, other shipments made it across France into banks in Spain and Portugal.[211] It seemed to be a quietly, yet commonly, held fact, during the war and after, that victims' gold had been looted on a massive scale by the Nazis. American and Allied diplomats knew this. This impression seemed clear well into the postwar period when American Embassy officials in Paris in 1947 quite explicitly reported " ... most non-monetary gold [is] definitely looted from concentration camp victims."[212]

According to the first Eizenstat Report of 1997, at least thirty-seven kilos of gold acquired from the Nazis' Melmer deliveries of victims' gold were in fact transferred to Switzerland. This gold was smelted, along with looted Dutch guilders, and sent to the SNB.[213] The Melmer deliveries began in May 1942, according to SS Captain Bruno Melmer, under whose name the account appeared in the Reichsbank. These deliveries, seventy in all, comprised confiscated gold from the personal possessions of Holocaust victims including eyeglasses, watches, other jewelry, and dental gold.[214] As Melmer testified in 1947, explaining how the Nazis understood the use of language and deception:

> About May 1942 SS—General (SS-Obergruppenfuhrer) Pohl ordered me to receive the valuables which were confiscated as Jewish property in the concentration camps Ausschwitz [sic] and Lublin and to take them to the Reichsbank Berlin. At an *oral* conference in which, as far as I know, Reichsminister [Walter] Funk, Reichsbankpresident Pohl and SS-Lt. General (SS-Gruppenfuhrer) Frank participated, and Reichsbank Berlin had been charged with realizing these valuables to the credit of the Reich and to transfer the equivalent amount to a newly opened delivery account at the Reich Main Accounting Office (Reichshauptkasse).(Italics, mine)[215]

Melmer's recollection of an 'oral conference' is significant. It shows the care taken by the Nazis to cover their actions.

While the SNB proved vital to the Nazis as their banker, the BIS proved important to the Nazis as a cloak for their international political and economic illegitimacy, especially in light of the economic war that was being waged against them by the Allies. "It was important for the Reichsbank to have the BIS as an international basis for its transactions," answered Emil Puhl, the former Vice-President of the Reichsbank, to Army investigators after the war. "Our situation was such that it was necessary for us to look for every possibility which possibly could give international help without too many difficulties."[216]

General Lucius Clay, Head of the U.S. Group Command Council sought help from the Treasury Department for further investigation of BIS accounts in September 1945.

> ... Reichsbank records and officials indicate ... that some of the gold looted by the Germans during the war was after resmelting sent to the Bank for International Settlements ... that the Principal of some of the old German debts to various European countries was at a time when such countries were occupied by the Germans ... repaid through the Bank for International Settlements in gold or foreign exchange which was subsequently looted or confiscated from such countries by the Germans.[217]

As the Germans moved east, the drive for amassing gold and general loot was included in a more comprehensive policy of economic despoilment. While the drive to annihilate Jews increased, the effort to meticulously gather their assets decreased. "... [T]he economic benefits extracted by the Germans from the rapidly over-run and basically wealthy Western economies," wrote Gerhard Weinberg, "were in reality considerably greater than those taken from the more heavily war-ravaged and in part less wealthy occupied portions of the U.S.S.R., [and] the intention was clearly different."[218] As much as the Nazis could have, and indeed wanted, to benefit from the exploitation of Eastern Europe and the USSR, complete destruction and eradication of everything down to the last morsel of the Soviet State was the overall driving ideological intent and purpose. Poles, too, as Nazi-defined the "inferior" Slavs and their cousins in Eastern Europe, were also scheduled for destruction. The organized looting and ransoming that occurred in the West took second place to the outright destruction of the culture and people of the Slavic nations. Toward this end, M.Y. Raginsky, Assistant Nuremberg Prosecutor of the USSR, explained that the orders of Hitler found:

> concrete expression in the wrecking of cultural institutions, the looting and destruction of cultural treasures, and the suffocation of the national cultural life of the peoples in the territories temporarily occupied by the German armies, that is, the territories of the U.S.S.R., Poland, Czechoslovakia, and Yugoslavia.[219]

There would be no time for legal structures. Destruction was the plan.

In Poland, following the division agreed to in the Nazi-Soviet Pact of August 1939, the Jewish population there was left to the mercy of the Nazis. When it came to dispossession of their assets, however, they initially faced the same procession of decrees and threats Jews in the West faced. As in Western Europe, some Polish public and private assets were, however, transported to safety in the West.[220] By September 17, 1940, that state of conditions changed dramatically when Hermann Göring issued a decree that went beyond the gradual dissipation of assets, and called for the confiscation of all the assets of all Poles, particularly Jews. Now, everything of possession to Jews, "among other things, large quantities of gold and silver objects, jewels, etc.," was to be taken for the good of the German State and "folkdom."[221] The fate of Poland's Jews was sealed.

As the Einsatzgruppen units advanced into the Soviet Union following the Nazi invasion of June 1941, there was an organized effort to round up Jews in great numbers and exterminate them. Their assets, left behind, were gathered and reported cumulatively to Berlin. Great amounts of gold, currency, jewelry, household goods, and other materials found were gathered en masse for delivery into the Melmer and Reichsbank processes.[222] The watches and jewelry were inspected and separated into lots determined to either be usable and unusable for either resale and redistribution purposes. Not all of the material confiscated from Jews was, of course, usable and this was, in part, a result of the more haphazard process of its accumulation. As an unidentified official at the Berlin Pawn Shop, the official agency responsible for evaluation and utilization of the loot, wrote, they were not entirely satisfied with the condition of the looted material:

> After experts looked over our stores, the professional group declared that no gold can be expected for the largest part of our stored materials. Most of the watches need repairs, they are old fashioned, used up and of foreign origin. We sure could obtain gold from the purchasing public but for new style and good watches, and not for old and bad ones.
>
> We would like here to mention that most of your watches have not been stored, but had to be salvaged because of their condition (rusty mechanism, missing parts). The specialists consulted by us consider storing in wet places as responsible for this condition.
>
> ... We regret not to be able to fullfill [sic] your wishes. You consider your consignments delivered to us as of very high value, while we must treat it as means to provide foreign currency and raw materials.[223]

In March 1944, the Pawn Shop wrote to the Reichsbank urging the proper utilization of labor for the vast amount of incoming goods. "Considering the large amount of incoming foreign currency as a result of the sale of these objects in foreign countries," wrote a Herr Kroop, "and the considerable acquirements of gold and silver not fit for export from smelting—the immediate settlement for this problem seems to be very advisable."[224]

What remained usable of Jewish household goods and furniture was requisitioned for military usage, and personal effects were resold to the general population in Germany and elsewhere in an effort to raise funds to pay occupation costs.[225]

When it came to art, the Nazis relied less on decrees and more on taking what they liked, and believed to be theirs, to repatriate to Germany, or their own private collections, regardless of where it was found. In France they found a rich haul of vast art collections which Nazi officers pilfered with utter glee.

Once France fell, French-speaking German officers began their triumphal "tours" of French museums and private collections. These officers, members of the Kunstshutz, were units that answered to a Commission especially designated to scourer Europe for art. They were, in some ways, acting on the unofficial dictates of the Kümmel Report. This report was a three-volume set, begun in 1939, featuring artwork looted from Germany by numerous European armies, including Napoleon's. From the 1500s, through World War I, up until the 1930s, Germany lost a number of historical works of art, and the Nazis were intent on repatriating them.[226]

At the command of Hitler, declared Hermann Bunjes one of the officers now roaming Paris for art:

> the German High Command, therefore, gave orders to the Military Commander in Paris dated June 30, 1940 to take over for the time being the safeguarding not only of the works of art owned by the French State but also the works of art and antiques owned by individuals, especially Jews, in order to prevent their removal and /or concealment.[227]

Soon the members of the Einsatzstab Reichsleiter Rosenberg (ERR) were canvassing France looking for valued art collections. Bunjes explained:

> When the organization in charge of examining the contents of Jewish archives and apartments (Gestapo, the Einsatzstab Reichsleiter Rosenberg, and 'Devisenschutz-kommando' traced the whereabouts of mainly Jewish owned works of art, hidden in a wide range of different places, and when the whereabouts of numerous works of art were reported by troops and headquarters in the Jewish castles and palaces in Paris and environs, Staatsrat Dr. Turner who was at that time chief of the Paris Military Administration, gave orders to the Administration of French Museums to set aside a few large rooms in the Louvre to which all works of art located were transferred.[228]

The ERR, the unit under the direction of early Nazi theorist Alfred Rosenberg, who, as an ethnic German born in Talinn, first discovered the "joys" of the fraudulent, *Protocols of the Wise Men of Zion* in 1917,[229] was tasked by Hitler to bring back to Germany all that was deemed "culturally holy" to the German

Volk. The ERR made sure that nothing would escape its tentacles, especially as Party theorist Rosenberg also found it necessary to expound on the reasoning behind his units' actions. In November 1941, the ERR produced a tract, once again using the same language the Nazis previously used to convince Germany of the righteousness of their cause suggesting, as Lynn Nicholas wrote, "The Jews, by their amassing or riches, had prevented the German people from "having their proper share of the economic and cultural goods of the Universe." Since most of the Jews in France had come originally from Germany, the "safeguarding" of their works of art should be considered "a small indemnity for the great sacrifices of the Reich made for the people of Europe in their fight against Jewry."[230]

Rosenberg and the ERR made the surrender of Jewish artwork appear as "the least possible gesture the Jews could do" to help the Nazis supercede them as the new "chosen people."

Later, seized artwork would be segregated into those acceptable to the Germans, and that which was viewed as "degenerate" Jewish art which was to be sold off to a stable of cooperative German, Swiss, and collaborationist French dealers. The art pleasant to the Nazis, crafted by artists "capturing the Volk spirit" such as the ethnic Germans and formerly German lands Hitler sought to recapture, were to be repatriated and brought back into the Reich.

"The Fuhrer wishes that the art objects seized by your staff," wrote Reichsleiter Martin Bormann to Rosenberg in 1943, "be transferred as soon as possible to the Furhrer's experts for further handling."[231] These pictures would be transferred to Hitler's grand museum in Linz.

While Jewish collections were being seized and 'repatriated' to Germany, some were being 'repatriated' to other places as well, namely the ever-growing collections of Hermann Goering and other high-ranking Nazis. With the conquest of Europe, Hitler sought to keep the various branches of the German occupation government throughout the expanding Reich in competition with each other, all vying for his attention and praise. This competitive division of labor created problems for Goering in that he sought to enrich himself with confiscated Jewish artwork. Now he had to take the initiative and seek artwork from a variety of sources, including the spoils of competitors within the various branches of the government, military, and diplomatic core, to enhance his collection.[232] As the analysts of the U.S. Foreign Economic Administration wrote:

> Unfortunately, Nazi organizations concerned with systematic looting soon made use of the Kunstshutz, which had been established in Norway, Holland, Belgium, France, Italy, Greece and Serbia. Such groups were little more than personal agents of high-ranking Nazis ... [233]

Goering never hesitating to use the Kunstshutz, as well as other sources, to "grow" his collection. Writing to Rosenberg in the guise of providing further instruction as to the disposition of seized works of art he wrote:

> In addition, I should like to call to your attention that I have been able to obtain especially valuable cultural goods from Jewish owners. I obtained them from hiding places that were very difficult to find; I discovered these a long time ago, by means of bribery and the employment of French detectives and criminal agents. This activity continues, as does the activity of my foreign exchange investigation authorities in scrutinizing bank vaults.[234]

Prominent Jewish families across Europe saw their collections scattered around the globe for sale or "auction," much of it lost through seizure. Paul Rosenberg of France, [235] the head of one of these families, saw a number of paintings from his collection end up in the hands of Arthur Wiederkehr, the infamous middleman for ransom payments extracted from Jews seeking freedom out of Holland and other occupied countries. Alois Miedl, the liquidator of the Goudstikker collection, claimed this transaction after the war during interrogations by U.S. personnel. Miedl confessed transferring six of Rosenberg's paintings to Wiederkehr after obtaining them from the ERR.[236]

Wiederkehr received a great amount of money in payment for his ransom work. While in contact with a number of wealthy Jews, one alternative method of payment for exit permits was the transfer of artwork. Another "client" who paid through the "sale" of his artwork was Nathan Katz, a Dutch art dealer and father of Sybilla Katz-Goldstein, who described the confiscations of her family by the ERR above. Katz had worked through the wife of the deceased former Swiss Consul in Amsterdam, Otto Lanz, who was described as a "great friend" of Wiederkehr by Allied Intelligence. It was Lanz who had introduced Wiederkehr to Miedl.[237] Lanz was instrumental in helping the Katzes to get out of Holland and into Basle, Switzerland.[238] Once there, intelligence officials were said to have been very interested in talking to Katz concerning any possible role he had in selling off paintings from the Goudstikker collection or in other transactions to which he might have been privy.[239]

German policy in looting artwork varied in Europe. Experience and necessity dictated the processes and measures taken. As the conditions of the war progressed, as with other forms of assets the Nazis acquired, the swiftness and methodical nature of their work changed. "In the Eastern part [of Europe]," U.S. Foreign Economic Administration analysts wrote, "particularly in Poland, the Germans apparently made a clean sweep of collections, both public and private." They continued, "In the western countries, France, Belgium, Holland, national museums were left comparatively intact while private collections owned by Jewish dealers and art collectors were confiscated outright."[240]

As the Nazis spread their conquest, and the Reich became too large to control by direct means, Nazi-allied forces joined them in the plunder using many of the same methods. While combating the spread of Nazi economic plunder, the Western Allies, inadvertently, as an unintended consequence, did the same.

Plunder by Proxy

"When reminded of this claim," wrote Professor Richard Goldschmidt, in 1943, "the Swiss company answered that first they will pay only in Berlin and in German marks, second, they will hand over the money [for an insurance policy] to the German government according to what they call German 'law'."[241] Helmuth Bloch also saw two of his life insurance policies handed over to the Nazi authorities as did Martha Mandelbaum and Paul Graupe, all losing their policies to the Swiss Insurance Company Basler Lebensversicherungs Gesellschaft under the same circumstances.[242]

Insurance companies outside Germany heeded Nazi confiscation laws accepting the legitimacy of mere promises when, in fact, they were not legally or even morally obliged to do so. As the authors of the final report of the Swiss Bergier Commission found:

> Another controversial area was the willingness of Swiss insurance companies to pay out on German Jews' confiscated policies. The companies were offered a declaration stating that in the event of later repayment claims by the policy-holders concerned, the German state would indemnify the companies. Some Swiss insurance companies were satisfied with this assurance ... [243]

Jews lost their assets in banks, insurance companies, and other institutions, simply because other agents, acting out of respect for or fear of the Nazis, or even out of simple or admiring respect and recognition of the assumed overwhelming Nazi legitimacy and by association, their rule, abided by German wishes to sequester or confiscate Jewish assets. Yet, their acquiescence to this, and acceptance of it, was done in an almost religious manner. As will be seen, French banking and Swiss insurance officials and others collaborators freely accepted Nazi rule. There was no necessity for them to carry out their observance of Nazi rules, much less do so in such a subservient manner, yet they did with religious affirmation and zeal.

As Henri Gadd, the French Counsel for Chase Bank in France, wrote Albert Bertrand the head of Chase in France, regarding Jewish accounts, "it seems to me that in connection with these accounts it would be advisable to observe, as you have in the past, not only the provisions of the French laws and decrees but also those of the ordinances of the occupying authorities."[244]

Gadd, and even more so the new head of the Paris branch of Chase, Swiss-born Carlos Niedermann, were all too willing to please the Nazis and this willingness, according to the U.S. Treasury Department, quickly extended into outright collaboration.[245] The example set by British, and American banks in Occupied France, is illustrative of the role overeager proxies played in the expropriation of Jewish assets.

Chase, the well-respected New York-based bank, led the pack of exuberant proxy expropriators. Chase was described after the war by rivals at another New York-based bank, Guaranty Trust, as "the beloved child" of German bank Administrator Hans Joachim Caesar.[246] Chase was not alone in their zealousness to cooperate and collaborate with the enemy.

An official at the British bank, Barclay's in France, inquired of Caesar what he should do with his Jewish employees.[247] Barclays later volunteered to loan as much as 16.5 million francs to quarries supplying the Herman Göring Works. Lloyds Bank also made a loan to a French armament company supplying the Nazis in France.[248]

Thinking their actions would perhaps benefit their companies, their social standing within the "new order," and simply out of their own convictions, these banking institutions acted on behalf of, and respect for, Nazi rule and against European Jews. Even officials of the American bank, J.P. Morgan and Co., took great pains to express to German administrators their hatred of Jews and their historic unwillingness to employ them.[249] Non-Germans like this were all too willing to accept the Nazis as the new agents of authority, regardless of their lack of acceptance by the majority of others, even in their own countries.

Bankers were not the only zealous agents in the Nazi expropriation effort. H.A. Dörflinger, a Swiss-born bookkeeper, reported the American Consul General in Basel in 1942 had disclosed forty presumably Jewish-owned accounts to Nazi officials. The accounts were then withdrawn from Credit Suisse in Basel and turned over to the Germans.[250] The sudden transfer of so many accounts to German hands, brazen as it was, caught the eyes of the Swiss National Bank and Credit Suisse who alerted the Swiss Political Police who arrested him for espionage.

Foreign banks in France and Holland gladly agreed to, and many times volunteered, to help the Nazis, but they were not alone. Bankers at the Nederlandsche Bank in Holland, described as "quislings," freely accepted German rule and "treated letters of the Reichsbank, which assumed a right of disposition of the gold, as orders."[251]

The Swiss too, played a central role as both bankers for the Nazis, as well as launderers of their looted gold. As has been explained above, the individual Swiss banks, insurance companies, art galleries, and attorneys providing services as middlemen for Jewish emigres' ransom cases and foreign bank accounts, all influenced the largely acquiescent attitude of the Swiss government to Nazi policies. They did so all in the name of "neutrality," cementing the central role Switzerland played in Nazi looting and the outright robbery of Jewish assets across Europe. The lure was too great for them. As Stanley P. Lovell of the OSS reported to his superiors from Switzerland in 1944, "neutrality pays off too well to ever be abandoned."[252] This neutrality, however, was dependent on the leading role the Nazis played in Europe. Were it not for their murderous rule on the continent, the Swiss and others likewise acting under the supposed banner of neutrality, would not have been able to take advantage of a windfall of Jewish assets. Beyond collaborating, they were also equally guilty in the process the Nazis engineered. These issues remained hidden for nearly fifty years until the mid-1990s when their exposure led to an explosion of revelations and recriminations against all of Switzerland. Switzerland, in many ways, became the ultimate collective enabler of the Nazis robbery of the Jews during the Holocaust.

While the Nazis' institutions of robbery changed as the circumstances warranted in each country, the basic practices remained the same. Sometimes it was not the Nazis or the German people that directly benefited from the plunder, but others in their place. Sometimes, the beneficiaries, however, were not the immoral agents the Nazis and their allies were, but those participating for bureaucratic and institutional reasons following self-created practices to defend themselves against the very policies the Jews suffered from as well. The Western Allies, who created structures to combat the Nazis' economic confiscation policies, themselves caused harm to the Jews they were ostensibly trying to help due to the unintended consequences stemming from the practice of the rules they constructed for this purpose.

A case in point was that of Max and Licco Haim. In Bulgaria, the American Car Company, owned in part by Max Haim and his son Licco Max Haim, was confiscated by the Bulgarian authorities on November 22, 1944. With his father dead, Licco was sent to a forced labor camp at Plovdiv, Bulgaria. Surviving the war, he emigrated along with his family to Sao Paulo, Brazil.[253]

What made Mr. Haim's case more complicated though, was the fact that after the war, some of the assets of the American Car Company were held by American companies. These assets, in the form of deposits, were held by the American companies General Tire, Kelly Tires, and General Motors. The deposits dated back from at least 1939, according to Haim.[254] After the war, when he wrote General Motors seeking to obtain possession of a blocked company account for $5,110.92, he was denied because of lack of proof, as well as the freeze placed on Bulgarian assets by the U.S. Government during the war.[255] Three years later, in January 1952, Henry G. Hilken, Chief of the Intercustodial and Property Branch of the Alien Property Division of the Justice Department informed Haim that "It is not the present policy of this Office to release property in which there is a Bulgarian interest."[256] The difference in Haim's case is he wrote to former U.S. Senator Alfonse M. D'Amato, "... that in my case, the money was not taken by Nazis nor by Communists, but by the U.S. Government!" Unfortunately, Haim's case was not the only one to surface detailing assets taken by the U.S. Government.

Nehemiah Robinson of the World Jewish Congress discussed the problem of assets in the United States in a memo to Irving Dwork, who during the war served as an intelligence analyst for the OSS and supervised the Jewish desk there. Seeking Dwork's opinion on legislation in New York to alleviate the problem, Robinson wrote:

> In consequence of the policies initiated by the Nazis and followed by their satellites, the greatest portion of the Jews of Austria, Czechoslovakia, Estonia, France, Germany, Greece, Holland, Hungary, Latvia, Lithuania, Luxembourg, Norway, Poland, Ronamia, and Yugoslavia were extirpated; quite large numbers of them were killed in Bulgaria, Denmark, and Italy. In these countries, especially those listed in the first category, whole families including parents, children, brothers, and sisters, and more distant relatives were killed or died an unnatural death. Obviously, the assets persons without heirs have in this country became masterless, while others will be unclaimed because the heirs do not know of the existence of the assets. Some of these assets were taken into custody by the Alien Property Custodian, almost all others were frozen (blocked) when the United States entered the war.[257]

According to the Alien Property Custodian, based in the U.S. Justice Department, the total amount of these properties came to $594,708,000, which included vested (confiscated) and blocked properties.[258] These sums included at least, but probably more, than $6 million in heirless bank accounts to which Maurice Golay, above, had referred. The other assets were later returned in tranches, bond series issued for sale in foreign countries, to the various other countries over a number of years. Heirless bank accounts, however, were a different story.

In 1950, the Congress held hearings on legislation to free these heirless funds and turn them over to international relief organizations for the use in settling displaced persons in Europe, as the U.S. and other nations were required to do by post-war treaty. Yet, despite the initial estimate, that sum was reduced based on Congressional testimony from former Secretary of War Robert Patterson, then in the context of the War Claims Commission in 1950, to a ceiling of $3 million. Legislation appropriating this sum failed to become law that year.

In 1954, another attempt was made to appropriate funding and it succeeded. The sum of $3 million was provided, as proposed four years earlier. Over the next several years, an insignificant number of claims were filed, amounting to roughly $500,000, with not even one actually being paid due to the difficulty of proving the claims. Many in Congress became suspicious that with so few claims, perhaps this amount was too much to have been set aside for the problem. Moreover, they were all too eager to have Americans, who also suffered material and financial damages during the war, settle their claims out of these and other blocked funds. In 1960, with this in mind, Congress passed further legislation amending and drastically cutting the $3 million figure to $500,000.[259]

While Congress was restricting the amount of available heirless funds, other parts of the government were doing the same with blocked funds. As of 1957, following a series of blocking orders issued by the U.S. Justice Department, assets belonging to nationals of Bulgaria like Haim, and from other "satellite" countries (Soviet satellites), remained blocked due to continued enemy status. These assets amounted to $225 million.[260] From the three countries of Romania, Hungary, and Bulgaria, the sum was $31.9 million.[261] Because of these numerous and overlapping freezing orders, Haim was not able to obtain his funds, and the claims procedure ended in 1989.[262] In reducing the amount to be paid to claimants, and by paying individual Americans' war damages out of those funds, the United States participated, not as directly or as intentionally as the Nazis and their allies, but nevertheless partook in the plunder of the Holocaust. Worse yet, as will be shown later, the United States did not make it easy, simply through neglect during the Cold War, for survivors to obtain their assets. The U.S. record, however, is far superior on any scale, to that of the Europeans. History bares this point out.

Plunder by Use of Slave and Forced Labor

"For six years of incarceration and other indignities and suffering inflicted on me, I was awarded by the Germans, the great sum of $1,695," wrote Morris Krakowski. "This was calculated at the rate of 5 DM per day (at the time the DM was worth about $.25)."[263] In today's values, Morris Krakowski would not have fared much better, earning perhaps $12.00 per week for the slave labor he performed at the Hasag munitions factory in Poland.

Industrial magnates such as Alfried Krupp, Friedrich Flick, and hundreds of others served as the purveyors of the final form of plunder: the use of forced and slave labor. These men were in fact not one-time offenders, but triple offenders of Europe's Jews. They were the first parties to benefit from the mass Aryanizations of Jewish factories, businesses, and real estate. Then they benefited by the surrender, under duress, of still more to expand their industrial empires, buying up the proceeds at bargain-based prices. Finally, as the demand for war production rose precipitously, these industrialists financially benefited again, quite literally on the backs of Jewish forced and slave laborers.

Physically captive labor, by the millions made available by the Nazis, were supplied to the great munitions, steel, and other factories of Germany. Jews and others formed an intentionally disposable supply of labor. If Jews and others were not working for the Wehrmacht, they worked for private companies which paid the Nazis pennies per day per inmate and benefited so far above that.[264] With Himmler intent on working the Jews to death, they suffered horribly and were overworked to the extreme. Slave and forced laborers were ill-fed, poorly clothed, poorly bunked, and treated as mere fodder for German war production. Laborers were moved around from one labor camp to the other where they faced sadistic guards who took pleasure at inflicting pain and suffering.

"In March 1941," wrote Dolores Finder Berkowsky explaining the plight of her father Alex Finder:

> the Jewish ghetto [in Krakow] was liquidated. Children and elderly people (including his mother) were shot on the spot. Since everyone had to be employed somewhere, he and many others were placed by the German Labor Office in the labor camp at Plaszow. During this time he lived in Emalie Camp, and was assigned to work at Chmielewski Baracken Bau, where they had to unload lumber, nails, cement, and field kitchens for the Army, and many kinds of building materials used for building army barracks, wooden ammunition boxes, and railroad cars. From there, he was sent to Zakopane, in the Tatry Mountains, where he had to build a hydroelectric station in the dead of winter. The Kommandant there was a cruel beast named Strojewski. Six weeks later, they were returned to Plaszow, and from there he was shipped to Mauthausen in Austria. He worked for a few days there in the stone quarry, where they had to carry heavy pieces of stone up the steep slope to the top. The Kapos enjoyed greasing the steep steps and then kicking [them back down]—they jokingly called these unfortunate victims "paratroopers."[265]

Alex Finder was one of more than 6.6 million foreigners put to work for the German war effort, against their will. This number included civilians and prisoners of war.[266] Forced and Slave laborers fell into five categories:

a. A person who was in at least one concentration, labor camp, and/or ghetto who was compelled to perform labor for a governmental, or industrial entity.
b. A person relocated under discriminatory conditions to perform forced labor.
c. Children of such people, who were either separated from or accompanied their parents.
d. A person who like those in 'A' above was force to work, but that work was not limited to government or industrial use.
e. A person who was relocated under discriminatory conditions and forced to work as domestic or agriculture labor.[267]

Of these forced and slave laborers, it is estimated that as of August 1999, there were 2.3 million surviving.[268] These survivors, it is suggested, not only suffered from physical and mental abuse at the hand of the Nazis, but suffered the loss of real wages and to be sure, a real lack of any fringe benefits. The product of their labor was not theirs, but the Nazis'. According to figures worked out by the economic forecasting firm of Nathan Associates, it is surmised that the Nazis benefited, in 1999 real terms, by $22,850 per forced laborer for each year of work.[269] Moreover, statistics bare out that nearly two-thirds of all slave laborers performed on average, two and three-quarters years of work.[270]

While these figures are in present-day terms, they nevertheless are enlightening in as much as the clear benefit the Nazis gained from these unfortunate people when it came to meeting their overwhelming labor needs. These needs were fulfilled by forced labor, giving the Nazis a multiplying effect, freeing up more men for the military, which in turn made it possible for the "capture" of more people to perform forced labor. With this constant influx of laborers, as Robert Gellateley wrote, the Nazis could afford to murder them without fearing the loss of a steady supply of workers.[271]

Slave labor is the final form of plunder. It is the easiest to quantify with available economic figures, yet the most difficult for which to obtain equitable compensation. There is only a return for their labor, rather than for something which had a value based upon a sliding index. Labor however, as mentioned, provided the Nazis with the ability to not only wage war, but do so with minimal labor costs. Slave labor, for those who endured it, was more than a humiliation, it was a robbery of their abilities, their strengths, and talents. More than a piece of gold, it was their very sweat that was lost with their labor.

Those who endured it many times suffered the horrors and indignities of Nazi rule and were, by the very nature of this institution, double victims. Many times they, too, faced the same losses of assets as other victims and survivors, but their losses were multiplied by the loss of the potential taken from them by their involuntary labor. These people were first robbed, then exploited. As Joseph Borkin wrote, companies like " ... I.G. Farben reduced slave labor to a consumable raw material, a human ore from which the mineral of life was systematically extracted."[272]

Notes

1. Samuel Johnson, *Rambler* # 161, October 1, 1751.
2. Letter of Sybilla Katz-Goldstein to Gregg Rickman, September 16, 1998.
3. Hannah Arendt, *Antisemitism* (San Diego: Harcourt Brace Jovanovich, Publishers, 1968), p. 9.
4. Arthur Ruppin, *The Jewish Fate and Future*, translated by E.W. Dickes (London: Macmillan and Col, Limited, 1940) reprinted, CT: Greenwood Press, Publishers, 1972), p. 135.
5. "The Jews of Austria," Duker/Dwork Papers, RG 226, Records of the Office of Strategic Services, Entry 191, Box 6, Folder 112, p. 10, NARA.
6. Ruppin, *The Jewish Fate and Future*, p. 155.
7. Ibid, p. 145.
8. W.D. Rubinstein, "Jews in the Economic Elites of Western Nations and Antisemitism," *The Jewish Journal of Sociology*, vol, 42, nos. 1 and 2, 2000, p. 1.
9. Siegfried Moses, *Jewish Post-War Claims* (Tel Aviv: Irgun Olej Merkaz Europa, 1944), pp. 3, 16.

10. Nana Sagi, *German Reparations, A History of the Negotiations* (Jerusalem: The Hebrew University of Jerusalem, Institute of Contemporary Jewry, 1980), p. 7.
11. Nehemiah Robinson, *Indemnification and Reparations* (New York: Institute for Jewish Affairs of the American Jewish Congress and the World Jewish Congress, 1944), p. 83.
12. Nehemiah Robinson, *Spoilation and Remedial Action, The Material Damage Suffered by Jews Under Persecution, Reparations, Restitution, and Compensation* (New York: Institute of Jewish Affairs, 1962) reprinted from "The Institute Anniversary Volume, (1941-1961)," p. 17.
13. Letter of Nathan Stein, American Federation of Jews From Central Europe to Dr. Charles [sic] Dwork, OSS, Office of Strategic Services, May 21, 1945, RG 200, Duker/Dwork Papers, Box 26, NARA.
14. Letter of Louis Lipsky to Secretary of State James F. Byrnes, February 5, 1946, RG 56, Records of the U.S. Department of Treasury, International Statistics Division, Box 84, National Archives and Records Administration, College Park, MD (hereafter referred to as NARA) p.1.
15. Sidney Jay Zabludoff, "And It All But Disappeared," (New York: Institute of the World Jewish Congress Policy Forum No. 13, 1998), p. 5.
16. Helen Junz, "Report on the Pre-War Wealth Position of the Jewish Population in Nazi-Occupied Countries, Germany, and Austria," in *Report on Dormant Accounts of Victims of Nazi Persecution in Swiss Banks* (New York: Independent Committee of Eminent Persons, December 1999), p. A-130.
17. There have been other, less then accurate estimates of the economic losses sustained by the Jews of Europe. In 1976, Tuvia Friedman, then Director of the Nazi War Documentation Center in Haifa, declared that there was $980 billion in Jewish property taken by the Nazis in the Holocaust; cited in Alexander Zvielli, "A Demand for the Final Installment," *Jerusalem Post*, August 10, 1990.
18. Jeanette Greenfield, "The Spoils of War," in *The Spoils of War, World War II and Its Aftermath: The Loss, Reappearance, and Recovery of Cultural Property*, ed. by Elizabeth Simpson (New York: Harry N. Abrams, Incorporated, 1997), p. 38.
19. "Himmler's October 4, 1943 Posen Speech, 'Extermination,'" The Nizkor Project, translated by the Nizkor Project, available online at http://www.nizkor.org/hweb.../oct-04-43/ausrottung-transl-nizkor.html .
20. Hitler's First Antisemitic Writing, September 16, 1919, translated by Richard S. Levy, available online at http://www2.h-net.msu.edu/~german/gtext/kaiserreich/hitler2.html.
21. Letter of Donald W. Curtis, Chief, Analysis & Reports Section, External Assets Census Branch, Headquarters, U.S. Group Control Council (Germany), to Chief, Financial Investigations Division, "Procedures and Records, Confiscation of Jewish Property," September 26, 1945, RG 260, Records of the Office of the Military Government of the United States in Germany, Headquarters, Finance Division, 1945-1949, Box 181, NARA.
22. Jewelry from Jewish families, once taken, was then handled by German firms for resale, either in Europe, South America, or in one case, in New York. See, "Appraisal of Jewish Jewelry. Release of The Two Lots of Diamonds from U.S. Customs," Letter of September 19, 1941 from the Prufungstelle Metallwaren to the Reich's Minister of Economics, Section V, in RG 260, Records of the Office of the Military Government of the United States in Germany, Finance Division, Interrogations of Nazi Financiers, Box 58, NARA, translated by Brian Hufker, office of Senator Alfonse M. D'Amato.

23. In addition to the cataloging that occurred through the forced property declarations mentioned below, cataloging occurred at the Concentration Camps, as well as round-up points where Jews were forced to report the personal property that was on their person, watches and other types of jewelry, wallets, lighters, photos, small change, and the like. Upon liberation of Dachau by American forces, it was reported that there were "seven containers comprising thousands of separate, sealed envelopes, each identified by name, nationality and number of prisoner, and bearing indications as to contents." See, "Records and Funds of Dachau Concentration Camp, September 10, 1946, RG 260, Records of the Office of the Military Government of the United States in Germany, Chief, Property Control Branch, NARA. Not all the assets were made available for centralized recording. According to Oskar Diegelmann, Senior Inspector of the Reich Railways in Lublin, reported that some valuables were traded among the staff at Belzec and others were offered to prostitutes for sex. See Klee, Dressen, Reiss, eds., p. 234. In Salonika, 166 Jews were lined up by German forces and forced to empty their pockets of all their belongings. See "Materials on Jews of Salonika, including inventory of funds deposited with German officer by listed individuals, and appeal from Archbishop of Salonika to Germans (March 1943) to refrain from cruelties in deportation," RG 226, Records of the Office of Special Services, Intelligence Reports, 115,650-115,731, Entry 16, Box 16, NARA.
24. Frank Bajhor, "The Beneficiaries of 'Aryanization': Hamburg as a Case Study," *Yad Vashem Studies*, Vol. XXVI, 1998, p. 186.
25. Cited in Rainer Sanvoss, *Widerstand im Steglitz und Zehlendorf* (*Resistance in Steglitz and Zehlendorf*), Berlin, 1986, p. 186, translated by Sybil Milton.
26. Kurt Burch, *"Property" and the Making of the International System* (Lynne Reiner Publishers, Boulder, CO, 1998), p. 26.
27. Ibid, p. 145.
28. Ibid; Kurt Burch, "Toward a Constructivist Comparative Politics," in Daniel Green, editor, *Constructivism and Comparative Politics* (M.E. Sharpe: Armonk, New York, 2002), p. 75.
29. Christopher Simpson, *The Splendid Blond Beast, Money, Law, and Genocide in the Twentieth Century* (New York: Grove Press, 1993), p. 5.
30. Kershaw, p. 65.
31. Cited in Simpson, p. 66.
32. Clifford J. Hynning, *Germany, Preliminary Report on Selected Financial Laws, Decrees and Regulations*, Vol. 2 Appendices... (Washington, DC: Treasury Department, Office of the General Counsel, 1944), p. E-48.
33. Ibid, p. E-43.
34. "Law Changing the Regulations in Regard to Public Officers," in Ibid, p. E-46.
35. Ibid, p. E-49.
36. Ibid, p. E-50.
37. Ibid, p. E-51.
38. Robert D. Scott, *Preliminary Study of Certain Financial Laws and Institutions, Austria* (Washington, D.C.: Department of the Treasury, September 1944), pp. 125-126.
39. Hynning, p. E-53.
40. Ibid, p. E-51.
41. Felicitas Heiman-Jelinek, "Of Aryanization and Restitution: The Fate of the Rothschild Art and Other Properties, in Vienna," in Theodore Brückler, *Looted Art, Recovery of Art and Restitution in Austria 1938 until Today*, 1999, in *Appendix of Declarations and Exhibits, Dorit Whiteman, et al, Plaintiffs v. Republic of Austria, et al, Defen-*

dants, Civil Action No. 00CIV.8006 (SWK), United States District Court, Southern District of New York, p. 4.
42. Robert Gellateley, *Backing Hitler, Consent & Coercion in Nazi Germany* (Oxford, United Kingdom: Oxford University Press, 2001), p. 143.
43. Grunberger, p. 459.
44. Scott, pp. 123, Appendices, p. F-1.
45. Hynning, p. E-31.
46. Otto Nathan, "Nazi War Finance and Banking," *Our Economy in War Series*, National Bureau of Economic Research, Financial Research Program, United States Federal Reserve, September 10, 1943, p. 39.
47. Ibid.
48. Avraham Barkai, *From Boycott to Annihilation, the Economic Struggle of German Jews, 1933-1943*, translated by William Templer (Hanover, New Hampshire: Brandeis University Press, 1989), p. 100.
49. Letter of Leonhard Hildebrand to the United States Department of State, "Subject: Report of property, cash and securities lost during Nazi Regime in Europe," September 27, 1946, RG 260, Records of the Office of the Military Government in Austria, US Allied Commission, Austria (USACA), Property Control Branch, Correspondence to Claims, 1945-50, Box 2, p. 4, NARA.
50. Based upon calculations used by United States Intergovernmental Commission Preliminary Report, coordinated by Amb. Stuart E. Eizenstat, rates for currency conversion from 1946 when Mr. Hildebrand wrote to the State Department, are multiplied by a factor of 8.2 to arrive at a current value. See Stuart E. Eizenstat, Ed., *U.S. and Allied Efforts To Recover and Restore Gold and Other Assets Stolen or Hidden by Germany During WWII, Preliminary Study* (Washington, D.C.: United States Government Printing Office, May 1997), p. xxxix. Hereafter referred to as Eizenstat I.
51. Letter of David Detmar Loewenstern to the Finance Division, Property Control Branch, U.S. Military Government for Germany, March 9, 1947, RG 260, Office of the Military Government for Germany, Property Division, Correspondence Pertaining to Claims, 1946-48, Box 79, NARA; Scott, p. 130.
52. Nathan, fn. #53, p. 43.
53. David Martin Luebke and Sybil Milton, "Locating the Victim: An Overview of Census-Taking, Tabulation Technology, and Persecution in Nazi Germany," *IEEE Annals of the History of Computing*, Vol. 16, No. 3, (1994), p. 29.
54. Ibid, p. 31.
55. Edwin Black, *IBM and the Holocaust, The Strategic Alliance Between Nazi Germany and America's Most Powerful Corporation* (New York: Crown Publishers, 2001), p. 73.
56. Simpson, p. 73.
57. Scott, p. 128.
58. Declaration of Elisabeth Grünbaum, Verzeichnis über das Vermögen von Juden, 27 April 1938, Österreichisches Staatsarchiv, Vienna, Austria. The Österreichisches Staatsarchiv in Vienna holds more than 50,000 similar case files. Each provides rich details as to the wealth of the Jewish community in Vienna at the time. Declarations detailed all of the person's wealth. Those wealthy like the Grünbaums down to the less wealthy like Bertha Kaufmann were forced to declare all they owned. Declaration of Bertha Kaufmann, attachment of Letter of Robert M. Kaufmann to Gregg Rickman, August 28, 2002.
59. Property declarations were required in nearly every area the Nazis conquered. The requirement for these declarations were either carried out directly by the occupying German authorities or by the collaborationist, proxy authorities, such as in France,

Romania and elsewhere. See Frederick Cohen, "The Jews in the Channel Islands During The German Occupation, 1940-1945," Jersey Heritage Trust and the Institute of Contemporary History and Weiner Library Limited, 2000, pp. 7-11, available online at .Aleksandar Matkovski, *The Destruction of Macedonian Jewry in 1943*, Yad Vashem Studies, (1959), Vol. III, pp. 213-214.

60. Scott, p. 130.
61. Bergier, p. 107.
62. Passport of Max Chowdowski, courtesy of the Estate of Max Chowdowski, via the Law Firm of Cohen, Milstein, Hausfeld, and Toll. See Appendix 3. See Gregg J. Rickman, *Swiss Banks and Jewish Souls* (New Brunswick, N.J.: Transaction Books), p. 173; Jean François Bergier, Ed., *Switzerland and Refugees in the Nazi Era* (Bern, Switzerland: Independent Commission of Experts, Switzerland—Second World War, 1999), pp. 73-85.
63. "The Second Regulation Under the Law Re The Changing of Family and Given Names," August 18, 1938, in Hynning, p. E-70.
64. Radu Ionid, *The Holocaust in Romania, The Destruction of Jews and Gypsies Under the Antonescu Regime, 1940-1944* (Chicago, IL: Ivan R. Dee, 2000), p. 259.
65. Marilyn Henry, "Victims of Omission," *Jerusalem Post*, July 29, 1999; "Descendants of father of Isaac and Menachem Schachne," A genealogy of the Schachne Family, distant cousins of the author, n.d.
66. Bergier, p. 20.
67. "Nr. 81 from 5.12, According to 23 November R 23552 Statement I," December 5, 1938, RG 242, Captured German Documents, NARA, translated by Brian Hufker, Office of Senator Alfonse M. D'Amato. German diplomats reported back to Germany that the Swiss people were upset, first that Jews had emigrated to Switzerland but had moved on "avoiding the risks of the remaining Swiss population." There was little respect for the plight of Jewish refugees seeking the temporary safety of Switzerland. Telegram of Jahnke to the Foreign Office, September 11, 1944, Captured German Records, Microfilm, NARA. Moreover, the Swiss Government erected over thirty labor camps in which to house the refugees. Once in Switzerland, the refugees were forced to perform menial labor, as they were barred from gainful employment. They were supported by funds from the Jewish community in Switzerland. By 1942, there were said to be over 6,000 Jewish refugees in Switzerland and there was talk of relocating them from Switzerland due to overcrowding and the expenses associated with caring for them. "30 New Labor Camps Set Up In Switzerland To Meet Refugee Influx," Intercepted letter from W. Levy of Santiago, Chile to Senor Dagobert de Levie, New York, RG 165, Records of the War Department General and Special Staffs, Entry 77, Box 2998, NARA; "Evacuation of Refugees from Switzerland," Memorandum from J. Edgar Hoover, Director of the Federal Bureau of Investigation to Adolf A. Berle, Jr., Assistant Secretary of State, May 15, 1942, RG 165, Records of the War Department General and Special Staffs, Entry 77, Box 2998, NARA.
68. Based on an exchange rate in 1938 of 2.5 RM to $1 US. Letter of Fire Insurance Branch of the German Association of Property Insurers, Addendum prepared by Bobby Brown, Senior Advisor to the Chairman of the Jewish Agency for Israel. Gellateley, *Backing Hitler, Consent & Coercion in Nazi Germany* (Oxford, U.K.: Oxford University Press, 2001), p. 127; Gilbert, p. 71.
69. Memorandum No. 490, *Documents on German Foreign Policy 1918-1945, Series C, "The Third Reich: First Phase," Vol. V, March-October 1936* (Washington, DC: U.S. Government Printing Office, 1966), p. 861.
70. Hynning, pp. E-86-87.

71. Letter of Fire Insurance Branch of the German Association of Property Insurers, Addendum.
72. Dr. Vitka Toshkova, "Anti-Semitic Legislation in Bulgaria, 1940-1944," paper presented at the London Conference on Nazi Gold, December 2-4, 1997, London, England, p. 3.
73. Radu Lecca, the director of the wartime Office for Jewish Problems in Romania, "demanded and received millions of lei from the Jewish community of Iasi, for example, at least part of which he kept for himself." See Ioanid, p. 285; and "Relief and Rescue Work for Jewish Refugees," Headquarters Africa-Middle East Theater, Office of AC of S, G-2, March 22, 1945, in RG 226, Duker-Dwork Papers, Entry 191, Box 4, p. 4.
74. Jean Matteoli, *Interim Report of the Prime Minister's Commission for the Study of the Spoilation of Jews in France*, December 1, 1997, pp. 17-18.
75. Letter of Fire Insurance Branch of the German Association of Property Insurers, December 12, 1938, RGVA Moscow Fond 1458-1-98, translated by the Jewish Agency for Israel, Bobby Brown, Senior Advisor to the Chairman.
76. "Stenographic Report on a part of the Conference on the Jewish question under the presidency of Field Marshall Goering at the Reich Ministry for Air on 12 November 1938–11 o'clock," RG 260, Office of the Military Government of the United States in Germany, Finance Division, Box 181, p. 1, NARA.
77. Ibid.
78. Peter Gay, "My German Question," *The American Scholar* (Autumn 1998), Vol. 67, No. 4, p. 39.
79. Hynning, p. E-91.
80. Feldman, p. 10.
81. Albert Fisher, "The Minister of Economics and the Expulsion of the Jews from the German Economy," in *Probing the Depths of German Antisemitism, German Society and the Persecution of the Jews, 1933-1941*, ed. by David Bankier (Israel: Yad Vashem and the Leo Baeck Institute, 2000), p. 222.
82. Simpson, p. 68.
83. Letter of Cornelia V. Paur to President Harry S. Truman, July 31, 1948, RG 59, Records of the State Department, Entry 1945-49, Box 4248, NARA. In most cases, duress was a means to an end when it came to aryanization. Imprisonment was considered a highly effective tool by the Nazis to achieve control of Jewish businesses through aryanization. In addition to the Paur case there was that of the Michaelis Washing Machine Factory in Munich, owned by Gustav Mannheimer who was imprisoned in Dachau on the night of Kristallnacht, November 10, 1938. His factory was then aryanized under duress on November 23, 1938, a little more than three weeks after his imprisonment. "Report of Investigation of Dr. Adolf Fischer, Munich, Germany," October 10, 1946, RG 260, OMGUS, Records of the Office of the Military Government of Germany, U.S. Occupation Headquarters, Office of the Finance Division and Finance Advisor, 49.00 Bank Deutscher Lander 1942, Box 219, NARA.
84. Barkai, pp. 99-100.
85. "Property Transferred Under the Nazi Regime in Germany," Foreign Economic Administration, Liberated Areas Branch, (June 1944), United States Federal Reserve.
86. Letter of M. Bally to Frederick B. Weissmann, October 19, 1945, RG 84, Records of the American Legation in Bern, Box 6, File of Frederick B. Weissmann, NARA.
87. Frank Bajhor, "The Beneficiaries of 'Aryanization': Hamburg as a Case Study," p. 186.

88. Toshkova, p. 1.
89. Fred B. Smith, *Preliminary Studies of Certain Financial Laws & Institutions, Czechoslovakia* (Washington, DC: U.S. Department of the Treasury, Office of the General Counsel, October 1944), p. 151.
90. Ibid, p. 152.
91. Ibid, p. 21; Stanford Schewel, "History and Present Status of Lippmann Rosenthal & Co. Sarphatistraat, Amsterdam, The Nazi Agency for the Confiscation of Dutch-Jewish Property," Report from the American Consulate General Amsterdam, Netherlands, April 7, 1946, RG 84, Records of the Department of State Posts, Hague Legation, 1946: 851 - 862.2, Box 41, NARA; Letter of A.J. Drexel Biddle, Jr. to A.F.I. van Troostenburg de Bruyn, Esq, Netherlands Foreign Office, Dutch Government in Exile, London, January 9, 1943, RG 84, Records of the Department of State Posts, American Mission to the Dutch Government in Exile, General Records - 1940-44, 350-885.91, Box 3, NARA.
92. Inter-Allied Reparation Agency, "Eleventh meeting of the Committee of Experts in matters of enemy property custodianship held at the Office of the Inter-Allied Reparation Agency, Brussels, on Wednesday June 26th, at 3 p.m.," RG 131, Foreign Funds Control, General Correspondence, 1942-1960, Entry NN3-131-94-001, Box 219, NARA, p. 7.
93. Interview of H.J. Caeser with the Office of Strategic Services, January 8, 1945, RG 131, Records of the Office of Alien Property (United States Department of Justice), File, France: Investigation of U.S. Banks & Enterprises - Vol. II, p. 1, NARA.
94. *Interim Report of the Prime Minister's Commission for the Study of the Spoilation of Jews in France*, p. 8.
95. Susan Zuccotti, *The Holocaust, the French, and the Jews* (New York: Basic Books, 1993), pp. 90-91; Interview with Mina Parsont, February 11, 2001, Rockville, Maryland.
96. Jean Ancel, "Confiscation and Seizure of Jewish Property in Romania," *Symposium, Confiscation of Jewish Property in Europe, 1933-1945, New Sources and Perspectives*, Center for Advanced Holocaust Studies, United States Holocaust Memorial Museum, Washington, DC March 22, 2001, p. 2.
97. Ibid, p. 16.
98. Telephone and discussions and email communications with Dr. Jacqueline Vlodinger Waldman, May 2002; Letter of Jacqueline Vlodinger to Gregg Rickman, June 27, 2002, with chronology and documents concerning her father's property in Romania.
99. Emily W. Thomann, *Preliminary Study of Certain Financial Laws and Institutions, Belgium* (Washington, DC: Department of the Treasury, July 1944), p. vii.
100. "The Jews of Belgium," RG 226, Duker-Dwork Papers, Folder 122, Box 6, p. 10, NARA.
101. Ibid, pp. 152-170.
102. Rickman, pp. 279-280.
103. Gay, pp. 35-36.
104. Letter of Susana David, Buenos Aires, Argentina, to U.S. Senator Alfonse M. D'Amato, August 1, 1996.
105. Tom Bower, *Nazi Gold, The Full Story of the Fifty-Year Swiss-Nazi Conspiracy to Steal Billions from Europe's Jews and Holocaust Survivors* (New York: HarperCollins Publishers, 1997), p. 261.
106. Treasury Department, Office of the Secretary, *Census of American-Owned Assets in Foreign Countries* (Washington, DC: United States Government Printing Office, 1947), p. 49.

107. On February 8, 1945, American Legation officials in Bern reported to the State Department a Zurich newspaper story which declared "Considerable amounts Jewish capital doubtless included in 1940 flight of capital since Jews had particular grounds to protect their property..."Telegram of Huddle, American Legation in Bern to the Secretary of State, February 8, 1945, RG 59, Records of the State Department Decimal File, 1945-1949, # 840.51/FC54/2-845 CS/EG, Box 5845, NARA.
108. According to Federal Reserve Records declassified only in the late 1990s, "[i]t is known that during the war substantial amounts of refugee capital flowed into Uruguay. The capital inflow in 1943, the latest year for which figures are available, amounted to 26 million dollars." The Uruguayan economy apparently was so dependent upon this inflow, that officials there worried about its impact. Letter of Wendall E. Thorne, International Section, United States Federal Reserve, to Mr. H. Lubin, Central Paint & Varnish Works, December 11, 1945, p. 1,
109. There was a suggestion of Jewish assets, either assumed or stolen by Albert Blume, a German immigrant, thought by some to have been a Nazi, and found in 1997 in Brazil. Blume's safety deposit box was found following the creation of a government commission established to locate Jewish assets there. In the box was found some $4,000,000 in luxury watches, rings, gold bars and gold teeth. Upon examination by an historian Dieter Strauss, it was found that there seems to have been no connection between Blume's background and the assets found in his safety deposit box. See, Diana Jean Schemo, "A Nazi's Trail Leads to a Gold Cache in Brazil," *New York Times*, September 23, 1997, p. 1, 14; and Stan Lehman, "No Apparent Link Between Fortune Left in Brazilian Bank and Nazis," *Associated Press*, January 7, 1998.
110. According to Professor Ronald Newton of Simon Fraser University in British Columbia, Canada, "perhaps as many as 100,000 Jewish refugees from Hitlerism were received in Latin America, almost half of them by Argentina." See Remarks of Ronald Newton, "Latin America and the Holocaust," International Conference, War Criminals and Nazism In Latin America: 50 Years Later," Sponsored by B'nai B'rith International and the Washington College of Law, University of Maryland, October 20, 1996, published July 1998, p. 11. More importantly, Newton suggested, regarding Argentina, "Private capital movement or flight did occur and it is suggested here [in the report] that much of it did not leave a paper trail to be found in the U.S. National Archives. German government restrictions on capital leaving Germany applied to all Germans but particularly to assets of Jews. It is suggested here that some other Germans utilized the same methods for shielding assets as did refugees from the Nazi regime." See Ronald C. Newton and Christel K. Converse, "Nazi Investments in Argentina Through Front Companies with Particular Emphasis on the Cases of The Wehrli Bank and Mandl Group Companies," p. 27, Final Report of the Commission of Enquiry into the Activities of Nazism in Argentina, Buenos Aires, 1997-1999.
111. Rickman, p. 30.
112. Letter of Yaakov Altman to the Office of Public Relations, Treasury Department, Jerusalem, October 5, 1962, translated by the Congressional Research Service, Foreign Ministry Archives, Jerusalem.
113. Letter of Maurice Golay, General Manager of the Swiss Bank Corporation, Basel to W. Sholes, Consul General of the United States, Basel, May 3, 1943, RG 84, Records of Foreign Service Posts, 851.6, NARA.
114. Ibid, p. 3.
115. Demand Accounts, Swiss Bank Corporation Final Report of Investigation, 1941, RG 131, Records of Foreign Funds Control, NARA.

116. Omnibus accounts could be divided up between a general account and a numbered or code-named account and even sub-accounts. Letter of Bernard Bernstein to L. S. Lessor, July 3, 1942, RG 56, Records of the Department of Treasury, Entry 56-77-52, Subject Files, 1942-72, Box 5, NARA.
117. In a letter to Treasury Department investigators, the Managers of the New York branch of the Swiss Bank Corporation declared their assertion, "Several of our branches, quite correctly, point out that the safekeeping of all bonds and non-American shares with your Agency under 'rubrique deposits' is simply a measure of our internal organization...the 'rubrique deposits' have always been considered as part of our ordinary collective deposits and can by no means be compared to the special deposits opened for certain clients upon their own request." See Criminal Report, Re: Swiss Bank Corp., Swiss Bank Corporation Final Report of Investigation, 1941, RG 131, Records of Foreign Funds Control, p. 6 fn., NARA.
118. Rozell, "Refugee Dollar Funds: Effect on Balance of Payments," Memorandum to the Files, U.S. Federal Reserve, New York Branch, June 7, 1940, Federal Reserve Bank, Washington, DC.
119. Ibid, p. 3. According to the Treasury investigative report, "To 'cloak' the identity of the owners of such capital the Swiss Banks conceived the idea of numbered accounts, i.e.accounts designated on the records of the bank and referred to by the bank by a number or code symbol only."
120. W.H. Rozell.
121. Letter of Maurice Golay.
122. List of Dormant Account Holders, Swiss Bankers Association, *New York Times*, November 10, 1997, p. 15.
123. "List of Swiss Lawyers in Lucerne Said to be Hiding German Assets," OSS Report, May 14, 1946, RG 226, Records of the Office of Strategic Services, SI, Special Funds, Box 23, NARA.
124. In an OMGUS Finance Division report of July 11, 1947, a bookkeeper and former inmate at Dachau suggested that the Deutsche Wirtschaftsbetriebe G.m.b.H. was a holding company for the SS and that the company held an account in Switzerland. Relatives in Switzerland covered their actions for them. See Report of Albert F. Bender, Jr., Chief External Assets & Intelligence Branch, Finance Division, Office of the Military Government for German, July 11, 1947, RG 260, Office of the Military Government of the United States in Germany, Records of the Property Division, 1945-1949, Box 538, p. 1.
125. Letter of Maurice Golay.
126. Letter of Wilhelm Kleemann to the U.S. Military Government in Germany, January 18, 1948, RG 260, OMGUS, Records of the Office of the Military Government of Germany, Ardelia Hall Collection, Restitution Claims, Wiesbaden, Box 116, NARA.
127. Nicholas, p. 83.
128. Telephone discussion with Marei von Saher (daughter-in-law of Jacques Goudstikker), January 1998, August 2, 2001; Nicholson, pp. 83-84, 104; Telephone discussion with Andrew Bursky, Managing Director, Interlaken Capital, Inc., Greenwich, Conn., March 5, 1998; Alan Riding, "Heirs Claim Art Lost To Nazis in Amsterdam," *New York Times*, January 12, 1998, p. B1; Letter of Dutch Foreign Minister Hans van Mierlo to U.S. Senator Alfonse M. D'Amato, in re: Marei von Saher, March 25, 1998; Major E.K. Waterhouse, "The Goudstikker Firm," Monuments and Fine Arts-Netherlands, n.d., RG 260, OMGUS, United States Occupation Headquarters, Records of the Property Division, Ardelia Hall Collection, Box 49, NARA; Looted Art in the Occupied Countries, Neutral Countries, and Latin America, May 5, 1945, RG 226, OSS, Records of the Office of Special Services,

Washington SI/Special Funds Records, Entry 183, Box 2; "Memorandum: Activities of Alois Miedl, Art Agent, September 26, 1944, RG 84, Records of the State Department Posts, 1942-1949, Box 64, NARA; "Looted Art in Occupied Territories, Neutral Countries and Latin America, Preliminary Report," May 5, 1945, Foreign Economic Administration, Enemy Branch, RG 226, OSS, Records of the Office of Strategic Services, Washington SI, Special Funds Records, Entry 183, p. 21, Box 2, NARA..

129. Andrew Decker, A Little Justice in Austria," *Art News Magazine* (May 1998), p. 49.
130. Letter of Lillian Politzer-Weingast to Gregg Rickman, August 18, 1997; Letter of Lillian Politzer-Weingast to United States Senator Alfonse D'Amato, June 26, 1997.
131. Letter of Lillian Politzer-Weingast to The Honorable Agnes Hamilton, Second Secretary of the Embassy of France in Washington, DC, May 26, 1997.
132. Letter from Isabella Rottenstreich to the U.S. State Department Office for Claims Against Germany and Austria, August 14, 1946, RG 260, OMGUS, Office of the Military Government of the United States Forces in Austria, U.S. Allied Command, Austria (USACA), Property Control Branch, Correspondence to Claims, 1945-1950, Box 3, p. 2, NARA.
133. Letter of Frederick William Koerner to the State of New York, December 4, 1946, RG 260, OMGUS, Office of the Military Government of the United States Forces in Austria, U.S. Allied Command, Austria (USACA), Property Control Branch, Correspondence to Claims, 1945-1950, Box 1, p. 1, NARA.
134. Letter of Hugo Mayer to the U.S. Department of State, December 3, 1946, RG 260, OMGUS, Office of the Military Government of Germany, Records of the Property Division, Box 84, NARA.
135. Letter of Milton S. Koblitz to General Dwight Eisenhower, October 13, 1945, RG 260, Office of the Military Government of the United States in Germany, Records of the Property Division, Reparations and Restitution Branch, Box 721, NARA.
136. Letter of Margit Freud to the Director of Claims, OMGUS, RG 260, Office of the Military Government of Germany, Records of the Property Division, Box 82, NARA.
137. Translation of the Statement of Frederick B. Weissmann, May 30, 1946, RG 84, Records of the American Legation in Bern, Box 6, File of Frederick B. Weissmann NARA.
138. Letter of Ignatz I. Rosenak on behalf of Mr. Arthur Sussmann and Mrs. Wera Elfriede Klipstein, nee Sussmann, to the Office of the Military Government of Germany, Finance Division, Property Control, June 23, 1947, RG 260, Office of the Military Government of the United States in Germany, Records of the Property Division, Box 84, NARA.
139. "Household Effects and Furnishings Confiscated during the Nazi Period, as well as the Business Activity of the Dorotheum, 1938-1945," an unpublished report by the Aunlaufstell of the IKG, *Appendix of Declarations and Exhibits, Dorit Whiteman, et al, Plaintiffs v. Republic of Austria, et al, Defendants, Civil Action No. 00CIV.8006 (SWK), United States District Court, Southern District of New York*, p. 6.
140. Walter V. Robinson, "Art from collector with a Nazi past puts Yale on spot," *Boston Globe*, January 22, 2001; Telephone discussion with Willi Korte, February 27, 2001.
141. Auction houses like the Government-owned Dorotheum in Vienna, which was entrusted with compulsory auctions. "Household Effects and Furnishings Confiscated during the Nazi Period, as well as the Business Activity of the Dorotheum, 1938-1945," p. 10.
142. Nicholas, p. 165.
143. Robinson; Korte; Bob Jackman, "Yale Acknowledges Possibility of Nazi Looted Art," *Antiques & The Arts Weekly*, February 2, 2001.

144. "The Jewish Property Contribution," Private Papers of Major Joseph Landow, Budget Specialist, Public Finance Branch, OMGUS, Office of the Military Government of Germany, Finance Division, p. 2.
145. In 1996, Christoph Meili, a private security guard at a Union Bank of Switzerland (UBS) branch in Zurich pulled two reams of documents from a document shredder in the basement of the bank. For his noble act, he was fired and forced to flee to the United States for the security of his family. Some of the documents he saved from destruction were lists of properties owned, in part, by Jews in Germany that following their default on the property, devolved through sales to the Eidgenössiche Bank (later absorbed by UBS). List of Twenty Items of Real Estate from the Reichsbank Management to the Eidgenössiche Bank, September 24, 1934, translated by the Law Office of Fagan & Associates.
146. Britta Bopf, "Economic Discrimination and Confiscation: The Case of Jewish Real Estate," Paper presented at the conference, *Confiscation of Jewish Property in Europe, 1933-1945: New Sources and Perspectives*, United States Holocaust Memorial Museum, Washington, DC, March 22, 2001.
147. Landow Papers, "The Jewish Property Contribution," p. 2.
148. "Household Effects and Furnishings Confiscated during the Nazi Period, as well as the Business Activity of the Dorotheum, 1938-1945," pp. 4-5.
149. Alfons Kenkmann, "The Supervision of Jews and The Plundering of Jewish Assets by the Regional Financial Administration: The Examples of Westphalia," Paper presented at the conference, *Confiscation of Jewish Property in Europe, 1933-1945: New Sources and Perspectives*, United States Holocaust Memorial Museum, Washington, DC, March 22, 2001.
150. Letter of Hugo Lowenfeld to Mr. Laurence C. Frank, Consul General of the United States of America, Vienna, Austria, September 21, 1946, RG 260, OMGUS, Records of the United States Military Government in Austria, U.S. Allied Command, Austria (USACA), Property Control Branch, Correspondence to Claims, 1945-1950, Box 2, NARA.
151. The passport of Max Chowdowski has a stamped and signed declaration that his assets were placed in a blocked account in the Deutsche Bank.
152. Raul Hilberg, *The Destruction of the European Jews*, Revised and Definitive Edition, Volume One (New York: Holmes & Meir, 1985), pp. 141-142.
153. Susanne Meinl, "The Expropriation of Jewish Emigrants from Hessen During the 1930s,"Paper presented at the conference, *Confiscation of Jewish Property in Europe, 1933-1945: New Sources and Perspectives*, United States Holocaust Memorial Museum, Washington, DC, March 22, 2001, pp. 5-6.
154. Kenkmann, p. 5.
155. Meinl, p. 6.
156. Letter of Fred and Herta Rosendorff to the Department of State re: Properties Abroad, August 8, 1947, RG 260, Office of the Military Government of the United States in Germany, Records of the Property Division, Box 86, NARA.
157. Martin Dean, "The Finanzamt Moabit-West and the Development of the Property Confiscation Infrastructure, 1933-1945," Paper presented at the conference, *Confiscation of Jewish Property in Europe, 1933-1945: New Sources and Perspectives*, United States Holocaust Memorial Museum, Washington, DC, March 22, 2001.
158. Eric A. Johnson, *Nazi Terror, The Gestapo, Jews, and Ordinary Germans* (New York: Basic Books, 2000), p. 91.
159. Complaint of Susie Bernheimer, RG 260, OMGUS, United States Occupation Headquarters, Records of the Property Division, Ardelia Hall Collection, Box. 341, NARA; Gellateley, p.128.

160. Letter of Walter Aufhauser to Colonel Allen, Restitution Branch, O.M.G. for Germany, August 26, 1947, RG 260, OMGUS, United States Occupation Headquarters, Records of the Property Division, Ardelia Hall Collection, Box. 340, NARA.
161. Letter of Bernard Rosenthal to The Department of State, April 25, 1947, RG 260, Office of the Military Government of the United States in Germany, Records of the Property Division, Box 84, NARA.
162. Memorandum of Leland Harrison, American Legation in Bern, Switzerland to the Secretary of State, October 28, 1942, RG 131, Records of the Office of Alien Property, United States Department of Justice, Foreign Funds Control, Accession number 61-A-109, Box 357, File, Ransom Cases, 1942, NARA, p. 1.
163. Letter of Claude G. Bowers, American Embassy in Santiago, Chile to the Secretary of State, December 3, 1942, RG 131, Records of the Alien Property Custodian, United States Department of Justice, Foreign Funds Control, General Correspondence, 1942-1960, Box 195, NARA.
164. Telegram of John G. Winant, American Embassy, London to the Secretary of State, October 29, 1942, RG 131, Records of the Office of Alien Property, United States Department of Justice, Foreign Funds Control, Accession number 61-A-109, Box 357, File, Ransom Cases, 1942, NARA, p. 1.
165. Bernhard Feiler, a German Jewish refugee was forced to transfer accumulated rent from property he held on the Kurfürstendamm and Tauentzienerstrasse in Berlin, collected on his behalf since 1938 when he left, to an account in Cuba and thereafter to the Reichsbank in Berlin. "Sweden: Economic, Enemy Capital in Sweden," August 14, 1944, RG 226, Records of the Office of Strategic Services, Report No. T-2202, NARA.
166. Telegram of John G. Winant, American Embassy, London to the Secretary of State, November 2, 1942, RG 131, Records of the Office of Alien Property, United States Department of Justice, Foreign Funds Control, Accession number 61-A-109, Box 357, File, Ransom Cases, 1942, NARA, p. 1.
167. Letter of James Somerville, First Secretary of the Embassy Economic Warfare Division, American Embassy in London, to the Secretary of State, November 2, 1942, Telegram of Winant, American Embassy, London to the Secretary of State, October 29, 1942, RG 131, Records of the Office of Alien Property, United States Department of Justice, Foreign Funds Control, Accession number 61-A-109, Box 357, File, Ransom Cases, 1942, NARA, p. 1.
168. Letter of John G. Winant to the Secretary of State, November 16, 1942, RG 131, Records of the Office of Alien Property, United States Department of Justice, Foreign Funds Control, Accession number 61-A-109, Box 357, File, Ransom Cases, 1942, NARA, p. 2.
169. Press Release of the Department of State, November 24, 1942, RG 59, Records of the Department of State, Main Files, File 862.5151/231B PS/LIC, Box C369, NARA, p. 2..
170. Wiederkehr and Hochberg were recommended for inclusion on the Proclaimed List on November 2, 1942, in a memorandum to the Secretary of State. See Somerville to the Secretary of State. Notice of the blacklisting was placed in the major London newspapers, including the *Evening Standard*, *The Times*, the *Daily Telegraph*, and the *Daily Mail*, in the days following the release of the Allied ruling. See RG 59, Records of the Department of State, Main Files, File 862.5151/231B PS/LIC, Box C369, NARA.
171. One successful "client" of Wiederkehr, a Sigmond Jacob was said by Bern Legation officials to have recommended other Jews wishing to leave Holland to Wiederkehr. See Telegram of Leland Harrison, American Legation in Bern to the Secretary of

State, December 23, 1942, RG 59, Records of the Department of State, Main Files, File 862.5151/231B PS/LIC, Box C369, NARA.

172. Memorandum by the American Legation in Bern, September 28, 1942, RG 84, Records of Foreign Posts of the United States Department of State, Conference File 1938-49, 1942: 892.3, Folder 811.11-824.5, Box 3, NARA.
173. Letter of James Sommerville.
174. Letter of Leland Harrison, October 28, 1942; and E.F. Ferdinand, Memorandum for the Files, re: Werener Carl Gabler, Erich Fischer, George Boochever, and Rudolf Callmann, June 17, 1943, RG 131, Records of the Office of Alien Property, United States Department of Justice, Foreign Funds Control, Accession number 61-A-109, Box 357, File, Ransom Cases, 1942, NARA, p.1.
175. Interview with Michael Ra'anan, Washington, DC, July 15, 2002, whose grandfather entered Switzerland in 1938 on a forged work permit; and Interview with Dr. John Graz, Director of Religious Liberty, World Headquarters, Seventh Day Adventist Church, May 30, 2002.
176. Various British newspapers, upon announcing the new policy of adding intermediaries to the Proclaimed List, identified Anna Hochberg as a "Dutch Jewess."
177. Memorandum of Gardiner S. Platt of the Office of Strategic Services to Walter S. Surrey, Chief of Division of Economic Security Controls, Department of State, "Subject: Jacques Salmanovich [sic]," June 5, 1946, RG 226, OSS Central Files, Entry 92, Box 612, Folder #2, NARA.
178. Letter of Paul C. Squire, American Consul General to Roswell D. McClelland, Special Assistant to the Minister, Representative of War Refugee Board, American Legation, Bern, April 10, 1945, RG 59, Records of the State Department, Decimal # 848, "Buchler, Stefan," NARA.
179. Letter of Jonathan Greenblatt, Attorney for SGS Société Générale de Surveillance Holding, S.A. to U.S. Senator Alfonse M. D'Amato, April 21, 1998. Jacques Salmanowitz's name graced a documentary film program first at the George Washington University in Washington, DC, then at Boston College. The program funds documentary films highlighting moral courage and sacrifice and is named after the "Swiss businessman who was instrumental in bringing individuals trapped behind German lines in WWII to safety in Switzerland." See The Jacques Salmanowitz Program at George Washington University at and at Boston College at http://bc.edu/bc_org/avp/cas/fnart/film/salmanowitz/Pages/Salmanowitz.html.
180. Research being done in Holland suggests that Salmanowitz did in fact help a great number of families there. Historian Friso Hoenfeld has written to this author suggesting that the diary of a young Dutch boy, that he is editing and translating, suggests help being given the boy's family during and after the war by Salmanowitz (E-mail correspondence to Gregg Rickman from Friso Hoenfeld, August 1, 2002).
181. Letter of Jonathan Greenblatt, Attorney for SGS Société Générale de Surveillance Holding, S.A. to U.S. Senator Alfonse M. D'Amato, August 1, 1996, p. 9, Preface to a Coopers & Lybrand study of 182 credit balances held on account with SGS., based on two requests for explanation of said accounts by Senator Alfonse M. D'Amato to Jonathan Greenblatt, Shearman & Sterling, April 10 and June 12, 1996. The accounts were found in Safehaven Report No. 121.00, "Supplementary Report on Funds Held for Others by Sociéte General de Surveillance S.A., Geneva, RG 319, Records of the Army Chief of Staff, Reports and Messages, 1918-1951=State Department, Switzerland 7/2/45-8/31/45, Box 1056, NARA. For an account of the details surrounding the finding and use of this document early in the Senate Banking Committee's investigation of the Swiss Banks, See Rickman, pp. 48-49. The accounts, numbering 115 in all, totaled $2,375,483 in values expressed in 1945, p. 7,

Greenblatt, August 1, 1996. Some accounts, roughly 10%, according to Jean Pierre Mèan, SGS General Counsel, were in fact held as numbered accounts in Swiss banks, Meeting with Jean Pierre Mèan, Washington, DC, May 8, 1996. Upon conclusion of the investigation for SGS by Coopers & Lybrand, all but two of those who made this arrangement with Salmanowitz survived the war, Greenblatt, August 1, 1996, p. 8.

182. See Letters of Louise MacMillan, British Embassy in Berne [sic] re: Nissim Hasan, to W.A. Brandt, Economic Warfare Department, Foreign Office, London, November 26, 30, and December 21, 1945 on behalf of The Societe Generale Surveillance, Treasury Files, "Axis Satellites," T236/578/OF117/27/1, Public Records Office, London, through the British Embassy in Washington, DC to the Office of Senator Alfonse M. D'Amato; Letter of Winant to the Secretary of State re: Nissim Hasan, October 30, 1945, RG 59, Records of the Department of State, General Records, 1945-1949, Box 4192, NARA; and Letter of Société Générale de Surveillance to Mr. Walter Ostrow, re: "Release of property of Mr. A. Immerglùck, deceased,"American Legation, Berne [sic], August 19, 1948, RG 131, Alien Property Custodian, Foreign Funds Control, General Correspondence, 1942-1960, Box 217, NARA.
183. "Looted Art in Occupied Territories, Neutral Countries and Latin America, Preliminary Report," p. 13.
184. Platt to Surrey; and Letter of Paul Squire, American Consulate in Geneva to J. Klahr Huddle, American Legation in Bern, October 13, 1942, RG 84, Records of the American Legation in Bern, 1942, 800.1-824.8, Box 6, NARA..
185. Letter of Oscar Perlberger to Jacques Salmanowitz, September 18, 1942, RG 84, Records of the American Legation in Bern, 1942, 800.1-824.8, Box 6, NARA.
186. *Biographical Directory of the United States Congress, 1774-1989* (Washington, DC: Government Printing Office, 1989), p. 909.
187. Letter of Leland Harrison, American Legation in Bern to the Secretary of State, November 5, 1942, RG 84, Records of the American Legation in Bern, 1942, 800.1-824.8, Box 6, NARA. It had been previously reported that sums of up to $7,000 were being requested for the same. See Letter of Walter Sholes, American Consul General, Basel to Charles B. Dyar, Financial Attaché, American Legation, Bern, October 8, 1942, RG 84, Records of the American Legation in Bern, Confidential Files, 1938-1949, 851.5, Box 3, NARA.
188. Telegram of Leland Harrison to the State Department, December 2, 1942, RG 84, Records of the American Legation in Bern, 1942, 800.1-824.8, Box 6, NARA.
189. Memorandum of David L. Barrett to Charles H. de Zevallos, U.S. Treasury Department, April 26, 1943, RG 131, Records of the Office of Alien Property, United States Department of Justice, Foreign Funds Control, Accession number 61-A-109, Box 357, File, Ransom Cases, 1943-44-45, NARA, p.2.
190. Letter of W. Ritchie, British Embassy in Washington to John Pehle, Foreign Funds Control, April 27, 1943, RG 131, Records of the Office of Alien Property, United States Department of Justice, Foreign Funds Control, Accession number 61-A-109, Box 357, File, Ransom Cases, 1943-44-45, NARA, p.2.
191. Letter of David L. Barrett to Charles H. deZevallos, Treasury Department, July 9, 1943, RG 131, Records of the Office of Alien Property, United States Department of Justice, Foreign Funds Control, Accession number 61-A-109, Box 357, File, Ransom Cases, 1943-44-45, NARA, p.1.
192. Political Memorandum from American Embassy in Stockholm to the American Embassy in London, August 22, 1944, RG 84, Records of the American Legation in Bern, NARA.

193. Safehaven Report, "Looted Art Stated to Belong to Baronne Elisabeth Weiss and to Andre and Steven Herzog, Budapest, Hungary," January 30, 1946, OSS, RG 226, Washington X-2 Files, Box 532, NARA.
194. Letter of Leland Harrison to the Secretary of State, July 24, 1944, RG 84, Records of the American Legation in Bern, NARA.
195. Hilberg, Vol. II, pp. 740-741.
196. Tad Szulc, *The Secret Alliance, The Extraordinary Story of the Rescue of the Jews Since World War II* (New York: Farrar, Straus & Giroux, 1991), p. 32.
197. Shabtai Teveth, *Ben-Gurion and the Holocaust* (New York: Harcourt Brace & Company, 1996), p. 174.
198. Hilberg, Vol. III, pp. 1132-1139; Teveth, p. 197.
199. Ibid, p. 184.
200. Hilberg, Vol. III, p. 844.
201. In one correspondence found in the archives of the former German Democratic Republic, Oswald Pohl, an SS General who was a high official in the slave labor program and played a very large role in the expropriation of Jewish assets, confirmed that a Jew, Kaufmann, was allowed to emigrate to Sweden against a payment of 102,000 Sfr. to the Swiss Bankers Association, the official association of Swiss banks, public and private. See Pohl, SS Obersturmführer, General of the Waffen-SS to the Central Security Board of the German Reich, November 23, 1942, translated by Brigit E. Blingge, Dr. Tatzkow and Partner, Packet of documents from the Office of Cohen, Milstein, Hausfeld & Toll, P.L.L.C., June 12, 1997.
202. *Final Report of the Independent Commission of Experts, Switzerland-Second World War*, "Switzerland, National Socialism and the Second World War," 2002, p. 162.
203. Letter of Siegfried Politzer to the Department of State, October 27, 1946, RG 260, OMGUS, United States Forces Austria, U.S. Allied Command Austria (USACA), Property Control Branch, Correspondence to Claims, 1945-1950, Box 1, NARA.
204. Feldman, pp. 9-10.
205. Ibid, p. 8.
206. Robert Vogler, *The Swiss National Bank's Gold Transactions with the German Reichsbank from 1939 to 1946*, Swiss National Bank, 1985.
207. The Bank of International Settlements was founded in May 1930 and acted as the Central Bank for all national Central Banks. It also was designed to administer the Young Plan payments from Germany to account for the restitution required of Germany from the First World War.
208. Undated draft memo from the American Embassy to the State Department, RG 59, Records of the Department of State, Office of Financial Operations Records Relating to the Tripartite Commission for Restitution of Monetary Gold, 1942-1962, Box 29, NARA.
209. *German Economic Penetration of Switzerland*, RG 43, Records of International Conferences, Lot File No. M-88, Council of Foreign Ministers Conference on German External Assets and Looted Gold, January 1953, p. 21, Box 203, NARA.
210. Interrogation of Herr Karl Gaupner, at Frankfurt, August 16, 1945, RG 260, OMGUS, Office of the Military Government of Germany, Office of Finance Advisor, General Records of the Financial Intelligence Group, 1945-1949, Box 204, Box 204.
211. Rickman, pp. 111-112.
212. Letter of Lovett to the State Department, December 30, 1947, RG 84, Records of the Foreign Service Posts, Entry 3221, Safehaven Subject Files (1942-1949), Box 6, NARA.

213. Stuart Eizenstat and William Slany, eds., *U.S. and Allied Efforts To Recover and Restore Gold and Other Assets Stolen or Hidden by Germany During World War II, Preliminary Study*, May 1997, p. 170.
214. Testimony of Oswald Pohl, at Nurnberg, June 7, 1946, RG 260, OMGUS, Office of the Military Government of the United States in Germany. Office of the Finance Division, 80.00 Charter/International Military Tribunal Trial, Nurnberg-94.02, SS Economic Enterprises, Box 225, p. 78, NARA; Statement of Albert Thoms, September 19, 1945, RG 260, OMGUS, Office of the Military Government of the United States in Germany. Office of the Finance Advisor, General Records of the Financial Intelligence Group, p. 2, Box 204, NARA. Documents from the archives of the former German Democratic Republic. Like similar archives in the West, former East German archives carry dental gold delivery documents and accounting statements for looted gold and other assets. Letter from Dr. Tazkow & Partners, of the Scholarly Documentation Services, Berlin, to Senator Alfonse M. D'Amato, May 12, 1997.
215. Bruno Melmer, "Sworn Statement regarding my activities in the SS - Economics and Administration Main Office, Berlin -SS - Wirtschafts und Verwaltungshauptamt Berlin)," July 15, 1947, RG 260, OMGUS, Records of the Office of the Military Government of the United States in Germany, Finance Division, General Records of the Intelligence Group, 1945-1949, Box 169, NARA.
216 ."Interrogation of Puhl," October 17, 1945, RG 260, OMGUS, Records of the Office of the Military Government of the United States in Germany, NARA.
217. Telegram from General Clay to the Treasury Department, September 27, 1945, RG 260, OMGUS, Office of the Military Government of Germany, Property Division, Box 649, NARA.
218. Gerhard L. Weinberg, *A World At Arms, A Global History of World War II* (Cambridge, UK: Cambridge University Press, 1994), p. 190.
219. Presentation of State Counsellor of Justice of the Second ClassM.Y. Raginsky (Assistant Prosecutor for the U.S.S.R., Nuremberg Trail Proceedings, Vol. 8, Sixty-Fourth Day, Thursday, February 21, 1946, Morning Session, *The Avalon Project*, Yale Law School, available online at .
220. In 1944, $45 million of the remaining gold reserves that had not already been removed to the United States, Canada, or Great Britain, after a five-year 10,000 mile journey, finally made it safely to the United States. "The Strange Delivery of the Polish Gold," July 12, 1944, Documents of the Federal Reserve Board.
221. "Order concerning treatment of property of Nationals of the former Polish State of 17 September 1940," Web Genocide Documentation Centre, Dr. Stuart D. Stein, Faculty of Economics and Social Sciences, University of the West of England, available online at . "Gold and silver objects of the Main Board of Trustees East," The Reich's Marshall of the Greater Reich, Deputy for the Four Year Plan, March 19, 1944, Order signed by Dr. Gramsch, RG 260, OMGUS, Records of the Office of the Military Government of the United States in Germany, Finance Advisor, General Records of the Financial Intelligence Group, Folder-Reichsbank, Box 204, NARA. While small amounts of movable property were ostensibly exempted from this order, over one hundred pass book accounts from Polish banks were found after the war in the underground mine at Merkers salt mine. "Savings-account Passbooks in Melmer Deliveries," Report to Major Klepper, Chief, Intelligence Unit, Financial Intelligence and Liaison Section, Financial Branch, OMGUS, RG 260, OMGUS, Office of the Military Government of the United States in Germany, Finance Division, Box 423, NARA.
222. Martin Dean, "Research Note: Jewish Property Seized in the Occupied Soviet Union in 1941 and 1942: The Records of the Reichshauptkasse Beutestelle," *Holocaust and Genocide Studies*, Vol. 14, No. 1 (Spring 2000).

223. Unsigned Memorandum from the City Pawn Shop, Berlin to the German Reichsbank, Hauptkasse, Berlin, September 14, 1943, translated by the U.S. Army, RG 260, OMGUS, Records of the Office of the Military Government of the United States in Germany, Finance Division, General Records of the Foreign Intelligence Group, Folder-Reichsbank, Box 204, NARA.
224. Memorandum of Herr Kroop, City Pawn Shop to the Reichsbank, March 31, 1944, translated by the U.S. Army, RG 260, OMGUS, Records of the Office of the Military Government of the United States in Germany, Finance Division, General Records of the Foreign Intelligence Group, Folder-Reichsbank, Box 204, NARA.
225. Martin Dean, "The Expropriation of Jewish Property in Reichskommissariat Ostland,1941-1944, 2000, p. 7, from the author.
226. Hector Feliciano, *The Lost Museum, The Nazi Conspiracy to Steal the World's Greatest Works of Art* (New York: Basic Books, 1997), p. 25; Nicholas, pp. 121-123.
227. Translation of Statement written by Dr. Hermann Bunjes," nd, RG 260, OMGUS, Office of the Military Government of the United States in Germany, Property Division, Ardelia Hall Interrogations, Looted Art in France, Box 469, p. 1, NARA.
228. Ibid, p.2.
229. Heiden, pp. 4-5.
230. Nicholas, p. 137.
231. Letter of Reichsleiter Bormann to Reichsleiter Alfred Rosenberg, April 21, 1943, translated by the U.S. Army, RG 200, Duker-Dwork Papers, NARA.
232. Feliciano, pp. 32-33.
233. "Looted Art in Occupied Territories, Neutral Countries and Latin America, Preliminary Report," p. 5.
234. Letter of Reichsmarschall Goering to Reichsleiter Alfred Rosenberg, November 21, 1940, translated by the U.S. Army, RG 200, Duker-Dwork Papers, NARA.
235. "Looted Art in Occupied Territories, Neutral Countries and Latin America, Preliminary Report," p. 16.
236. Memorandum of Charles H. Sawyer to Bernard Towell, June 20, 1945, RG 226, OSS, Records of the Office of Strategic Services, NARA.
237. "Looted Art in Occupied Territories, Neutral Countries and Latin America, Preliminary Report," p. 37.
238. Letter of Sybilla Katz-Goldstein.
239. Report of March 26, 1945, on Arthur Wiederkehr, Economic Warfare Department, London, RG 1136, James Surkamp Collection, 88, BV, 12/9, Folder 29, YIVO, New York. Nathan Katz, while getting 58 of his relatives out of Holland, largely through the sale and surrender of paintings to the Nazis, was nevertheless considered questionable in his dealings, as he was 'tolerated' by them. Lynn Nicholas, in the *Rape of Europa*, says quite forthrightly, that "[t]he Germans tolerated this because Nathan Katz was the conduit for major works from several extremely important private collections." She goes on to say that he procured pictures for Göring (Nicholas, p. 108). These accusations were vehemently denied to this author by the son-in-law of Nathan Katz in both a phone call on September 15, 1998, as well as a letter in which S. Sid Goldstein wrote, "As per our discussion I explained to you the so-called allegations that my father-in-law, Nathan Katz, did business with the Nazis. The enclosed packet with english [sic] translations confirm that the allegations were totally wrong. In addition, Queen Juliana of the Netherlands decorated him in Switzerland with the highest honors in 1947 after the war," (Letter of S. Sid Goldstein to Gregg Rickman, September 16, 1998).

240. "Looted Art in Occupied Territories, Neutral Countries and Latin America, Preliminary Report," p. 3.
241. Letter of Professor Richard Goldschmidt to the State Department, June 7, 1943, RG 59, Records of the State Department, General Records 1940-1944, Box 1206, NARA.
242. TFR-500 Report for Census of Property in Foreign Countries, Report of Helmuth S. Bloch, RG 265, TFR-500 Series Property Declarations, Foreign Funds Control, Box 1192, NARA; Letter of Mrs. Martha Mandelbaum to the Property Control Branch, Office of [the] Military Government for Germany, July 31, 1947, RG 260, OMGUS, Office of the Military Government of the United States in Germany, Records of the Property Division, Box 86, NARA; Letter of Manfred Zobl and Markus Weisskopf of Rentenstalt/Swiss Life, to U.S. Senator Alfonse M. D'Amato, July 1, 1997.
243. *Final Report of the Independent Commission of Experts, Switzerland-Second World War*, "Switzerland, National Socialism and the Second World War," 2002, p.290.
244. Letter of Henri Gadd to Albert Bertrand, Chase Bank, France, January 15, 1942, Exhibits copied to Report on the Activities of the Chase Bank Branches in France, April 3, 1945, RG 56, General Records of the Treasury Department, Accession 67-A-1804-OASIA (Office of the Assistant Secretary for International Affairs, Box 5, NARA.
245. Report on the Activities of the Chase Bank Branches in France, April 3, 1945, RG 56, Records of the Treasury Department, Accession 67-A-1804-OASIA (Office of the Assistant Secretary for International Affairs, p. 2, Box 5, NARA.
246. Thomas Dougherty, Memorandum for the Files, Subject: French Branches of the Guaranty Trust Company during the German Occupation, February 20, 1946, RG 131, Records of the Office of Alien Property, United States Department of Justice, Foreign Funds Control, Accession number 61-A-109-FFC, File, France: Investigation of British Banks, p.1, Box 138, NARA.
247. Majorie Farber, "Report on the Activities of The British Banks Operating in France During the Period of the German Occupation," July 19, 1945, RG 131, Records of the Office of Alien Property, United States Department of Justice, Foreign Funds Control, Accession number 61-A-109-FFC, File, France: Investigation of British Banks, p.11, Box 138, NARA.
248. Draft Report, "British Banks in Occupied France," RG 131, Records of the Office of Alien Property, United States Department of Justice, Foreign, Funds Control, Accession number 61-A-109, France: Investigation of British Banks, p. 3, Box 138, NARA.
249. Matthew J. Marks, United States Treasury Department, Memorandum for the Files, Subject: Investigation of Morgan et Cie, April 28, 1945, RG 56, Records of the Treasury Department, Accession 67-A-1804-OASIA (Office of the Assistant Secretary for International Affairs, p. 4, Box 5, NARA.
250. Walter H. Sholes, American Consul General, Basel, "German Agents in Swiss Banks," December 7, 1942, RG 84, Records of Foreign Posts, General Records, 1936-1949, 1942: 851.2-860.7, Box 79.
251. Letter of McCombe, British Embassy in Lisbon to Gerald Villiers, Economic Warfare Department, London, November 15, 1947, Treasury Records, T236, 1449, Public Records Office, London.
252. Memorandum of Stanley P. Lovell to Homer Hall, OSS, June 5, 1944, RG 226, Records of the OSS, Office of Strategic Services, Miscellaneous Washington, DC Office, Entry 146, Box 170.
253. Letter of Licco Max Haim to Senator Alfonse M. D'Amato, n.d.,1997.
254. Ibid.

255. Letter of G.N. Blue, General Motors Overseas Operations, General Motors Corporation to Licco Haim,, August 1, 1949, enclosure of Letter to D'Amato.
256. Letter of Henry G. Hilken, Chief of the Intercustodial & Property Branch, Office of Alien Property, United States Department of Justice to Licco Max Haim, January 10, 1952, enclosure of Letter to D'Amato.
257. Nehemiah Robinson, World Jewish Congress, "Memorandum on Masterless Foreign Assets in the United States," in a letter to Irving Dwork, October 15, 1946, RG 56, Records of the Department of Treasury, Accession 56-66A816, Folder, Miscellaneous Case Work-Dwork, Dr. Irving, Box 63, NARA.
258. Abby L. Gilbert, "Alien Property Custodian - Bureaucratic History," United States Department of Treasury, unpublished June 2000, p. 24.
259. Ibid, p. 26; "Plunder and Restitution, The U.S. and Holocaust Victims' Assets, Findings and Recommendations of the Presidential Advisory Commission on Holocaust Assets in the United States and Staff Report," December 2000, pp. SR-170-171; Statement of Mr. Seymour J. Rubin, Professor, Hearing before the Committee on Banking and Financial Services, "The Eizenstat Report and Related Issues Concerning United States and Allied Efforts to Restore Gold and Other Assets Looted by Nazis During World War II," United States House of Representatives, June 25, 1997, pp. 100-101.
260. Ibid, pp. 15-27.
261. Ibid, p. 24.
262. Ibid, p. 35.
263. Morris Krakowski, *Memoir*, unpublished, June 1995, p. 26.
264. Albert Speer was influential in the decision to bring industry into the picture, as well as for the idea of bringing the inmates to the factories where engineers and other experts were located. See Robert Gellateley, p. 207.
265. Questionnaire of Dolores Finder Berkowsky for Friedman v. Union Bank of Switzerland (Swiss Banks lawsuit), 1996, Law firm of Cohen, Milstein, Hausfeld & Toll, P.L.L.C.
266. "Results of the Slave Labor Program," Nazi Conspiracy and & Aggression, *The Nizkor Project*, available online at: http://www1.us.nizkor.org/hweb/imt/nca/nca-01/nca-01-10-slaves-04.html.
267. Dr. John C. Beyer and Dr. Stephen A. Schneider, Nathan Associates, "Forced Labor Under the Third Reich," Part One, August 20, 1999, p.9.
268. Ibid, p. 10.
269. Dr. John C. Beyer and Dr. Stephen A. Schneider, Nathan Associates, "Forced Labor Under the Third Reich," Part Two, August 20, 1999, p.6.
270. Ibid, p. 11.
271. Gellateley, p. 207.
272. Joseph Borkin, *The Crime and Punishment of I.G. Farben* (New York: Pocket Books, 1978), p. 160.

2

Crusaders and Conferences: U.S. Policy on Restitution, the Beginning

"If all is not to be lost, there can be, then, in place of the positive idea of a world republic, only the negative surrogate of an alliance which averts war, endures, spreads, and holds back the stream of those hostile passions which fear the law, though such an alliance is in constant peril of their breaking loose again."—*Immanuel Kant* [1]

Morgenthau's Crusaders

Henry Morgenthau, Franklin Delano Roosevelt's Secretary of the Treasury saw the peril of Germany in the late 1930s and began to direct his Treasury investigators against this growing threat. Bernard Bernstein, a Treasury Department Attorney at the time, explained Morgenthau's intentions,

> I think it is fair to say that Secretary Morgenthau, beginning in about 1937, made of the Treasury Department—and the Legal Division in particular—a workshop to assist President Roosevelt in formulating plans to protect the security of the United States ... as a result of his own foresight and sound judgment, as well as his close personal and official relationships with the President, [he] began to be increasingly concerned about the dangers to the democratic nations of the world of Nazism and aggressions on the part of Germany and Japan. He was continuously studying and seeking ways and means of building up the strength of the United States, of the Western democracies, and of China, and of weakening the power of Germany and Japan. He directed his top staff to focus on the problems and to bring him suggestions and ideas.[2]

Morgenthau was the son of the American Ambassador to Turkey during World War I, and came to understand the ways of the Germans before they became Nazis.

> ... What the Turks did to the Armenians made a terrific impact on me. Later on when the Germans did the same things to the Jews, I remembered the feelings I had had in Turkey during World War I. And I also always remembered on Christmas Eve at the

> Dardanelles. There was a German officer there sitting and talking who didn't know that I understood German. I heard him damming Americans in foul language. This made a great impression on me.[3]

That Morgenthau was a close personal friend of the president going back to 1915, helped greatly in Morgenthau's rise to prominence. As Secretary of the Treasury, he was in a unique place to act against the evil he foresaw coming from Germany. Morgenthau was in the center of FDR's inner circle of advisors and this close relationship ensured a trust that afforded him a breadth of independence and power that other Cabinet Secretaries could not attain. More importantly, his power transcended his Department's normal jurisdiction. His influence spilled into the field of foreign affairs, normally a purview of the State Department, enabling him to leave his mark upon the affairs of state to a level unequaled by most others short of the president, who as then-State Department official Elbridge Durbrow suggested, usually acted as his own Secretary of State.[4] Morgenthau's influence and drive led Secretary of State Cordell Hull to refer to him as an aspirant for the position of "a second Secretary of State."[5] Morgenthau's prominent policy position, however, would eventually place him in a direct policy clash with Foggy Bottom.

John Morton Blum described Morgenthau as sitting atop an extraordinary department of the Federal Government, "whose combined activities took the full time of the largest police force and one of the largest staffs of lawyers in the federal establishment..." Morgenthau needed, Blum added, " ... practical men who had 'trading experience.'"[6] As such, "his description of the kind of man he wanted hired," Dean Acheson wrote, "was: "Does he want to lick this fellow Hitler.... Does [he] hate Hitler's guts?'" As for Morgenthau, himself, Acheson concluded, "Henry did."[7] These men would go on to serve the Treasury and the nation quite well throughout the war and after.

Together, Morgenthau and his men settled down to work on ways to contain Hitler and the Nazis. Between the economic exchange controls they would construct, and the complex investigations of German economic penetration of the West they would lead, they would have more than their share of work to do. It would be these plans, economic exchange controls, that gave the policymakers the tools they would utilize to counter the growing Nazi military and financial threat to the United States and her allies. As Sim C. Binder wrote of Nazi foreign economic policies in 1941:

> The distortion by Germany of exchange control into a totalitarian offensive economic and political weapon has finally brought about the corresponding reaction of American democracy, to wit, the use of foreign exchange control, as part of foreign property control, first as a defensive and later as an offensive weapon.[8]

More importantly, Nazi foreign economic policy became, as Kenneth S. Carlston declared, " ... an instrument of political power for economic penetration and political persuasion of specific countries ..."[9] As shown by the decrees passed by the Nazis and their allies, Nazi ruled within Germany and beyond, was geared toward the absolute enrichment of the Reich and the impoverishment of its conquered foes. The Allies did not wish to fall victim to that manipulation.

Morgenthau's men began this work in earnest in December 1937, not against Germany, but Japan when Japanese pilots bombed the U.S. gunboat, *The Panay* on the Yangtzee River in broad daylight, killing two and strafing the survivors.[10] With this attack, Morgenthau's General Counsel, Herman Oliphant, drafted orders and regulations to enable the president to impose monetary exchange controls on Japanese funds in this country.[11] Because the situation calmed, the controls were never imposed. The drafts were, however, saved and Oliphant's work would not to be wasted.

Along with Oliphant, Morgenthau created an able staff that Tom Bower would call "Morgenthau's Crusaders."[12] In a heroic article for the *Saturday Evening Post* in 1944, by Francis Rufus Bellamy, and also written with the concurrence of the Treasury Department, the "Crusaders" were heralded for their foresight and wisdom into enemy intentions. "Where the United States is concerned," wrote Bellamy, " ... In Washington, DC there is a group of men who foresaw it [enemy economic sabotage and looting] too and did not need a Pearl Harbor to make them gaze into the crystal ball of the future."[13]

Bernard Bernstein was one of Morgenthau's Crusaders. John Pehle, who worked in the General Counsel's Office and would later direct the Office of Foreign Funds Control, was another. Edward Foley ,who worked closely with Morgenthau early on combating Axis financial influence in the United States until he entered the Army in 1942, was an important part of Morgenthau's staff.[14] Many of his crusaders gained greater acknowledgment than others. One of those that went largely unheralded and greatly impacted the work, first to restrict Axis financial influence in the U.S. and later in Europe, was an intrepid investigator by the name of Sam Klaus.

Sam Klaus

Sam Klaus, born in Brooklyn in 1904, was the son of a tailor who died of cancer soon after his birth. His mother remarried, this time to a grocer who, for his stepson, insisted on a strong Jewish education and commitment to Jewish causes.[15] Klaus graduated from City College in 1924, and went on to study law at Columbia University, graduating in 1927 as a Phi Beta Kappa. He later joined the Law Faculty there.[16] He was a stickler for detail, kept elaborate files, was multi-lingual, a collector of rugs, and according to all who knew him, possessive of "one of the finest investigative minds in or out of government."[17] Most of all, Klaus was the epitome of a "crusader."

In 1934, Klaus left Columbia to work for the Department of Treasury. The first time he appears in the Treasury personnel manuals is as Special Assistant to the General Counsel, Herman Oliphant.[18] While working for Oliphant, Klaus led a staff of lawyers who spent five years deciphering the books of Moses L. Annenberg, who had built his fortune through a national syndicate furnishing race track information.[19] Annenberg tried to defraud the government by encoding his books. After a relentless five-year effort at cracking Annenberg's books, Klaus and his men delivered ten hand trucks of records on Annenberg's operations and profit-making to a Federal Grand Jury, which indicted Annenberg. Seeing the weight of evidence against him, Annenberg plead guilty and paid a fine of $8 million.[20]

In 1937, Klaus transferred to the Legal Division at Treasury where he investigated the "whiskey trust," alleging a price fixing arrangement between fourteen distillers in the United States. His report to Morgenthau concluded that these distillers produced 95 percent of the liquor in the country. Their connections extended to British and French cartels and Canadian firms as well as with manufacturers of bottles, corks, and barrels.[21] Following his domestic criminal work, Klaus moved over into intelligence work and, in coordination with the FBI and other agencies, settled into a job that would become the core of his future endeavors and until now, unheralded success.

As such, by 1940, Morgenthau, impressed with Klaus' previous work, requested that he secretly and without staff, begin collecting information on the transit of funds to and from Europe for legitimate and subversive intent.[22] In October 1940, Klaus began his mission by seeking the help of the Federal Bureau of Investigation (FBI), as he was instructed to do by Morgenthau. The Secretary wanted Klaus to have the FBI do the detective work in uncovering the subversive financial role of the Axis and Axis-occupied powers by having Klaus indirectly navigate the FBI's investigation via subtle suggestion and gentle tasking. In a report to FBI Director J. Edgar Hoover, Agent H. H. Clegg explained Klaus' interest in an "investigation of the planning and direction of propaganda, espionage, etc. organizations."[23] Clegg informed Hoover of Klaus' interest in gaining the cooperation of the FBI in obtaining the inflow and outflow of funds from Germany, Soviet Russia, Italy, Japan, and their economically controlled countries of France, Spain, and Rumania.[24] In a memorandum to staff, Director Hoover addressed the matter further by adding that Klaus was interested as well in the FBI's "coverage" of Swiss bank accounts in this country, which the FBI was also watching.[25] This added coverage, as time would tell, would greatly add to the available intelligence on Axis financial subversion in the United States.

Agreeing in principal to such a request was one thing for Hoover, but fulfilling it to the fullest was yet another thing entirely. Ever the stickler for detail and for proper accreditation due the FBI, Hoover made no secret of his dislike for these kinds of projects, let alone his direction at the hand of another agency. On January 18, 1941, Hoover explained his reluctance in supplying information to the Treasury obtained from confidential sources to the Treasury. He complained, following an independent Treasury contact of a confidential FBI source at Riggs Bank in Washington, DC, "The success of the Bureau's operations in the intelligence field can only be maintained in so long as it is possible to keep the channels of the Bureau's information open and cooperative."[26] Less than a week later, the Treasury official who made the contact with Riggs, John Pehle, was quoted as saying that, to date, he had to act on his own because he had not received any information "worth sticking in your eye."[27]

By October of that year, however, Pehle's pejorative reference to FBI cooperation proved, in Klaus' estimation, to be quite different and vastly more important. Klaus wrote to Morgenthau:

> In consequence of my liaison work with the FBI a complete new, and large, unit was set up by Mr. Hoover to investigate for the Treasury the amounts, the sources, and the uses of Axis and Soviet funds in the banks and brokerage houses of this country. ... The Treasury now has intimate, friendly relations with the FBI to such an extent that FBI officials have told me that there is no other agency in the Government with whom they are able to engage in so effective cooperation as with Treasury. I may recall that prior to the beginning of this work relations between FBI and Treasury were highly strained. As a result a large amount of material on Axis funds in this country was received in this office, collated, and indexed.[28]

The structure Klaus created, with the apparent support and trust of the FBI, served as a model for that which he would later help create to track and gain control of Nazi-looted assets throughout Europe and beyond.

The volumes of intelligence information gained from first the FBI, and later the Coast Guard, IRS, Office of Naval Intelligence, Justice and Commerce Departments, and other governmental intelligence agencies, filled 14,000 index cards of contacts. The information found in this time also revealed millions of dollars in Axis funds were being transferred in and out of the country. Moreover, more than 700 income tax investigations were opened, the funds of numerous subversive groups' in the U.S. were frozen, the abuse of the diplomatic pouch by the Axis powers for subversive purposes was discovered, and the discovery of a German plan to switch nominal ownership of German businesses in the U.S. to American ownership was made, thereby avoiding confiscation during wartime. Also important was the discovery of two alleged German agents in the Bureau of Standards, as well as two more in Foreign Funds Control and in Personnel.[29]

Foreign Funds Control

It was in Foreign Funds Control (FFC) that Morgenthau's men created, "the instruments," Edward Foley declared in 1941, "which this country can employ in its economic defense." Based on the *Trading with the Enemy Act of 1917*, and bolstered by the *1933 Emergency Banking Act*, as well as the *First War*

Powers Act of December 18, 1941, that the Foreign Funds Control was formerly authorized to "freeze," or more accurately subject to Treasury Department license, all transactions suspected of abetting the enemy cause in time of war.[30] These transactions could be those of German or other origin.

Morgenthau, however, lacked a blank check regarding the freezing program. Numerous intergovernmental meetings took place to decide when and against whom to impose the orders. Secretary of State Cordell Hull repeatedly and jealously argued against their use, arguing that they should be imposed only as a last resort. Hull and his State Department aides feared reciprocal acts against American funds in these countries were the United States to act. With the United States officially "neutral," acts like this would be seen, they feared, as hostile. Both he and Morgenthau repeatedly and competitively tried to gain the advantage with FDR in policy discussions concerning the imposition of these types of exchange controls. By 1940, however, Morgenthau gained the upper hand.[31] These disputes, common to FDR's style of governance, bred competition between the two departments and their respective staffs as well, and lasted well beyond the war years. The fundamental divide over the conduct of various economic programs against the Nazis and their allies carried over to the post-war period, greatly affecting the delicate formation of the restitution policies the United States would pursue immediately before and during the Cold War.

The FFC brought the Treasury the full-time apparatus and resources to further investigate Axis financial schemes, the likes of which Klaus was uncovering, and the workforce to restrict them. The FFC's work also expanded the ability of the General Counsel's Office lawyers to work on freezing controls of enemy firms and funds. As the written history of FFC would explain:

> It was the one agency responsible for seeing that the Axis reaped no benefits from the billions of dollars for the acquisition of war materials; that the Axis were deprived of money necessary for espionage, sabotage and propaganda; that rewards to collaborationists and cloaks for their services to dictators were adequately cut off; that as territory commenced to be liberated by our forces the controls were used as a firm basis from which our armies moved forward, and for further weakening the enemy's position.[32]

Freezing controls, Foley explained, had four purposes:

1. To protect assets placed here in confidence from Axis realization of their full benefits.
2. To minimize the liabilities of American banks and others against conflicting claims to property arising out of invasion and other "revolutionary" changes in the over-run European countries.
3. To prevent the importation into the United States of Nazi-looted assets.
4. To prevent the Nazis and Axis powers the benefit of the frozen funds to finance subversive activities in this country.[33]

Moreover, vesting, or confiscation of enemy property, was a staple of the *1917 Trading with the Enemy Act*. With many of the same goals of preventing enemy access to public, as well as personal, looted assets, vesting was a procedure that was extended to the new acts coming out of Morgenthau's Treasury Department. This time, however, with over $7 billion in European capital having been transferred to the U.S. from 1935-1940, there was a very real need, as Foley said, to secure those assets from enemy use.[34] With freezing orders having gained a legislative blessing by the U.S. Congress through the passage of the *First War Powers Act*, vesting became another economic tool for defense against the Nazis.

Originally, the vesting powers rested with Morgenthau, but with a further Executive Order in March 1942, vesting was separated from the overall economic powers granted to him. Now, enemy property would rest with the Alien Property Custodian, namely John Pehle, his former Treasury aide.[35] With the Treasury Department much more concerned with the control of liquid, rather than hard, assets, this jurisdictional divide was acceptable to Treasury.[36]

First Warnings

Hitler's conquest of Czechoslovakia proved to be an important test case for the United States. When Vladimir S. Hurban, the Czech Ambassador in Washington, DC complained about the fate of numerous Czech bank accounts in Chase National Bank in New York in March 1939, he warned of the principle of the non-recognition of looted assets.

As Minister of Czechoslovakia to the United States, I wish to notify you that my country is occupied by foreign armed forces and that officials of its Government and its citizens are or may be acting under duress thereof. Specifically, withdrawals, or attempted withdrawals, of funds on deposit in your bank made or purported to be made in the name of the Government, the National Bank of Czechoslovakia (Narodni banka Ceskoslovenska), or any other instrumentality of the Government may be made under duress. This is to inform you that in the event any such withdrawals ordered under duress are permitted to be made by you, you will be held liable for any and all loss or damage caused thereby.[37]

Hurban's warning to Chase, however, lacked legitimacy as the State Department refused to help.[38] As such, Bernstein and the others in the legal office were relegated to continue working within the usual framework of intergovernmental correspondence and meetings, alternately pleading and arguing for the need for Executive Orders to freeze enemy and occupied Allied finances. "Thereafter, for I would say three years to about...April 1940," Bernstein declared:

> every time there was a crisis in international affairs, generally speaking precipitated one way or another by Hitler and the Nazis, I would take out these old documents,

> redraft them in terms of the current crisis, and we always were ready with our written plans as to how to proceed.... In April 1940, the Germans invaded Denmark and Norway. We had another one of these meetings in the Secretary's office that was typical when a crisis in the world arose. At the meeting there were officials from the State Department, Federal Reserve Board and the Treasury to consider financial and economic matters that we might engage in view of the Nazi invasion. As usual, I had taken the old documents that had been drafted and rewrote them to apply to Denmark and Norway. [39]

Morgenthau continued to fight with the State Department over the need to issue freezing orders that would have satisfied the Czech Ambassador's plea. To Morgenthau's displeasure, Hull continued to hold sway with the president. By 1940, though, freezing orders became unavoidable with the obvious course of Nazi policy and were finally imposed by Executive Order against all German-controlled countries, Axis and Axis-allied countries, and unoccupied countries following the Nazi invasion of first Northern, then the European, Low Countries.

As the German armies progressed, so, too, did the freezing orders: on May 10, 1940, against the Netherlands, Belgium, and Luxembourg; on June 17, 1940, against France; on July 10, 1940, against Latvia, Estonia, and Lithuania; on October 9, 1940, against Romania; March 4, 1941, against Bulgaria; on March 13, 1941, against Hungary; on March 24, 1941, against Yugoslavia; and on April 28, 1941, against Greece.

Finally, on June 14, 1941, President Roosevelt issued an Executive Order freezing the assets of the remaining belligerent countries, all invaded or occupied countries, and the remaining unoccupied states of Europe: Finland, Czechoslovakia, Poland, Albania, Austria, Danzig, Germany, Italy, San Marino, Japan, USSR, China, Portugal, Spain, Andorra, Sweden, Switzerland, and Lichtenstein.[40]

Morgenthau and his men, John Morton Blum wrote, "revealed the belief that someday the frozen assets could be returned to their rightful owners, [and] that someday the Germans would be driven out."[41] As time would show, the latter belief would certainly be fulfilled, but the former would prove much more difficult to achieve.

Access to the Swiss Banks

With the June 14, 1941 order, arming Treasury Department auditors and investigators, in combination with Klaus' FBI-directed intelligence, access was gained into all the files, account information, secret account numbers, and ledger books of the three Swiss banks in New York. Credit Suisse, Swiss Bank Corporation, and Swiss American Corporation files were now all available to Morgenthau's eager Treasury Department investigators, and what they showed alarmed them.

With FDR's freezing order, the banks had been operating under special license, with their actions restricted. Now Foley wrote Morgenthau seeking permission to place a group of investigators in the offices of the Swiss banks in New York on a permanent basis. Foley's concerns were many. Investigators had found even more documentary information, complimenting Klaus on Swiss-German industrial relations in the United States, as well as the camouflaging of German businesses by Swiss companies and banks, formerly the purview of Hoover and the FBI.

More ominously, Foley explained to Morgenthau that a former top executive of the Swiss Bank Corporation in Switzerland, who then moved to the United States, wrote to a colleague in a letter the Treasury obtained, that he resigned because of the fact that "certain high officials of the Swiss Bank Corporation were allowing themselves to be unduly influenced by Germany's apparent success in establishing a new European order."[42] This was all that Morgenthau needed to hear to get him to give the "green light" to his men to act.

Within days, Foley sent his investigators into the Swiss banks and immediately began to search the files, even opening private files. This was clearly too much for George Ludwig of the Swiss American Corporation. Ludwig wrote to Foley, "while we have no idea as to what information is being sought, we notice that special attention is being paid to what might be described loosely as refugee accounts ... we are being placed at a definite business disadvantage with respect to our foreign clients."[43]

Morgenthau's men had gained the opening they needed to analyze and work to break up a variety of German economic schemes in the United States. With America's entry into World War II, the focus of U.S. foreign economic intelligence expanded to include the role the Axis' economic subversion would play in Europe and how the Nazis' new economic and financial resources would affect the U.S. overseas, now that its troops would be engaged in combat against them.

Leaking Information

In the course of further investigations into Swiss-German cooperation, on July 16, 1942, an interdepartmental meeting between the Justice, State, War, and Navy Departments was held to discuss the role of Swiss insurance companies and the leakage of vital shipping information through insurance channels. In October, Acting Secretary of the Treasury Randolph Paul, wrote the Attorney General:

> In the course of the investigation of Swiss insurance companies currently being made the Foreign Funds Control certain information has come to our attention, illustrating: (1) the manner in which specific information with respect to ship movements and losses is disseminated in the normal course of business operations of insurance com-

panies, and (2) the manner in which information regarding ship movements and losses during specified periods is collated so that it is readily available to the employees of seventy-two insurance companies in this country.[44]

Reports like this caused deep concern inside the government and pointed toward the problems that needed to be urgently addressed, not only as they related to Germany, but to its declared and undeclared allies as well. The need to control these economic relationships became an issue that weighed heavily on policy makers' minds, causing them to seek solutions for control at home and abroad. As Foley explained:

> Foreign funds control is so flexible and dynamic an instrument of economic defense that we may reasonably assume its growing usefulness as new situations arise. We may likewise reasonably assume that freezing control will be a most useful instrument in dealing with several of the inevitable post-war economic and financial problems.[45]

Prevention of Flight: *Operation Safehaven*

As a Special Assistant to the Administrator of Foreign Economic Administration (FEA),[46] Henry H. Fowler highlighted the growing problem to which Morgenthau's men were dedicated, especially with regard to post-war policy formulation.

> There was a dispute between [Henry] Stimson, the Secretary of War, and [Henry] Morgenthau, the Secretary of the Treasury, as to what would be done with the German economy. Morgenthau was for, well, the catch phrase was, "pastoralizing" it, and Stimson wanted to reconstruct it on a peaceful basis, but to have a mix of industrial and agricultural operations with which to restore the economy along a very peaceful bent.
>
> Roosevelt solved the dispute between these two by asking Leo Crowley, the head of the Foreign Economic Administration, to conduct a series of studies on how to carry on the economic and industrial disarmament of Germany so that it would never be in a position to make war again. That approach didn't take either position between these two disputees. I organized a group of about thirty-five task forces that went into trying to, as I put it, deal with the economic and industrial disarmament, but to restore, on a peaceful bent, a consumer-oriented, rather than a heavy industrialized militarily-oriented economy.[47]

Now, with the creation of The Foreign Economic Agency, the task of analyzing the Nazi subversive economic threat abroad was begun, and soon analysts from all over the government, especially the Treasury, were detailed to the FEA to form the backbone of Allied efforts against the Axis. Klaus, who would become a Special Assistant to the General Counsel, would continue to work on foreign intelligence matters as a sort of "jack of all trades."

Throughout the next two years, the FEA published detailed studies on the extent of German economic penetration into the occupied countries of Europe. The FEA's work formed the backbone of economic intelligence about the enemy and would lead Klaus, in 1944, to begin work on the formulation of plans for a program that soon came to be known as *Operation Safehaven*.

The FEA's research and findings prompted Morgenthau to pursue an aggressive policy promoting Allied declared non-acceptance of Nazi-looted property, especially gold—not unlike the Czech Ambassador's warning concerning Czech bank accounts. The focus would move to the formulation of policies designed to deny the Axis powers access to large caches of looted public and private assets, soon to be defined as "external assets," which obviously had been taken from victims and others trapped under Nazi occupation. As U.S. forces would later liberate territory from Nazi-occupied Europe, they would be directed to impound these "external" and "internal assets," those taken by the Nazis in Germany.

This much was warned about on January 5, 1943, when eighteen nations, including the United States, issued a joint warning to the neutral nations that the Allies would not recognize the legality of their purchases of German-looted gold anywhere in the world. Like the Proclaimed List, this declaration portended the force of law in Allied dealings with the neutral countries, but it would remain, in this case, an expression of a future policy that would be binding upon the nations of the world.

Not all the Allies, however, accepted this warning. The British, came to the conclusion "that it would be undesirable for His Majesty's Government to issue an official warning to neutrals about receiving Axis-owned gold, saying:

> ... We are assured that difficulties of identifying bar gold would be considerable. If therefore allied [sic] governments (who are parties primarily interested) were to ask our help in recovering looted gold we should probably be unable to do so directly nor of course should we be prepared to seize for their benefit other neutral gold of equivalent value within our jurisdiction. ... On the other hand our belief is that existing German gold reserves have been looted from various European countries and Germany is certainly using gold as a means of payment in neutral countries.[48]

Not all the neutrals accepted the warning either. This much was made very clear in a November 6, 1943 memorandum by Pehle, then Director of the FFC, to Harry Dexter White, Assistant Secretary of the Treasury and a close confidant of Morgenthau.

> Although our information is, of course incomplete, it is significant to note that transfers during the past six months total more than 100 million dollars and that such transfers have increased both in frequency and amount. It is evident that Germany is becoming more and more dependent upon sales of gold for the purpose of obtaining critical materials from European neutrals and that her credit position is growing progressively weaker. Accordingly, I believe that we should arrange for the issuance of our statement on gold as soon as possible in order to limit Germany's ability to dispose of her gold holdings in the future.[49]

As the months proceeded, Morgenthau's men convinced him that a second warning was needed. On February 22, 1944, Morgenthau issued the second declaration, this time in cooperation with the British and the Soviets which said in part:

> The United States Treasury has already taken measures designed to protect the assets of the invaded countries and to prevent the Axis from disposing of looted currencies, securities, and other looted assets on the world market. Similarly, the United States Government cannot in any way condone the policy of systematic plundering adopted by the Axis or participate in any way directly or indirectly in the unlawful disposition of looted gold.
>
> In view of the forgoing facts and considerations, the United States Government formally declares that it does not and will not recognize the transference of title to the looted gold which the Axis at any time holds or has disposed of in world markets ... [50]

With the war running decidedly against the Nazis, thoughts turned to what efforts were needed to be undertaken to prevent a Nazi state, bent on vengeance, from resurfacing following its downfall and defeat. As Morgenthau would argue, there had to be a total defeat and elimination of German war potential in order to erase any chance of this occurring. To assure that it did not, a world-wide program imposing total economic controls on Germany and its identifiable assets, wherever they might be, would need to be instituted and continued on into the post-war era.

Something toward this goal began in April 1944, when FDR ordered a study prepared on the effects and reach of international cartels to reduce their influence in the post-war world.[51] This was, of course, only a study, but it formed the precursor to efforts in various places throughout the government to plan for the future and to gather information on just what the Nazis had done. The FEA wanted to know how great the international robbery really was.

A month later, Klaus, now Special Assistant to the General Counsel at Treasury Joseph J. O'Connell, wrote a memo to the Assistant Administrator of the Foreign Economic Administration, Frank Coe, outlining the basic principles of a program to provide those controls. That program would come to be known as "*Operation Safehaven*" or *"The Safehaven Project."*[52] *Safehaven* was to locate and prevent the spread and hiding of Nazi finances to prevent the rise of a "Fourth Reich."

Two months later, Klaus described in a "Memorandum to the File," the need for such a program. "The New York office," he wrote, "should interview informants who could tell us, of their personal knowledge, the facts concerning German rearmament and the concealment of assets abroad in connection with the defeat in the last war." Klaus explained:

> It is reported that as early as 1917, Gen. Von Bernhardi and others, anticipating a German defeat, began plans for a concealed rearmament. These plans or similar plans,

became widespread after the Armistice. By the time of the Treaty of Versailles, the organization had already been formed in a secret way to maintain Germany's military potential within Germany and abroad for use in Germany at the appropriate time.[53]

Morgenthau later echoed these sentiments by warning:

I would also say that in this way the Germans could save their Army and be ready for another war in the next generation. ... The German war machine has plans for survival. ... We can be sure of that. Such plans have worked before. ... It is an easy guess that Germany may offer Hitler and the Nazi gang to bribe conditions out of us. We won't be bribed. Our terms are unconditional surrender.[54]

Under a plan of action then, approved by Morgenthau, *Operation Safehaven* was begun. Klaus is considered to be the "father" of *Safehaven*. Margaret Clarke, in her unpublished monograph history on the program, *The Safehaven Project*, wrote that while many contributed to the formulation of the project, "internal evidence from the records, however, supports the testimony of many participants in the project's work that Samuel Klaus must be credited with formulating the concepts upon which the program was based."[55]

At the same time as *Safehaven* was forming, from July 1-22, 1944, in direct reference to the goals of the program, the Allies met at the United Nations Monetary and Financial Conference to address post-war international economic affairs. In the conference's set of final resolutions came Resolution VI, "Regarding Enemy Assets and Looted Property," which said in part:

Whereas, In anticipation of their impending defeat, enemy leaders, enemy nationals and their collaborators are transferring assets to and through neutral countries in order to conceal them and to perpetuate their influence, power, and ability to plan future aggrandizement and world domination, thus jeopardizing the efforts of the United Nations to permanently maintain peaceful international relations.[56]

With the goal of preventing this, the conference recommendations (assertive speech acts), then called upon all neutral countries to prevent the movement of looted assets and those of Nazis and Nazi leaders. They were also called upon to prevent the concealment of the same and to deliver them to the post-armistice authorities.[57]

Bretton Woods lent further international legitimacy to the *Safehaven* concept. Now coupled with Klaus' rich background and experience with intelligence gathering on German and other Axis assets and economic plots in the United States, he began the work of creating the apparatus to accumulate the right type of information for *Safehaven*. He explained to State, War, and Treasury officials that it was important for as much information to be gathered as soon as possible, and that it was vital for the Allies to track that information through coordinated efforts as well. In that way, a better picture of the economic penetration could be deciphered and used to the benefit of all the Allies.

Others saw the wisdom and ultimate use of the information *Safehaven* might yield. In London, the Chief of Secret Intelligence, William J. Casey, wrote to Dean Acheson that:

> While it is true that Safehaven information will be one of the most important yields, and also an important cover, this activity should be firmly and specifically aimed at recruiting agents or cutouts and developing lines for the intelligence penetration of German financial and industrial circles–a penetration which should yield all kinds of political and commercial intelligence in addition to Safehaven information.[58]

This intelligence information, in Klaus' estimation, and no doubt Casey's and others, included, "a thorough review of censorship intercepts, intelligence, cables, enemy trade papers and investigations into the field including interrogation of the European underground and of Allied sympathizers in neutral countries."[59] The search would be wide and in-depth.

Moreover, recalcitrant neutral countries like Switzerland and Argentina had to be persuaded to control German assets, in many ways in the same manner that the United States had done in 1940-1941. "We have every reason to believe," wrote Leo Crowley, Administrator of the FEA:

> that the Germans and perhaps the Japanese are using, and will, if permitted continue even more to use, the territories of sovereign nations outside Germany (and Japan) as places in which they may, with some impunity, conduct the transactions and activities that frustrate and even evade allied controls over them following defeat.[60]

Plans for searching for and preventing the utilization of these assets would have to be worked into the overall post war economic and political governance plan for Germany, as Foley had suggested in 1941. With the occupation of Germany, economic controls would indeed play a role in reversing what the Nazis had created. In all, *Safehaven* called for joint action, coordinated intelligence, political will, and diplomatic effort. At the end of the day, *Safehaven* was a plan, every bit important as others used to win the war, only its use was dedicated to winning the peace as well. Whether that would be allowed to happen or not was a question left open to debate.

Once *Safehaven* was approved, Klaus was tasked to go to Europe to canvass the problem there. In advance of his mission, European Embassies and diplomatic missions in London, Madrid, Ankara, Lisbon, Stockholm, Tangier, and Bern were alerted to the rationale behind *Safehaven,* and were informed as to what information Klaus was seeking.[61]

Klaus arrived in Madrid on September 13, 1944 on the first leg of his trip. With disputes as to which agency would provide the lead on *Safehaven*, bureaucratic battles and confusion mounted. In his candid report on his meetings with Klaus and Herbert J. Cummings of the State Department, sent along with Klaus on the trip, Carlton J. H. Haves, described his discussions with Klaus on this trip.

Klaus told Haves that when FFC officials learned of Klaus' impending departure, and the assignment of Cummings, they feared an encroachment on their own jurisdiction. They expressed the belief that the mission's work would overlap to a considerable extent with that which they had been performing during the war. They jealously moved to attach their own representatives to accompany Klaus on his trip. Klaus was adamant about not wanting "company" and refused the "offer," departing as quickly as possible for Europe intending to visit as many capitals on his itinerary as possible before the FFC representatives could overtake him.[62]

Eventually, the FFC representatives did catch up with Klaus and Cummings, much to their chagrin. Klaus did not hide his displeasure at their arrival, complaining to Haves, of "the utter incapacity" of either of the two Treasury men to "contribute anything" to their mission.[63] Klaus held various meetings with Embassy officials and counselors on the movements of gold and other looted assets into and out of Spain. Following his mission there, he and Cummings continued on to Barcelona and to Lisbon, unable to travel on to Tangier.

Haves' memo highlighted an important problem that would go on to plague *Safehaven* until the end, namely the bitter jurisdictional disputes, today commonly known as "bureaucratic turf wars." An unsigned *Safehaven* update by officials at FEA for November 1944, read:

> we must admit that the over all accomplishments during the current month have not been very gratifying inasmuch as we have failed to conclude satisfactorily any of the broad problems or matters which must be disposed of before the program can go into high gear.[64]

While Klaus had created the mechanism to investigate, track, and locate German external assets, it became clear that with the bureaucratic battles that enveloped *Safehaven*, the program, while moderately successful, would never amount to the ambitious effort Klaus had envisioned. Results were achieved, but due to intense rivalries both within the U.S. Government—especially between Treasury and State—and between the Allies as well, *Safehaven* would have to wait fifty years to see the true realization of its creator's goals.

The Morgenthau Plan

While *Operation Safehaven* was to prevent the rise of another Nazi state by stopping the flight of Nazi looted assets. Morgenthau and his men also developed a plan to eliminate Germany's physical and material ability to wage war. The "Morgenthau Plan," as it became known, and derisively referred to by its critics—of whom there were many—as "pastoralization," was a comprehensive plan for post-war Europe and the Allied Occupation of Germany. Others would be less kind calling it "hysterical,"[65] "superficial and silly"[66] and even costly in terms of American lives.[67] In a 1971 interview, one State Department official described Morgenthau as simply "crazy" for promoting it.[68]

In an extraordinarily frank expose entitled, *History of Treasury Participation in Formulation of German Occupation Program*, expressly prepared for the use of future historians, Morgenthau's men sought to explain their rationale behind their plans. This remarkable study detailed the evolution of Treasury's plans for post-war Germany, as well as the internecine conflicts behind its partial implementation.[69]

The nexus of the problem, and the reason that it engendered so much opposition, was the plan's abject severity toward Germany. The Treasury's idea of Germany in the post-war world, and how that approach would effect restitution and reparations, ran counter to all other U.S. policymakers' plans. While hindsight looks with a critical eye toward its content, one cannot, in the context of the time, completely argue with its intent or formulation in light of the experiences of those who wrote it and when they wrote it. The intense debates and struggles behind the campaign to encourage the plan's adoption caused a bitter divide, perhaps a result of early disputes emanating from the Morgenthau-Hull disagreements over the imposition of exchange controls. Hints too, of a resentment of Morgenthau's intrusion into the jurisdiction of the State Department also, quite logically, played a role.

Morgenthau and Hull argued strenuously about the plan, with personal animosities guiding the disputes. Morgenthau called Hull's opposition to his plan and his insistence on leaving Germany intact, "appeasement." Hull answered that it was only humanitarian. To that, Morgenthau retorted that he agreed, only his plan was the one that was humanitarian because it would prevent the inevitable German rearmament and revenge, thereby precluding World War III. Hull's answer was simply that the plan was nothing more than "Jewish vengeance."[70] This sentiment would be voiced from other quarters as well. Others, while not as hostile, reasoned that such a harsh plan would only stiffen German resolve and cost American lives.

Morgenthau's plan, in essence, called for the decentralization of Germany. Total disarmament and de-industrialization would be the operating feature of the state. In reference to restitution and reparations, the Treasury men wrote, there would be:

> no reparations from future production or in the form of future payments. Past experience ... dictated that 'Restitution and reparation shall be effected by the transfer of existing German resources and territories,' e.g., by the restitution of property looted by the Germans in occupied territories; by the transfer of German territory and German private rights in industrial property, situated in such territory; by the removal and distribution among devastated countries of Industrial plants and equipment; by using Germans as forced labor in former occupied zones; and by confiscation of all German external assets 'of any character whatsoever outside of Germany.'[71]

As the authors concluded their description of this section of the plan suggesting, "This paragraph was loaded with controversy."[72] This was surely an understatement.

While integral parts of the Morgenthau plan were in fact asserted in Occupation policy plans announced at the Quebec Conference between FDR and Prime Minister Churchill in September 1944, as well as at the later Yalta Conference in February 1945, plans for a policy of de-industrialization would wither as time and events passed. As the Treasury authors accusingly referred, the State Department, not Treasury, was being represented at Yalta. They ominously suggested, "It is important to realize this because it was the first obvious official suggestion of the fundamental schism between the British and the State Department, on the one hand, and the Treasury and the Soviet Union, on the other." As they concluded, "The single word 'control' was the wedge with which the opponents of the Morgenthau Plan began their hard-fought and successful struggle to prevent it from becoming official U.S. and Allied policy."[73] Subtle references to the alignment of the players on both sides was also mentioned, portending ominous tones as well.

Control

The argument over "control" would dictate all future discussions. For the State Department and the British Foreign Office, control would mean control of German production for Allied use against the Soviet Union, a contention that Morgenthau did not ignore, though calling it merely an expression of the fear of Communism.[74] While on a trip to Europe in August 1944, Morgenthau met with General Eisenhower, who promised him no preferential treatment for the Germans and offered little sympathy either. Eisenhower observed that demands for a soft peace came from "those who wanted to make Germany a bulwark against Russia."[75]

This, however, was not the intention of Morgenthau and his men at Treasury. They envisioned a Germany prostrated, being able only to produce for itself and no one else. Morgenthau strongly disputed the State Department contention as naive that de-industrialization would leave Germany weak, declaring that:

> Now, as soon as you start arguing with me, and I begin to give way, let this in or that in, or let that area or that population continue their skills, they will do just what they do in the hills of Pennsylvania—they will mine bootleg coal. ... A fellow will have a coal mine in his basement, and those fellows are so clever and such devils that before you know it they have got a marching army.[76]

The Treasury was not completely isolated in its opinion. Similar sentiments came from Julius Hirsch of the Federal Reserve, when he explained to his superiors that:

> the protection of the Allies against another attack from Germany is quite different. Since the time of Caesar, there have been long-term occupations. Do not forget that last time the occupation terms were deliberately shortened. Basically they did not exceed

> much the ten years. I would strongly advise everyone to have a very close economic control. The Germans themselves have developed devices that can be used to our advantage, if applied with energy and intelligence.[77]

Yet, those in opposition to his plan had gathered a far greater political counterweight than Morgenthau could muster, despite his close relationship with FDR. Not only was the opposition too great, but those opposing his plan felt sufficiently threatened by it to use all the tools available to them to defeat it. The "fear of Communism" to which Morgenthau referred, would be the dividing line between the two sides of this policy process. While not uttered aloud, the accusation began to surface toward the Treasury that Morgenthau's team harbored "Communist sympathies."[78] It may have still been too soon to suggest that the atmosphere of the Red Scare of the Cold War had been completely developed, but the realization of the emergence of two very different agendas—those of the Western Allies and their Soviet counterparts—were beginning to take shape.

"Lefty Language"

By that time, American planners at State Department had arrived at a fairly good and personal appraisal of the behavior of the Soviets in the international arena and as a result, they had developed a growing sense of distrust. "We in the Division said," elaborated Elbridge Durbrow, "'Try it, but be sure you look every horse in the face very carefully and count his teeth and everything else, because remember the past, etc., etc.' We had been burned; we'd been there. We'd seen these things happening all the time and by 1944 they had gone back on a lot of things."[79]

After all, by late November 1943, State Department planners, already ingrained with experience with the Soviets, had begun to layout plans for post-war Germany and partition was not part of those plans.[80] With Soviet obstructiveness and Morgenthau's strident, albeit unintentional, defense of similar post-war aims, it was easy to mistrust anyone adhering to this overall tone. With this kind of history, it was not surprising then, that this philosophical alignment prevailed.

Paul R. Porter, then the Chairman of the Shipbuilding Stabilization Committee of the War Production Board in Washington, DC, and soon thereafter the Chief of the Economic Mission at the U.S. Embassy in London, commented on these sentiments.

> Well we must be very careful to distinguish between those that were consciously carrying out a Communist plan, and those who just favored harsh treatment of Germany. Most people were in the latter category. I'm convinced, or at least I've never had any reason to believe, that Morgenthau himself was in the slightest influenced by any disposition to be pro-Communist. Some of the people in the Treasury were pro-Communist, but there weren't very many. And they had very definitely infiltrated the

Manpower Division of military government. I never spotted any in the Treasury division of military government. Well the Treasury took a very hard line, but I don't think they were in the least bit influenced by any Communist objective. At least I never identified any of those that were influenced at least.[81]

The Soviets had long pressed for harsh treatment of the Nazis and Germany upon defeat, harsh reparations and the punitive treatment of Nazi leaders were their standard demands. They were not alone. Churchill himself hinted at harsh treatment during a Parliamentary debate when he declared that "It should not be assumed that the procedure of trial will be necessarily adopted."[82] Moreover, while there was opposition to the dismemberment of Germany, among Churchill's advisors there existed strong, yet quiet, sympathy for partition of Prussia and the Ruhr valley from the rest of Germany. Economic partition from Germany, and extinguishing the historic Prussian militaristic culture, were two ideas foremost in their minds.[83]

Morgenthau, had reasoned as well that with German military and economic power destroyed, Britain and the United States would fill the gap in production and supply in Europe, Britain in particular with coal and steel.[84] Yet, despite this complicated economic calculation, State Department planners viewed the plan as too onerous, too reminiscent of a vindictive Stalin, and too helpful towards Soviet post-war plans. With memories of post-World War I harsh reparations plans all too fresh in their minds, they feared the Morgenthau Plan would be but a repeat of a bad mistake, only this time driving Germany into the arms of the Soviet Union.[85] With so much at stake, the plan could not be allowed to become active policy.

This, as history has shown, was the case. The State Department, and arguably British planners as well, viewed these as "overtones" of postwar policy. As Bruce Kuklick has written, "[t]he total plan envisioned a strong Germany and a strong Russia in a completely reconstructed world."[86] Yet, what was undeniable, however, was the tone taken by adversaries of the Morgenthau Plan. American troops serving in the Military Government in the U.S. Occupation zone in Germany even spoke of "speaking in lefty language of wiping out the German economic ties."[87] While suggestions of harboring views contrary to those of the establishment were attacked in a subtle, yet suggestive, way, no one could openly accuse Morgenthau of support for Communism. As Kuklick wrote, "Morgenthau's idea was not "pro-Soviet in a way detrimental to American interests."[88]

The Morgenthau Plan, in the end, was a plan to render Germany harmless for the future. It was an attempt at creating operative policy that in the end failed to gain the necessary support to win the day. While it had coherence, it was seen as too harsh to be acceptable to those implementing it. Moreover, as events would unfold, conditions in Germany would obviate any remaining reasons to allow the Morgenthau Plan to be fully implemented.

Occupation and Debate Over Policy

"They'll say the pictures are faked," wrote British Captain Robert Barer MC to his wife on May 3, 1945. "No picture on earth could ever convey one millionth of the real horror. One felt no pity for these people, only loathing and disgust."[89] Captain Barer's revulsion at the horrors committed by the Nazis is ever present in his letters home. These sentiments were shared by so many from the victorious Allied armies that brought Hitler's messianic vision to an end. Yet, with the end of the fighting came the need to rebuild, salvage, and restitute that which to their every ability, Allied forces, and Governments, could practically accomplish.

As Germany was formally occupied by the Allies with its defeat, there would be four zones of occupation, American, British, French, and Soviet—zones first arrived at during the Quebec Conference and further solidified five months later at Yalta, in February 1945. At Yalta, FDR, Churchill, and Stalin agreed on the need to completely destroy German war-making ability, punish war criminals, disband the armed forces, eliminate or control German war-making industries (less than the Morgenthau Plan's call for elimination or destruction[90]), and exact reparations[91] (the Soviets requested $10 billion). Finally, identical to the Combined Chiefs of Staff Directive 551 of April 28, 1944, the Nazi party, laws, and institutions were to be wiped out.[92]

There were other issues as well that deeply impacted the Cold War, such as the agreement on situating the borders of Eastern Europe, which led to the sphere of Soviet influence there that did not end until the end of the 1980s with the fall of the Communist regimes there. Clay noted that it was also at Yalta where the expulsions of German origin was agreed upon, and solidified later at Potsdam, leading, in his words, to a "new and difficult problem of absorption."[93]

Vital to post-war control was the agreement that a central Control Commission, administered jointly by the victorious powers' Supreme Commanders and headquartered in Berlin, would be created. With further details worked out by the European Advisory Commission (a joint American-British-Soviet Commission formed out of the Foreign Ministers Conference in Moscow in 1943), the Allied Control Council was created and Lt. Gen. Lucius D. Clay would soon become its U.S. Representative.[94]

Throughout the autumn of 1944, there were a variety of other plans being worked out for the Occupation including more in-depth implementation plans for *Safehaven*, and War Department plans for the Military Government for General Eisenhower to administer in Germany. Included as well were the same contentious issues that surfaced during discussions on the Morgenthau Plan, the Quebec Conference, and at Yalta, namely the material shape Germany would constitute in a post-war world. As the Treasury and State Department planners bickered over the degree of pacification, decentralization, and de-

Nazification, each side jockeyed for inclusion of its points in the final directives. The Treasury, as predicted, took the harsher line and State Department took the ostensibly "softer" line. The result, however, was, in essence, a loss for the Treasury in the zero-sum game that was in existence at the time. As was suggested in the Treasury history itself, if the Treasury did not get all that it sought, then it was assumed by them that they lost the battle altogether. With the issuance of Joint Chiefs of Staff Directive 1067 on April 26, 1945, and its full implementation on May 14, 1945, General Eisenhower had his orders and his plan for the administration of the U.S. Zone of Occupation. As General Clay described:

> Germany was to be occupied as a defeated nation under a just, firm, and aloof administration which would discourage any fraternization. The German economy was to be controlled only to the extent necessary to meet the needs of the occupation forces or to produce the goods which would prevent disease and unrest, which might endanger the occupying forces.[95]

For the Treasury, however, any control of the German economy was wrong and inadvisable. Price, wage, and other controls of the economy would only serve to increase the chance of a recovery, which to them was unthinkable. The Treasury, for a number of reasons, however, lost this argument to the State and War Departments as mediated by the president. FDR's policy on controls was simple, and while not practiced, indicative of some of the hard-line policy Morgenthau had tried to instill in him. "We'll get a committee of say three Germans," FDR was said to have quipped. "We'll tell them to do thus and so. If they don't do it, we'll shoot them and get three more."[96]

Policy by Directive

Joint Chiefs of Staff (JCS) Directive 1067, the official Occupation policy document, was the "first official statement of restitution policy for the loss of personal property under the Nazi regime."[97] In JCS 1067, the U.S. Commander was instructed to impound a variety of categories of internal assets, as distinguished from external ones, to be found through *Safehaven.*

JCS 1067 was also designed as an Anti-Trust decree, mandating the decartilization and break-up of Nazi economic monopolies. German industrialists too were to be removed and de-Nazified.[98] That these requirements were mandated was admirable. That they were accomplished was yet another. Failure to achieve these goals, along with many others, would resurface in the near future.

It would be through the Allied Control Council (ACC) then, that decrees would now again rule Germany. This time, however, the directives would be specifically designed to reverse the actions and results of those issued by the Nazis. As Hitler's decrees enriched the Nazis and their supporters, ACC directives would do the opposite. This much was inherent in directives predating those of the ACC, such as CCS 551, which as the Treasury authors derided when they explained its call for "the institution of a thorough-going rehabilitation program, and to that end ordered the establishment of a most paternalistic and extensive control over the German economy."[99]

U.S. Occupation personnel initially were to operate under the directives of JCS 1067 as well as a Presidential Determination of Policy of March 23, 1945. In doing so, part of the flavor of the Morgenthau Plan persisted and the German economy was to meek out an existence with no overall help by the occupying powers, hence the reliance upon the term "aloof." Yet with the Potsdam Declaration of August 2, 1945, the policy of aloofness would fade and the development of a balanced, self-sufficient economy would take its place. The Potsdam declaration would also dictate the procedures to be taken with reparations in regard to industrial plant removals, declared to be "surplus to Germany's peacetime needs," and removed within two years after the final determination of the amount needed. Procedures for the war crimes trials of Nazi war criminals were mandated.[100] There was also an extensive list of prohibited and production-restricted industries such as synthetic, metallurgical, chemical, machine tools, engineering, electro-engineering, and transportation engineering, spare parts, agricultural, machinery, optical and precision equipment, mining, and electrical power.[101]

What made Potsdam's call for reparations different than that made a generation before at Versailles, was that they were not assessed or exacted in currency, only in kind, and done on a zonal basis, allowing each occupation power a choice, and not the mandatory extraction of, all industrial development within the respective zones, thus essentially softening the blow on post-war Germany.

Truman and a Change in Policy and Direction

Potsdam came after FDR's death and the end of the war. With FDR gone, Truman was president and he brought with him an administration with different views, different personnel, and facing different threats. "The people who had had the greatest influence and developed the occupational powers went out," wrote Clay, "and Mr. Truman's administration came in with the people that he brought to run the Government. I don't think that the so-called 'destroy Germany' policy was ever one that President Truman personally believed in. He had nothing to do with its creation and I don't think he ever believed in it."[102] No longer would Morgenthau have the president's ear and no longer would his power transcend his office.

Morgenthau's men agreed with this assessment and mourned the loss of their influence on the process toward a harsher treatment of Germany as well as efforts at de-Nazification and industrial pacification. "After the President's death," they wrote, "Treasury lost its court of appeal, and the result should have been quite foreseeable."[103]

With the change in administrations, those leaving office following FDR's death left because, in Judge Samuel Rosenman's belief, Truman either did not share their views or held no confidence in them.[104] Morgenthau was one such case. Truman, according to Blum, was irritated at Morgenthau and those advocating similar views on Germany, complaining...'they couldn't keep from meddling in' German questions."[105] Morgenthau, according to Rosenman, the Special Counsel, first to FDR and then to Truman, explained that he had sought a reassurance of his position as Secretary before Truman left for Potsdam, but was denied it. Morgenthau then worked out the details and timing with Truman for his eventual resignation.[106]

With Morgenthau's departure from the scene, a weight was lifted from all those at the State Department who had been overshadowed by Morgenthau and more shrewdly by FDR, whose "free-lance style circumvented normal bureaucratic channels," wrote Amos Perlmutter, disheartened many at the State Department.[107] As James W. Riddleberger, then Chief of the State Department Division of Central European Affairs, explained, "In a sense that there was a new power conferred upon the State Department. Now, of course, this was all a very interesting period. ... Roosevelt, even up until his death was still postponing decisions on Germany, because he still hadn't decided. He would decide on these matters later, he said. But he died in April, 1945."[108]

Now, the role and trajectory of U.S. Occupation policy would change. If the policymakers were going to change, so, too, did the policy and the events to which they would have to react. "Six months after Potsdam," Clay wrote, "the Soviet expansion program was under way. The Communist drive to power in the satellite countries was gaining in form and strength; agreement in Germany was no longer possible."[109]

Military Government

"I think that it was something that I had to grab and do. ... Nobody had had any experience in this kind of job," reasoned Clay. "After all, we hadn't had this kind of occupation of a major country."[110] Just as Bernard Bernstein and Morgenthau's Crusaders had done through the creation of new methods to combat the Nazis, so, too, would General Clay's men. Occupation policy was to be created out of whole cloth.

In the first of three directives by the ACC, the *Declaration Regarding the Defeat of Germany*, Clay wrote, "the four occupying governments eliminated the last vestige of national government in Germany and replaced it with four commanders in chief."[111] The second proclamation decreed that the supreme legal authority in each of the four zones would be the respective Occupying powers' Commanders-in-Chief. The third proclamation defined the borders of the occupation zones.[112]

Clay's situation was, to say the least, difficult. Never before had the U.S. approached this kind of effort, and on such a scale. Now, they had to do so under the watchful eye of their ostensible Soviet allies who were increasingly voicing divergent opinions on occupation policy, including repeated refusals for Allied Occupation officials' transit through their zone. This, coupled with the use of combat officers as Occupiers, and the rotation out of Germany of other veteran officers, in part for the ongoing war in the Pacific, made for difficulties of administration and practice in the American Zone of Occupation. Paul Porter, who at the time was serving first in the U.S. Embassy in London, asserted that:

> ... most of the combat officers were wholly unsuited for military government and they wanted out as quickly as they could, and the men who were assigned there were largely second-string men, who had not been used for combat because they were not first-class officers. We got some awfully poor quality men as military commanders then. I don't know how you run a military government suitably. It's a pretty difficult thing to do. Certainly the combat officers would not have been the right people; but neither were the men that were chosen, other than Clay, who was a man with very real ability, and a few others, but particularly the men out in the field were not.[113]

Frank J. Miller, of the Property Control Division of the Office of Military Government (OMGUS), echoed Porter's description of Occupation personnel with respect to the Division, which was designed to articulate and conduct the early restitution program in the U.S. zone in Germany.

> I think my conclusions on this program are that we were inexperienced. That we had never confronted such a situation before and we didn't know exactly what we wanted to do, that we bit off much more than we could properly chew...They didn't ask me if I knew anything about it. I got a job and by one means and another I hung onto it. I don't think that is a very intelligent way for a country to run a program of this size. I think that's a pretty serious mistake that was made that in view of all planning that was done in foreign funds in 1940, 1941, 1942, and 1943, that we should have taken people with years of training in precisely this kind of work and had them come over here.[114]

While FFC advisors did spend some time in Germany, the Property Control officers were largely left on their own.

Important too, was the fact that between Soviet demands for reparations, and Allied disagreements over the types of property to be included under any restitution programs, the ACC did not arrive at a unified definition of the term until January 1946.[115] It was in this environment that Military Occupation and restitution efforts began.

Property Control

"At the inception of occupation," wrote the authors of the March 1946 Status Report on Military Government of Germany (OMGUS), "Military Government detachments were stationed in every Stadkreis and Landkreis in the U.S. Zone. As operating field units for Military Government, they exercised complete control over every phase of German life. Today ... the burden has been shifted to the German civilian administrations."[116] Yet, the shift was neither complete, nor speedy.

Restitution began cautiously with Property Control investigators taking control of the property largely taken from the Jews by the Nazis in duress, as well as that belonging to citizens of Allied nations. Yet, the issuance of Military Government Decrees and Laws did not take long to shape Property Control's work. In July 1945, Military Government Law 52 was issued declaring that the German authorities were obligated to comply with all directives regarding property and assets. Military Government Law No. 53 mandated the blocking of assets, in particular gold. OMGUS had the authority to formerly begin to take control of properties. Beginning with 2,600 properties taken under control in the early months, the number swelled to 110,000 properties at the program's peak. By that time, Property Control officers were taking 10,000 properties each month.[117] Of all these properties, 14,600 were properties of citizens of the United States; 31,500 were those taken under duress, and the rest were largely those belonging to Nazis.[118] The properties under their control totaled $5.6 billion.[119]

As properties were being taken over, census lists had to be accumulated, reports had to be filled out, and with never more than 300 men assigned to Property Control, it was a logistical nightmare. Lists for such properties were extensive. They included appraisals of the properties' condition and the present owner. In most cases that owner was a private German citizen. In others, found on Property Control lists assembled by OMGUS investigators in the Hesse region of the American Zone, there were corporations, including Dresdner Bank, Allianz Insurance, I.G. Farben, Degussa, and even the NSDAP, the Nazi Party that had taken over Jewish property.[120]

Decontrol, or the turning over of property to either the rightful owners, or to auction, was intricately complicated with investigations required for each, and claims having to be recorded and verified. International organizations were accumulating claims collectively and for individuals alike. The remnants of entire cities in Germany were accumulating information as to the losses suffered at the hands of the Nazis, including confiscated and damaged buildings, hospitals, cemeteries, orphanages, and community investments.[121]

In some cases, Property Control officers were assigning properties to displaced persons and GIs. These homes, in some cases, were turned over completely furnished only to be emptied later by their new inhabitants when they moved on. These instances only added to the officers' problems when actual claimants later surfaced.[122]

Law No. 5 and the Neutrals

As haphazard as this process began, the officers were given further authority with the issuance of ACC Law No. 5, the "Vesting and Marshalling Decree," on October 30, 1945. With this Law, the Allies formally took title to, and blocked all the external, German assets, "including corporations organized under the laws of Germany or having their principal place of business there," thought to be in the range of $200 million, and declared their intention to "divest the assets of their German ownership."[123] These assets, taken outside of Germany in many cases, were brought back into Germany. That which was not was not brought into Germany was sent to neutral countries such as Switzerland, Sweden, Turkey, Portugal, Spain, and to countries in Latin and South America was thought to be some 28 percent of the total of all German external assets.[124]

The vulnerability of the Allied position with regard to the extraterritoriality of Law No. 5 made it difficult for some to argue the point. "Any legal opinion given to the Swedes," wrote Otto Fletcher of the State Department to Seymour Rubin, a *Safehaven* negotiator:

> can omit a legal justification for the request of giving extraterritorial effect to Law No. 5 and should be limited to a legal explanation of the legal basis of the supreme authority of the ACC and of the reason why seizure of German assets is a justified action that has nothing to do with 'violent departure from what has been deemed impregnable rule of international law' and 'inroad on private property' as Professor Borchardt put it. This relieves us of the necessity of arguing about legality of Law No. 5 and its extraterritorial effects, the latter one being the most vulnerable of our positions anyway.[125]

Gaining physical control of assets located in the neutral countries would be an added trouble for *Safehaven* investigators who would endure endless diplomatic torture due to Law No. 5. Neutral countries, hiding behind the veneer of extremely legalistic explanations, simply refused to recognize the legitimacy of this decree and refused to return that which was not theirs to keep.

As advisors explained to Morgenthau's successor at Treasury, Fred Vinson, a Truman friend:

> The problems of uncovering German assets in neutral countries is tremendously complicated because the Germans have been so methodical in hiding their assets through complicated and intricate cloaking devices. This means that even if the neutrals agree to cooperate with us in implementing the German vesting decree (Law No. 5), the actual task of corralling and selling such assets will be extremely difficult.[126]

Treasury advisors further warned Vinson about the difficulties of gaining hold of these assets, beyond the legal impediments.

> The neutrals have in fact for many years been an integral part of the German economy. They still feel that their economic future depends upon doing business with the Germans as they have in the past. The evidence is overwhelming that the neutrals will do everything they can to prevent us from uncovering and disposing of German assets.[127]

These warnings were true then, and in light of the history of the past fifty or more years, they still are. The neutrals became the most difficult nut for the Allies to crack. Each proved nearly impossible for the Allies, mostly the Americans, to force into relinquishing these assets. Heirless assets of Holocaust victims, politically mixed in with those of the Germans, would become the crux of the restitution battles a half-century after this warning was made to Vinson. Assets entrusted with companies in neutral countries were shielded by their governments who stubbornly refused access to Allied investigators ignoring numerous entreaties to surrender them.

Defining Properties

On December 3, 1945, the War Department issued rules for a definition of the types of properties subject to restitution. Now, all Allied currencies, works of art, cultural and religious works, books, manuscripts and documents, archives, industrial and agricultural machinery, transportation such as ships, trains, and barges, livestock, and other valuables, excluding financial instruments, were subject to removal.[128] These assets fell under the jurisdiction of an order dating back to March 1945, by the Supreme Headquarters Allied Forces (SHAEF), as Allied forces were liberating more and more of Europe. Forces finding these items were to immediately turn them over to financial and/or Military Government detachments for immediate deposit in secure facilities in U.S.-controlled, then formally occupied, territory.

Blocking of assets was the first step in establishing the control mechanism. Based on the measures taken in the United States by Morgenthau's men before and during the war, they were to be repeated this time under occupation. Once assets were under Allied control, the next process was to catalogue them and begin the complicated effort to establish a claims procedure and apparatus with which to sort and adjudicate claims.

Reparations

From November 9 to December 21, 1945, representatives from eighteen Allied nations,[129] excluding Poland and the Soviet Union, met in Paris and established the Inter-Allied Reparations Agency (IARA), to be seated in Brussels. On January 14, 1946, they formally signed the agreement. The IARA was formed to administer the collection and distribution of German reparations to the Allies on a pro-rated share basis, with the Western Allies taking 75 percent of German external assets, split by nineteen countries, and the Soviet Union eligible for the other 25 percent.[130] A procedure for the return of "monetary gold," taken by the Nazis from the treasuries of Europe, was to be affected. Additionally, two categories of assets were arrived at, industrial equipment in order to demilitarize Germany, and capital equipment and property such as ships. There were thoughts of further dividing these categories into more, but the idea was abandoned due to a desire for simplification.[131]

In all, the concept of economic security, through the elimination of German war-making potential, overrode other concerns. The application of German external assets located through *Safehaven* and other channels, would be made as long as those assets were to satisfy the requirements of economic security for the Allied powers.

At Paris, reparations issues were largely instituted, yet the subject of restitution began to take shape first with the application of German external assets to their respective countries of origin, and then the setting aside of not more than $25 million for refugees[132] from a pool comprised, in part, of these assets in addition to all non-monetary gold assets found and all assets retrieved from and deposited in neutral countries and left heirless because of the death of their original owners. Refugee funds would be controlled by the Inter-Governmental Committee on Refugees. As stated in the Final Report written for the State Department:

> The Signatory Governments assume no obligation to prevent their nationals from seeking to obtain satisfaction of such claims [private claims] directly against a German Government or its Agencies through means which do not require support from the Signatory Government concerned.[133]

Private claims then, were not forbidden, only not supported by a participating government. The only way private claims could be supported by a participating government would be for them to be made to that government, and their payment would be subsumed under the overall reparations total for that country's share. In essence, this qualification placed an artificial ceiling on the number and amounts of claims to be paid, presuming that each country was willing to handle private claims out of their national totals.[134] This stipulation was made because the participating countries did not want to separate the two issues for fear of the possibility of distributing the property of one claimant nation to that of another. Additionally, because of the extent of personal property lost to the Nazis, and because of the desire of all the nations involved to pro-rate the amount of damages by a mutually agreed upon share basis, this careful balance would have been upset. There were already enough problems caused by Soviet mistrust of Allied intentions, their seizures of formerly enemy assets in Eastern Europe, and their overwhelming claims for damages. To re-open this carefully negotiated formula agreement further would have caused serious, perhaps harmful, disagreements.[135] Important, too, was the agreement that claims for social security payments to forced laborers, sought by victimized countries on their behalf from a future German government, were to be considered as property interests and subsumed as reparations as well.[136]

Two vitally important features of future reparations policy were sacrificed to expediency. Private claims were not excluded, nor would they be supported by national governments. Payments in return for unpaid benefits arising out of forced labor were also lost on a private basis. Both forms of payments to victims were forgotten in the chaotic post-war policy of expediency, and would slowly fester for decades tainting the shape of other plans for victims' restitution. It was not a mistake then, that the U.S. delegation was authorized to only discuss the restitution of monetary gold.[137] In the end, the fact that private claims were "subsumed" for the ostensible 'greater good' of all concerned, showed the future of individual claims in the immediate post-war world.

Resettlement Funds

On June 19, 1946, the governments of the United States, the United Kingdom, France, Czechoslovakia, and Yugoslavia formally agreed on a fund of $25 million for refugees and "Since the overwhelming group of eligible victims were Jewish, the conference allocated $22.5 million out of German assets in neutral countries, 90 percent of the non-monetary gold and 95 percent of all the heirless funds for the rehabilitation and resettlement of Jews."[138] None of the funds would be used for compensation, only resettlement. Moreover, it was expected that the "authorized Jewish field organizations will use a large part of these funds for the rehabilitation of refugees and for the resettlement in Palestine. The remaining amount would be used for non- Jewish refugees.[139]

Restitution

As the early conferences on reparations proceeded, the tide slowly turned toward the implementation of restitution for victims. Restitution came internationally and from within Germany, at the start, imposed by occupation authorities. Internationally, and as a product of *Safehaven* work, the Allies pursued the fulfillment of their commitments at Paris.

The Swiss

As an ostensibly neutral country, because of their deep role in attracting Jewish assets from before and during the war, Switzerland was an obvious target of Sam Klaus and the *Safehaven* investigators. Following years of investigation, veiled and sometimes not-so-veiled threats, and heated discussion, the Allies and the Swiss signed the *Washington Accord of May 25, 1946*, whereby the Swiss agreed to turn over some $58 million in gold and Sfr. 250 million, evenly split between the Swiss and the Allies, keeping half in return for claims they made on the Germans. On the issue of heirless assets, the Swiss negotiator Walter Stucki promised that his government would enact procedures to search their banks for dormant assets. Stucki even committed this to writing when he signed a letter to the Chiefs of the Allied Delegation stating that his government would:

> examine sympathetically the question of seeking means whereby they might put at the disposal of the three Allied Governments, for the purposes of relief and rehabilitation, the proceeds of property found in Switzerland which belonged to victims of recent acts of violence of the late Government of Germany, who have died without heirs.[140]

In reality, however, the Swiss were neither sympathetic nor willing to look for heirless assets. In a report to the Federal Political Department, Litigation, Financial Affairs, and Communications Division, the government's Justice and Police Department reported the legal determination that "We do not believe that this accord makes it possible to impose on the banks an obligation to announce all assets that they manage on behalf of owners who have not given any sign of life since May 9, 1945..."[141] The Swiss stalled, dodged, and applied overly legalistic interpretations to the entire process. As Morton Bach, a U.S. Foreign Service officer serving in Bern at the time explained, " ... [I]t's a nation of lawyers and if you came up with a piece of paper that established your viewpoint, well, that helped."[142] Essentially the Swiss never intended to search for these or any assets.[143]

Later in 1952, after much discussion and persistent claims of the inadequacies of the first agreement, and after more than a year of diplomatic exchanges, conferences, and negotiations, the Allies and Switzerland came to another agreement. On August 26, 1952, The Government of Switzerland and the Federal Republic of Germany (FRG) concluded an agreement by which the Swiss Government received 121.5 million Swiss Francs from the Federal Republic of Germany. Two days later, on August 28, 1952, in another agreement, concluded between the U.S., U.K., and France, acting on behalf of the Inter-Allied Reparation Agency and Switzerland, the Swiss agreed essentially to turn over the 121.5 million Swiss Francs (Sfrs.) received from the FRG. Of this sum, 17.2 million Sfrs. were turned over to the Liquidating Trust for the International Refugee Organization, with 90 percent available to Jewish refugees,[144] but not for restitution.[145]

The Swiss refused to acknowledge of the existence of any further heirless assets, but Allied negotiators essentially forced the Swiss to commit to dedicating any heirless assets they ever found in the future towards the rehabilitation of victims of Nazi persecution.[146]

Waiving Claims

In February 1947, Rumania, Hungary, and Bulgaria—as former allies of the Nazis—concluded bi-lateral treaties with the Allies, waiving all claims against Germany nationally, and for their citizens. In a climate still pervaded by the punitive approach to reparations, these treaties prevented the diminution of the overall pool of German external assets, but shut out victims of the Nazis from these three countries from submitting claims for restitution, again closing out consideration for their suffering.[147]

Law 59 and Mandated Restitution

Following the treaties waiving restitution rights for survivors in the three Eastern European countries, in November, Law 59 was issued in the American Zone by OMGUS. After fruitless efforts to achieve restitution for property abandoned under duress through the varied levels of the Allied Occupation apparatus, it was decided to pursue a policy of restitution unilaterally in the U.S. Zone. With this law, mandatory restitution was, for the first time, ordered by the Military Government. With this law, the structure necessary to affect internal property restitution put into place. W.J. Dickman, Deputy Chief of the Property Control and External Assets Branch explained:

> It is the purpose of the Law to effect to the largest extent possible the speedy restitution of identifiable property to persons who were wrongfully deprived of such property within the period from 30 January 1933 to 8 May 1945 for reasons of race, religion, nationality, ideology, or political opposition to National Socialism.[148]

Law 59 was to apply throughout the American Sector, but not in Berlin. The law was later extended there under separate authority under the Berlin Komandatura, Order 49, in July 1949. In addition to the restitution mandate came the requirement for the creation of an agency to take custody of heirless property in Germany. Property, personal and cultural/religious, with no successors, was going unclaimed with no agent to take control and disposition of it because no specific successor organization had been recognized.

Heirless Property and a Successor Organization

From the time before the end of the war, and continuing on past the immediate surrender, American Jewish groups were pressuring the U.S. and Military Governments for a process whereby property of Holocaust victims, with no identifiable heir, could be collectively identified and title claimed. Yet, these same groups were, in the words of Col. L. Wilkinson, Acting Director of the Economics Division of the Military Government, " ... far from unanimous in their ideas with respect to the disposition of such religious and cultural objects" and that seemed to be the crux of the disagreement.[149] Communal properties amounted to more than synagogues and unmovable properties, but also millions of books ,[150] torah scrolls, manuscripts, and other religious items. Jewish institutions all over the world bid for them but OMGUS could not simply give the materials away, either morally or legally, at least in the beginning.

In the case of books without identification, by 1952, over 150,000 unidentifiable books had been turned over to seventeen priority libraries across the United States, including the Library of Congress in Washington., DC[151] Hundreds of Torah scrolls were later sent to Israel.[152]

Communal property was one issue, but personal property that was heirless caused greater concern. Clay was apprehensive about the amount of heirless property that needed to be processed and returned. "... [I]nternationally known and recognized Jewish Organizations" Clay wrote in June 1946, "might prepare [a] comprehensive and detailed plan for disposal of all Jewish ownerless property in Germany indicating particularly suggested beneficiaries [for] such property."[sic][153] These kinds of cables went back and forth for a year, while the material continued to accumulate in the various depots, and collecting points OMGUS created to house these properties. Initially, there were numerous depots and collecting points. By June 1946, these were consolidated to only four: Offenbach, Munich, Weisbaden, and Marburg. Offenbach was the primary collecting point for looted items of Jewish origin and according to Seymour J. Pomrenze, a Property Officer with OMGUS, U.S. officials worked quickly, once the depot was established, restituting over 98 percent of the Nazi-looted materials that came under U.S. control, 60 to 70 percent in the first three months alone.[154]

One month later, following discussions among various Jewish organizations in the United States, the Commission for European Jewish Cultural Reconstruction was created and immediately began consultations with Clay's representatives in the Military Government on various options to take title to unclaimed properties. Clay communicated the suggestions being made.

> Plans also contemplate OMGUS creating tribunals [to] pass upon claims. Proposals for distrib[ution] [to] provide identifiable Pvt. Owners would get property; Jewish communities and institutions only to [the] extent capable making full use thereof with due regard [to] percentage [of] former Jewish populations surviving.[155]

In 1947, the Jewish Restitution Successor Organization (JRSO) was incorporated in New York State in order to file claims for heirless property. On its board sat Jewish representatives from the United States, Palestine, and Europe.[156] This was an important requirement in Clay's mind because, as he wrote in October 1946, "if claims are to be filed by an International Agency on behalf of Jewish interests in general it is considered imperative that the Agency be truly representative of Jewish interests throughout the world with adequate provision in particular for the representation of Jewish interests now in Germany."[157] The need for a successor organization to be universally representative, in order to act as trustee for heirless property, was also vitally important due to quadripartite agreements mandating identifiable items be returned back to their countries of origin. This point was impressed upon OMGUS, and would have material and policy consequences for the heirless, yet identifiable, property for years to come.

Soviet intransigence led Allied officials to change course in the direction first, a tripartite process, then to an individual, and no longer national, restitution policy.[158] Moreover, heirless property from Eastern Europe would have to go to the JRSO/JCR as well.[159] Movable property with identifying traits, such as financial instruments (stocks, bank accounts, and non-bearer bonds[160]) would be caught in the confusion of this definition and requirement.[161] Later, when *Safehaven* investigators and diplomats would argue for the restitution of heirless bank accounts from Switzerland, and other property from Portugal, Spain, Sweden, and Turkey, this procedural requirement would prevent the transfer of title for resettlement and restitution purposes.[162]

With deadlines for filing claims approaching on December 31, 1948, Clay finally issued Regulation 3 to Law 59 authorizing an application process for charitable organizations to be accorded the status of a successor organization for unclaimed Jewish property. Inherent in this regulation was a specific recognition of a successor organization, which would soon come to be the JRSO as the body "which will be entitled to file petitions for restitution in all cases not claimed by individuals or special Restitution Successor Organizations heretofore appointed by Military Government."[163] On September 12, 1949, JRSO's eligibility to act as a successor organization was extended to the Berlin Sector of Germany.[164]

What is important to understand about Clay's decree, however, was that Clay issued it over the objections of his legal division which did not concur, citing the unilateral proposal as "ambitious and [one which] could result in a legalized form of looting..."[165] They, like many others, felt the legal need to avoid any unilateral decisions and seek quadripartite agreement for all such actions.

In April of the same year, the Jewish Cultural Reconstruction, Inc. was incorporated in New York. Soon the two would form a partnership with the JCR, forming the cultural arm of the JRSO handling individual heirless claims.[166] By inviting major American Jewish organizations to join its board, the JCR sought to ensure a moral and legal authority necessary to act as a trustee for heirless cultural objects.

The JCR sought access to all storage depots in the American Zone of Occupation as well as logistical and transportation help necessary to take title to these objects. Moreover, they sought the authorization for the commanding generals in the occupations zones of Germany and Austria wrote Jerome Michael, to "seize and take into their possession Jewish religious and cultural objects..." and "... all Hebraica, Judaica, and other Jewish religious and cultural objects which are owned by or in the possession of German and Austrian state, municipal, and other publicly owned or maintained libraries, archives, museums, and similar institutions."[167] Michael believed that with the death of so many Jews, and the dispersal of the survivors from Europe, the heirless assets that remained should be completely, and entirely, removed from Europe because that continent held no hope of ever again attaining the status of being a center of Jewish life.[168] This belief guided his actions in seeking control over these assets. Despite this, though, the request for the seizure of these items, however, would inflame some at State Department. Their reaction would only further show why restitution would prove, in reality, to be a difficult proposition.

"Acts of Revenge" and Open Theft

Ralph Simpson at the State Department was given Michael's letter and reacted with hostility expressing short-sightedness toward the proposal and suggestion of the appointment of a trustee. Like Clay's OMGUS Legal Division lawyers, he, too, felt that the idea of a trusteeship was a legal violation. "It gives the impression," he wrote, "of an act of revenge on the part of the Jews using the American Army and American officials as a reverse version of the Einsatzstab Rosenberg." Simpson continued derisively suggesting that:

> Jewish organizations acting in a spirit of revenge could loot with the assistance of United States troops, German public museums, libraries, and archives, of any cultural treasures which, in the opinion of the personnel of the Jewish mission, had a Jewish character. It is contrary to elementary principles of justice that a claimant be the judge of his own claim. Government agencies, and especially troops, should not be placed under the direction of private claimants.[169]

These expressions of disagreement over Jewish custody of the recovered property were unfortunate, but they were overcome. There were other obstacles to restitution as well.

U.S. Army personnel found themselves, like children in a candy store, staring at the ill-gotten gains of the Nazis from a pillaged continent sitting in the various American depots. With Germany laid in waste, and with no German governmental authority, "all of Germany belonged to us," exclaimed Seymour Pomrenze, the first Commander of the Offenbach depot from February-May 1946. "There were no rules on taking anything home. There was not a close handle on the situation there."[170]

In U.S.-Occupied Austria, similar circumstances seemed to reign. "The position of Fine Arts Officer in USFA was eliminated in July 1946 and from then until October 1947," wrote Eve Tucker, of the Monument and Fine Arts and Archives section of OMGUS-USACA, from Vienna in 1949, "the negligence of this explosive situation was hardly short of being criminal."

> (These are strong words, I know, but hear me out.) There was no control then on what American officers sent home and there is very little now. I did what I could from my office position in Vienna to control the situation (though of course I could do nothing on what was sent to the States). Finally in October 1947 the job was recreated and I was officially appointed fine arts officer. The same man sits in control now in Salzburg

who had been there since 1946—he was Chief of Property Control and Restitution - now, besides keeping control of this office he is also Deputy Chief of Military Govt. [sic] As such in his first capacity he is custodian of my art depot in Salzburg—which he has used as a requisition dump for officers homes and clubs. He is of course a great favorite with the Generals, being among other things a good poker player. Efforts on my part to protect the art depot in Salzburg from these inroads have been without avail—I have not been able to get a letter out of this Division (This man's name is Vernon Kennedy—he was formerly in Labor circles in California and then with UNRRA).[171]

Tucker objected that "... with three art depots in Austria, all containing unidentified loot, no investigations having been made of officers clubs and villas, with scores of outstanding art claims unsettled—USFA is just eliminating the job—why?"

The Salzburg Gold Coin Collection was looted while in the possession of the Military Detachment of Hallein, Austria; several truckloads of fine arts were brought to Vienna by General Clark (for his quarters here) from Castle Klessheim in Salzburg; seven paintings were stolen from Lauffen Mine, including a Rubens and a van Dyke, while under protection of U.S. personnel; seven valuable engravings four of them by Durer, were stolen from Alt-Aussee saltmine while under protection of US personnel. Most of these have had no investigation—but all is carefully documented by the Austrian Government.[172]

Pomrenze suggested, like Tucker, that "probably there were Generals and the entire military that had privileges of taking and mailing materials home. I could have taken books, manuscripts, etc. home, but I didn't. It was a free-for-all." Nevertheless, Pomrenze said of Eve Tucker's claims, "our experience in Germany was at variance with that of Tucker's letter."[173]

Tucker's accusations of improprieties were not the first to be heard, as real acts of cultural robbery by Americans in Occupied Germany and Austria would increase. As researchers for the *Presidential Advisory Commission on Holocaust Assets in the United States* concluded of the actions of U.S. forces in 1945, "[h]igh ranking American officials took assets from the [Hungarian] Gold Train for their own personal use and assets from the train were sold through the Army Exchange. There is also evidence that assets from the Gold Train were stolen outright."[174]

Other members of the military sought to avail themselves as well of the riches that came to them courtesy of the U.S. occupation of Germany, including such riches as the Quendlinburg Bible dating back to the tenth century. The Bible and was taken out of Germany by Lt. Joe T. Meador and sent home to Whitewright, Texas in the summer of 1945, and was discovered in 1989 by the art provenance researcher Willi Korte.[175] Still other German-origin works of art were packed and sent to the United States for display, and only later returned to Germany or Israel and other locations if their provenance was identified.[176]

Bill Daniels, Chief of the Property Division of the High Commissioner for Germany, writing in a private letter of July 14, 1950, confided to a friend that there were real problems when it came to returning cultural property, although he made no accusations of criminal action, he nevertheless agreed with the notion that the pace of restitution was just too slow. "The cultural property situation is still bogged down badly." Hiring was slow and OMGUS seemed more interested in exhibiting recovered pictures than restituting them.[177]

More importantly, as the Property Control men earlier complained, there was a lack of preparation, and moreover, those placed in charge of the process of restitution had varying views on the subject, as well as varying commitments to policy.[178] Processes for restitution varied as well. For example Ardelia Hall, the MFA and A adviser to OMGUS, according to Pomrenze, a trained archivist, reorganized the order of some of the archival materials to which she had access according to her own system, thereby destroying the original order of the collections, misplacing some materials in the process—simply due to error.[179]

In sum, Pomrenze suggested four reasons why restitution did not progress as smoothly as they might have wished. First, he explained, it was difficult to get countries to send authorized representatives to the depots to file claims. The Soviet Union did not send an authorized representative until late 1947. At Offenbach, though, fifteen nations eventually sent representatives.

Second, the items necessary to carry out restitution were not readily available. Transportation was scarce, as were the number and flexibility of personnel available to work on restitution. "The positions at Offenbach were 'civilianized' and people couldn't get what they needed to live and work. As a captain," Pomerenze stated, "I could go to the PX and get what I needed. Civilians could not."[180]

Third, there were so few people to which they could return material, and there were far too many items that were found unmarked. Blindly returning heirless material to countries of their native origin could result, in the case of whole collections, in the dispersion of that collection.[181] Vanished communities presented a particular problem in places like Lithuania from which books and hundreds of torah scrolls were recovered.[182] Many countries claimed written materials found in their language, yet language could not logically be the sole determinant for restitution, as book collections were international in nature and not segregated by their origin.

Finally, there were serious questions as to whether restitution could be made of items to former enemy countries. This proved to be an added difficulty in a long series of logistical problems. Nevertheless, Pomrenze, stressed the absolute good that came out of this process, despite all the problems encountered, and compared the American experience to that of other countries. "The

Russians," he said, "never gave anything back, and the Vatican is still holding things from the Roman times."[183]

Restitution Courts

At the same time, in Law 59, there was the explicit mandate to the German courts to adjudicate claims for property. As stated in the instructions from the Property Group, charged with overseeing the program:

> Immediate responsibility for the execution of the Restitution Program rests with the German authorities, through the Minister-Praesidenten in the US Zone. It is carried out by and through Restitution Agencies and Courts established under Military Government Law No. 59, which are administered by officials selected or approved by the Minister-Praesidenten. Supervision of the program should, therefore, be conducted without interference with the actual operation of Restitution Authorities and in such a manner as not to cause unnecessary friction which may adversely affect the program.[184]

In various sectors of the American Zone, Breman, Hesse, Bavaria, and Wuerttemberg-Baden, the Minister President of the region, was to issue regulations to implement Law 59. The courts, while supervised by OMGUS officials, were supposed to be of German composition and the restitution chambers were spread all over the American Zone. There was a right of appeal through the German Courts of Appeals, and eventually to the Board of Review, the highest venue for appeal, staffed by American judges.[185]

While claims were due to be filed by December 31, 1948, before all properties escheated to German claimants or Germany itself, the courts were to keep going through the process of deciding cases. OMGUS Property Control went out of operation on June 30, 1949, having accomplished much in the identification and confiscation, but not enough in the return of heirless property. The duties of the agency were transferred to the German state government in Munich.[186] In the end, the JRSO itself obtained payments, in lieu of title for 2,084 claims and obtained title for 1,587 properties.[187] As for the restitution agencies overall, as of November 1949, in only eighteen months, only 6,625 cases out of 55,208, or only 12 percent, were finally cleared. At that rate, it was estimated that the chambers would have needed more than eight years to clear the others.[188] The restitution courts were mandated, however, only until December 31, 1951.[189]

The return of cultural property, as well, was to pass from the jurisdiction of OMGUS to the High Commissioner for Germany, and eventually on to Germany itself, as with other properties restitution jurisdiction. Recommendations for the transfer also involved the establishment of requisite claims termination dates, and other procedures. These features were part of a stabilizing effort by the Allies in creating a new Germany, capable of standing on its own and running its own affairs, yet, with the requisite responsibilities as a defeated power, to continue and finish the restitution efforts first mandated by the occupation authorities. Restitution itself would, in fact, be formally passed to German jurisdiction on April 1, 1950. These efforts, overall, would evolve into a series of treaties that would come to be known as the *Transition Agreements* that would, as the title suggests, transition Germany to an eventual reintroduction into the family of nations.

The program dragged on, the reason for this being due largely to the fact, as described at the time by Frank J. Miller, that "the Restitution Program was not a popular one and that, as time goes by, it would become even less popular."[190]

Backlash

Saul Kagan, an early OMGUS property investigator working with Bernard Bernstein immediately after the war, moved on to the JRSO and began working for the cause of restitution for survivors.[191] Kagan directed a confidential report to Miller at Property Control detailing the reasons for the slow progress of restitution courts. The descriptions of the process by an unidentified American lawyer representing claimants attests to the attitude of the German officials entrusted with the restitution program at the time, and would prove to be symbolic of the overall attitude of restitution, not only in Germany, but across Europe, even into the 1990s.

> In contrast thereto settlements are reached to a much smaller percentage and are far less satisfactory in such districts, where the German officials in a more or less open manner make known to the defendants that they approve of their standard defenses, i.e. that the respective laws are unjust, that they constitute new unlawfulness and that they could not stand enforced for all times.
>
> German officials which I have met in the courts or restitution agencies in all three zones, but particularly in the American and French zone, are rarely free from such considerations, even when they do not (as it has happened in a number of cases) openly and flagrantly make a point to state their opinion as definitely opposed to those restitution laws.[192]

According to the report, when decisions that were administratively determined, one such German official, a Dr. Fixon, was said to have remarked to a notary making such an administrative decision, "Why are you giving back so much to the American Jews, aren't you in the first place a German? I must protect the German interests, as I have been forced to leave my homestead in East Prussia.[193]

Dr. Fixon's attitude would become all too common. OMGUS officials, operating along plans to phase out American participation from the very beginning, were turning over an overwhelmingly large process to a less than willing partner in the German civil bureaucracy. With far too many cases to handle, OMGUS officials had called for a one-third increase in the number of legal officers to handle cases.[194] With a complimentary and ongoing program of de-Nazification, there were fewer German officials available to help adjudicate restitution cases than OMGUS officials had hoped. In some cases, those left in the role of handling cases were the very ones who, twenty years earlier, were acting as the confiscating authorities on behalf of the Nazis.[195] In these cases, with intimate knowledge of the property in question, there was little doubt upon which side the German adjudicator would fall.

There were also reports of defendants holding out hope that time would act as their greatest ally, and that the program and severity of the occupation would dissipate. Organizations were even founded, OMGUS officials reported, that were dedicated to this very purpose. Others simply exhibited open hostility to the process, seeking an end to it altogether.[196] "Hitler was right when he promised us a 1,000-year Reich," went a joke circulating in Germany, "twelve years of nazification under Hitler and 988 years of de-Nazification under the Americans."[197] Many other Germans failed to show any "general feeling of war guilt or repugnance for Nazi doctrine and regime," Clay wrote, and there were other Germans, who were not Nazis, who feared that as the Occupation waned, the Nazis would return.[198] They feared a counter-reaction against any cooperation with the Allies.[199]

Other problems arose due more to the complexity of the process of restitution itself. For those acquiring legitimate title to heirless properties that were found to have been confiscated, the problem of counter-confiscation by OMGUS authorities arose. While they were not considered "black restitutors," or those guilty of "aggravated confiscation," they were, nevertheless, in receipt of confiscated property. These "gray" classes caused, at the very least, definitional confusion for restitution officials at OMGUS, and later German offices as well.[200]

In all, a lack of experience and exposure to a restitution program of this scale on the part of OMGUS officials, little cooperation from neutral countries in returning assets, Allied political expediency, and overall German hostility to the process, together made early restitution a real difficulty right from the start.

Recriminations and Delay

While certain definable steps were taken to commence restitution from the successors of the Nazi state, these steps were halting at best. They represented what could be determined as a respectable, yet incomplete, effort on the part of the Allies. Not only was restitution incomplete, but Europe itself was left so as well. "It has suddenly been brought home to Americans," wrote Anne O'Hare

McCormick in the *New York Times* in July 1945, "that this Europe is not only a charge upon us but a danger."

> The boys who fought there are coming back, shipload after shipload, division after division. ... For most of them homecoming is only a furlough between battles and this puts restraints upon their exuberance—this, and the haunting feeling that what they have left behind is not peace. "We've broken it up all right," said a veteran of twenty-three who landed a few days ago. "But I've been wondering all the way home who's going to put the pieces together."[201]

There were, of course, impediments placed in the Allies' way in putting those pieces together. While extremely conscious of German attitudes and reactions, the Allies were all too aware of the growing strength of the Soviet Union, its encroachment on freedom in Eastern Europe, and its increasingly hostile attitude toward anything resembling agreement with the Allies. The Allies, too, while largely united in their opposition to the Soviets, were, nevertheless, not wholly unified toward the concept of restitution due, in part, to old prejudices and economic reality. They too, could plainly see that the Soviets were on the rise, yet they realized also that the war that had taken such a toll on their own people and economies necessitated the reinstitution of trade within Europe, and the resuscitation of Germany in some form, quickly. Buildup of their armies too, in light of the growing Soviet threat, loomed large to their economic planners as well. With this in mind, the Allies could no longer carry on the pretension of abiding by any plan that approached the harshness of the Morgenthau Plan, much less the plans agreed upon within the ACC. In August 1947, western zone occupying powers agreed to a revised level of industrial development for Germany and prepared a new list of industrial plants affected. According to the revised level, Germany was to achieve roughly the same industrial capacity as it possessed in 1936, instead of the originally designated 75 percent of the 1936 level. The United States was particularly concerned that the dismantling program not be conflict with its efforts to promote European redevelopment. In developing the policies underlying these changes, U.S. planners discovered the simple truth that keeping Germany in a state of economic collapse required the United States to incur enormous costs for food and other subsistencelevel aid, not to mention the growing premise of the need for an American-sponsored defense of the continent.

Past decisions of the Allies regarding the harsh economic treatment of Germany were found, in practice, to be virtually impossible to enforce. Instead, what was promoted, and in fact practiced, was far less harsh than those inclined toward the Morgenthau idea of "pastoralization" had hoped. Even a few OMGUS officials expressed their disgust at the relaxation of the treatment given to Germany as a whole.

One such official, Russell Nixon, abruptly resigned from his investigatory post in OMGUS and soon afterward testified before Congress on the Allied decision to weaken the policy of de-industrialization and to pursue trade instead of German external assets. Nixon, who interestingly was no admirer of the Morgenthau philosophy toward Germany, nevertheless, bitterly attacked the lagging de-industrialization by Allied officials, as mandated by ACC and other decisions, defiantly declaring:

> Our failure to act in this instance augurs ill for the carrying out of a vigorous policy with respect to other important segments of German industry which have not been so specially treated. In the United States Military Government, these deficiencies between action and policy developed from the fundamental fact that the officials responsible for the program did not support the directives to destroy Germany's war industry potential. Their energies and imagination have been expended in the direction of finding excuses for inaction and devices for evasion of orders. If we are to eliminate Germany's war resources, this condition must be charged. We must have a staff there which without being pushed will aggressively proceed to carry out the letter and spirit of the Potsdam Agreement to the end that Germany will never again be able to threaten the peace of the world.[202]

Moreover, Nixon complained of the lack of effort to reign in German external assets.

> I charge that elements in the United States, British, and French foreign offices have consciously maneuvered to prevent all four powers from being involved in the search for external assets in the neutral countries, because that would lay bare the fascist or reactionary regimes in countries such as Spain, Portugal, Switzerland, Sweden, and Argentina, and would reveal all the elements of collaboration of certain interests in the Allied countries with these regimes. Such genuine quadripartite action would completely upset the applecart for plans of compromise regarding Germany's external assets in the interest of trade and commercial advantages, and in the interest of avoiding the creation of too radical regimes in the future.[203]

Nixon found the two weakest points of Allied policy regarding Germany, and the two points that would most impact U.S. efforts on restitution. While reparations would aid in the implementation of restitution from Germany, the lack of enforcement of policy to achieve the reparations had a deep effect on the implementation of restitution. The very fact that reparations were not achieved to the extent required at Potsdam could be directly tied to the Soviet Union's growing aggressive policies and actions. The fact that Potsdam would be the last Allied conference said a great deal about the fragility of the very nature of alliances to which Kant referred. Organized to fight and defeat Nazism, "such an alliance is in constant peril of their breaking loose again."

The potential for this fact was already being seen at the war's end in Germany, by Germans, no doubt retarding the restitution process. "The P.W.s generally are speculating very much about another possibility," reported an unnamed OSS agent infiltrated into a Prisoner of War camp near the end of the war:

> i.e. when Germany has been defeated militarily the Allies will start quarreling about the booty. Some of them expect war between the Allies because they can't agree about their share in the booty, others hope that one or other of the allied powers will make greater concessions to the Germans in some part of occupied Germany. All these are very vague, but they all expect the Allies to quarrel.[204]

P.W.'s expressing these beliefs could not have known just how correct they were in their opinions.

Settling these "quarrels," and countering this new threat, would preoccupy the Allies and put issues of restitution on the back burner of political necessity. While there would be efforts at restitution, some successful, attempts at full restitution would have to wait for an end to those "quarrels" which would go on for the following half-century. For the interim, countering the Soviet Union would take precedence over finding and returning the assets of the Jewish people.

* * *

In the essay, "The Sense of Reality," Isaiah Berlin wrote of the extreme nature of the Morgenthau Plan and the seeming incredulity it engendered.

> In 1944 a plan was submitted at the Quebec Conference by Henry Morgenthau, US Secretary of the Treasury, whereby German industries were to be dismantled and the entire country turned back to pasture. It was a plan which could scarcely be taken seriously, although Roosevelt is said—I do not know how reliably—to have briefly inclined towards it. Nevertheless, those who were horrified by it and resisted it conceded that it was practicable. Yet the very notion that some such plan could be put into operation would have struck most historians, philosophers, statesmen, most intelligent men in the late nineteenth century—say at any time before 1914—as wildly Utopian.[205]

Equally, the plans of Hitler, with all the attendant ideational mutations, were more utopian than any plan Morgenthau could have ever devised. Yet his plan, conceived as a way to prevent the Hitlerian immoral ideational mutation from ever rising again, was condemned by friend and foe alike. Morgenthau's idea of pastoralization seemed so threatening because it was so extreme, but it was also one that had not been seen before. As a dialectic, Morgenthau's concept was a defense, and in his mind a legitimate historical reaction, against the Nazi's. "The relationship of ideas and history," wrote Thomas Sowell, "has been one of reciprocal interaction, rather than one-way causation..."[206]

The search for asset restitution would soon move from Germany to the countries in which *Safehaven*, for numerous reasons, failed to work. Heirless assets, like those transferred at times en masse from the depots in the American zone of Germany, were not as accessible elsewhere. With pressure, diplomatic and otherwise, restitution would become an exceedingly more difficult proposition in the years to come. The only real reason that the policy had any chance of succeeding in Germany, and to a lesser extent in Austria, was the simple fact that United States forces occupied these countries and forced the policy on the population and developing administrations. What would prove an eminently greater problem from this point on was the onset of the Cold War.

Notes

1. Immanuel Kant, *Perpetual Peace: A Philosophical Sketch*, 1795, available online at http://www.constitution.org/kant/perpeace.htm.
2. Oral History Interview with Bernard Bernstein, by Richard D. McKinzie, Harry S. Truman Presidential Library, June 20, 1989, available online at www.trumanlibrary.org.
3. John Morton Blum, *From The Morgenthau Diaries, Years of Crisis, 1928-1938* (Boston, MA: Houghton Mifflin Company, 1959), p. 7.
4. Oral History Interview with Elbridge Durbrow, by Richard D. McKinzie, Harry S. Truman Presidential Library, May 31, 1973, available online at www.trumanlibrary.org.
5. Michael Beschloss, *The Conquerors, Roosevelt, Truman and the Destruction of Hitler's Germany, 1941-1945* (New York: Simon & Schuster, 2002), p. 52.
6. Blum, *From the Morgenthau Diaries, Years of Crisis, 1928-1938*, pp. 78, 81.
7. Dean Acheson, *Present at the Creation, My Years in the State Department* (New York, W.W. Norton & Company, 1969), p. 22.
8. Sim C. Binder, "Practical Aspects of Foreign Property Control," *New York University Law Quarterly Review* (Vol. XIX, No. 1) November 1941, p. 2.
9. Kenneth S. Carlston, "Foreign Funds Control and the Alien Property Custodian," *Cornell Law Quarterly* (Vol. XXXI, No. 1), September 1945, p. 1.
10. Thomas Bailey, *A Diplomatic History of the American People*, Tenth Edition (New Jersey: Prentice-Hall, Inc., 1980), p. 705.
11. *A History of the Foreign Funds Control*, United States Department of the Treasury, Counsel's Office, Declassified in October 1996 at the request of the Office of Senator Alfonse M. D'Amato.
12. Bower, p. 30.
13. Francis Rufus Bellamy, "The Treasury's Fight Against Axis Looting," draft article in RG 131, Records of the Alien Property Custodian, Foreign Funds Control, 1942-60, Box 475, NARA, p. 4.
14. Bernstein interview, p. 5.
15. Bower, p. 29.
16. Obituary, Samuel Klaus, *New York Times*, August 3, 1963, p. 17.
17. Tom Bower, *The Paperclip Conspiracy, The Hunt for the Nazi Scientists* (Boston: Little, Brown and Company, 1989), p. 164.
18. "Bureaucratic History of Samuel Klaus' Career With Treasury," by Francine Barber, a Special Report prepared for the Office of the General Counsel, U.S. Department of Treasury, November 15, 1996, p. 3.
19. See Elmer L. Irey as told to William J. Slocum, *The Tax Dodgers, The Inside Story of the T-Men's War with America's Political and Underworld Hoodlums* (New York: Greenberg Publisher, 1948).
20. John Morton Blum, *From the Morgenthau Diaries, Years of Crisis, 1928-1938* (Boston, MA: Houghton Mifflin Company, 1959), p. 96.
21. Blum, p. 111.

22. Letter of Samuel Klaus to Secretary Morgenthau, October 15, 1941, RG 59, Aircraft Incidents, 1944-62, Lot File 64D551, Box 105, NARA.
23. "Memorandum for the Director," H.H. Clegg, Federal Bureau of Investigation, October 18, 1940, FBI Response to the Document Request of the United States Senate Banking Committee, 1997, p. 1.
24. Ibid, p. 6.
25. "Memorandum for Mr. Tamm, J. Edgar Hoover, Director, Federal Bureau of Investigation, November 20, 1940, FBI Response to the Document Request of the United States Senate Banking Committee, 1997, p. 10; Rickman, p. 4.
26. Letter of FBI Director J. Edgar Hoover to John Wiley, Treasury Department, January 18, 1941, p. 2, RG 59, Aircraft Incidents, 1944-62, Lot File 64D551, Box 105, NARA.
27. Unsigned "Memorandum for the Files, Conversation with Mr. Pehle re his plan to make copies of confidential FBI reports," January 23, 1941, found in the files of Sam Klaus, RG 59, Aircraft Incidents, 1944-62, Lot File 64D551, Box 105, NARA.
28. Letter of Samuel Klaus to Secretary Morgenthau, p. 1.
29. Ibid, pp. 3, 5.
30. Judd Polk, "Freezing Dollars Against the Axis," *Foreign Affairs* (October 1941), p. 116; Edgar Turlington, "Vesting Orders Under the First War Powers Act, 1941, *The American Journal of International Law* (Vol. 36), July 1943, p. 460.
31. John Morton Blum, *From the Morgenthau Diaries, Years of Urgency, 1938-1941* (Boston: Houghton Mifflin Company, 1965), p. 137.
32. *A History of Foreign Funds Control*, p. 2.
33. Foley, p. 2.
34. Polk, p. 115.
35. Turlington, p. 461.
36. Carlston, p. 11.
37. Letter of Vladimir S. Hurban, Envoy Extraordinary and Minister Plenipotentiary of Czechoslovakia to the Chase National Bank in New York, March 27, 1939, RG 56, Records of the Department of Treasury, Accession No. 67-A-245-OSIA, Box 36, NARA.
38. Letter of the Czechoslovak Legation to the Secretary of State, April 15, 1940, RG 56, Records of the Department of Treasury, Accession No. 67-A-245-OSIA, Box 36, NARA.
39. Bernstein interview, pp. 4, 6.
40. Binder, p. 3; Polk, p. 114.
41. Blum, *From the Morgenthau Diaries, Years of Urgency, 1938-1941*, pp. 332-338; Memorandum to File of Bernard Bernstein, October 8, 1940, RG56, Records of the Department of the Treasury, Entry 66-A-816, Box 55, NARA, p. 1.
42. Treasury Department Inter Office Communication from Edward Foley, General Counsel of the Treasury Department to Secretary of the Treasury Henry Morgenthau, 2 June 1942, RG 131 Foreign Funds Control, NARA.
43. Letter from George Ludwig, Swiss American Corporation to Edward Foley, General Counsel of the Treasury Department, 15 June 1942, RG 131 Foreign Funds Control, NARA.
44. Memorandum for the Files, "Conference on Swiss Insurance Companies Held at the Office of the Solicitor General, July 16, 1942, at 3:00 p.m.," RG 131, Foreign Funds Control, General Correspondence, 1942-1960, Entry NN3-131-94-001, Box 219, NARA; Letter of Acting Secretary of the Treasury Randolph Paul to the Attorney General, October 10, 1942, RG 60, Records of the Antitrust Division, Economic Warfare Section, Entry 285B, Box 95, NARA.

45. Foley, p. 4.
46. The FEA was formed by Executive Order 9380 signed by FDR on September 25, 1943, RG 131, Records of the Foreign Funds Control, Records and Analysis Division, Entry 170, Box 991, NARA.
47. Oral History Interview with Henry H. Fowler, by Niel M. Johnson, Harry S. Truman Presidential Library, June 20, 1989, www.trumanlibrary.org.
48. Memorandum from the Ministry of Economic Warfare to the British Embassy, Washington, D.C. June 3, 1943, Records of the Alien Property Custodian, RG 131, 1942-60, Box 51, NARA.
49. Memorandum from J.W. Pehle to Mr. White, "Treasury's Gold Statement," November 6, 1943, Foreign Funds Control, NARA.
50. Telegram to Certain American Diplomatic and Consular Officers," Records of the State Department, RG 59, The Legal Advisor, Box 13, pp.1-2, NARA.
51. Marc Jean Masurovsky, *The Safehaven Program: The Allied Response to Nazi Post-Defeat Planning 1944-1948*, a Masters' Thesis, American University, May 4, 1990, p. 24.
52. Margaret Clarke, *The Safehaven Project*, Foreign Economic Administration Study, #5, 1945, RG 169, Entry 170, NARA.
53. Memorandum to the File of Samuel Klaus, June 17, 1944, RG 59, Aircraft Accidents Files, 194460, Lot File 64D551, Box 97, NARA.
54. John Morton Blum, *From the Morgenthau Diaries, Years of War, 1941-1945* (Boston: Houghton Mifflin, 1967), p. 333.
55. Clark, *The Safehaven Project*, p. 25.
56. *Proceedings and Documents of the United Nations Monetary and Financial Conference*, Bretton Woods, New Hampshire, July 1-22, 1944 (Washington, DC: United States Government Printing Office, 1948), p. 1082.
57. Ibid, pp. 1083-1084.
58. Memorandum from W.J. Casey, Chief of SI, HQ & HQ Detachment, Office of Strategic Services, European Theatre of Operations, to Dr. Acheson, March 19, 1945, RG 226, Records of the Office of Strategic Services, Entry 183, Washington SDPF-Int.-1, Box 24, NARA. Casey, the Chief of Secret Intelligence for the OSS in London during WWII went on to become the Director of the Central Intelligence Agency in the first Administration of President Ronald Reagan.
59. Letter of Sidney Homer, Jr., FEA to Orvis Schmidt, Foreign Funds Control, Department of the Treasury, June 13, 1944, RG 131, Foreign Funds Control, Entry NN394001, Box 27, p. 3, NARA.
60. Letter of Leo Crowley, Administrator of the FEA to the Secretary of State, February 14, 1945, RG 59, Records of the Department of State, Entry 1945-1949, Box 4179, NARA.
61. Circular Airgram, "Mission Re Flight of Axis Capital," RG 131, Foreign Funds Control, General Correspondence 194260, p. 2, NARA.
62. Memorandum to the Secretary of State by Carlton J.H. Haves, Madrid, September 30, 1944, RG 59, Records of the Department of State, Decimal File, 194044, 800.515/5-3044, p. 2. NARA.
63. Ibid, p. 3.
64. Records of the James Surkamp Collection, RG 1136, Box 1 of 9, Loc. (T) 87, BV: 13/9, Folder 2, "Safehaven Reports, p. 1, YIVO.
65. Testimony of Russell A. Nixon, former Acting Director, Division of Investigation of Cartels and External Assets, Office of Military Government in Germany (United States), Hearing of the Subcommittee of the Committee on Military Affairs, *Elimination of German Resources for War, United States Senate*, 79th Congress, February

25, 1946 (Washington, DC: United States Government Printing Office, 1946), p. 1571.
66. Oral History Interview with James W. Riddleberger, by Richard D. McKinzie and Theodore A. Wilson, Harry S. Truman Presidential Library, June 24, 1971, available online at www.trumanlibrary.org.
67. Blum, *From the Morgenthau Diaries, Years of War*, p. 382.
68. Oral History Interview with James W. Riddleberger.
69. *History of Treasury Participation in Formulation of German Occupation Program*, RG 56, Records of the Department of the Treasury, Correspondence of the Office of the Secretary of the Treasury, Entry 199C, Box 1, NARA, p. 1.
70. Blum, *From the Morgenthau Diaries, Years of War*, pp. 376-377.
71. *History of Treasury Participation in Formulation of German Occupation Program*, p. 4.
72. Ibid.
73. Ibid, p. 7.
74. Blum, *From the Morgenthau Diaries, Years of War*, p. 394.
75. Ibid., p. 335.
76. Ibid.
77. "Memo of Julius Hirsch to Mr. E. A. Goldenweiser, "Reparations, and European Exports," June 15, 1945, Records of the Federal Reserve, p.6.
78. One who did fall under suspicion of Communist sympathies during the Red Scare was Morgenthau's close Treasury aide, Harry Dexter White. White was accused of being a Communist sympathizer. After giving testimony before the House Un-American Activities Committee in August 1948, White suffered a fatal heart attack. There are, today, disagreements over whether White was in fact a sympathizer, spy, or simply wrongly accused. See James M. Boughton, "The Case against Harry Dexter White: Still Not Proven," *IMF Working Paper*, WP/00/149, August 2000.
79. Interview with Durbrow.
80. Oral History Interview with E. Allan Lightner, Jr., by Richard D. McKinzie, Harry S. Truman Presidential Library, October 26, 1973, available online at
81. Oral History Interview with Paul R. Porter, by Richard D. McKinzie and Theodore Wilson, Harry S. Truman Presidential Library, November 30, 1971 , available online at www.trumanlibrary.org.
82. "Summary Judgment [sic] Seen, Churchill Hints Execution of Reich Leaders Without Trial," *The New York Times*, October 4, 1944. According to Judge Samuel I. Rosenman, Special Counsel to FDR and later Truman, "They wanted to treat the seven or eight top Nazis the same way they had treated Napoleon, namely, as a military or political matter. They had sent Napoleon into exile without any trial, just as a political matter, and they didn't want to try these Nazis. They just wanted to announce one day that all of them had been shot. Oral History Interview with Samuel I. Rosenman, by Jerry N. Hess, Harry S. Truman Presidential Library, April 23, 1969, available online at www.trumanlibrary.org.
83. Lothar Kettenacker, "British Post-War Planning for Germany: Haunted by the Past," in *Conditions of Surrender, Britons and Germans Witness the End of the War*, ed. By Ulrike Jordan, (London: German Historical Institute and Tauris Academic Studies, 1997), p. 16.
84. Bruce Kuklick, *American Policy and the Division of Germany, The Clash with Russia Over Reparations* (Ithaca, New York: Cornell University Press, 1972), p. 65.
85. Ibid, p. 64.
86. Ibid, p. 66.

87. "Property Control Interview, External Assets," RG 260, Records of the Office of the Military Government of the United States in Germany, Records of the Property Division, General Records, 1944-1950, Box 11, NARA.
88. Ibid, p. 65.
89. "Extracts from Contemporary Correspondence and Diaries," in *Conditions of Surrender, Britons and Germans Witness the End of the War*, p. 89.
90. *History of Treasury Participation in Formulation of German Occupation Program*, p. 8.
91. Reparations to be differentiated from restitution. Reparations would be payments actual or in kind to the aggrieved party, in this case the Allies, particularly the Soviets who demanded large sums in payment in return for the massive amount of damage done by the Germans. Restitution would be defined as the return of property taken by the Nazis. While the two are sometimes mixed in this context, it is important to know that each impacted upon the other. Reparations policy became caught up in the Cold War as did restitution. Restitution however, became mixed up in the context of reparations.
92. Lucius D. Clay, *Decision in Germany* (Garden City, New York: Doubleday & Company, Inc., 1950), p. 12; *History of Treasury Participation in Formulation of German Occupation Program*, p. 8; Greg Murphy, "U.S. Restitution Policy Towards Holocaust Victims' Assets," *Working Paper*, Presidential Commission on Holocaust Era Assets, 2000, pp. 9-10.
93. Clay, p. 12.
94. Clay, pp. 7-8.
95. Ibid, p. 17.
96. *History of Treasury Participation in Formulation of German Occupation Program*, p.22.
97. Murphy, p. 10.
98. Christopher Simpson, pp. 196-197.
99. *History of Treasury Participation in Formulation of German Occupation Program*, p. 1.
100. F.H. Klopstock, "The German Reparation Problem," Foreign Research Division, United States Federal Reserve, January 9, 1946, p. 1, Records of the United States Federal Reserve.
101. "Summary of Multipartite Agreements & Disagreements on Germany, 2nd Revised & Supplemented Edition, 15 September 1948," Council of Foreign Ministers Secretariat, Civil Administration Division, Office of the Military Government for Germany (US), RG 466, Records of the High Commissioner for Germany (HICOG), Historical Division, Publications Relating to the U.S. Occupation of Germany, Box 1, NARA, pp. 248-250.
102. *History of Treasury Participation in Formulation of German Occupation Program*, p. 1.
103. *Ibid,* p. 12.
104. Oral History Interview with Samuel I. Rosenman.
105. Blum, *From the Morgenthau Diaries, Years of War*, 1941-1945, p. 464.
106. Oral History Interview with Samuel I. Rosenbaum; Blum, *From the Morgenthau Diaries, Years of War*, pp. 464-476.
107. Amos Perlumutter, *FDR & Stalin, a Not So Grand Alliance*, 1194301945 (Columbia, Missouri: University of Missouri Press, 11933), p. 213.
108. Oral History Interview with James W. Riddleberger, by Richard D. McKinzie and Theodore A. Wilson, Harry S. Truman Presidential Library, June 24, 1971, available online at www.trumanlibrary.org.

109. Clay, p. 43.
110. Oral History Interview with Lucius D. Clay, by Richard D. McKinzie, Harry S. Truman Presidential Library, July 16, 1974, available online at www.trumanlibrary.org.
111. Ibid, p. 14.
112. Ibid, pp. 14-15.
113. Porter Interview.
114. "Property Control Interview, External Assets," p. 43.
115. Clay, p. 306.
116. "Status Report on Military Government of German, U.S. Zone," Office of Military Government for Germany (U.S.), March 15, 1946, RG 466, Records of the High Commissioner for Germany (hereafter abbreviated as HICOG), Historical Division, Publications Relating to the U.S. Occupation of Germany, Box 3, NARA.
117. "Property Control Interview, External Assets," p. 8.
118. "Property Control," estimated date 1949, RG 260, Records of the Office of the Military Government of the United States in Germany, Records of the Property Division, General Records Division, 1944-1950, NARA, p. 1.
119. Helen Junz, "Property Control: OMGUS Property Management Corporation?," Working Paper, Presidential Commission for Holocaust Era Assets in the United States, 2000, p. 5.
120. Property Control Division, Lists of Former Jewish Owned Properties, Numerous lists dated from April 1947 to August 1947, RG 260, Records of the Office of the Military Government of the United States in Germany, Hesse Property Division, General Records, 1945-1949, Box 1261, NARA.
121. Letter of Nathan Stein, American Federation of Jews from Central Europe, Inc."; "Registry of Property of Former Jewish Communities in Germany," Submission of the city of Worms to the American Federation of Jews from Central Europe, Inc., Reported by Isidor Keifer, and Letter of Rabbi Helmut Frank to the American Federation of Jews from Central Europe, Inc., February 11, 1945, AR-C.1751, 4420, A11/8; American Federation of Jews from Central Europe, B.XVI-XIX, Box 3, Leo Beck Institute, New York.
122. "Property Control Interview, External Assets," p. 10.
123. "Control Council Law No. 5," Enactments and Approved Papers of the Control Council and Coordinating Committee, Germany, For Year 1945, Vol. 1, Compiled by the Legal Division, Legal Advice Branch, Drafting Section, Office of Military Government for Germany (U.S.), RG 260, Library of Congress; "Final Report on the Paris Conference on Reparation, Nov. 9, 1945 to Dec. 21, 1945," RG 59, General Records of the Department of State, The Legal Advisor, Records Relating to Postwar Settlement Issues 1939-1963, IARA, Entry NN359-96-74, Box 2, NARA, p. 11;"Memorandum for Secretary Vinson,"RG 56, Records of the Department of Treasury, Correspondence of the Office of the Secretary of the Treasury, Entry 199C, Box 1, NARA, p. 3.
124. "Control Council Law No. 5."
125. Otto Fletcher, Memorandum, "Paper on Legal Basis of our Safehaven Demands to the Neutrals," to Seymour Rubin, United States Department of State, Division of Economic Security Controls, April 22, 11946, RG 43, Records of International Conferences, Lot File No. M-88, Council of Foreign Ministers, Conference on German External Assets and Looted Gold, January 1953, NARA, p. 1.
126. "Memorandum to Secretary Vinson," p.3.
127. Ibid, p. 4.

128. "Restitution in the Four Zones," Office of Military Government for Germany (US) Finance Division, RG 56, Records of the Treasury Department, 69A4707, German Restitution, Box 84, NARA, p. 2.
129. Invited by the United States, Great Britain, and France were : Albania, Australia, Belgium, Canada, Czechoslovakia, Denmark, Egypt, Greece, India, Luxembourg, Norway, New Zealand, Netherlands, South Africa, and Yugoslavia.
130. Rudolf Dolzer, "The Settlement of War-Related Claims: Does International Law Recognize a Victim's Private Right of Action? Lessons after 1945," Stefan A. Riesenfeld Symposium 2001, "Fifty Years in the Making: World War II Reparation and Restitution Claims," *Berkeley Journal of International Law* (Vol. 20, No. 1, 2002), 318.
131. "Final Report on the Paris Conference on Reparation," p. 16.
132. It was thought that there would not be more than $25 million in heirless funds found and therefore it was possible that less than this amount could have been allocated. Moreover, the United States delegation believed that there were at least 100,000 refugees that would eligible for this aid. Ibid, pp. 80, 235.
133. Ibid, p. 23.
134. This kind of arrangement would surface again over fifty years later in the agreement to pay insurance claims against European insurance companies as part of the overall Slave Labor agreement in 2000.
135. Ibid, pp. 22, 129-130.
136. Ibid, p. 26.
137. Ibid, p. 131.
138. Press Release, United States Department of State, June 19, 1946, No. 436, RG 59, General Records of the Department of State, Records Relating to Postwar Settlement Issues, 1939-1963, IARA, NARA, p. 1.
139. Ibid.
140. Rickman, p. 16.
141. Letter of the Federal Justice and Police Department, Justice Division to the Federal Political Department, Litigation, Financial and Communications Division, Bern, Switzerland, E 2001 (E)/1962/113, Bd. 374, Swiss Federal Archives, translated by Mark J. Masurovsky, Cybertrans Translation Service.
142. Interview with Morton Bach, Washington, DC, November 7, 1996.
143. Rickman, p. 16.
144. Refugee funds went to housing, relocation, clothing, children's services, including education, supplies, and teachers' salaries. See Accounting Memorandum #251, Reparations Bill, American Joint Distribution Committee, RG 59, Records of the Department of State, Lot 53D307, Entry Reparations, Schwartz Report, Box 14, NARA.
145. Letter of Seymour J. Rubin to Moses Leavitt, American Joint Distribution Committee, April 8, 1953, American Jewish Joint Distribution Committee, New York City Archives, AR 45/64, #1208.
146. Rickman, p. 29.
147. On August 23, 1953, the government of Poland agreed that: "Regard being had to the fact that Germany has complied with her obligations to effect reparations to a substantial extent already and that an improvement of Germany's economic situation is in the interest of her own peaceful development, the government of the People's Republic of Poland has taken the decision with effect from January 1, 1954 to waive all claims of reparations." The question arose whether the 1953 Soviet and Polish waivers applied to individual claims of forced laborers. Evidence based on relatively recent exchanges suggest that such claims were not waived. In 1993 Germany and the Russian Federation entered into a com-

pensation arrangement through the vehicle of a Reconciliation and Understanding Foundation. A March 30, 1993, note of the Russian Federation with respect to the Foundation closes with the sentence: "Both governments agree, that this creates no limitation of the rights of citizens of both nations." An October 16, 1991, agreement between Poland and Germany establishing a PolishGerman Reconciliation Foundation provided that: "The government of the Republic of Poland will assert no further claims of Polish citizens that arose in connection with Nazi persecution. Both governments understand that this creates no limitations of the rights of citizens of both nations."

148. Memorandum of W. J. Dickman, Deputy Chief, Property Control and External Assets Branch, Property Division, Office of Military Government For Germany (U.S.), June 8, 1946, RG 260, Records of the Property Division, General Records Division, 1944-1950, Office of the Military Government of the United States in Germany, Box 110, NARA, p. 1.
149. Memorandum of Col. L. Wilkinson, Acting Director, Economics Division, Office of Military Government For Germany (U.S.), May 27, 1947, RG 260, Records of the Property Division, General Records Division, 1944-1950, Office of the Military Government of the United States in Germany, Box 110, NARA, p. 1.
150. Following the war, of the millions of books found by U.S. forces, hundreds of thousands of them remained unclaimed and unrepatriated. Of these books, over 79,000 made their way back to the United States where some were housed in the Library of Congress. There is a dispute as to whether these books were universally unrepatriateable or less than satisfactory efforts were made to return them. Discussion with Eli Rosenbaum, United States Department of Justice, Office of Special Investigations. See Robert G. Waite, "Returning Jewish Cultural Property: The Handling of Books Looted by the Nazis in the American Zone of Occupation, 1945 to 1952," *Libraries and Culture* (Summer 2002), Vol. 37, No. 3, pp. 213-228; and Michael Dobbs, "Epilogue to a Story of Nazi-Looted Books, Library of Congress Trove of War Propaganda Included Many Stolen Jewish Works," *Washington Post*, January 5, 2000, Sec. C, p. 1.
151. Waite, p. 223.
152. Telephone Interview with Seymour Pomrenze, former Property Officer, OMGUS, December 4, 2002.
153. Outgoing Message of [Lt. General Lucius] Clay to AGWAR, June 15, 1946, RG 260, Property Division, Central Collecting Points (Ardelia Hall) JRSO Correspondence, Box 66, NARA, p. 1.
154. Seymour J. Pomrenze, "Personal Reminiscences of the Offenbach Archival Depot, 1946-1949: Fulfilling International and Moral Obligations, "in *The Proceedings of the Washington Conference on Holocaust-Era Assets, November 30-December 2, 1998* (Washington, DC: United States Government Printing Office, 1999), p. 526; Interview with Pomrenze.
155. Outgoing Message of [Lt. General Lucius] Clay to AGWAR, July 15, 1946, RG 260, Property Division, Central Collecting Points (Ardelia Hall) JRSO Correspondence, Box 66, NARA, p. 1.
156. Michael J. Kurtz, "Resolving A Dilemma: The Inheritance of Jewish Property," *Cardozo Law Review*, (December 1998), Volume 20, Number 2, p. 639.
157. Outgoing Message of [Lt. General Lucius] Clay to AGWAR, October 16, 1946, RG 260, Property Division, Central Collecting Points (Ardelia Hall) JRSO Correspondence, Box 66, NARA, p. 1.
158. Michael J. Kurtz, "The End of the War and the Occupation of Germany, 1944-52, Laws and Conventions Enacted to Counter German Appropriations: The Allied Control Council," in Elizabeth Simpson, p. 116; Department of State, Division of

Foreign Correlation, "Book Message to Clark and McNarny from Joint Chiefs of Staff," March 4, RG 59, General Records, Department of State, Records of the Fine Arts & Monuments Adviser, Ardelia Hall Collection, Box 18, NARA.

159. General Hays, OMGUS, EUCOM for Property Division: Reparations and Restitution Branch, OMGUS Karlsruhe," Department of the Army Staff Message Center, RG 59, General Records, Department of State, Records of the Fine Arts & Monuments Adviser, Ardelia Hall Collection, Box 28, NARA.
160. Bearer bonds would be title-less bonds payable on demand to those who bore them. These bonds were of particular interest to the Nazis when they were available. Ordinarily, bonds and securities could be de-listed and considered as being of no-value once reported lost. Throughout the war, Foreign Funds Control investigators and State Department officials made strenuous efforts to compile long lists of looted securities and other financial instruments.
161. Swiss Justice and Police Department, "Stoppage of Payments Germany," Memorandum to the Swiss Office of Compensation, June 7, 1945, translated by Brian Hufker and David Skelly, Congressional Research Service,, E7160 (A) a 1968/54, BD.9 Swiss Federal Archives.
162. Rickman, pp. 21-25.
163. Phillips Hawkins, Director, Property Division, Office of Military Government for Germany (U.S.), "Establishment and Appointment of a General Successor Organization Under Military Government Law No. 59 for Heirless Property not Claimed by Special Successor Organizations or Individuals," RG 260, Records of the Office of the Military Government of the United States in Germany, General Records 1944-1950, Box 2, NARA, p. 2.
164. Memorandum of F.S. Hannaman, Assistant to Acting Director, Provisional Office of Economic Affairs, Berlin Kommandatura to General Hays, "Successor Organization Pursuant to Berlin Restitution Law," September 12, 1949, RG 260 Records of the Office of the Military Government of Germany, Records of the Property Division, General Records of the Director, Box 15, NARA.
165. Loyd [sic] V.Steele, "OMGUS Proposed Cable in Reply to WX-81072," October 1, 1946, RG 260, Records of the Office of Military Government of the United States in Germany, Records of the Executive, 1945-1949, Adjutant General Restitution Reports, Box 111, NARA, p. 2.
166. Kurtz, p. 640; Col. John M. Raymond, Outgoing Cable to the Department of the Army, September 5, 1948, RG 260, Records of the Property Division, General Records Division, 1944-1950, Office of the Military Government of the United States in Germany, Box 110, NARA..
167. Letter of Jerome Michael, Commission on European Jewish Cultural Reconstruction to General J.H. Hilldring, Assistant Secretary of State, August 26, 1946, RG 59, Records of the State Department, Fine Arts & Monuments Adviser, Ardelia Hall Collection, Box 28, NARA, pp. 1-4. Within time, JCR would also take title, among other things, to Jewish Cultural properties in Palestine. See Phillips Hawkins, Deputy Economics Advisor, OMGUS to James Cantenbein, Office of the Political Advisor, July 19, 1949, RG 260, Records of the Office of the Military Government of the United States, Records of the Property Division, General Records of the Director, 1944-1950, Box 15, NARA.
168. Waite, pp. 218-219.
169. Memorandum of Conversation and Supplementary Observations, "Jewish Cultural Treasures in Germany and Austria: Comments on one phase of the proposal for an International Jewish Trustee Corporation submitted by the Commission on European Jewish Cultural Reconstruction," September 24, 1946, RG 59, Records of the

State Department, Fine Arts & Monuments Adviser, Ardelia Hall Collection, Box 28, NARA, pp.2, 7.

170. Interview with Pomrenze.
171. Letter of Eve Tucker, Headquarters United States Forces in Austria, USACA Section, Reparations, Deliveries and Restitution Branch, to Ardelia Hall, Fine Arts & Monuments Adviser, January 6, 1949, RG 59, Records of the State Department, Fine Arts & Monuments Adviser, Ardelia Hall Collection, Box 28, NARA, pp. 1-2. Planning for the identification and repatriation of looted artwork was to be accomplished through the Monuments, Fine Arts, and Archives section (MFA&A). Members of the MFA&A were in many ways akin to the art experts of the ERR, but in reverse. MFA&A officers came from University and Museum backgrounds and they, like their opposites in the ERR were expert in the provenance of the wide range of looted personal and cultural artwork. See Craig Hugh Smyth, "The Establishment of the Munich Collecting Point," in Simpson, pp. 126-130.
172. Tucker letter, pp. 2-3.
173. Interview with Pomrenze.
174. "Progress Report on: The Mystery of the Hungarian 'Gold Train,' " Special Report of the *Presidential Advisory Commission on Holocaust Assets in the United States*, October 7, 1999. In 2001, Hungarian survivors filed a class-action lawsuit against the United States Government over the Hungarian Gold Train. On December 22, 2005, Judge Patricia Seitz of the U.S. District Court for the Southern District of Florida signed an order implementing a settlement of $25 million and an apology from the government.
175. See Willi Korte, "Search for the Treasures," and Thomas R. Kline, "Legal Issues Relating to the Recorvery of the Quedlingburg Treasures," both in Simpson, pp. 150-152, 156-158.
176. See Walter I. Farmer, "Custody and Controversy at the Wiesbaden Collecting Point," in Elizabeth Simpson, pp. 131-134.
177. Portion of a Confidential letter of July 14, 1950, to Mr. H.K. Dreman from Bill Daniels, RG 59, Records of the Department of State, Records of the Fine Arts & Monuments Adviser, Ardelia Hall Collection, Box 28, NARA, p. 1; Press Release, "Restitution Program Reviewed,"United States Political Advisor for Germany, April 29, 1947, RG 59, Records of the State Department, FW 800.515/4-2947, Box 4228, NARA. Pomrenze confirmed that this tendency was present in some cases among Occupation officials.
178. Letter of Thomas C. Howe Jr., Central Collecting Point Landesmuseum, Wiesbaden to Ardelia Hall, April 20, 1951, RG 59, Records of the Department of State, Records of the Fine Arts & Monuments Adviser, Ardelia Hall Collection, Box 28, NARA, p. 1.
179. Interview with Pomrenze.
180. Ibid.
181. Waite, p. 218.
182. According to Pomrenze, many were sent to Israel.
183. Interview with Pomrenze.
184. Frank J. Miller, Chief, Property Group, Office of the Economics Adviser, Office of Military Government for Germany (US), "Supervision of the Restitution Program Under Military Government Law 59," RG 260, Office of the Military Government of the United States in Germany, General Records of the Property Division, 1944-1950, Box 15, NARA, p. 2.

185. "Organization and Functions of Restitution Authorities in the US Zone,"RG 260, Office of the Military Government of the United States in Germany, General Records of the Property Division, 1944-1950, Box 10, NARA.
186. Form letter response of the Property Group to filed claims, OMGUS, RG 260, Office of the Military Government of the United States in Germany, General Records of the Property Division, 1944-1950, Box 15, NARA.
187. Junz, p. 28.
188. "Conference Held at Bad Nauheim December 14, 1949," Office of Economic Affairs, Property Division, Internal Restitution Supervision Branch, Office of the United States High Commissioner for Germany, RG 260, Office of the Military Government of the United States in Germany, General Records of the Property Division, 1944-1950, Box 10, NARA, pp. 2-3.
189. Ibid, p. 4.
190. Ibid.
191. Kagan would later work on the same issues for the Conference on Material Claims Against Germany, otherwise known as the Claims Conference. He is still involved as an advisor to this day.
192. Confidential Report of American Restitution Lawyer as an enclosure to a Letter from Saul Kagan, Director, Plans and Operations Board, Jewish Restitution Successor Organization to Frank G. Miller, Chief of Property Division, OMGUS, RG 260, Office of the Military Government of the United States in Germany, General Records of the Property Division, 1944-1950, Box 15, NARA.
193. Lawyer Report, p. 4.
194. "Conference Held at Bad Nauheim December 14, 1949," p. 4.
195. Discussions with Willi Korte.
196. "Conference Held at Bad Nauheim December 14, 1949," p. 6.
197. Cited in Richard J. Barnet, *The Alliance, American, Europe, Japan, Makers of the Postwar World* (New York: Simon & Schuster, 1983), p. 20.
198. *The Conquerors,* p. 273.
199. "Testimony of Russell A. Nixon," p. 1503.
200. Memorandum of E.J. Cassoday, Deputy Director, Property Division, OMGUS to [Lt.] General Clay, "Heirless Property Under the Restitution Law, Not Claimable by JRSO," RG 260, Office of the Military Government of the United States in Germany, General Records of the Property Division, 1944-1950, Box 10, NARA.
201. Anne O'Hare McCormick, "Too-Little, Too-Late Policy Will not Win Peace, Either," *New York Times*, July 23, 1945, p. 18.
202. Ibid, pp. 1538-1539.
203. "Testimony of Russell A. Nixon," p. 1585.
204. "What Germ P.W.s think about the war," RG 226, Records of the OSS, Entry A1-170, Entry 210, Box 175, NARA, p. 5.
205. Isaiah Berlin, *The Sense of Reality, Studies in Ideas and their History*, ed. By Henry Hardy (New York: Farrar, Straus and Giroux, 1996), p. 11.
206. Sowell, p. 356.

3

"Memory Dethroned": U.S. Policy on Restitution, the Cold War

"During the war, in the ghetto and camps, we often fantasized about how good the world will be after the Germans are defeated. We thought that the "world" will be full of sympathy for the Jews and try to atone and make up for all the harm and crimes committed against us and how the Germans and their accomplices will be made to pay for their misdeeds. Illusions. We envisioned the "good Germans" taking revenge on the murderers, hanging them from the lamposts. No such things happened. There were no "bad Germans," no Nazis. Few admitted any knowledge of the crimes committed by them or their sons, brothers or husbands."[1]—Morris Krakowsky, a survivor from Poland

De-Nazification

Judging Their Fellow Germans

With the war's end, Germans of all stripes and from all levels of power, civilian and military, were fleeing retribution. Most preferred the relative safety of the custody of the Western Allies, being "awfully frightened of the Russians," in the view of an American OSS agent reporting from inside a prisoner of war camp in 1945.[2] U.S. troops were stumbling over, first hundreds, then thousands, of suspect Germans every day. In May and June, 1945, U.S. troops were arresting 700 a day; and 18,000 per day by August. By September, 82,000 were being held in internment camps.[3] Fleeing Germans were held as well in other European countries such as in the Netherlands, where at least 25,000-45,000 Nazis or sympathizers were interned as late as August 1946.[4]

As the occupation of Germany by the Allies proceeded, there were numerous issues of administration and political import. While restitution was one of those issues, it was not the primary one. One of the chief aims of the Allies in Germany following victory over the Nazis, very simply was to win the peace.

In light of the growing belligerence of the Soviet Union, keeping Germany whole and secure quickly took precedence in the minds of not only the occupation officials but of the policymakers in the Truman Administration as well. As General Lucius Clay wrote:

> We were convinced that the restoration of a normal economy in Europe would revive the will to be free and that it could come about only with our financial assistance. The provision of such assistance to the free countries of Europe would change our course of action from a passive defense against Communist penetration along our eastern occupation border to an active attack with ideas and economic benefits from a revived western Europe.[5]

The plan to revive Germany would have many aspects, not the least of which was de-Nazification. With so many Germans interned for their role during the war, the need spread beyond a political one to a practical as well. In this respect, the Allied Control Council declared in Directive No. 24, of January 12, 1946:

> The Tripartite Conference of Berlin included among the purposes of the occupation of Germany: the removal from public and semi-public office and from positions of responsibility in important private undertakings of all members of the Nazi Party who have been more than nominal participants in its activities, and all other persons hostile to Allied purposes. Such persons shall be replaced by persons who, by their political and moral qualities, are deemed capable of assisting in developing genuine democratic institutions in Germany.[6]

While de-Nazification was the goal, and called for originally at Potsdam, many in the Allied governments as well as Occupation forces, quickly came to understand that replacing all those Nazis "hostile to Allied purposes," was functionally impractical. They would have to determine levels of "hostility" examining who could be excluded from the harshest elements of the established policy. In this regard, General Clay, as John McCloy, the U.S. High Commissioner for Germany, would later write whittle "away the unworkable clauses of JCS 1067 empirically and piecemeal."[7] As such it would become a foregone conclusion that the harshest dictates of the Occupation would fade, and the fate of de-Nazification would follow soon afterward. "Whether they advocated passing a hard or a soft judgement on Nazis," wrote Earl F. Zeimke in a U.S. Army history of the time, "—a few argued for the latter—military government officers generally agreed that if they made a completely clean sweep of the party members, they were going to have to run the country with old men until the next generation grew up."[8]

This realization did not, however, put to rest the obvious conclusions of many at the time as to German complicity. For Hannah Arendt who wrote prophetically in 1945 that complicity went further than simply the Party, down to the level of the German people themselves. Moreover, she wrote this total complicity would, in the end, make proper punishment impossible.

> The greater the military defeats of the Wehrmacht in the field, the greater becomes that victory of Nazi political warfare which is so often incorrectly described as mere propaganda. It is the central thesis of this Nazi political strategy that there is no difference between Nazis and Germans that the people stand united behind the government, that all Allied hopes of finding part of the people uninfected ideologically and all appeals to a democratic Germany of the future are pure illusion. The implication of this thesis is, of course, that there is no distinction as to responsibility, that German anti-Fascists will suffer from defeat equally with German Fascists, and that the Allies had made such distinctions at the beginning of the war only for propaganda purposes. A further implication is that Allied provisions for punishment of war criminals will turn out to be empty threats because they will find no one to whom the title of war criminal could not be applied.[9]

Arendt's assumption of the "empty threats" of de-Nazification became a reality not long after this statement was written. Clay made it clear that the lessening of the reigns on de-Nazification had deeper meaning. "I had become convinced," he wrote, "that this real task could not be accomplished by occupation officials without at some time making martyrs out of those we sought to condemn in the eyes of their countrymen..."[10]

Yet, Arthur Kahn, the former Chief Editor of the Intelligence Information Division of OMGUS, suggested that fears of Germany falling under the grip of Communism was what truly drove policy makers in Washington, DC to soften the tone on de-Nazification.[11] "There is complete economic, social and political collapse going on in Central Europe," Kai Bird wrote quoting McCloy's description to Truman of the situation there, "the extent of which is unparalleled in history unless one goes back to the collapse of the Roman Empire..."[12] There was chaos there and out of that could come only more trouble. In this sense, then, as Kai Bird suggested, "[o]ne could not simultaneously punish Germany and rebuild her economy."[13]

With the exception of the hardcore Nazi criminals, tried at Nuremberg and the associated trials, the responsibility for the process was quite soon turned over to the Germans. For as Clay wrote, quite naively;

> The decision to turn over to the Germans further denazification was controversial when it was made. Factual analysis of the administrative problem was sufficient to convince me that there was no other solution to this problem. Moreover, it seemed to me of major import that German officials had voluntarily assumed the responsibility of judging their fellow Germans who had supported the Nazi party and enabled it to bring destruction to so much of the world and to the German people. They were far better able than we to determine the real Nazi who had profited from the misdeeds of the Nazi regime.[14]

Like the case with restitution courts and their return to German administration, the Military Government turned over control of important authority to

Germans who, for reasons quite understandable to them, could not and would not fulfill the intent of the mission entrusted to them. Once again, expediency took precedence over justice and the survivors paid the price.

The Cold War as Anomaly

Coral Bell has written of the disillusionment after World War II of the people of Europe with their respective national states, "which had protected them neither from the Great Depression, the rise of fascism and the trauma of conquest and occupation, nor the later depredations of Soviet power."[15] Because of this, they rejected colonialism and advocated "anti-sovereign" structures, including those of their own government. Yet, this concept was contradicted by the notion of an ideologically predatory Soviet Union seeking, of all things, a colonial, supra-sovereign existence on the very same continent so newly freed from the same practices of the Nazis.

The United States, like much of Europe, agreed with this sentiment. Rupert Emerson commented on the need to oppose colonialism in an FEA report in June 1944, to FDR's close friend and advisor Lauchlin Currie.

> Tying up the "colonial problem" with liberated areas, I gravely fear that in both cases the United States, having become prosperous and powerful, is now going to play it safe and work primarily with the responsible and established elements in all parts of the world. In both Europe and the Far East the results of such a policy are likely to be fairly disastrous, inasmuch as we will fail completely to capture the imaginations and spirits of the new elements that must be arising everywhere.[16]

These sentiments were no different than the idealistic concepts espoused after World War I by Woodrow Wilson. The victorious powers after World War I sought to establish the principals such as liberalism, anti-colonialism, and collective security in the form of the League of Nations, but failed to gain acceptance for these principles. The outbreak of World War II demonstrated this failure. Just as the effort to establish these principles as rules of international behavior were instigated by the slaughter of World War I, so, too, were efforts begun anew to reinstate them again after the carnage of WWII. Equally, just as with the emergence of World War II, the attempt to facilitate these principles was blocked by another occurrence, the beginning of the Cold War and the imposition of Communism in Eastern Europe by the Soviet Union.

The Cold War then, can be seen as an unintended consequence of World War II. The argument could be made that the Nazis made the Cold War possible by engulfing the Soviet Union in a cataclysmic war that, despite their own visions of grandeur, could not be won. At the time of the Nazi attack in June 1941, the Soviet Union faced severe internal conflicts including a politically and materially decimated army and Party structure, and a populace gripped with paranoia and fear.[17] It is questionable then, facing these factors and the very real possibility that they could have increased in intensity during this time, whether the Soviet Union could have even survived in its post-World War II form. But with the German attack, the Soviet Union was fighting for its life in defeating the Nazis, not only within the USSR, but in all the lands between them. As is popular today, counterfactuals,[18] or the concept of an alternative history, suggesting what might have been, could conceive of the possibility that the Cold War might not necessarily have come about had not the Soviet Union, otherwise in turmoil, been as such, and particularly oddly enough, "saved" by its war with Germany. As Williamson Murray has written, "The fate of Operation Barbarossa (the code name for the invasion) determined the course of World War II and the face of our world."[19] At the very least, the Soviet Union, absent an attack by the Nazis, certainly would not have been in the geopolitical position achieved precisely because of the war that it occupied in May 1945.

As such, the Cold War arguably might not have taken the form that it did. With this argument then, the notion that the Cold War was an anomaly can be advanced. That the Soviet Union indeed survived and prospered through tragedy, and ultimately victory, over the Nazis, enabled it to challenge the West and particularly the United States. While the Allies were triumphant in their war against Fascism and Nazism, as James Bowman has written, "All peace coexists with various sorts of dissatisfaction which, for one reason or another, are not for the moment erupting into war."[20] True enough, the dispute between the United States and its allies and the Soviet Union did later erupt into war, not between them directly but between their allies—proxy war—the kind of war to which neither was accustomed. As such, it was the reactions of the Allies, and to the rules which they themselves created, and to a great extent, extended from their practice against the Nazis to apply to Communism, that prevented the proper fulfillment of the process of restitution that began in the early years following the end of World War II.

Growing Insecurity

As it relates to Soviet belligerence, the concept of political tolerance is inversely related to one's sense of security.[21] As such, the Allies felt exceedingly insecure with the rise and growing threats posed by the Soviet Union. As the Allies' insecurity rose, their ability and willingness to advance the progress of restitution waned in equal proportion. This retreat formed the basis for an extended condition known as "silencing." Silencing was, in this period, a crime of three parties. In the case of Germany, it revolved around Germans' lack of acceptance of responsibility for the Holocaust and its crimes and its reluctance to fully restitute its victims for their losses and suffering. For the United States and its allies, it was the failure to push restitution strong enough on its own initiative or that of its allies. For the neutrals, who evaded U.S. and Allied inspection of their Holocaust-era holdings and the level of their cooperation, it was the belief that they were bystanders and therefore not taking sides, neither of the defenders nor of the aggressors.

As James Booth wrote, quoting Tzvetan Todorov, "Memory is dethroned, not in the interests of forgetting, of course, but of certain universal principles and the 'general will.'"[22] For the Allies, as the exigencies of the times and the abiding "general will" to counter the Soviet Union in the Cold War gained coherence, the pace of restitution slowed out of necessity to preserve the status quo with the Soviet Union and to deny the Soviets any victory in the zero sum game that the Cold War became. The Cold War and the need to fight it, politically and militarily, necessitated the formation of principles that brought about this silencing.

For Germany, it was in Booth's words, the "seduction of the normalizers of German history."[23] While the crimes of the Nazis could not be wholly forgotten, a disassociation with them became coherent and acceptable. Just as those administering the German-run restitution courts felt the indignation of the tasks imposed upon them, so, too, did Germans as a whole feel the indignity of the crimes of the Nazis being imposed upon them. As such, shame for those humiliations resulted in a shutting off of history, a willful denial. Officially it was not a denial, as some would later contend, but a pattern of dismissal of responsibility for the past.

Restitution was never an easy proposition after the end of the war, but with this policy of silencing, it would now be even more difficult. Those seeking the return of property ran headlong into the realities of the Cold War.

Silencing

It has been written of Germany's notion of an "immaculate conception," of the year 1945 as being "year zero."[24] Of course German history did not begin with the end of the war, but for Germans it might as well have. For Germans, this nightmare period of history, one for which they were responsible, was far less acceptable to them than the appellation of "victims" arising from post-war retaliation and occupation. In the creation of their new cultural and national identity, they sought to believe that the Nazi years were a kind of fog, something that was seen yet not quite able to be grasped or soon to dissipate.

Germans, sought to separate themselves from the Nazis both out of shame and of necessity. As Occupation authorities sought to weed out Nazis from "ordinary Germans," there were, at times, almost understandable attempts at distancing oneself, omitting any collective connection to the previous regime out of disgrace, and at others, being a purposeful choice to avoid capture and punishment. "The remarkable thing," wrote Zygmunt Bauman:

> is that we are not unable to recognize wrong acts or gross injustices when we see them. What amazes us is how they could have come about when each of us did none but

harmless acts. ... It is difficult to accept that often there is no person and no group that planned or caused it all. It is even more difficult to see how our own actions, through their remote effects, contributed to causing misery.[25]

More than individually, the inability to recognize "wrong acts" was extended collectively as well. If "[i]t takes a community to remember a crime," it "also takes a community to forget a crime," wrote Michael Walzer. "Repressing the memory, wiping out the traces: this, too, is cooperative work and probably easier to accomplish."[26] The memories of the recent German past were collectively, and conveniently, erased. In this respect, many times the two categories of needs for forgetting merged and, due to the widespread acceptance of Nazism in the population, a blurring of the two, many times, was arguably unavoidable. As such, the very existence and extent of the avoidance of blame only lent credence to the widespread culpability of the German population as a whole.

The German people were not, however, alone in this endeavor. There were needs, collectively, the West asserted, for putting the past behind them as well. As James Booth wrote, "there are times when, for individuals and communities both, life and the future require that we forget, let the past go..."[27] Western officials began asserting that the people of America and Europe recognize that not all of these Germans were bad, and moreover, that "we needed them." "The struggle is immediate and intensive," declared the U.S. High Commissioner for Germany (HICOG), John McCloy, in testimony before Congress. "We in Germany feel that we are facing a critical point in history..."[28] In a highly classified plea to Secretary of State Dean Acheson on April 25, 1950, McCloy went even further explaining, "I have strong feeling that our present approach [read idealistic approach] to problem of preventing Germany from 'again becoming threat to peace of the world' is unrealistic [sic]."[29]

To this end, however, questioning of the present course was forbidden. In setting the proper course, a proper policy was needed. "In the course of history," Jeannine Gramick, wrote that:

repressive regimes, including modern-day fascist and totalitarian states, have used silencing to control the behavior and even the thoughts of the masses. Because public discussion can challenge the status quo and question the rule of the current government, these regimes fear and forbid dialogue. Dissenters are silenced or disappeared. The power of the autocrats must be maintained at all costs. Religious authorities, no less than secular ones, have used silencing as a method to enforce orthodoxy.[30]

In this case, however, it would not be a repressive regime or modern-day fascist or totalitarian clique to silence the Nazi past or forbid dialogue, but a group of elected democracies fearing the resumption of conflict on an apocalyptical scale, which did all they could to enforce the orthodoxy of the prevention of Soviet aggression.

Policies were created which established the "official line" from which public deviation was unacceptable. To this point, Nathan Becker, a State Department economic advisor at the time, commented on the policies towards instilling a policy of silencing.

> It becomes a compromise position, but you have to add one other factor that I mentioned before. We have certain pet phrases, as I indicated before, certain pet concepts, and you just dare not write three pages without including one of these somewhere, even if it's only a sort of a distant bow ... [31]

Only through highly classified documents and cables then, could U.S. officials express their true feelings between themselves as to the nature of the threats emanating from the east without challenging the orthodoxies prevalent at the time. Any idea of openly disclosing how policymakers were acting in response to them was out of the question. As for the idea of discussing German rearmament, in the words of Secretary of State Acheson in June 1950, "large segments of American opinion would undoubtedly be thrown into very active opposition."[32] The policy of rearmament, however, would be implemented.

For the neutrals, a stubborn adherence to the concept that they acted impartially in favor of neither side was the standard defense. That they sided with no one in the war was their claim in the avoidance of responsibility for having even lent aid to the Nazis and their allies. In a war of such magnitude and of such violence, to the victors, having helped the Nazis at all was a brand of direct guilt. Cries of neutrality rang hollow with Allied policymakers. If only they had gained the right of inspection and verification of the neutrals' holdings and deeds, could they have properly countered these claims. Fifty years later, neutrality would therefore come to be known as another method for the silencing of one's wartime actions.

"In many cases," wrote Gerrit W. Gong, "underlying political economic, security, and social-cultural trends will be expressed in the vocabulary of historical relations and national identity, including the emotional language of past and future." Through the purposeful amnesia of the German people and the statements of Western diplomats mitigating German war guilt, the commutations of Military Tribunal sentences on Nazi war criminals, and the diplomatic treaties foreclosing restitution claims as well as the rewriting of Occupation decrees and Military Laws, silencing was achieved on the widest scale.

The reasons for silencing were many, and through all of them came the willful abandonment of responsibility for both the collective past and the collective future. The silencing of Nazi responsibility was a continued rejection of its survivors as people as well as a rejection of their suffering, and by connection, their claims for restitution.

Because of actions taken by the vanquished Germans and the victorious Allies alike, survivors as individual and collective agents were denied the respectability, acceptability, and even the legitimacy due them for their suffering. They were powerless to assert themselves to the full measure necessary to achieve satisfactory restitution. Survivors' assertions of suffering was, in part, denied acceptance institutionally by practices designed to restrict their claims. In this manner then, Germany and her allies, as well as later on the neutrals, would successfully evade their full responsibility for complete the restitution of personal property to Holocaust survivors.

Flight to the West

As the Allies scoured their respective zones of occupation for Nazis, they began to find that there were some who posed an abiding interest in them and it became a necessity to get them out of Europe and back home where they could be put to work for the benefit of the Allies. If these Germans possessed some scientific, military, or intelligence value to the United States in the years to come, they could provide much needed help in the struggle that was about to evolve with the Soviet Union. To gain custody of them, if for no other reason than to deny their expertise to the Soviets, was vitally important for U.S. and Allied security.[33] For the Allies then, securing fleeing Nazi scientists and intelligence officials, took precedence over securing restitution for these same Nazis' victims.

In August 1945, this effort began as *Operation Overcast*, but would come to be called, and now more commonly known as *Operation Paperclip*. To spirit them out of Europe, however, they simply could not bring them into the country without following the proper procedures, as Sam Klaus, later a member of the State Department's Legal Advisor's Office, would soon notify them. Bringing them into this country caused legal, if not political, problems. "This Government has made international commitments with other American Republics," wrote Klaus, who was brought to the State Department by the Special Assistant to the Secretary of State for Intelligence, Colonel Alfred in spring 1946. Klaus explained that the United States:

> ... has asserted similar doctrines in dealings with such countries as Spain, Portugal, Sweden, and even China, looking toward the repatriation or strict control of Germans outside of Germany who might engage in conspiracies and other activities for the rebuilding of German war potential and aggressive movements. We have, however, in this respect neglected to practice in our own country what we preach to others.[34]

Klaus concluded one section of his memo warning of the peril of bringing Nazis into the United States, by declaring "I have become convinced that there is a grave danger of embarrassment to the Department and to the Government, nationally and internationally, in the present uncoordinated handling of this problem."[35]

Due to his vast experience with German security problems, McCormack chose Klaus to serve as the State Department's representative of the Joint Intelligence Objectives Agency, a Joint Chiefs of Staff organization, created to implement the State-War-Navy Coordinating Committee (SWNCC), directive on the scientists. The SWNCC was the precursor to today's National Security Council.

Upon examination of the files, Klaus soon came to the conclusion that as it was the State Department that had sole control over the immigration question, and he would make a conscious effort to fulfill the SWNCC directive which stated that the State Department was to be the facilitator of the entry of the scientists, "but consistently with the law regarding issuance of visas."[36]

Klaus feared that the purposeful lack of coordination between the Army and Navy on the one hand, and Immigration officials on the other, would lead to unlimited and illegal immigration of Nazis and war criminals to the United States—war criminals who "may now be associated in movements to conduct espionage in the United States, or to restore German military potential."[37] Only in August 1946, with the advent of the expanded *Paperclip* program did the policy change. The problem was that the rationale of the methods by which the Army and Navy wanted to bring in the scientists, did not.

The military's view was diametrically opposed to Klaus' proposal to bring the Nazis in through the formal visa process. Klaus suggested that the Army formally take custody of the scientists bringing them here in that way, thus bypassing the visa process and the investigative procedures that were a prerequisite for the receipt of a visa. He opposed the blanket authorization of visas for the Germans and he eventually drafted just such a policy directive for the Office of Controls.[38]

The Army, however, continued to push for the issuance of visas, but without the formal investigations. Fearing, and rightfully so, that the subjects they sought to bring in would never clear the security investigations because of their war-time records of murder, torture, use of slave labor, and membership in the Nazi party. Klaus suggested the custody route to allow them to actually bring more scientists in, not less as he would soon be accused of doing. In the end, he pushed for, and ultimately obtained, an expansion of the original plan to bring in the scientists so that none could be taken by the Russians.

Operation Paperclip was not the only route for the former Nazis, yet it had some legitimacy in that the government sought to establish it in principle if not in practice. For others, however, seeking freedom from justice in a less official manner, there were other routes as well. As has been the subject of legend, various Nazi criminals made there way to North America, South America, and Australia, and escaped justice either entirely, or for years until their discovery and capture. Notable among those captured was Adolf Eichmann by

Israel in 1961. Others, over 2,000,[39] have been discovered during the past half-century by a variety of Nazi hunters, news organizations, and Nazi War Crimes Commissions, notable among them, the United States Justice Department's Office of Special Investigations.[40]

Review and Release

In 1948, a series of events occurred in rapid succession that brought about the realization, as James Bowman said, that this new peace would not be a satisfying one. On June 26, the Soviet Union instituted a blockade of Berlin, causing the United States to initiate thousands of airlift flights to continually furnish the German people of West Berlin with the daily needs of food and fuel to survive.

With the end of that blockade on May 12, 1949, peace again reigned, but the Allies understood, clearly now, that they had a new enemy with which to deal. With this in mind, on April 4, before the blockade had even ended, the United States and her allies signed the treaty establishing the North Atlantic Treaty Organization (NATO). Three weeks later, in the culmination of the effort to return Germany to the family of nations, the Federal Republic of Germany (FRG) was formed out of the Western occupation zones of the French, British, and the United States. Although a state, the FRG remained subject to the previous Occupation statutes and other laws and decrees.[41] Konrad Adenauer, the former Nazi opponent and Mayor of Cologne, became the Federal Chancellor of a truncated, and again divided, Germany. Roughly six months later, in direct response to the formation of the FRG, the Soviets established the communist government and satellite regime of the German Democratic Republic (GDR) in the areas of its occupation zone.

On June 16, 1949, the Allies agreed to form an Allied High Commission, establishing a High Commissioner for each of the former zones of occupation. The U.S. High Commissioner was John McCloy. The former Assistant Secretary of War during WWII, and "loyal workhorse," McCloy had worked on Wall Street with Averill Harriman and Dean Acheson.[42] He had a loyal following and many long-established and strong friendships among the many old hands of the Cold War U.S. bureaucracy.

As U.S. High Commissioner for Germany, McCloy would be remembered, beyond his towering intellect and deal-making abilities, for his commutation of the sentences of Nazi war criminals and wartime industrialists in the face of a Cold War turning hot. These commutations provided the sharpest break yet in contrast to the reversals from the harsh residual "pastoralization" policies of Morgenthau. The easing and eventual break with de-Nazification angered many, and reflected the wholesale change in U.S. policy to come. Fairness, the likes of which they did not grant their victims, was in the offing for the former Nazis.

> Since my arrival in Germany, McCloy declared on January 31, 1951, I have received many letters and petitions asking clemency for war crimes prisoners convicted at Nuremberg and confined in Landsberg Prison. It is a fundamental principle of American justice that accused persons shall be given every opportunity to maintain their innocence. If found guilty, it is recognized that they should be permitted to establish mitigating circumstances. In conformity with this latter principle I decided to appoint an impartial board to review these petitions, to examine each case and to consider whether any basis existed for clemency.[43]

This was McCloy's explanation for the process he created to pave the way for the eventual commutations that he would grant. The Board shared the blame for the commutations, according to Brigadier General Telford Taylor, the Chief U.S. Prosecutor at Nuremberg, for its slow-moving, overly deliberative consideration of cases involving men who committed mass atrocities and whose guilt was beyond question.[44] Ten of the fifteen prisoners convicted at Nuremberg, held at Landsberg Prison, and sentenced to death, had their sentences commuted to life. Seventy-eight of eighty-nine who had been convicted and sentenced to terms of prison, but not death, received reductions in their terms, including all eight of the Krupp Industrial Concern Management, with Alfried Krupp and Friedrich Flick (released in August 1950[45]) among them, seven S.S. officers who had run the Concentration Camp system, and four S.S. officers convicted of war-time atrocities. McCloy, to make matters even worse, took the further step of reversing the confiscation of Krupp's vast properties and subsequent compensation for these holdings, to which the Labour Party Executive of Britain later reacted with "alarm and disgust."[46]

"All of my decisions," McCloy declared, "have been rooted in the firm belief in the basic principle of the rule of law which all are answerable. With this principle, I have striven to temper justice with mercy."[47]

With Krupp's release and the restoration of his property, he was again the owner of vast properties, and according to Benjamin Ferencz, another former U.S. prosecutor at Nuremberg, and even millions in foreign bank accounts.[48]

That mercy, however, had been based on a number of factors. There were numerous requests for clemency. "In view of this it is to be regretted that according to newspaper reports," read one from the Most Rev. A. J. Muench, the Bishop of Fargo, Regent, Apostolic Nunciature in Germany, "certain organizations are writing you to reject proposals for an amnesty. "Such an attitude," Bishop Muench continued:

> will keep alive a spirit of vindictiveness that is not good for peace and prosperity. It will reawaken racial resentments that in the interest of these very organizations should be weakened and done to death as quickly as possible.[49]

Appeals like this only added to the general sense that the Germany the Allies had planned for before Germany's defeat, would not be the Germany they would, in the end, establish. Moreover, for Germany's victims, this shift in reality placed justice ever more distant from them.

Korea and a "Divided World"

On June 25, 1950, North Korean troops crossed the border with South Korea and headed for Seoul. Tensions that had risen to a fever pitch in Berlin in 1948-1949 and spread fear in Europe now burst forth with the outbreak of war in Asia.

Just as U.S. policymakers were working to re-integrate Germany back into a democratic Europe, so, too, were they attempting to conclude a treaty with Austria to do the same. Allied troops had jointly occupied Austria and the proposal being considered in the beginning of the 1950s was to seek the withdrawal of all of them. There were some 20,000 Western troops and some 43,000 Soviet troops in the country in the two occupation zones.[50]

On this point, B.D. Kimpel of the Western European Bureau at the State Department questioned the wisdom of U.S. efforts to achieve a joint withdrawal of troops from Austria in a Memorandum of January 31, 1951 (the same day of McCloy's mass pardon of Nazi war criminals):

> The invasion of South Korea has taken place since the last examination of the U.S. policy towards Austria, and this policy should be re-examined in the light of the following considerations. ... The issue therefore is reduced to the following question: Is it more desirable, from the point of view of Western security, to maintain the status quo in Austria and to continue indefinitely the ever-present opportunity for the Soviets to unilaterally partition Austria, or to obtain the withdrawal of all occupation troops, leaving Austria a free country with a small army? In other words, would the withdrawal of Western occupation troops mean a danger of Soviet control of Western Austria which would outweigh the advantage of the withdrawal of Soviet occupation troops from Eastern Austria?[51]

There were, in fact, very real fears of Soviet or Soviet-inspired military actions breaking out in other places and while Berlin had already faced threat and was now surrounded by a hostile Communist East Germany, many feared that the North Korean invasion was simply a dress rehearsal for Europe. "Surprise invasion South Korea by North Korea," read a "For American Eyes Only" warning from the U.S. Department of the Army written three days after the war began, "may indicate riskier Soviet policy henceforth of using satellite armed forces in attempting to reach limited objectives for expansion Communism."[52]

Now, with fears of Soviet intentions in Austria, German policy was again affected. To this charge, McCloy vehemently denied any connection. "There's not a goddamn word of truth in the charge that Krupp's release was inspired by the outbreak of the Korean War..."[53] According to Walter Isaacson and Evan Thomas, McCloy did oppose rearmament but the advent of war in Korea brought him around to supporting the notion.[54] The release of Krupp, then served that purpose. "... [T]here can be no question," Isaacson and Thomas wrote, "McCloy was worrying far less about Nazis than about making Germany strong enough to resist the Soviets."[55]

Krupp and Rearmament

On August 1, 1950, Secretary of State Acheson wrote to McCloy asking him to communicate to the other High Commissioners the notion that "scope of defense effort required by current international situation cannot be managed without finding means to utilize German productive capacity to turn out non-combat types of equipment ... "[56] The United States needed then, to bolster its defenses in Germany in light of its large troop withdrawals immediately after the war and the fear of further Soviet aggression perhaps in Germany or elsewhere. Germans expressed the urgent need to be able to defend themselves in the view that any war would be fought on their territory. As such they would have to rearm.[57] In order to rearm, they would need the industrialists, Krupp, Flick, and all the others pardoned.

That critical point in history then, could not and would not be interfered with in light of present developments. In this regard, de-Nazification was more symbolic than anything else to the Western allies. As Kai Bird, McCloy's biographer wrote, "the Nazis were a residual issue left over from the war..."[58] As early as August 1947, so soon after the end of the war, the State Department's Policy Planning Board called for the termination of de-Nazification.[59] Again, in 1948, the British Commonwealth Relations Office blithely suggested the same, commenting that:

> In our view, punishment of war criminals is more a matter of discouraging future generations that of meting out retribution to every guilty individual. Moreover, in view of future political developments in Germany envisaged by recent tripartite talks, we are convinced that it is now necessary to dispose of the past as soon as possible.[60]

McCloy's actions epitomized the concept of silencing. He minimized Krupp's role, suggesting that he had only inherited the affair from his father who was the real Nazi.[61] Yet, this was contradicted by his own staff. John A. Bross, in a HICOG Memorandum, suggested that Krupp's properties were not his to have been confiscated at all, but those of his mother Bertha (the namesake of the WWI artillery behemoth "Big Bertha"). In another act of minimizing German guilt, Bertha Krupp cast herself as a victim, claiming that the Krupp properties were, in fact, taken from her and her husband "under duress" by the Nazis and that they therefore could not have been legally confiscated from her son in the first place.[62]

Regardless of the sanctity of the confiscation, Alfried Krupp would, only six years after the commutation of his sentence, stand proudly in a different light, gracing the cover of *Time*, under the appellation, "Industrialist Krupp." Of Krupp, *Time* would write:

> Amid the magnificent trappings of the Villa Hugel, his 200-room ancestral mansion above the valley of the Ruhr, Alfried Krupp regally receives visiting heads of state such as King Paul of Greece, Brazil's President Kubitschek, Cabinet ministers and businessmen, extends his hospitality to men who once vowed to destroy him. In a gesture that symbolizes the rehabilitation of the Krupp empire and name, the U.S., which has long refused to admit convicted war criminals, last fortnight granted Alfried Krupp a visa to visit the country.[63]

While Krupp was entertaining heads of state and international businessmen, those survivors who toiled in slave labor for him were initially denied compensation for their work. While Krupp would later agree in 1958[64] to provide token payments, the idea that he was again living in the lap of luxury while the surviving victims of his crimes were denied real compensation for their suffering is more than distressing.

McCloy, nevertheless, in commuting the sentences of Krupp and the other Nazis, went to a considerable extent to distance himself from any political motives, as he did in a letter to Eleanor Roosevelt in March 1951, explaining that the Clemency Board he set up to undertake reviews of the Nuremberg sentences, "was set up in March 1950, long before there was any thought that Germany might participate in Western defense and its appointment was clearly not related to that issue."[65] McCloy continued by suggesting that he was "not passing judgment upon the degree of their incrimination as Nazis, but upon the extent of their guilt in terms of the offences for which they were convicted by the U.S. Military Tribunals."[66] He was, in simple terms, mitigating their guilt. There was no question that they were Nazis, only whether and of what they were guilty.

As conditions worsened, McCloy and Acheson continued exchanging views on German requests to create a federal police force. They needed to do so not simply to ease the transition, but to also alleviate fears of a reinstitution of a Gestapo-like force. From a police force evolved the idea of Labor Service Unions, formerly industrial police. All too aware of the threats inherent of again arming Germans, HICOG staff wrote, confiding their discomfort with the action:

> Outstanding danger to our position from propaganda viewpoint is that LSU will be first Germans to be given semi-military training with Western approval since end of war. Soviet propaganda will make capital of fact that first Germans bearing arms not members of European army or even German army or police force but are rather American "mercenaries." This is worst possible Berlin introduction to rearming Germans, which in itself is ticklish public relations matter.[67]

Days after these discussions, came conversations about, and approval for, the purchase abroad of light weaponry for a German armed force; weaponry. however, not permitted to be produced in Germany.[68] Within two months, discussions were then held on Germany joining a common Western defense of Europe. Acheson, however, wanted it plainly understood by the Germans, particularly Adenauer, that any suggestion of German participation in a common defense was the basis of "a formal request of Germany." He wrote, "We desire [to] avoid any basis for growth of [the] idea that proposals had been made by us ... "[69] These discussions were concluded in confidence and not released in violation of the official policy regarding Germany.

The Marshall Plan and Economic and Political Recovery

"This government opposes," Harry Dexter White wrote in April 1945, "any policy of reparations which will put the United States in a position where it will have to assume the sustained responsibilities for relief to the German people."[70] White, adhering to the tough Treasury Department line on Germany, was saying nothing his compatriots in the other agencies had not heard before in Treasury Department policy pronouncements. The Treasury, in the emerging Cold War, however, would not carry the day.

In a series of written correspondences involving both explanatory statements as well as questions as to the evolution of the policy, Ambassador Averill Harriman discussed the planning for what would eventually become the Marshall Plan with its namesake, the Secretary of State, General George C. Marshall. "We must not permit Germany to be drawn into the Soviet orbit," Harriman warned, "or be reconstructed as an instrument of Soviet policy."[71] In short, Harriman summarized what was one of the main sentiments of the early years of the Cold War, worries over the political sway of Germany. This sentiment played a large role in dictating policy with regard to reconstituting that defeated nation. Fears of riding them too hard, driving them into the arms of the Soviets, were all too prevalent among policymakers at the time. Rebuilding Germany—a democratic Germany—and the other war-ravaged countries, was paramount. "Our objective," wrote Dean Acheson, "was not relief, but to revive agriculture, industry, and trade so that stricken countries might be self-supporting."[72]

In the end, despite a great deal of bickering with the Congress and internally within the U.S. Government, the Marshall Plan proceeded. As President Truman's close adviser, Clark Clifford, would write years later, "[t]he most wonderful part of the Marshall Plan was that it *worked*."[73] With the provision of $10 billion to Europe and other devastated areas in the world, nations that might have been ripe for the picking in the U.S.-Soviet contest for influence, was avoided.

The Demise of *Safehaven*

" ... State was not tough. ... [the] Treasury was tough."
—*W. Averill Harriman*

State vs. Treasury

The divisions within the government would, however, continue and would play a strongly inhibitive role in the effort to achieve the restitution of assets to survivors. "We didn't clash so much with State as we did with Treasury," explained Harriman of the planning for the Marshall Plan. "Of course," he reasoned, "you had to get Treasury's agreement on some of these things—God knows why—but we did. The economic side of State was not tough; the financial side of the Treasury was tough."[74]

The State Department surely had much to worry about with the global contest with the Soviet Union. The Marshall Plan, a direct effort to deny the Soviets opportunities to expand, was successful, yet there was more than playing a successful offense in this economic phase of the Cold War, there was the need to play a successful defense as well. To do that, the U.S. needed our allies' help. In Europe, this would be tough as most countries were recovering themselves and were ill-prepared to provide anything in this way.

Of all the countries in Europe, Switzerland, however, was economically whole, in fact flush, as a result of its dual trade with the Axis and Allies alike during the war. While Allied intelligence had reams of documents detailing Swiss banks' and other Swiss industries' complicity with the Nazis, harsher measures planned against them, declared Seymour Rubin, were thought to be "excessive [and] could annoy" them.[75] The State Department felt, like the international bankers that were helping to rebuild Europe, "that keeping them neutral," was an advantage, he explained.[76] Because of this, the State Department demurred when it came to criticizing Switzerland and actively sought to silence any threats to that endeavor.

Walter Ostrow, a Treasury Representative in Bern, bitterly complained to his superiors in the Treasury Department that State Department officials were "systematically sabotaging our efforts to look after the Treasury's interests."[77] Thus, the problem was being circumvented from within the U.S. government and criticism of Switzerland was intentionally being muted. As Nathan Becker had explained, the "smothering" of contrary ideas was becoming routine.

With the transition to peace, U.S. allies began to care for themselves. In the case of Britain, this was all the more true.

Safehaven Unravels

When it came to fear of criticizing Switzerland, the State Department was not alone. "I am very much afraid," wrote James H. Mann, another Treasury representative in the U.S. Embassy in Bern, "that the British have concluded that good will and trade are the only things which matter insofar as their relations with the Swiss are concerned and that some of the war objectives which were so forcefully proclaimed can now be forgotten."[78] The British, badly in need of loans with which to rebuild their nation, looked to the Swiss for that help. In return, however, it was understood in London that pressure on the Swiss would now be quite impossible if their loans were to be granted. Now the British were subject to Swiss demands, and Allied unity on *Safehaven* was no longer possible. Soon, on issue after issue, the British abandoned her previously harsh economic controls policies. As Mann would write about British cooperation, "[o]ther cases could be cited of how the British are attempting to undermine the concerted Safehaven effort here."[79]

The Swedes, the Spanish, and the Portuguese

In August 1941, the FBI was alerted by the Office of Naval Intelligence to "large sums of money" from Spanish and Portuguese sources being transacted through Swiss banks in New York "destined for 'anti-U.S.' uses."[80] In the years following, the FFC, and later the FEA, directed great resources to following these and other transactions, with these countries as the European "neutrals" being heavily utilized by the Nazis, with the help of the Swiss, to launder looted public and private assets. Three years later in September 1944, D.W. Bell, Under Secretary of the Treasury, responding to a question of FDR's close political adviser, Harry L. Hopkins, explained, "There is increasing evidence that the Nazis are transferring assets to neutral countries for concealment. These assets are going principally to and through Spain, Switzerland, Sweden, and Argentina. We expect that the volume of assets leaving Germany will increase as final defeat approaches."[81]

Sweden. Following the difficult and quite inadequate agreement with the Swiss in May 1946,[82] the Allies began to close negotiations with Sweden in an effort to finalize yet another case of a European neutral aiding the Nazis. On July 18, 1946, Allied negotiators concluded an agreement by which Sweden would pay $66.5 million to the Allies, with one-quarter of that sum going to the rehabilitation of refugees. While the Swedes steadfastly disagreed with the Allies claim on German external assets, specifically Law No. 5, they nevertheless agreed on the need for the rehabilitation of war-ravaged countries in Europe.[83] As R. Simons of the Federal Reserve noted in a memo to his superiors at the time, the Swedes' "greater readiness to recognize and act in accordance with the political and strategic purposes of the Allies resulted in less difficult negotiations and a settlement more satisfactory to the Allies."[84] Unlike the Swiss, who very grudgingly recognized the Allies' authority and legitimacy, the Swedes much more readily understood and recognized it.

Spain. ... [S]hading the meaning of these figures slightly," wrote Francis McCombe, a British Economic Warfare Officer based in Madrid, was necessary in order to bring the Spanish to agree to return German looted gold "because we have to convince Spain that she is getting a very good bargain, as all the neutrals have done in getting something of immense capital value to their economy if they choose to exploit it..."[85] Like the Swiss before them, but unlike the Swedes, the Spanish were difficult to negotiate with and a careful hand was necessary in order to obtain a deal with them. Spanish banks were in possession of tons of German looted gold transmitted through France and into Spanish and Portuguese banks.[86]

Despite being in receipt of $138 million in gold from Germany, the fact that the gold had been transhipped through Switzerland, disqualified most of it due to the requisites of the Bretton Woods resolutions that specified that the gold was to have been received directly from Germany. Spain, as McCombe complained, was able to provide legalistic explanations for its gold stocks, excluding vast amounts of it in order to keep that which was left, claiming reparations from the war due to the Nazi intervention during the country's Civil War. By May 1948, Spain had agreed to turn over a mere pittance of all the gold, $114,329 worth, to the Allies. At the same time, Spain agreed to turn over some $24 million in German external assets to the Allies, roughly three-quarters of the total estimate of the Allies had made for Spain.[87]

Portugal. "I regret that I have no settlement to report," McCombe wrote six months later from Lisbon, "but after a full week of battling with our stubborn Allies, I feel that we are nearing the climax when the telegraph can be used."[88] McCombe explained further:

> Discussion wobbles between heated argument on "principles" and irrelevant but intense comparisons of this and that system of procedure of following stolen property, with marked refusal of the Portuguese to admit anything. ... Arguments drawn from other cases, the Swiss and Swedes, are not admitted. These were they say "political" settlements, and they will only settle on "principles".[89]

Due perhaps to the complexity of the negotiations, and the stiffness of the Portuguese negotiators, Allied cooperation with Portugal on concluding an agreement to close *Safehaven* matters there was exceedingly difficult. The Allies, fractured due to different goals and wariness of so many overlapping negotiations, could not agree on a common approach with the Portuguese. "The American delegates went home in time for 'Thanksgiving' and are not returning;" wrote another British official, "and the French, who as a matter of fact have throughout done extraordinarily little to help, also sent their principal men home, with the result that McCombe is the only special delegate left to negotiate with the Portuguese."[90] The French, the diplomat moaned, " ... do not care much either way about German assets but fuss terribly about looted gold." Moreover, he concluded, "... it is not worth risking our present favourable [sic] position for the sake of the French."[91]

Negotiations churned on and off for the next eleven years with the Portuguese stubbornly refusing to recognize their responsibility for repayment of either looted gold or German external assets. After the war, Allied intelligence had concluded that the Portuguese had accepted some $52.6 million worth of gold from the Nazis, including a very real possibility of gold from private French citizens,[92] and in external assets. When the negotiations were finally over in June 1958, the Portuguese had concluded a series of agreements with the FRG by which their claims were settled from wartime debts and claims and they, in fact, made money on the deal, receiving more than they claimed. The Allies even contributed their share of that settlement to the International Refugee Organization.[93]

Hurdles to Agreement

It became apparent to Allied negotiators that compared to dealing with the Swiss and later the Swedes, the Spanish and later the Portuguese were infinitely more stubborn. U.S. Ambassador Lincoln MacVeagh explained in a letter to the Secretary of State in 1949, that Dr. Antonio Faria, the Acting Director-General of the Portuguese Foreign Ministry, complained to Seymour Rubin, then representing a number of Jewish organizations on assets and refugee issues, that his country had "been treated very badly," during this period and blamed the Allies for the slow pace of the negotiations.[94]

Despite Faria's claims, there is a kernel of truth to the criticism of the time taken by the Allies to negotiate the arrangement. As 1948 approached, the negotiations, not yet entirely bogged down in the minutiae imposed upon them by Portuguese intransigence, were suddenly dropped out of U.S. fears of a disruption in the negotiations over a lease of the Portuguese-owned Azores islands upon which the U.S. had intended to place airbases, out of necessity due to the Cold War. Negotiations were practically halted to accommodate these concerns.[95] Only after the successful conclusion of the lease were negotiations restarted, only to be stalled again in 1951 until the lease for the Azores was renewed.[96]

Portugal, however, was not the only country with which negotiations were soft-peddled due to concerns for the Cold War. In Spain, the British wanted to hold a stronger line on the subject of Spanish wartime trade with the Nazis. J. Scullen of the Treasury Department, in a Memorandum to the Files, made a point to record the remarks of a State Department representative to a meeting a March 1945 *Safehaven* meeting suggesting a different approach.

> The group was still in complete agreement that Safehaven demands should be made part of the war trade negotiations, and felt that every effort should be exerted to

> convince the British of our position. Mr. Oliver pointed out, however, that while State was prepared to take a strong position with the British, it felt that this Government had certain interests in Spain which were as important as our Safehaven objectives, and that it was not prepared to subordinate everything to Safehaven. He mentioned specifically that State was extremely interested in acquiring landing rights in Spain.[97]

Inherently then, silencing pervaded U.S. and Allied operations in *Safehaven* after the war. In negotiations that evolved from *Safehaven*, silencing, too, was the guiding force. When issues arose that took precedence over reparations or restitution—and that was many times—survivors lost out. "I did not believe that during the intensified cold war [sic]," wrote Nahum Goldmann, at the time, Chairman of the Jewish Agency Executive and the President of the World Jewish Congress, "the Western Allies would compel a strong Germany, against its will, to commit itself to any large-scale fulfillment of the Jewish demands."[98] The orthodoxies of the Cold War were predicated then, on combating the Soviet Union at every turn and in all too many ways, restitution did not fit the definition of contributing to the fight against Communism.

"Our people cannot be helped if the 'red tape' is going on"

> Mr. Steinberg presented a somewhat pathetic picture and appealed for sympathetic understanding. He informed the meeting that prior to Hitler there were 7 ½ million Jews in Europe and that the number had been reduced through murder, etc., to 1 ½ million, and that from this number none wished to remain in Europe because Jewish people had suffered there too much and felt that they could not go on living in places where they have suffered.[99]—I. Steinberg of the Freeland League to Ex-Surinamese Soldiers, June 1, 1947

Steinberg was discussing the reluctance of survivors of the Holocaust to return to Europe. They sought any avenue where they could be safe and productive, starting anew their lives that were so terribly wrecked. With Jews scattered from the United States to Europe, Aden to Afghanistan, the remnants of the Jews of Europe sought refuge in their reinstatement in Palestine.[100]

Israel

As leader of the Jewish Agency, David Ben-Gurion was about declare the birth of the Jewish state after 2,000 years, upon the expiration of the British colonial mandate over Palestine in 1948, and there were heated policy disputes in the Truman White House over the question of recognition. "I strongly urge you," recalled then Special Counsel Clark Clifford of his presentation to Truman in the presence of a sternly disapproving Secretary of State George C. Marshall, "to give prompt recognition to the Jewish state immediately after the termination of the British Mandate on May 14."[101] Clifford continued:

> This would have the distinct value of restoring the President's firm position in support of the partition of Palestine. Such a move should be taken quickly, before the Soviet Union or any other nation recognizes the Jewish state.[102]

Seen within the context of the burgeoning Cold War, Clifford's presentation of competition with the Soviet Union, could be chalked up to mere rhetoric—assertions lacking sincerity and at times meant as a bluff—simply to gain acceptance for his true beliefs of the need to influence Truman to recognize the nascent state.

Competition with the Soviets, however, was in fact one facet of the decision. With the Soviet Union vying with the United States and the West in Europe and Asia, policymakers were on the watch for every Soviet move, regardless of the location. "The main motive behind the Soviet support for the establishment of a Jewish state in Palestine," wrote Ambassador Arye Levavi, the First Secretary of the Israeli Legation in Moscow in 1948, "was probably the intention to weaken the British position in the Middle East."[103] With the eventual outpouring of support by Soviet Jews for the new Minister, Golda Meir, to that country on Rosh Hashana, Soviet leaders were taken aback and shocked at their political miscalculation. Walter Eytan, later the Director General of the Israeli Foreign Ministry, explained the depth of their surprise at their own strategic blunder.

> Had they thought for a moment that the creation of an independent Jewish state would have these domestic repercussions in their own country (it was like the sin against the Holy Ghost, against sacred, untouchable, infallible doctrine), they would never have supported Israel in the first place, not even as a means of weakening the British in the Middle East.[104]

Whether Soviet intrigue was aimed at Great Britain or the United States, the reaction was the same. Hence, Truman's decision to proceed in the face of stern disagreement with Marshall and numerous others in the State Department created yet another area into which the Soviet-American and Soviet-Western disputes could flow. Moreover, the ability of Holocaust survivors to obtain reparations would be both helped and hurt by the emergence of the State of Israel and the declaration of its inherent right to act as the protector of Jews wherever they might be threatened.

Refugees

The growing post-war rush of refugees, particularly Jewish ones, created a burden on the United States, as well as Jewish service organizations that sought to address the problem in Europe, the United States, and the new State of Israel.

Initially the refugees went home seeking to return to the lives they left for practical or professional reasons.[105] When they got there, they found their towns and cities empty of the people they had known. They found others living in their homes, engaging in "bitter quarrels ... over claims for the restitution of apartments or other property that had been plundered, stolen, or confiscated."[106] Thereafter, they faced retribution from native, non-Jews over their property, accusations of their harboring Communist sympathies, and simple anti-Semitism. As became all too obvious for returning Jews in Europe, particularly in Eastern Europe, they were not welcome. They had to go back to the West, or to Palestine then Israel.

Just as the senior policymakers at the State Department fretted about the creation of Israel, so, too, did they fret about the plight of refugees, not out of sympathy, but out of fear. Among the many problems of the mass movements of refugees, the State Department, as well as U.S. intelligence, worried about the slippage of "black sheep," and Communist agents into the flow out of Europe, estimating that "no less than 10 percent of all illegal emigrants passing through Italy are Russian agents."[107]

The State Department had opposed help for refugees even during the height of the Holocaust and now after the war, little had changed. "I did not hear anything from the State Department," wrote M. Schenkolewski to Eleanor Roosevelt a full year-and-a-half before the creation of Israel, "about these proposals [permission to admit 100,000 displaced Jewish refugees into Palestine]. The winter is already knocking on our door and something must be done immediately. Our people cannot be helped if the 'red tape' is going on."[108]

Jewish organizations, particularly the American Jewish Joint Distribution Committee (known more simply as the JDC), was responsible for administering to the needs of survivors in Europe. In camps all over Europe, survivors remained, trying to get either to Israel, the U.S., Canada, Australia, or South America. They needed rehabilitation, food, medical services, education, and workers training. All of these services were supplied by Jewish organizations subsidized by donations from the International Refugee Organization, the United Nations Relief and Rehabilitation Administration (UNRRA), and private citizens. "Our activities are by no means limited to the issuance of funds and supplies," read the JDC's 1947 Annual Report for Poland. The report continued:

> We work with the organizations hand in hand, and JDC has a decided share in every phase of the progress the Jewish community has made since liberation. Moreover, our activities are based upon the principle of helping the Jews to become productive and healthy regardless of whether they wish to stay in the country or intend to leave and establish themselves in Palestine or elsewhere.[109]

Jewish officials went to great lengths to raise funds, encourage extended care for refugees in their host countries, and lobby European governments as well as the State Department for continued assistance in these overwhelming endeavors. American Jewish groups were therefore spread thinly and widely working to help refugees.

While the argument could be made that restitution would aid in their efforts, IARA money was supposed to address resettlement first and these groups were hard pressed to pay attention to restitution any more than they were to the refugees' immediate needs. One example of this predicament was a plan by the JDC to use "a certain portion of reparations funds allocated for the resettlement of non-repatriable victims of German action by the Paris Reparations Agreement would be used to advance the cost of passage of visa immigrants to the United States."[110] This plan was approved in 1947 by both the Secretary of State and the Commissioner of Immigration. Resettlement, as was the case, came first, restitution and reparations would have to wait.

"What then shall Zionism do?": Claims Against Germany and Austria

Germany

In a telegram from Jerusalem back to the U.S. Embassy in Tel Aviv, a Foreign Service Officer, Tyler, reported back in 1951, on the first meeting of the Zionist Congress since Israel's independence.

> Jewish lamentations have resounded for 2,000 years. How shld they sing the Lord's song in a strange land. This was the basis of their literature; one of the central themes of their religion; stimulation of their zionist propaganda and activity and an integral part of their inmost being. It sets them apart from other peoples. Now Zion is theirs. Like an old beau who has long resigned himself to the refusal of his lady and has been accepted in that role by others, the lady's sudden "yes" throws him off balance. Some Jews never expected Israel to exist and almost none rpt almost none that it wld happen so soon. The creation of the State has been a profound psychological shock.... What then shall zionism do? [sic].[111]

This redefinition of the Jewish world and its duality of the Jews of the Diaspora and the hardened Jews of Israel was a product of a tortured history.

That history and the Jewish experience with the loss of its possessions and the redemption of the Jewish people, was explained by the Sages, wrote Rabbi Harris L. Selig in 1941. "The Sages prescribe three forms of renouncing lost property," he wrote:

> *yiush*, or completely despair of its return; *hefker*, or permitting tis [sic] appropriation by any finder; and *bittul*, or complete surrender of all rights and ownership, even as though the owner had never actually possessed it.
>
> In exilic lands we Jews often employ all three methods simultaneously. When persecution break out, and Jews are deprived of their goods and freedom, many of us—in

particular the assimilationists who have convinced themselves that their defection has assured them an unimpeachable place in their country's economy—fall into immediate deep despair and rush into suicide.

Others—and these will include the persons of means who have not altogether doffed their Jewishness but who have never been too close to their people—immediately give up their belongings to any who seek them, save what they can, and rush off wherever they find a turning. They wander into new lands to find a new life ... to remain there until the wave of anti-Semitism engulfs this country also, and compels the repetition of the process.

But nationalist and religious Jews do not despair and lose their courage. They pass off the tragic events as though they had never existed, and turn their thoughts to a new hope of redemption. They have always known that the Jew is like a sheep among the volves [sic] because he has been living in exile, everywhere a small minority. This fact has made it possible for corrupt political schemers to draw the general attention away from their own misdeeds and ascribe them to the helpless Jewish community.[112]

The question of what "shall Zionism do," then, was a valid one, particularly following the Holocaust and the establishment of the State of Israel. As Selig foretold, the new Jews, those of Israel, would not repeat the mistakes of the past. Israel would stand for itself, defend itself, and yes, even grudgingly seek restitution for the assets taken from the Jewish people. As Nahum Goldmann, affirmed, "To ask reparations for this people was as audacious as it was ethically justified."[113]

Despite the modest progress made to that point on restitution, more needed to be done. As Chaim Weizman explained:

It is submitted that the provisions for heirless property falling to the State were not designed to cover the case of mass-murder of a people. Such properties belong to the victim, and that victim is the Jewish people as a whole. The true heir, therefore, is the Jewish people and those properties should be transferred to the representative of the Jewish people, to be employed in the material, spiritual and cultural rehabilitation of the Jews. ... It is therefore submitted that a proper percentage of the reparations to be obtained from Germany should be allotted for the purpose of the resettlement in Palestine of Jewish victims of racial and religious persecution, and granted, in the form of suitable assets (e.g. plant, machinery, equipment, and materials), to the Jewish Agency for Palestine, as the body charged by international authority with the duty of developing the Jewish National Home.[114]

This vision would soon become the basis for a Jewish, then Israeli, claim on the FRG, as the successor to the Third Reich, for reparations for the crimes of the Nazis. Material restitution was one thing, heirless property would be another. Heirless property was to continue as a point of contention between Jewish groups and the FRG, the U.S. Military Government, and neutral countries holding Jewish assets.

Heirless Assets

While the JRSO had obtained title to heirless properties through the Military Government in Germany, gaining acceptance of that title (established through MG Law No. 5) in countries not under U.S. occupation would be a different matter entirely. There was nothing in the experience of the survivors, Rabbi Philip S. Bernstein, the Advisor on Jewish Affairs to the American Theater Commander, which could "reasonably lead Jews to hope that Germans will be just to them, particularly when these Germans themselves must be held to give account for property acquired from Jews."[115] Why then, they thought, would other countries cooperate any more than Germany?

To this point, it was surmised by Jewish groups seeking to help Israel and refugees alike, that their moral cause was just and if they only pled their case loudly and often enough, they would succeed. They needed, however, to transcend, in the words of President Truman, "strict adherence to legalistic conceptions which will result in ignoring just and honorable...claims..."[116] As such, they believed that it should be argued that "it must in all justice be admitted that the measure of compensation embodied in these acts [restitution measures] is hardly commensurate with the crimes committed and the damage caused by Nazi Germany. Nor is it commensurate with the profit derived by the Nazis by the spoilation of millions of people."[117]

Jacob Blaustein, President of the American Jewish Committee elaborated,

> It needs no emphasis that the Jewish communities of the world not destroyed by Hitler have contributed and continue to contribute to the limit of their ability toward the relief and rehabilitation of the victims of the Reich. Governments have done more, particularly the Government of the United States, whose participation in UNRRA, in IRO and whose liberation of its immigration laws need not be underlined here. It would appear only fitting that, in this context of voluntary contribution by individuals and by governments, the Government of Western Germany should make some payment in equity and in recognition of the transfer to it of Reich assets. The payment should be available for relief and rehabilitation where needed outside of Germany. It should be made as a simple act of justice and of law. It should be made promptly. The problem should no longer be neglected. If measures are necessary to permit such a payment to be made, they should be taken swiftly. In this area particularly, that surgery—if surgery is needed—is best which is quickest. And there has already been too much delay in the advancement of immediate solutions to settle matters which otherwise become festering sores.[118]

Restitution in the era of the Cold War would take two tracks. The first would concentrate on the return of heirless properties held in countries outside of Germany. The other track would concentrate on seeking compensation for the overall suffering of the Jews. Reparations, while not tied directly to physical individual robbery, were viewed on the level of a more collective return to the entire Jewish people in lieu of the recovery of heirless assets which seemed to be impossible to retrieve. On the latter, Truman's warning of adherence to legalistic conceptions would ring alarmingly true for the next forty years. On the former, reparations would be achieved to a larger extent, but would always be viewed as an inadequate substitute for real and just compensation because of technical exclusions and prejudices. That collective feeling of inadequacy would remain in the minds of claimants until the end of the Cold War.

"I have discussed this problem with Mr. [Ben] Ferencz, director general of the Jewish Restitution Successor Organization," wrote Max Isenburgh of the American Jewish Committee in November 1948, "and he agrees that the prospect of effective action in Germany would be greatly enhanced if the desired legislation in the other countries were to become a fact first."[119] Isenburgh explained, regarding legislation on heirless assets:

> Thus far, there has been no action in Sweden because the Swedes are awaiting resolution of the problem by the United States and other Western countries. Here again the significance of getting an heirless property law in Holland is apparent, as is also the need for pressing our American legislation as soon as Congress reconvenes.[120]

As was the case with the imposition of laws in Nazi-allied and Nazi-controlled areas to confiscate assets, the spread, or lack of spread, of laws to contribute to the reversal of them was dependent upon simple emulation. The idea of joining the "bandwagon" comes to mind as well, if only that bandwagon had begun moving.

The idea of "effective action" in Germany, as proposed there, seemed to ring hollow with some survivors and claimants. In 1949, both the Army and the State Department had proposed plans to sell off unidentifiable properties coming into their possession. Advisors to the several Jewish groups, Seymour Rubin among them, suggested the proceeds from such sales go to the IRO for refugee purposes.[121] Some survivors, including Hans F. Abraham, complained bitterly to the State Department about these plans. "First one sells the so-called [sic] unidentified Jewish property in auctions despite the protest of many Jews," Abraham wrote to Covey T. Oliver of the State Department, "telling them that they would receive damages from reparations. Then, after having disposed of the 'unidentified' property, one intends to give up the plan of granting damages from reparations and one wants to use the remainders of the 'unidentified property' after having disposed of the bulk of it already for other purpose!"[122]

Disposing of heirless property in Germany became difficult due to the lack of the now German-run restitution courts in settling cases; the reluctance of the German people, collectively, to restitute property; differences in the various the policies and procedures of the German Laender, (States) on restitution; and finally, because of legislation passed in Germany called the "Equalization of Burdens." This legislation was a tax on all property owners to provide benefits for Germans either born, or placed, in Eastern Europe by the Nazi regime and expelled following the Nazis' defeat and taken back into the FRG.[123] The tax provided a very real impediment to payments to Jewish survivors and organizations outside of the FRG. For those properties, and even funds of those who had moved out of Germany, this exchange control on payments outside of the country, not to mention the ban on the export of non-Deutschmark payments, or even investments of funds to survivors in Germany, prevented many survivors from obtaining just restitution.[124] In the words of the British *O'Sullivan Report:*

> The claimants hesitate to take back property which may be subjected to heavy taxation or to agree to a money settlement calculated on the basis that the property will be subject to this burden. Defendants, likewise, are reluctant to agree to settlements on the basis that the property will be exempt. Claimants urge strongly that it would be a manifest injustice to impose on victims of persecution any liability for burdens for which they bear no responsibility. It would facilitate settlements therefore, if an early decision were taken in this matter.[125]

The demand for indemnification awards and the exemption from this tax, therefore, became a chief point of contention between the various Jewish groups and the FRG, and to some extent, between the groups and the State Department, whom some of the groups accused of a lack of awareness of the problem, or worse, a lack of caring.[126] Based on the frequency and tone of the letters from Capitol Hill to the State Department at this time, whom the elected representatives the groups actively sought, shared in this belief. The State Department was flooded by complaints, as well as questions, from Members of Congress seeking answers to questions for years to come.[127]

"No indemnity, however large can make good the loss ..."

On October 24, 1950, the American Embassy in Tel Aviv presented a memorandum to the Foreign Ministry explaining that, due to the inability to unify the now two halves of Germany under Western auspices, the FRG alone could reserve the sole right to speak on behalf of the German people. With this in mind, the three allied Western governments would, therefore, take the steps necessary to bring a formal end to the state of war between them and Germany.[128]

This note, Richard Ford, the Charge d'Affaires perfunctorily commented, was received rather "stiffly," commenting that a Mr. Bendor of the Ministry did concede that there were questions as to "whether Israel is or has ever been at war with Germany." Fox concluded, however, that the Israelis might "brush-off, whether polite or otherwise" the Embassy note out of anger.[129] Nearly ten months later, the exchange of this memorandum was still causing ripples in the State Department, the U.S. Embassy in Israel, and in the Israeli Foreign Ministry. "I feel," scribbled E.P. Keeler at the bottom of a note to the American Ambassador, "that we have unnecessarily given the Israelis a peg to hang their reparations claims on—by implication, at least."[130] Nahum Goldmann, himself, concluded that any claim made on Germany was based on moral, not legal, circumstances such as those discussed by Ford.[131]

Most importantly, however moral it might be, that claim was based on Israel's basic need to survive. " ... Prime Minister Ben-Gurion, and Foreign Minister Sharett," wrote Ambassador Uri Lubrani, then Sharett's private secretary, "had to face the question whether to seek reparations from Germany in order to alleviate ... [at] least some of the most urgent economic problems which Israel faced at the time and use German funds primarily to build the very basic infrastructure of a modern state." Ben-Gurion's unbridled commitment to Israel's survival was based on his belief that "all other considerations should be secondary." Dealing with Germany, however onerous, was a necessity that had to be accepted.[132]

As such, on March 12, 1951, the Foreign Ministry answered the question of Israel's position on its qualification to claim reparations from Germany, not the least of which was its very reason for existence, having "been built up for the specific purpose of providing a refugé [sic] for all persecuted and homeless Jews."[133] The Ministry argued that "[i]t is surely no exaggerated claim to demand that the German people, who were responsible for all this misery and who continue in possession of the economic assets taken from the Jews, dead and alive, should [be] required to make reparation for the benefit of the survivors." As such, the argument concluded:

> The Government of Israel is not in a position to procure and submit full data of the Jewish property confiscated and plundered by the Germans, which, as previously stated, is authoritatively estimated to aggregate over six billion dollars. It can base its claim only on the expenditure incurred and anticipated in connection with the resettlement of the Jewish immigrants from the countries formerly under Nazi control. Their number is estimated at about 500,000, which would involve an overall expenditure of one and a half billion dollars. This figure corresponds approximately to the value of exports from Western Germany alone in 1950, which, in view of Germany's economic recovery, is likely to increase considerably during 1951.[134]

In April, Israeli officials stepped up their efforts to reinforce their case for reparations with the State Department. In a Memorandum of Conversation between the Finance Ministry Director General David Horowitz and Ambassador Abba Eban for the Israelis, and Henry Byroade of the German Affairs Bureau at State, the Israeli position was summarized as "not a purely legal one, and possibly there were certain legalistic gaps in it."[135] Byroade, was at the least, skeptical of the Israeli position.

He even suggested that what the Israelis were really asking for was reparations out of current production. This was a linguistic swipe at the Israeli claim. Taking reparations out of current German production resources was a strongly frowned-upon concept in Allied diplomatic circles intent on building Germany into a viable partner in Western Europe. Current production was considered sacrosanct in that every bit of it was needed to rebuild the state, not to mention provide the industrial cushion necessary to keep pace with Soviet moves and intentions. It was, however, disingenuous in some respects because Washington, DC, while castigating and opposing Soviet plans to do the very same thing, had similar plans as well for current production in Germany, despite any denials to the contrary. U.S. officials publicly claimed to be aiming only to rebuild Germany economically, but in fact were engaging in intense efforts to rearm Germany, through its own means. In this context, this remark smacked of hypocrisy. During the talks, Horowitz, when pressed, however, did admit to the claim, yet considered it "necessary retribution."[136]

Israeli negotiators were, nevertheless, all too aware of the Allied position in Germany. Israeli Embassy officials in Washington, DC in subsequent meetings in June 1951, made it clear that any reparations from Germany should not be financed indirectly by the aid the United States was providing the FRG. On this idea, they agreed that owing to the necessity to rebuild Germany, any final reparations plan could be stretched out over a period of years. They also expressed a willingness to accept commodities in place of foreign exchange. State Department officials expressed disagreement over this condition, saying it did not alter U.S. objections.[137]

In June as well, came the U.S. response to the Israeli note of March 12 which argued its inherent right to seek reparations from Germany. While not denying the Israeli right for compensation, the reply showed a snippiness, even an arrogance, as to the full measure of the Israeli claim, even if it was based on figures accounting for the resettlement of Jewish immigrants in Israel. "In bringing to the attention of the Government of Israel," read the reply:

> the reparations and indemnities thus far received by the Jewish refugees, the Government of the United States does not imply that it regards them as full compensation for their sufferings. It concurs in the view of the Israeli Government that no material compensation can be sufficient. It would point out, however, that many nations and peoples experienced tremendous losses and sufferings at the hands of the Nazis and that none can expect its reparations receipts to reflect compensation in any substantial measure.[138]

On the same day as the disappointing American response to the Israeli note, Abba Eban relayed to Henry Byroade at the State Department that a meeting had recently taken place between Horowitz and Chancellor Adenauer and that the Chancellor had expressed sympathy to the request of a German "gesture" in recognition of the Israeli claim against Germany. Adenauer feared, however, the reaction of the German opposition and declared that he was unable to act without U.S. approval since any decision would impact American assistance.[139] Horowitz's meeting with Adenauer was not the first between a representative of a Jewish organization or of Israel and a German official. At war's end, a delegation of German Jews had suggested that Adenauer offer $10 million to the Jews, an offer that never materialized due to its inadequacies.[140]

More concretely, between 1949 and 1950, Dr. Noah Barou, a Vice President of the British Section of the World Jewish Congress who had befriended Herbert Blankenhorn, a close Adenauer advisor, had conducted nearly forty trips to Bonn to discuss reparations from the FRG.[141] Blankenhorn had assured Barou that Adenauer was sincere about arriving at a settlement, and Barou was acting upon that assurance.[142] These quiet meetings helped to eventually pave the way for official meetings to begin.

Soon afterward, Acheson decided that in light of the persistence of Israel and the Jewish organizations, it would be prudent for the Germans to be approached with a request to make "a voluntary act of settlement covering all claims." This should be done, however, under the conditions that any settlement be spread out and delineated as to what Israel could receive; that there be no burden on the Allies as Occupying Powers; that it not disrupt the German economy or "prejudice the Ger [sic] defense contribution..."[143]

"Further restitutions will follow."[144]

On September 27, 1951, Chancellor Adenauer spoke before the Bundestag on the need for Germany to resolve the problems of restitution.

> The Federal Government is prepared, in conjunction with representatives of Jewry and of the State of Israel—which has admitted so many homeless Jewish refugees—to bring about a solution of the financial aspect of the restitution problem, in order thus to pave the way towards clearing the psychological atmosphere, blackened by untold suffering. The Federal Government is deeply imbued with conviction that the spirit of true humanity must revive and bear fruit. The Federal Government considers it the foremost duty of the German people to foster this spirit with all its power.[145]

Adenauer, who had vowed soon after his election as Chancellor to better relations with Israel,[146] had made a statement that, in the words of Congressman Jacob Javits, who would be a longtime advocate for restitution "should prove to be [a] landmark on [the] road toward strengthening free institutions and full enjoyment of human rights in [the] Ger[man] Fedrep."[147] Javits believed "Jews everywhere ... will be gratified by this statement." In truth, Javits' observation proved correct. Adenauer's speech paved the way for the commencement of talks between the FRG and Israel, providing the sanctions and near apology Israeli leaders needed to initiate the procedures necessary to begin talks.

Adenauer's personal history of opposition to the Nazis and his close friendships with Jews in Germany from before the war, made this a personal mission. " ... Adenauer's attitude," wrote Nana Sagi, "is highlighted when it is recalled that no pressure whatsoever was exerted on him by the victorious Powers to open negotiations," another indication of U.S. indifference to the effort.[148] Adenauer's motives were pure, according to Thomas Schwartz, but at the same time he "never lost sight of the political aspects of the question." Adenauer was keenly interested in his standing with the Allies, particularly with the United States.[149]

With the way clear to negotiation, a meeting was first held on October 1, in Jerusalem, between Nahum Goldmann and Israeli Foreign Minister Moshe Sharett.[150] The Foreign Minister sought unity from the various Jewish groups in the diaspora and asked Goldman to work toward that end. Two days later, Goldmann called for such a meeting and it was convened on October 25, at the Waldorf Astoria in New York City. Beyond a call for unity, the twenty-three Jewish communal and service organizations attending discussed the approach to be taken with the FRG and the very nature of the concept of reparations from Germany.

While most supported the contentious, and almost taboo, idea of directly negotiating with Germany, a few did not and what was supposed to be a short meeting simply to endorse Israel's decision turned into a very real debate on the issue. Beyond the difficult concept of negotiating with the Germans, it was agreed that a representative body should be created to negotiate and receive the proceeds from any future arrangement with Germany. That body was the Conference on Jewish Material Claims Against Germany. It was not a mistake that the term "material" was included in that the term meant just that, "material restitution." What was desired, even demanded, was not merely moral restitution, not a simple exchange of payment for forgiveness, but restitution as payment for financial repair of the damages done to the Jewish people. While no amount could adequately accomplish this (a debate that rages on to this day) the amounts expected were not meant to be only token payments.[151]

What would come to be called, for short, the Claims Conference, had a leadership body lead by Goldmann. Under him sat as Vice Presidents Jacob Blaustein of the American Jewish Committee; Seagram CEO Samuel Bronfman of Montreal, Canada; Britain's Barnett Janner; as well as Saul Kagan of the JRSO, as Secretary.[152]

While the formal decision to allow Israel to negotiate with the Germans had not yet been sanctioned by the Israeli Knesset. Israeli diplomats had begun to lay the groundwork for this eventuality. At the end of December, Ambassador Eban, returning to Israel from Washington, DC, expressed to the press, his belief that the "Israel must either negotiate directly with Germany or give up hopes [of] obtaining reparations."[153]

In January 1952, the Israeli Knesset accepted the German offer to negotiate after a bitter debate, far surpassing even that of the hostile atmosphere in New York the previous October with the Jewish organizations. Outside the Knesset there were riots on January 9, the day of the Knesset vote, and the police had to push back large crowds, whipped up into a frenzy by Menachem Begin and his Herut Party, who protested negotiating with the Germans, even for the purpose of obtaining reparations and restitution. In the end, however, the Knesset approved the notion for negotiations to go forward. Israel agreed to send a negotiating team and the Claims Conference did so as well. Both teams would negotiate with the Germans in Wassenaar, near The Hague in Holland.

After a difficult six months of negotiations beginning in March, on September 10, 1952, West Germany and Israel, and West Germany and the Claims Conference, signed agreements whereby the FRG agreed to pay DM 3 million (or some $722 million at the time) in annual installments to Israel in the form of goods and services. To the Claims Conference, the FRG agreed to pay DM 450 million (or $107 million at the time) in goods and services, which under a separate agreement with Israel, were transmitted to that country and then converted to cash and transferred on to the Conference in order to financially administer the resettlement of survivors.[154] The Conference would also monitor legislation that the FRG agreed to pursue that would provide additional payments to survivors around the world. Finally, the FRG was held liable for two-thirds of the financial obligations of the Third Reich to the Jewish community as a whole, and the other one-third obligation was ascribed to the GDR.[155] The GDR, however, claiming itself a collective victim of Hitler and part of the "anti-fascist group opposed to him," steadfastly refused to pay any reparations.[156] In the 1990s, the GDR did agree, in principle to pay reparations, but never actually paid anything.

On October 1, 1953, the FRG enacted the initial indemnification program for victims of Nazi persecution. The program was designed to pay reparations to individual victims and survivors of the Nazis. The law was later updated and expanded in 1956.

On June 29, 1956, the *Third Federal Law of Compensation of Victims of Nazi Oppression* ("BEG") was passed by the Bundestag. Slave laborers were not eligible for compensation but injuries such as death or physical harm caused by forced labor might be grounds for compensation.

"Excessively Technical and Hair-splitting"

True enough, there were problems with these indemnification laws. Inadequate and not far reaching enough, the laws were then, and perhaps still are, considered too legalistic.[157] Criteria for payments has been considered at times difficult, and at others simply not inclusive enough. In June 1959, Nahum Goldmann, explained these early problems.

> My report on the situation would not be complete if I were not to mention the fact that the indemnification authorities are by no means encouraged to a liberal administration of the Law by the Senate for Indemnification Cases of the Federal Supreme Court

> (Wiedergutmachungssenat des Bundesgerichtshofes). The present restrictive tendencies are, rather, strengthened by Karlsruhe. To this day, the indemnification authorities wait in vain for the broader interpretation of the indemnification law that the legislator assigned to the Bundesgerichtshof.[158]

According to Kurt Grossmann, the former Secretary General of the German League for Human Rights, who explained the details of the adjudication process for some 660,000 claimants . "It should be noted," Grossmann wrote, "that these documents are scanned and interpreted by German civil servants who are not particularly disposed to compassion for the claimants with the consequence that they are excessively technical and hair-splitting."[159] The claims process, while adequate, was still insufficient. For a good number of survivors, the process also could not move fast enough.

While the number of programs for survivors would increase, the numbers of problems would do so as well. In 1966, there was a temporary suspension of payments to survivors, due in part to a clerical error of the German Finance Ministry, which resulted in the loss of some $30 million annually due to the erroneous deduction of FRG taxes from survivors' payments, despite their tax-free status there.[160] What made matters worse for survivors was that due to budget shortfalls in the FRG, the error stood and survivors' pensions, the creation of amendments to the indemnification laws, were suspended temporarily.

In 1980, the FRG and the Claims Conference, under pressure applied by Jewish organizations, established a Hardship Fund in response to the large number of Jews who were permitted to emigrate from the Soviet Union and other Eastern European countries during the period of *detente*. These persons had not been able to apply for compensation before the filing periods had expired, and the Hardship Fund provided a measure of relief for them. A total of DM 535 million was turned over to the Claims Conference for this purpose.

By the end of the 1990s, the FRG had paid perhaps as much as DM 120 billion to survivors around the world. There were expansions of the definition of a survivor and exemptions for the requirements to receive payments. As always, changes were brought about through negotiations which were painstaking and lengthy, but in the end, the special relationship that had developed between West Germany and Israel, as well as the Claims Conference, which enabled the indemnification and restitution programs begun under Allied Occupation to continue on their own.

Throughout the years, an unmistakable feature of U.S. restitution policy during the Wassenaar negotiations was an avoidance of policy pronouncements for or against Jewish claims. "It was not so extensive as some of us had initially had hoped," Goldmann summarized, "and at no point did they make any statement concerning our concrete claims..."[161] The Germans, though, were all too aware of their responsibilities to history, the Western alliance to not having committed to some regime of payments to victims regardless of the input of the Americans. While the process brought a measure of restitution and reparations to survivors, it was by no means a full, or even perfect, justice. There were categories of recipients that would remain outside the evolving definitions eligible for aid from the FRG. These recipients would have to wait until the Cold War ended.

Austria

> The governments of the United Kingdom, the Soviet Union and the United States of America are agreed that Austria, the first free country to fall a victim to Hitlerite aggression, shall be liberated from German domination.—"Declaration on Austria," Moscow Conference, November 1943[162]

In May 1943, OSS agents interviewed Austrian trade unionists and businessmen on their views of the conditions in Austria five years after the *Anschluss*. "The shop people, who have taken over the former Jewish shops," the agent wrote:

> are, for the most part, Nazis. Their attitude to their customers breeds antagonism amongst the people. The Viennese call the[m] 'white Jews' and one often hears the assertion by the people that the Nazi owners of these aryanized (formerly Jewish) shops are 'worse than the Jews.'[163]

This attitude in Austria portrays the malevolence attached to the Jews during the war. At war's end, little changed.

With the defeat of Germany and the joint U.S.-Soviet occupation of Austria, the Government of Austria instituted three laws to effect the restitution of property from September 1946 to March 1947. The first law effected property already under the administration of the Austrian Government. The second effected property that had come into the possession of the Austrian Government. Finally, the third affected all other types of confiscated property, excluding claims of employees, leases of apartments and businesses, and patent and other commercial rights.[164]

Austrian reasoning for taking these steps was, however, less altruistic and more self-preserving. Reasoning that while there was no Jewish State to submit a claim on behalf of survivors, world Jewry might nevertheless bring their might, and that of the rest of the world, upon Austria.[165] Therefore, these first restitution acts cannot, in any way, be viewed as representing the fullest measure of help to the survivors. These first acts were only the opening moves in a protracted effort to obtain restitution for the Jewish survivors and victims from a country not at all willing to concede the errors and misdeeds of its past, or much of their past at all.

From the very start, the Austrians proved to be an entirely different case from the Germans when it came to restitution. Whereas, it might have been considered to be difficult to obtain restitution from the FRG for psychological reasons, there was nevertheless, no official or openly hostile presentation of denial as there was in Austria. In Germany any remaining hostility to Jews was more or less muted. In Austria, outright hostility was the norm. There was a proliferation of willful obfuscation and half-hearted excuses to avoid restitution. For example, Jews were described as ineligible because of confusion over their birth, inside or outside of Austria . Many were said to have not really been Jews at all, but baptized Catholics.[166] Jews who left Austria were viewed as disloyal for seeking safety during adversity.[167] As such, the only Jewish Austrians believed were eligible for restitution were those still in Austria, despite the fact that thousands left before and after the *Anschluss* and 60,000 were murdered in the Holocaust. As Robert Knight explained:

> In an ironically circular argument the fact that the inheritors were living abroad was taken as evidence that they would 'unfairly' sell, lease or sublet any premises returned to them before returning abroad. Yet at the same time the fact that there was no legal basis for regaining their accommodations or leased premises was a major disincentive to those—admittedly probably a minority—who might be contemplating return.[168]

In all, the Austrians, who viewed themselves as victims, and not as successors, to Nazi Germany, proved to be argumentative, legalistic, and outwardly hostile to the entire process.

That process begun in 1952 when the Committee on Jewish Material Claims Against Austria formed out of the Claims Conference, began meetings with Austrian Government officials to discuss substantive restitution of Jewish property. Israel chose to remain apart from these negotiations, much to the dismay and consternation of the Committee.[169]

A Wall of Denial

The Austrian Government's stubborn refusal to confront its past and accept its responsibility for its national role in the Holocaust was, and has been, the hallmark of Austrian intransigence since 1945, having gone through a strong wave of denial of its wartime complicity in the Holocaust. Silencing of this complicity became an officially sanctioned program. It was not the Austrians' fault, went the argument, but the Nazis'.

American inaction, charged some in Congress, only abetted the cause. "Mr. Javits," H.A. Land of the State Department's Bureau of German Affairs wrote concerning the Congressman's complaints:

> indicated his astonishment that the United States Government, paying substantial amounts in aid to the Austrian Government, should be reduced to the position of

writing what he called a little letter of protest to the Austrian Government; that we could simply cut off or substantially reduce our aid.[170]

Javits' complaints while noted, were put aside by the State Department despite that fact that they were entirely appropriate in light of the its inaction, or even willful avoidance of the issue. As Robert Knight wrote, fear of the Soviet Union played a large role in policy.

> As the Cold War intensified Western authorities became increasingly reluctant to press even their own economic claims against the Austrian government, for fear of offering ammunition to the Russians.[171]

Yet, when it came to policy on Austria, especially regarding Jewish restitution, the Soviet Union was not the only source of concern to the State Department. The Middle East mattered as well. When Hashim Khalil, the Chargé d'Affaires of the Iraqi Embassy in Washington, DC visited the Near East Bureau in August 1953, R. Funkhauser, noted the degree of U.S. apprehension.

> The Charge' stated that he had been instructed to make representations to the Department of State concerning Austrian reparations to Israel. He referred to reports of alleged U.S. Government pressure on Austria and expressed the hope that the U.S. Government would not encourage the Austrian Government to pay reparations to Israel.
>
> Mr. Jernegan informed Mr. Khalil that the U.S. Government had exerted no influence on the Austrian Government, taken no position with respect to Austrian reparations payments, and contemplated none. Hope was expressed that this point could be clarified for the Baghdad Government in order to avoid misunderstanding of the U.S. Government role in this matter.
>
> The Charge' presented an aide memoir from his Government and was informed that a brief written response would be given to him.
>
> The Charge' stated that his Government would be most relieved by this information. The referred briefly to the hope which his Government held towards the new Administration's approach to NE problems.[172]

Concerns over the Middle East were an ever-present American worry. Nearly two years earlier, Abba Eban, it had been reported by American Embassy officials, had reassured his government that in regard to the pressure at the time put on the Germans for restitution, relations with the United States, "had improved with [the] growing realization that assistance to Israel [was] not responsible for [the] worsening of the Wests [sic] relations with Arab States."[173]

Austrian officials no doubt understood this American reticence. As such, they made the most of the chance they were given. Clinging at every turn to the Declaration of the 1943 Moscow Conference, the Austrian Government abided by the proclamation of their innocence in the face of the Nazi onslaught. As the Allies had declared, they were the Nazis' first victims. With this seal of their innocence, Austrian soldiers returning home were granted amnesty and pensions by legislation, despite the veto of these acts by the U.S. Occupation authorities. Half of the 34,000 of Austrian Nazis were sentenced for war crimes were pardoned along with 4,000 civil servants, leaving only fifty Nazis remaining in prison by 1964.[174] Regarding these pensions, James K. Penfield, the Deputy Chief of the American Embassy in Vienna wrote back to the State Department in March 1955:

> According to figures collected by the Jewish organizations, the Austrian Government has, between 1945 and 1955, paid victims of National Socialism two hundred and sixteen million schillings under the Victims Welfare Law and one hundred forty nine million schillings as compensation for detention. To former National Socialists, the Austrian Government has allegedly paid, during the same period, the amount of two thousand and twenty million schillings ... for salaries and pensions which had earlier been denied under post-1945 legislation.[175]

The Austrian government was actively and arrogantly disavowing its country's immediate past. To make matters worse, the Austrian Chancellor Julius Raab sought to delegitimize Jewish claims, boldly declaring in a radio broadcast at that time:

> I wish to premise that the Jewish world organizations only represent Jews by faith, but that in those times other persons too, and a large number of them at that, suffered persecution. Therefore, the restitution laws, which I will discuss later on, only refer to persons subjected to political persecution. No difference is made between so-called racial, religious, or other persecutees.[176]

The government then, was providing members of the Nazi Party with pensions, even offering advance payments to them, with the Chancellor vowing to work for greater benefits, while undermining the restitution claims of these pensioners' Jewish victims.[177] Their willful silencing of both their responsibility and the victims' suffering was an unforgivable double sin on their part, and as the delegates of the Fourth Plenary Assembly of the World Jewish Congress resolved in 1959, "[t]his unwarranted mitigation diminishes confidence in the sense of justice of the competent Austrian authorities."[178]

When the Committee presented its claim to the government, it met a wall of denial. " ... [T]he Finance Minister did not believe that this claim was properly presentable against Austria," wrote Moses W. Beckelman of the Committee. "The property in question had been taken to Germany and the claim should therefore be presented to Germany rather than to Austria," was the answer they received.[179]

Beckelman furthermore explained that Finance Minister Kamitz had met in the United States with Dr. Armand Eisler, a former Socialist member of the

Austrian Parliament and the Chairman of the Association of Former Concentration Camp Inmates in the United States, who opposed the work and aims of the Committee claiming that they were not wholly representative of all the claimants and that the Claims Conference itself had the goal of monopolizing all of the negotiations.[180] Eisler, the Minister assumed, represented yet another claim to the heirless property held in Austria. Eisler, however, according to Penfield, was "a rather senile, ambitious old man."[181] Penfield suggested that he was acting alone, yet Kamitz, inviting him to negotiate along with the Committee, elevated him in stature to that of another representative, and therefore another legitimate voice in the debate. Dr. Robert Weissenstein, the representative of yet another group of claimants, the Association of Jurists from Austria, told an Embassy officer that he believed there were cynical reasons for Kamitz to invite Eisler, namely to feign the idea of negotiating with the Jewish groups.[182]

Kamitz also denied there were only Jewish heirless assets, implying that to turn all heirless assets over to Jewish claimants, especially when there were ostensibly counter claims, would simply be unjust. There were also, others argued, "restitution victims," or those they claimed had bought Jewish property purely out of selfless acts of mercy for the escaping Jews who, in reality, were subjected to forced sales of valuable property for pennies on the dollar.[183] To punish them, the logic followed, would be manifestly unfair. Finally, Kamitz suggested, to put forth an "advance" of 25 million shillings toward the Committee's claim of 300 million Schillings to help the survivors, would equally be unjust for the same reasons.

As their position on restitution hardened, Austrian officials made it clear that there would be no further movement on the issue until the decision on the long-discussed State Treaty, re-establishing Austrian nationhood, a treaty the Allies and the Soviets would have to grant Austria.[184] Jewish organizations, however, felt they "had been taken for a ride," by Austrian officials. In a meeting in December 1953 with State Department officials, Blaustein, Rubin, Kagan, and others, explained that were the Austrians to be granted a State Treaty, effectively freeing them from occupation, American influence would be reduced and the chance for success lessened, not enhanced.[185] They and other groups worked to impress upon State the need to lock the Austrians into an obligation before the signing of a State Treaty granting them their independence.[186]

This assumption was probably correct, in as much it concerned waning U.S. pressure on Austria, seen in some quarters as predicated upon overall U.S. policy toward the Middle East. There was great consternation on the part of the Israeli Consul in Vienna, Eshel, toward this end when he suggested that the United States had "shifted its support to the Arab world." The flurry caused by the State Department reaction to the Iraqi complaint no doubt fed this feeling.

Furthermore, he told representatives of the Jewish groups negotiating with the Austrians that they could no " ... longer count on the support of the United States Element in Austria, saying that the objective of gaining the support of former National-Socialists was much more on the mind of the United States than the support of political persecutees of the Hitler era."[187] Eshel urged measures to "correct" the Austrian position and suggested retaliatory measures to aid that correction. Due to these and other statements, at the U.S. request to "keep [him] out of the matter," the Israeli Government quickly recalled him.[188]

On May 15, 1955, the Austrian Government was granted its long awaited State Treaty. In the process of being granted independence, Austria nevertheless committed to returning the property confiscated from victims following the *Anschluss*. In Article 26 of the State Treaty, Austria committed to:

> ... in all cases where property, legal rights or interests in Austria have since 13 March 1938, been subject of forced transfer or measures of sequestration, confiscation or control on account of the racial origin or religion of the owner, the said property shall be returned and the said legal rights and interests shall be restored together with their accessories. Where return or restoration is impossible, compensation shall be granted for losses incurred by reason of such measures to the same extent as is, or may be, given to Austrian nationals generally in respect of war damage.[189]

Following their independence, the Austria, as it said it would do, agreed on July 6, 1955, to seek the appropriation of 550 million shillings, or $22 million,[190] over a period of ten years to provide to Jewish organizations to pay to Austrian-born survivors. On February 15, 1956, the Aid Fund Law, providing for the settlement, was passed by the Austrian Parliament.

Despite Article 26, the Austrians held out and obstructed the issuance of claims by survivors, objecting to payments for tenancy rights, bank accounts, securities, life insurance policies, or funds paid in discriminatory taxes. In October 1957, following further negotiations, the Government budgeted another 100 million shillings, or slightly over $4 million toward compensation for properties not yet returned. By 1958, however, Raab on a visit to the United States, sought a definitive "end to Jewish claims," and achieved a commitment from the State Department, whose officials assured him that "the United States would not support any such action after a satisfactory settlement was reached."[191] U.S. pressure, if there was much of it on Austria at all, would cease.

On June 5, 1958, the Austrian Parliament passed the War Damage Compensation Law which granted payments of up to $2,700 per person for the loss of household goods, furniture, and other work-related equipment. The Committee objected to its inadequate funding.[192]

In February 1959, the Austrian Government proposed the creation of another fund of $6 million to cover the confiscation of bank accounts and other properties not covered under Article 26 claims.[193] Jewish groups sought to add political persecutees, but the State Department objected saying that their inclusion would dilute the overall fund. The groups had hoped this category would increase the value of the fund. On March 22, 1961, the Austrian Parliament passed the legislation creating the fund.

Gustav Jellinek, one of the Committee negotiators described the Austrian grant of restitution as "tiresome and nerve racking ... with repeated interruptions." That the Austrians committed to any type of payment, from the beginning, was surprising. In the end, their offer, they explained, was not conditioned upon any concept of guilt or responsibility, but was a purely voluntary contribution to the Jews. This minimizing of responsibility would be repeated later in the 1990s when countries and institutions would take the same tone in granting restitution and reparations to survivors again, "purely out of a recognition of their need," not out of responsibility. As Robert Knight explained:

> This continuing tension between officially propagated myth and authentic experience makes it doubtful whether in Austrian restitution had the kind of cathartic or educative effects claimed for it for the German Federal Republic ... [194]

In sum, Nahum Goldmann described the experience of negotiating with Austria when he wrote, that "[o]ur completely inadequate achievements in the negotiations with Austria are another impressive illustration of how much was achieved in the long years of negotiations with Germany."[195]

Denial and Dismissal

> "... our Company is not subject to any obligation with reference to the policies issued prior to World War II in central and Eastern European countries, where all its assets and branches were expropriated after the war."—Assicurazioni Generali, S.P.A. Insurance Company, 1998[196]

Double Victims

Survivors from Western Europe were the focus of the settlements with the FRG and Austria. They were also the subject of the Military Government laws and decrees issued in the occupation zones. Their possessions were subject to review and return. In Eastern Europe, newly liberated from Nazi rule, survivors now were subjected to Communist tyranny and were blocked from applying for restitution as well. Survivors in Eastern Europe were to become "double victims," surviving plunder and persecution by the Nazis, and then by the Communists as well.

Another aspect of silencing, so rampant in Europe after the Holocaust, came the institutional denial of return of assets. Survivors, as already described, were forgotten, ignored, marginalized, and subjected to a complete lack of respect in seeking the return of what was morally and legally theirs to claim and receive. In this manner, those surviving the Holocaust faced this deliberate form of silencing, through the denial of access to their assets, in three manners: first denial by institution; the second by denial through legislation and treaty; and third, denial by the very survivors themselves.

Denial by Nationalization

Remaking Eastern Europe in their own cast, the Soviet Union sought to replace the notion of private property with that of collectivist state ownership. Largesse was denied and the recapturing of the same was viewed as a sign of the bourgeois nobility. Companies, their properties, their interests, and assets, were all taken under the "protection" of the state, nationalized for the benefit of the "people." Insurance and banking firms, offering people protection through investments, were viewed as gouging the people and inherently untrustworthy. As such insurance firms in particular, " ... became victim of the notion that it was the state's obligation to provide for the protection of individuals as well as the society against accidental damages and losses."[197]

"We are in possession of your letter of the 25th last," wrote an official of the Insurance firm Riunione Adriatica Di Sicurta to Zikmund Schmerler of Montreal:

> and beg to inform you that after the war all private Insurance Companies operating in the Czechoslovakian Republik have been turned by specific law dispositions into a State property and the czechoslovakian [sic] portfolios of these Companies with the respective properties, representing the premium reserves set up in Czechoslovakia, have been transferred to a State Institute ... [198]

Mr. Schmerler was seeking the proceeds from an insurance policy held by his father Max, an agent of Riunione in Rachov, Czechoslovakia. Marta Druckerova Cornell was told the same thing by Riunione and by Assicurazioni Generali, S.p.A. as was Helen S. Weiss and Martin Stern.[199] Martha Saraffian claimed four policies issued by Victoria Zu Berlin, issued as well in Czechoslovakia.[200] George Goldberg and John C. L. Szekeres, on behalf of their grandfather, were denied their claims by Generali for policies issued in Hungary, as was Judith T. Karmi for a Hungarian-issued policy by Riunione for her father. Dr. Thomas Lys tried to claim the Warsaw-issued policy of Zygmut Lis from Riunione.[201]

What all these people shared in common was a stiff refusal by the numerous companies to fulfill their obligations to pay on the insurance policies of their customers. Companies based their refusals on the nationalizations, for which, admittedly, it was difficult for them to seek redress. As Generali declared fifty years later, " ... the racial laws of the Nazi and fascist era followed by the state-led expropriations of the Soviet-dominated regimes in Central and Eastern Europe ended, for all practical purposes, Generali's ability to do business there."[202] Nevertheless, as Generali's position stated, the nationalizations, directive acts against the companies,[203] directly effected those companies' customers for whom, without them, the companies would not exist. Thus, those denied the proceeds of their policies were being punished again (through directive speech acts just as the Nazis had done). The nationalizations became the chief excuse for not paying customers their rightful claims. Yet, legal opinions handed down against these denials did not support the companies' actions.

In a claim filed by the mother of Judith Karmi against the government of Hungary, the United States Foreign Claims Settlement Commission, despite ruling against her claim for properties in Hungary in addition to the insurance policy, explicitly declared:

> The claimant's right, if any, to collect under the policy, is against the *Riunione Adriatica di Sicurtá*, the principal assets of which were and are outside of Hungary. Consequently, the nationalization of the corporation's assets within Hungary, if that was the case, does not affect the claimant's right to collect from the corporation in Italy or any other country where the corporation has assets.[204]

Through Communist nationalization, thousands of survivors were deprived of the proceeds from the insurance policies left for them by their parents or others. When they needed these assets the most, specifically for reconstructing their lives after the Holocaust, they were unable to obtain them. Moreover, approaching the various Communist states for the assets was out of the question, as payments by them for expropriated properties were rare and usually done only at the international level between nations.

Denial by Bureaucracy

The denial of assets by bureaucracy was an all too common occurrence in the years following the war. Governments, threatened with the possibility of thousands of returning survivors, as we now know, worked in a few cases to accommodate them, but more often than not, worked even harder to place obstacles in their way. In one fashion, simple bureaucratic inefficiency, and a very real lack of due diligence, was a cause for the denial of claims. A very good example of this indifference was the claim of Charles Sonabend. The Sonabends fled their native Belgium in August 1942 and were smuggled into Switzerland. Betrayed soon after their arrival, the Swiss police deported them across the border into Vichy France. Charles and his sister were sent to Paris to be held for deportation to the East, an action which luckily failed to occur. His parents, however, were sent to Auschwitz where they died two weeks later. Parisian families shuttled the two children between them until the city was liberated in August 1944. Charles later traveled to the United Kingdom where he eventually made his home. Sabine resettled in Belgium[205]

What makes the Sonabend case unique is a police report written in 1963 based on files located in the Swiss Canton of Bern concerning the Sonabend's arrest that dark day in 1942. The report was precipitated by a request of the Federal Justice and Police Department in Bern by Charles' sister Sabine. She made the inquiry after hearing that the Swiss Parliament had mandated a search through the archives of the Swiss banks for account information only weeks before.[206]

On December 20, 1962, the Swiss Parliament passed legislation which ordered a search for Holocaust victims' assets in the banks and other financial institutions. Claimants had five years to submit their claim and the entire process would last ten years. With the expiration of the Disclosure Decree ten years later, Swiss authorities disclosed the finding of slightly more than 10.8 million Swiss francs, or slightly more than $2 million, belonging to 1,048 owners. Close to 7,000 people filed claims that went unfulfilled.[207]

While the report Sabine requested did not explain the whereabouts of the equivalent of close to $50,000 in assets in Swiss banks Simon Sonabend was thought to have deposited during the war in anticipation of their escape to that country, it did disclose that he had deposited the balance of funds owed a friend, $200 in the cantonal bank of Bern, thus providing proof not only of their deportation, but that funds were actually deposited in a Swiss bank on their behalf. This fact alone showed that even though a nominal sum, there was still money in a Swiss bank under his name and it should have merited a more in-depth search for additional accounts.

While it is surprising that the report was written nineteen years after the Sonabend's arrest and death, what is more astonishing is that it laid silently and was not found until 1996 when researchers from Swiss Television found the report in the Swiss Federal Archives. Sabine had not been notified of the results of her request. No action had been taken by Swiss officials to find any assets belonging to Simon Sonabend in 1942 or 1963, even after the Swiss Parliament passed a law to search through the banks—the very act which triggered the request for the report in the first place. After suing the Swiss Government for the deportation of their parents, Charles and Sabine Sonabend received compensation for this callous act when the government settled out of court with them for $116,000.[208] This bureaucratic inefficiency is yet another example of the silencing that occurred at the time.

Another case involves again, the Swiss banks, but with a different twist. In this case, a Hungarian survivor, Miklos Griesz, in 1947 met with officials at a branch of the Union Bank of Switzerland, where his father had placed assets in trust before dying in the Holocaust. Surprisingly, the bank acknowledged his claim, and that of his mother, to the assets of his father, even helping them in a reinvestment plan in blue chip stocks.[209]

In 1949, however, Griesz and his mother, feeling threatened in Hungary tried, like the Sonabends before them, to flee. The Grieszes tried in August to cross the border into Austria but were apprehended by the Hungarian Security Forces and returned to Budapest and imprisoned by the Secret Police, the AVH. During the interrogation of both him and his mother, Miklos Griesz was searched and papers detailing their Swiss accounts were found. In return for his mothers' freedom, he was forced to sign a letter AVH officers drafted for him dated August 6, 1949, and a second one dated six days later, instructing the UBS branch in Zurich to forward the sum of 100,000 Sfr. to Eltis Inc., in Zurich for "'goods delivery' and pay it without further notification."[210] No account number was listed, only a request to sell his securities, at the highest price possible, was made.

Upon payment to Eltis, Griesz's mother was released three weeks later. Griesz, himself, was interned for another eight months and then released to house arrest. In December 1956, following the Hungarian Revolution, both mother and son escaped Hungary fleeing to Austria as part of the flood of 150,000 refugees.[211] Immediately upon arriving in Vienna, Griesz contacted UBS about his assets but was told that, as per his instructions, they were liquidated and transferred to Eltis. He continued to try to get his assets back and sought legal remedy once he emigrated to the United States, engaging attorneys in New York to pursue the case.

All along, he claimed that there was evidence that UBS should have known that because of the timing of his request and the very nature of it—a transfer to a company—they should have had at least a suspicion as to transfer request's real origins, and it should not have been granted. Alas, forty-eight years after this duress letter was sent and acted upon, officials at UBS confessed, only after the strong protest and intervention of Senator Alfonse M. D'Amato's office:

> In response to your claims, we have recently uncovered a formerly classified document kept in the Swiss national archives that reports rumors that Eltis Corp. may have had some connection with the Hungarian Communist Party.[212]

While denying any wrongdoing for their actions, UBS agreed to advance Greisz the sum of close to $30,000 owing to the fact that "the actions of the Hungarian Government have deprived you of the benefit of the proceeds of your account for nearly fifty years."[213] The Hungarian Government, despite efforts to seek restitution from them, never provided Griesz with restitution.[214]

What is intriguing about these two cases is that in both instances claimants encountered a corporate bureaucracy that failed to do the minimum of due diligence on behalf of its clients. Officials acted with indifference, with no one even bothering to ask a question or perform the proper checks necessary to substantiate the facts. For the Sonabends, there was not so much as a proper search, even when the facts were at least enough to warrant further investigation. For the Grieszes, when the transfer request came into the bank, conversely and interestingly enough it was paid all too quickly, despite the obvious adverse situation in Europe at the time, with no one posing the slightest question. Both cases highlight an abrogation of duty and an outward display of silencing. They also lead us to another form of denial—denial by unduly high standards and changing standards of evidence.

Denial by Unduly High Standards and Changing Facts

When claims could not necessarily be denied in the initial phase, other methods of silencing were employed. When seeking either their own assets, or those of family members, claimants were presented with requests for evidence they could not meet. They also were forced to face changing standards of evidence to prove ownership over accounts, and differing stories as to their fate and existence. The rules of the game were changed in the middle and the cards were stacked against the claimants from the very beginning.

The burden of proof was always shifted to the survivors, who were viewed with casual contempt. As such, those claiming their assets were viewed as a nuisance. One opposition Swiss Parliamentarian, Gottlieb Duttweiler in a post-war meeting at the U.S. State Department, blithely referred to the claimants as "little people" who were not considered "politically interesting" and therefore unable to convince the Swiss government to work on their behalf.[215] Claimants had no standing and no power.

When claiming assets, survivors were forced to prove that they had been victimized. "As we pointed out on the telephone it is necessary to prove what has been confiscated," wrote Dr. H.E. Fabian of the United Restitution Organization to Kurt R. Grossmann. Grossman had fled for his life from Nazi Germany less than a month after Hitler ascended to power in Germany. "The burden of this proof is yours," Grossman was told, "and you have to give full evidence and proof."[216]

Some of the chief practitioners enforcing this burden on survivors were banks, particularly Swiss banks. One of their infamous practices was to request from heirs death certificates of their relatives in order to gain custody of their accounts. This was surely an impractical request for following the Holocaust, those who survived to claim accounts from their families were lucky if they knew the banks, or even the cities they were in, much less the account numbers. At times, they knew the banks, but when those like Estelle Sapir presented themselves to request the account, while its existence might well have been acknowledged, they were also peppered with questions as to place and date of death, facts rarely known by survivors.[217] The Nazis surely did not issue death certificates at concentration camps. Callous and insensitive, bankers sought information that claimants surely did not possess and could not have known.

Anna Magos, the wife of Johannes Rohony, who had included passbooks from other accounts in other banks in the safety deposit box of a Swiss bank, was asked by Swiss government officials participating in a 1962 search for accounts, if she knew of her late husband's various accounts. She was then queried on his friends and business acquaintances and other possible residences. As the examination progressed, government investigators would ask increasingly more detailed questions with the full knowledge that she did not know the answers. Instead of treating her with any kindness, much less understanding, she was interrogated and forced to prove a connection to assets that she simply could not establish. Faced with these unanswerable questions, she was denied the assets.[218]

Even when claimants possessing the necessary account numbers sought access to their accounts, as Anny and Kurk Kadisch of Erie, Pennsylvania did when they sought access to their accounts in July 1939, they were refused by the Swiss Bank Corporation out of hand because the query was made by their attorney and not them.[219]

Alfred Selden, who sought the account proceeds of two of his uncles' accounts in Credit Suisse in the late 1930s, used a letter from one of them in an unsuccessful effort to secure his safe passage out of Germany by smugglers. After Selden safely emigrated to the U.S. in 1938, he waited until after the war to inquire, with another signed letter, about the account. In notifying the bank with the proper account name and number enclosed in the letter, he was informed that there was indeed an account, but that it had been assessed fees during the war years and that the account balance was insufficient.[220] In 1997, however, Selden was advised by Credit Suisse that they had no record of the account. Selden's case is one of many in which the standards changed along with the facts about the assets, and the claimants were the ones on the losing side in the effort.[221]

While institutions proved to be great practitioners of silencing through denial, governments were no less guilty of the same doing so through directive speech acts such as legislation. Worse, when acting in concert through an institutionally derived directive speech act, such as a treaty, silencing was not only spread, but legitimized through institutional acceptance.

Denial by Legislation and Treaty

Denial had been described thus far as the province of individual nations and institutions. Yet, when nation contracted with another nation in the form of a treaty, the denial of assets took on another more complicated form.

Treaties designed to manipulate the use of assets of Holocaust victims, either by actual commission or simple omission, placed the fate of these assets as a commodity, a bargaining chip to be used by the possessor nation as leverage with another in order to gain economic or political advantage. Nowhere was this more true than with a series of treaties negotiated in different stages between Switzerland and her eastern European neighbors.

The Swiss Indemnification Treaties

On June 25, 1949, the Government of Switzerland settled with the Communist Government of Poland on a treaty to indemnify Swiss citizens whose properties were nationalized by Poland only a year earlier. In an exchange of letters between Max Troendle of the Swiss Trade Ministry and head of the Swiss delegation, and Leon Kurowski, Chairman of the Polish Financial Delegation, the agreement was laid out. After a lapse of five years from the implementation of the agreement, Swiss banks would close the accounts and liquidate the insurance policies of Polish citizens missing since May 9, 1945. The balance of these accounts, and the proceeds from the liquidation of the victims' insurance policies as well, would then be deposited in the Swiss National Bank under the control of the National Bank of Poland.[222] At that point, Swiss businessmen could then apply for, and receive, compensation for their nationalized property in Poland—out of the accumulated sum of the assets of Polish Holocaust victims.

On July 19, 1950, a similar treaty with Communist Hungary was made. There, too, Swiss businessmen would be compensated for their nationalized property out of Hungarian Holocaust victims' assets.

Swiss negotiators later concluded deals with the Communist Governments of Czechoslovakia, Bulgaria, Yugoslavia, and Romania. In all these efforts, compensation for Swiss citizens was the goal. In the treaties accomplished after the Polish and Hungarian agreements, however, assets were not the payment option. Payment for imports from the respective countries was balanced off against the various debts incurred. Yet, in the case of Czechoslovakia, the Swiss first promised, then reneged after the Prague spring of 1968, on a provision to inform that country of any accounts that would later be found.[223]

The National Treatment of Assets

The Swiss were following a concept that, like with the Paris Treaty of 1946, called for the "national treatment of assets." In 1946, as in these treaties, the concept was simple: the assets should be returned to the nation from which the original owner, if deceased, was a citizen. At Paris, the responsibility for appropriating the respective share of assets to private claimants was to rest with that country. For the Swiss, this precedent proved to be quite useful in that through the consideration of the assets on the territorial basis, they could then take control of them. While in the hearts and minds of the Jewish groups working so hard to obtain them, the goal was to apply these funds to the displaced refugees in Europe, the Swiss had other thoughts in mind.[224]

The Swiss, and their Polish and Hungarian treaty partners, concluded arrangements that, beyond the cynical nature of their composition, violated, at the very least, Swiss banking laws forbidding the disclosure by the banks of assets of account holders to anyone, including the government. That ban, however, was flagrantly violated in these treaties. Banks that were forbidden from surrendering access to their holdings did so across the board by nationality, all in the name of paying damages its own citizens suffered due to the nationalization of their properties. Those whose insurance policies were denied to them for the same reason, were not as lucky. In concert with these countries, Swiss illegalities were institutionalized and normalized. In the end, Switzerland simply gave these assets away, placing them far outside the reach of claimants and heirs.

The London Debt Treaty of 1953

The Swiss were not the only participants in the process of the deprivation of reparations to survivors. On September 27, 1953, the Allies and the FRG signed a treaty aimed at recouping Germany's external debt resulting from both World Wars. The negotiations for the treaty were progressing at the same time as the negotiations between Israel and the Claims Conference with the FRG. German negotiators were keenly aware of the importance of a satisfactory conclusion of the reparations talks on those concerning the Debt Treaty. As such, the conclusion of both sets of negotiations went a long way toward the shoring up of the German economic position. Yet, as important as that was, there were aspects to the treaty that very negatively impacted the welfare of the surviving forced laborers of the Third Reich.

In Article 5, Sections 2 and 3 of the Treaty, entitled "Claims Excluded from the Agreement, the Allies agreed to the following:

2) Consideration of claims arising out of the second World War by countries which were at war with or were occupied by Germany during that war, and by nationals of such countries, against the Reich and agencies of the Reich, including costs of German occupation, credits acquired during occupation on clearing accounts and claims against the Reichskreditkassen shall be deferred until the final settlement of the problem of reparation.
3) Consideration of claims, arising during the second World War, by countries which were not at war with or occupied by Germany during that war, and by nationals of such countries, against the Reich and agencies of the Reich, including credits acquired on clearing accounts, shall be deferred until the settlement of these claims can be considered in conjunction with

> the settlement of the claims specified in paragraph (2) of this Article (except in so far as they may be settled on the basis of, or in connection with, agreements which have been signed by the Governments of the French Republic, the United Kingdom of Great Britain and Northern Ireland and the United States of America and the Government of any such country.) [sic][225]

Private claims against Germans then, as done at Paris seven years earlier, were forbidden. This time, however, there would not be another opportunity for restitution for the foreseeable future. As Michael Pinto-Duschinsky wrote of the treaty:

> At the time, Germany was divided into two states, one Communist, the other anti-Communist. There was no prospect of any end to the Cold War; it seemed unlikely that there could be a 'final settlement' of the War, since this would require agreement between all the victorious Allies, including the Soviet Union.[226]

Governments and corporations, in concert, had, before and during the Cold War, worked assiduously to avoid providing restitution and reparations to survivors.[227] Throughout the post-war recovery period, German negotiators participated in another form of silencing—silencing of their progress toward economic recovery. By denying, to the Allies, by assertions to the contrary, the true extent of their recovery, the FRG could plead poverty and lower the levels of reparations both demanded of, and agreed to, by them.[228] Any reparations claim then, that was considered too high would, as the warnings went, end up being financed by the American and other Allied taxpayers in the form of even higher aid to Germany, a politically unfeasible request. Indeed, this fear was placed by State Department officials at the feet of Israeli diplomats causing great consternation as they developed their claims against Germany, thereby limiting property restitution.

While restitution might not have been complete, it was nevertheless, the goal of U.S. policy. With the Cold War, however, restitution became less achievable and more of a weapon to be used by the source countries of restitution in the service of denial—denial of the past, the crimes of the Holocaust, and, quite simply, the very real inconveniences of the process itself. With restitution becoming inconvenient for political, economic, and to some, psychological reasons, that weapon was wielded by institutions, governments, and even the recipients with some effectiveness.

Denial by Recipients

Israel

Upon the formation of the state of Israel, the policy regarding Germany was summarized simply as "lack of contact." Israeli passports bore the inscription,

" ... not valid for Germany."[229] The reception of Germany in Israeli eyes was hostile. "In Israel," as Ambassador Uri Lubrani remembered of the 1950s:

> the memories of the Holocaust were fresh, deeply painful and vivid for a very meaningful number of citizens, and, therefore, the deep abhorrence and hatred of anything German, of any contact with Germany, deeply repentant as the voices emerging from there may have been at the time, was totally unacceptable. Actually, I do not believe that even at that time those totally anti-anything German people, constituted an absolute majority in the country yet there "*crie de ceur*" certainly was most compelling, vociferous and deeply emotional.[sic][230]

Apart from the size of the opposition, there was no argument as to its depth. Nahum Goldmann wrote that "[r]arely has an issue so divided the Jewish people." As such, there was a sizeable number of Jews in the Diaspora, and in Israel, that believed that to accept money from the Germans was to accept "blood money." Many times, Goldmann wrote, "[t]he discussion was carried on with great passion and ... during those months I required the protection of bodyguards, both in Israel, where I spent a lot of time, and during my travels in Europe and America."[231]

While the leaders of Israel and the Diaspora leaders, as represented in the Claims Conference, wholeheartedly supported negotiation, those opposing it made their feelings clear. Menachem Begin, the former leader of the Irgun, the group that fought to force British troops out of Mandatory Palestine, was one who bitterly opposed the idea of negotiating. Begin's protests against the Knesset's approval of the right to openly negotiate with the FRG had to be put down with tear gas. His Herut Party daily, on the same day as the Knesset vote on negotiation, reprinted a quote from Maimonides. "And one should take care not to take ransom from a murderer even if he gives all the money in the world and even if the blood avenger wishes to absolve him, since the soul of the victim is not the property of the avenger but the property of the Holy One, Blessed Be He."[232] As Neima Barzel has written, for Begin, "[t]he all-too-real threat from Germany against every Jew as an individual must be countered by unity in the hatred of Germans on the part of all Jews."[233]

Those opposed to negotiations with Germany did so out of the belief that to speak with, or even meet with, Germans was an indignity repugnant to the memory of those lost in the Holocaust. As the very existence of Israel was based upon the Holocaust, to negotiate with Germans, even for indemnification for suffering of the Holocaust, was to accept them as equals and, in essence, was as good as silencing the cries of the millions who were slaughtered. Both right and left in Israel used strong, emotion-laden language to ascribe the most vile of intentions to the German people. The difference in the tactics, however, were such that Ben-Gurion and his supporters used the assertive language to support the acceptance of reparations and Begin and his supporters used assertive language to oppose them.[234]

The Individual Survivor

"I have read or been told on many occasions," wrote Morris Krakowsky, "that we should tell our children all about it. How do you 'tell' a child or young teenager without poisoning their outlook on life? Must the children of survivors bear a heavier burden than the children of those who did not go through the hell? This is a terrible burden."[235]

For survivors like Krakowsky, questions like this were always a horrible choice. Survivors were always reluctant to talk about the Holocaust. They were reluctant to talk about the concentration camps, the suffering, the loss. They grieved for their loved ones, and they did not want to pass that pain onto another generation.

Many after the war, having tried to obtain their assets, went first went through the torture of coming to terms with such horrific human losses, then having to overcome the opposition presented to them by the authorities from whom they sought their family's assets, or even their own. Having been weakened so much by the effects of the war, the guilt, and the "sense of total helplessness and powerlessness," they kept it all in, silencing themselves and, as a result, gave up on trying to get the assets back.[236]

As Nancy Potter found, "[t]he initial harm done to a victim of violence is exacerbated when the audience fails to give uptake to the victim's experiences. ... The ability to perform speech acts of certain kinds can be a mark of political power. To put the point crudely," she wrote:

> powerful people can generally do more, say more, and have their speech count for more than can the powerless. If you are powerful, there are more things you can do with your words. ... If you are powerful, you sometimes have the ability to silence the speech of the powerless. ... But there is another, less dramatic but equally effective, way. Let them speak. Let them say whatever they like to whomever they like, but stop that speech from counting as action. More precisely, stop it from counting as the action it was intended to be.[237]

Some survivors like Jacques Neuville pressed his claim for his assets and bravely fought on to no avail, having been silenced by the practices created for the purpose of denying access to assets. Having given up when the fight dragged on for too long, Neuville, with the help of his family, reinstituted his fight in the 1990s.[238]

Others like Paul Baer, having given up on his efforts toward regaining the assets his family invested with the firm Fahnestock in Germany, passed the account information to his accountant before he died in 1972. The accountant, Charles Berg kept the information until he died in 1993 and the file passed on to his son who subsequently contacted Baer's son.[239]

While so many survivors had lost assets, they felt that the hurdles placed by governments and institutions alike after the war were so great it was nearly impossible to overcome them. As for the banks and other institutions holding assets, they preferred to not deal with the problem at all. As the Paris office of the American Jewish reported in 1952 regarding the Swiss banks' wishes with regard to heirless assets, "The attitude of the banks shows little comprehension of the total problem. ... The banks would keep the heirless assets."[240]

With requests for death certificates, impossible questions to answer posed, undue government regulations, restrictions, and overriding priorities, the survivors had few options at their disposal, and even fewer friends outside of the handful of Jewish organizations that were stretched thin by overwhelming priorities. Most survivors, although believing that while these assets were all that was left of their family, felt that moving on and starting a new life was more important and put this sad chapter behind them. As Morris Krakowsky had expressed, the hope that the sympathy of the world would be with them was an illusion. For them, their wait would last the duration of the Cold War.

* * *

While it was, indeed, the Cold War that laid the heaviest burden on the story of U.S. policy on restitution, it was also the key to its solution. With the fall of Communism in Eastern Europe and later the Soviet Union, the silencing would end and change would begin. Through the instigation of governmental and non-governmental officials and groups, a campaign was begun to recapture and return that which was cruelly taken from victims, survivors, and heirs.

Moreover, those countries, neutrals in particular, and institutions alike, that so artfully silenced their roles in, and their claimants from, the war, would now find that these tactics would no longer work. The campaign for the truth about the assets of Holocaust victims and their heirs would go public, using different tactics in a different international political climate. This campaign would spread across the United States and Europe, ending the silence of both governments and survivors alike, giving voice to long-withheld claims for justice that resulted in a measure of restitution for those deprived for so long.

Notes

1. Krakowsky, p. 26.
2. "What Germ P.W.s think about the war," p. 3.
3. Earl F. Zeimke, "Reckonings With the Past," in *The U.S. Army in the Occupation of Germany, 1944-1946*, Army Historical Series, Center of Military History (Washington, DC: United States Army, 1975), p. 380.
4. Letter of J. Webb Benton, Chargé d'Affaires, a.i. The American Embassy, The Hague, to the Secretary of State, August 15, 1946, RG 84, Records of the Foreign Posts, Department of State, Hague Legation, 711.7 - 841.5, NARA, Box 39, NARA, p. 1.
5. Clay, pp. 236-237.
6. *Summary of Multipartite Agreements & Disagreements on Germany*, Part I, Second Revised & Supplemented Edition, 15 Sept 1948, Prepared by CFM Secretariat, Civil Administration Division, Office of Military Government for Germany (US), RG

466, HICOG Historical Division, Publications Relating to the U.S. Occupation of Germany, NARA, Box 1, p. 85.

7. Walter Isaacson and Evan Thomas, *The Wise Men, Six Friends and the World They Made, Acheson, Bohlen, Harriman, Kennan, Lovett, McCloy* (New York: Simon and Schuster, 1986), p. 238.
8. Zeimke, p. 381.
9. Hannah Arendt, "German Guilt," (January 1945), in *Jewish Frontier Anthology, 1934-1944* (New York: Jewish Frontier Association, 1945), p. 470.
10. Clay, pp. 67-68.
11. Arthur D. Kahn, *Betrayal, Our Occupation of Germany* (New York: Beacon Service Co., 1950), p. 171.
12. Cited in Kai Bird, *The Chairman, John J. McCloy, The Making of the American Establishment* (New York: Simon & Schuster, 1992), p. 237.
13. Ibid, p. 309.
14. Clay, p. 70.
15. Coral Bell, "Normative Shift," *The National Interest* (Winter 2002/03), p. 48.
16. "Viner Memorandum on the 'Colonial Problem,' " Memo of Rupert Emerson to Lauchlin Currie, June 19, 1944, RG 169, Records of the Foreign Economic Administration, BEW, OEW Executive Director, Entry 128, August 1944 -October 1945, Box 62, NARA.
17. See "The Red Army on the Eve of Barbarossa," in Nikita Khrushchev, *Khrushchev Remembers*, trans. and ed. By Strobe Talbott (Boston: Little, Brown and Company, 1970), pp. 157-164.
18. An example of this popular new practice is Robert Crowley, ed. *What If?, The World's Foremost Military Historians Imagine What Might Have Been* (New York: G.P. Putnam's Sons, 1999).
19. Williamson Murray, "Barbarossa," in Robert Cowley, ed., *No End Save Victory, Perspectives on World War II* (New York: G.P. Putnam's Sons, 2001), p. 108.
20. James Bowman, "What Happened to Honor?," *The Bradley Lecture*, American Enterprises Institute, June 10, 2002, available online at
21. Serge Schmemann, "Us and Them, The Burden Of Tolerance In a World of Division," *New York Times*, December 29, 2002, Section 4, p. 1.
22. W. James Booth, "Communities of Memory: On Identity, Memory and Debt," *American Political Science Review*, Vol. 93, No. 2 (June 1999), p. 251.
23. Ibid, p. 254.
24. Judith Miller, "Erasing the Past, Europe's Amnesia About the Holocaust," *New York Times Magazine*, November 16, 1986, p. 32.
25. Bauman, p. 25.
26. Michael Walzer, "The Present of the Past," book review of *The Ethics of Memory*, by Avishai Margalit, *New Republic*, January 20, 2003, p. 36.
27. Booth, p. 259.
28. Cited in Bird, p. 336.
29. Priority Message of McCloy to Henry Byroade, U.S. Department of State, April 25, 1950, RG 466, HICOG, Top Secret McCloy Papers, 1949-1952, Box 2, NARA.
30. Jeannine Gramick, "Silencing no safeguard of truth; discussion of controversial issues," *National Catholic Reporter*, July 27, 2001, No. 35, Vol. 37; Pg. 22.
31. Oral History Interview with Nathan M. Becker, by Richard D. McKinzie, Harry S. Truman Presidential Library, June 19, 1973, available online at www.trumanlibrary.org.
32. Eyes Only Message from the Secretary of State to McCloy, June 21, 1950, RG 466, HICOG, Top Secret McCloy Papers, 1949-1952, Box 2, NARA.

33. American intelligence officials tracked the movement of a number of German scientists out of Europe, through Switzerland, Spain, Portugal, and Italy to South America, and in one case the movement of 150 technicians to India, via Switzerland. See, 820.02, Flights of Germans to Latin America, RG 84, Records of the Foreign Posts of the Department of State, American Legation, Bern, 1940-49, 1948: 811.3-820.02, Box 68, NARA; and numerous other documents from the same box on the same topic.
34. Memorandum of Samuel Klaus to Mr. Panuch, "German Immigration," June 20, 1946, RG 59, Aircraft Accidents Files, 194460, Lot File 64D551, Box 103, NARA, p.1.
35. Ibid.
36. Samuel Klaus, "German Scientists Program," Memorandum to the Files, July 17, 1947, RG 59, Aircraft Accidents Files, 194460, Lot File 64D551, Box 105, NARA, p.1.
37. Memorandum of Samuel Klaus to Mr. Langer, "Immigration of German Specialists, July 15, 1946, RG 59, Aircraft Accidents Files, 194460, Lot File 64D551, Box 103, NARA.
38. Ibid.
39. Dr. Efraim Zuroff, "Worldwide Investigation and Prosecution of Nazi War Criminals (January 1, 2001 - March 31, 2002)," Simon Wiesenthal Center, Jerusalem, April 2002, p. 1.
40. Since 1979, 71 Nazi war criminals have been stripped of their U.S. citizenship and 57 have been removed from the country by the Office of Special Investigations of the U.S. Department of Justice. See, "Federal Immigration Judge Orders Deportation of Castskills Man Who Served as Nazi Camp Guard," Press Release, Office of Special Investigations, United States Department of Justice, October 25, 2002.
41. Guy Lee, ed., *Documents on Field Organization of the Office of the U.S. High Commissioner for Germany, 1949-1951*, Historical Division, Office of the Executive Secretary, Office of the U.S. High Commissioner for Germany, 1952, RG 466, Records of the High Commissioner for Germany, Historical Division, Publications Relating to the U.S. Occupation of Germany, Box 3, NARA, p. 1.
42. Isaacson and Thomas, p. 135.
43. Statement of U.S. High Commissioner, Landsberg, A Documentary Report, Office of the US High Commissioner for Germany, January 31, 1951, RG 466, Records of the High Commissioner for Germany, General Records, 1949-1952, 321.5-6, Box 12, NARA, p. 3.
44. Taylor, p. 170.
45. Office Memorandum, "Case of Friedrich Flick," Office of the High Commissioner for Germany, RG 466, Records of the High Commissioner for Germany, General Records, 1949-1952, Bonn, Box 13, NARA, p. 1.
46. Incoming Message of American Embassy in London to the Office of the U.S. High Commissioner for Germany, October 2, 1952, RG 466, Records of the High Commissioner for Germany, General Records, 1949-1952, 321.5-6, Box 12, NARA.
47. Ibid, p. 4.
48. Benjamin B. Ferencz, *Less Than Slaves, Jewish Forced Labor and the Quest for Compensation* (Cambridge, Massachusetts: Harvard University, 1979), p. 75.
49. Letter of Most Rev. A. J. Muench, Bishop of Fargo, Regent, Apostolic Nunciature in Germany, to John J. McCloy, U.S. High Commissioner for Germany, December 19, 1949, RG 466, Records of the High Commissioner for Germany, General Records, 1949-1952, 321.5-6, Box 12, NARA.
50. B.D. Kimpel, Memorandum, "Re-examination of Austrian Policy in the Light of the Korean War," RG 59, Records of the Department of State, Miscellaneous Files, Files

relating to the Austrian Occupation and Peace Treaty, 1949-1955, Box 8, NARA, pp. 1-2.

51. Ibid, pp. 2-3.
52. Priority Message, Department of the Army to Mr. McCloy, June 28, 1950, RG 466, HICOG, Top Secret McCloy Papers, 1949-1952, Box 2, NARA.
53. William Manchester, *The Arms of Krupp, 1587-1968* (Boston, MA: Little, Brown and Company, 1968), pp. 641-642.
54. Isaacson and Thomas, p. 517.
55. Ibid.
56. Cable of Secretary of State Dean Acheson to McCloy, August 2, 1950, RG 466, HICOG, Top Secret McCloy Papers, 1949-1952, Box 2, NARA.
57. Thomas Alan Schwartz, *America's Germany, John J. McCloy and the Federal Republic of Germany* (Cambridge, MA: Harvard University Press, 1991), p. 127.
58. Ibid.
59. W. C. Haraldson, Memorandum for the Record, "Paris Discussions on the Marshall Plan, August 4 to August 6, 1947," RG 84, Records of the Foreign Posts of the United States, U.S. Political Advisor in Berlin, Top Secret Correspondence, 1944-1949, Box 1, NARA, p. 4.
60. "Trials of Suspected German War Criminals," Outward Telegram from Commonwealth Relations Office, July 13, 1948, Ministry of Defense, United Kingdom courtesy, Office of Special Investigations, United States Department of Justice.
61. Schwartz, p. 169.
62. Office Memorandum of John Bross, Office of the High Commissioner for Germany, January 19, 1950, RG 466, Records of the High Commissioner for Germany, General Records, 1949-1952, 321.5-6, Box 13, NARA, p.3.
63. "The House that Krupp Rebuilt," *Time*, August 19, 1957, p. 69.
64. On December 23, 1959, Krupp Industries agrees to a supplemental lump sum payment of DM 6 million, which later grew to a total of DM 10.1 million, for slave laborers. See, Translation of Agreement between Alfried Krupp von Bohlen und Halbach and the Conference on Jewish Material Claims Against Germany, December 23, 1959, RG 59, Office of the Legal Adviser, Office of Educational, Cultural and Public Affairs, Subject Files, 1945-1997, Lot File 96D244, Box 40, NARA; Michael Pinto-Duschinsky, *Nazi Slave Labour: The Unfinished Campaign for Compensation, A Preliminary Account* (London, United Kingdom: The Holocaust Educational Trust, December 1998), p. 19.
65. Letter of John McCloy to Eleanor Roosevelt, March 12, 1951, RG 466, Records of the High Commissioner for Germany, General Records, 1949-1952, 321.5-6, Box 12, NARA, p. 1.
66. Ibid, p. 3.
67. HICOG Secret Emergency Message from Berlin to Frankfurt, October 7, 1950, RG 466, HICOG, Top Secret McCloy Papers, 1949-1952, Box 3, NARA.
68. HICOG Routine Message, Bonn to Frankfurt, October 21, 1950, RG 466, HICOG, Top Secret McCloy Papers, 1949-1952, Box 3, NARA.
69. HICOG Top Secret Message, Acheson to McCloy, December 14, 1950, RG 466, HICOG, Top Secret McCloy Papers, 1949-1952, Box 3, NARA.
70. "Reparations," Draft Paper, April 1945, attached in a memorandum from Assistant Secretary of the Treasury, Harry Dexter White to W.L. Clayton of the State Department, James Perkins of FEA, General J.H. Hilldring of the War Department, Isador Lubin of the White House, and Francis X. Downey of the Navy Department, April 10, 1945, RG 84, Records of the Foreign Posts of the United States, U.S. Political Advisor in Berlin, Top Secret Correspondence, 1944-1949, Box 1, NARA, p. 2.

71. Marshall - Harriman Conversations, December 8, 1948, United States Department of State, RG 84, Records of the Foreign Posts of the United States, U.S. Political Advisor in Berlin, Top Secret Correspondence, 1944-1949, Box 1, NARA, TAB 5.
72. Acheson, p. 229.
73. Clark Clifford with Richard Holbrooke, *Counsel to the President, A Memoir* (New York: Random House, 1991), p. 145.
74. Oral History Interview with W. Averell Harriman [sic], by Richard D. McKinzie and Theodore A. Wilson, Harry S. Truman Presidential Library, 1971, available online at www.trumanlibrary. org/oralhist/harriman.htm.
75. Interview with Seymour Rubin, Washington, DC. December 17, 2002.
76. Ibid.
77. Rickman, p. 12.
78. Letter of James H. Mann, Treasury Department Representative in the American Embassy in Bern to Harry D. White, Assistant Secretary, Records from the United States Department of Treasury delivered to the Office of Senator Alfonse M. D'Amato, October 1996.
79. Ibid.
80. Letter of John Edgar Hoover, Director of the FBI to Assistant Director K. J. Connelley, August 25, 1941, delivered to the Office of Senator Alfonse M. D'Amato, December 1996.
81. Letter of D.W. Bell to Harry L. Hopkins, September 14, 1944, RG 131, Foreign Funds Control, General Records, NARA.
82. Two of Seymour Rubin's deputies at the State Department at the time of the first treaty with Switzerland, Walter S. Surrey and Otto F. Fletcher, accepted a decision beyond their control regarding the settlement with Switzerland. They wrote in a memo, declassified only in December 1996:

    "We were compelled to strike a bargain with the Swiss for reasons which are known to you, in spite of the fact that we knew that figure reached with them was far below the figure of looted gold acquired by them—far below even the Belgian looted gold acquired by them, the amount of which was exactly known at the time. So far there is in the drafts no legal ground on which to fight the Swiss and the appeal to their "morality and justice" was made in an exhaustive manner at the time of the negotiations, the results of which are known to you." See, Inter-Office Memorandum of W.S. Surrey and O.F. Fletcher, United States Department of State, 17 March 1947, RG 59, Department of State Office of Financial Operations, Entry NN3-59-69-59, Box 23, NARA.
83. Seymour Rubin, "Swedish Negotiations With Respect to German External Relations," July 24, 1946, RG 59, Records of the Department of State, Decimal File 1945-1949, 80.515/7/3046, Box 4212, NARA.
84. Research Memorandum of R. Simons to Mr. Knoke, Federal Reserve, August 9, 1946, delivered to the Office of Senator Alfonse M. D'Amato, 1996.
85. Letter of Francis McCombe to R.C. Goodchild, British Foreign Office, May 21, 1947, F 3371/67901 xc/A61253, Public Records Office, London; Rickman, pp. 112, 247.
86. Rickman, p. 111.
87. Stuart E. Eizenstat, *U.S. and Allied Wartime and Postwar Relations and Negotiations With Argentina, Portugal, Spain, Sweden, and Turkey on Looted Gold and German External Assets and U.S. Concerns About the Fate of the Wartime Ustasha Treasury* (Washington, D.C.: Government Printing Office, June 1998), pp. 75-81; hereafter known as Eizenstat II.

88. Letter of Francis McCombe to G.H. Villiers, November 15, 1947, T236/1449, Public Records Office, London.
89. Ibid.
90. Abbott to the Foreign Office, January 25, 1947, OF 837/1159 xc/A61253, Public Records Office, London, p. 2.
91. Ibid.
92. Stirling to the Foreign Office, October 5, 1946, Public Records Office, London.
93. Eizenstat II, pp. 45-58.
94. Letter of Ambassador Lincoln MacVeagh to the Secretary of State, "De-blocking of German Assets Earmarked for Refugee Purposes: Visit of Mr. Seymour Rubin to Lisbon and Embassy Assistance, August 8, 1949, RG 59, Records of the State Department, 800.515, Box 4257, NARA.
95. Eizenstat II, p. 48.
96. Ibid, p. 54.
97. J. Scullen, Memorandum for the Files on the Safehaven Meeting of March 9, 1945, RG 131, Foreign Funds Control, Safehaven General Correspondence, Box 382, NARA.
98. Nahum Goldmann, *The Autobiography of Nahum Goldmann, Sixty Years of Jewish Life* (New York: Holt, Rinehart, Winston, 1969), p. 252.
99. Letter of Dale B. Maher, American Vice Consul, American Consulate, Paramaribo, Surinam, June 2, 1947, RG 59, Records of the State Department, Refugees, 840.48 Refugees 12-146-840.48 Refugees /3-1247, Box 5698, NARA.
100. "Memorandum for the Files, Visit to Aden of Mr. Harry Viteles," January 1948, report accompanying Letter of Charles C. Sidney, Jr. American Consul, Aden, Arabia to the Secretary of State, June 18, 1948, RG 59, Records of the State Department, Refugees, 840.48 Refugees 12-146-840.48 Refugees /3-1247, Box 5697, NARA; Letter of Ely E. Palmer, Legation of the United States in Kabul, Afghanistan to the Secretary of State, May 30, 1947, RG 59, Records of the State Department, Refugees, 840.48 Refugees 12-146-840.48 Refugees /3-1247, Box 5698, NARA.
101. Clifford recalled " ... the thunder clouds gathering—Marshall's face getting redder and redder." Cited in David McCullough, *Truman* (New York: Simon & Schuster, 1992), p. 615.
102. Clifford, p. 11.
103. Letter of Ambassador Arye Levavi to Gregg Rickman, February 12, 1988.
104. Letter of Ambassador Walter Eytan to Gregg Rickman, February 12, 1988.
105. Walter Laqueur, *Generation Exodus, The Fate of Young Jewish Refugees from Nazi Germany* (Hanover, New Hampshire: Brandeis University Press, 2001), p. 247.
106. Marrus, p. 335. Forty years later, after the end of the Cold War, descendants of those returning would again come to claim their properties.
107. Chief, Dissemination Branch, SO, to Major D. T. Kellett, War Department Intelligence Division, October 30, 1946, RG 319, Army Intelligence ID Files, 110-317451 to 317650, Box 2090, NARA, p. 4; Vincent La Vista, "Illegal Emigration Movements in and Through Italy," otherwise known as "The La Vista Report," RG 59, Records of the State Department, 800.0128/5-154, NARA, p. 3..
108. Letter of M. Schenkolewski to Eleanor Roosevelt, November 29, 1946, RG 59, Records of the State Department, Refugees, 840.48 Refugees 12-146-840.48 Refugees /3-1247, Box 5697, NARA.
109. American Joint Distribution Committee, "Budget and Research Report No. 48, Annual Report of the JDC in Poland for 1947," June 1, 1948, RG 59, Records of the State Department, Refugees, 840.48 Refugees 12-146-840.48 Refugees /3-1247, Box 5699, NARA, p. 3.

110. Letter of Ugo Carusi, Commissioner of Immigration, United States Department of Justice to the Secretary of State, January 22, 1947, RG 59, Records of the State Department, Refugees, 840.48 Refugees 12-146-840.48 Refugees /3-1247, Box 5697, NARA.
111. Telegram, Tyler to the State Department, August 20, 1951, RG 84, Records of the American Embassy in Tel Aviv, 1950-52, 350-360, Box 9, NARA.
112. Rabbi Harris L. Selig, *The Eternal Fount* (New York: Hebrew Publishing Company, 1941), p. 268.
113. Goldmann, p. 251.
114. Letter of Chaim Weizman to the Secretary of State, September 20, 1945, RG 59, Records of the State Department, 740.00119 EW/9-2045, Box 3667, NARA, pp. 2-3.
115. Memorandum of Rabbi Philip S. Bernstein, Advisor on Jewish Affairs to the Theater Commander to General Joseph T. McNarney, July 1, 1946, RG 260, Records of the Office of Military Government of the United States in Germany, 1944-1950, Box 12, NARA, p. 2.
116. Letter of President Harry S. Truman to Edwin W. Pauley, United States Representative, Allied Reparations Commission, August 12, 1947, White House Central Files, Harry S. Truman Library, Appendices, Eizenstat I.
117. Letter of Jacob Blaustein, President of the American Jewish Committee to Henry Byroade, Director, Bureau of German Affairs, Department of State, September 11, 1950, RG 59, Records of the State Department, 262.0041/9-1150, 1950-1054, Box 1044, NARA, p. 2.
118. Ibid, p. 6.
119. Max Isenburgh, Memorandum to the Files, "Restitution and Related Matters," November 17, 1948, AJC Records, Series FAD, 1941-1946, RG 347.7 1941-46, New York, p. 2.
120. Ibid.
121. See, Department of State Airgram from the American Embassy in Rome, September 14, 1949, 800.515/6-949, 1945-1949, Box 4256, NARA.
122. Letter of Hans F. Abraham to Covey T. Oliver, State Department, August 3, 1949, 800.515/8-349, 1945-1949, Box 4257, NARA.
123. Nana Sagi, *German Reparations, A History of the Negotiations* (Jerusalem: The Magnes Press, The Hebrew University, 1980), p. 46.
124. Telegram of McCloy to the Secretary of State, April 9, 1950, RG 59, Records of the State Department 262.0041/9-1850, 1950-1954, Box 1046, NARA, p. 2.
125. *Report of the O'Sullivan Committee on the progress made in the disposal of internal restitution claims in the British Zone of Germany,* 30th June, 1951, (London: His Majesty's Stationary Office, 1951), p. 14. Included in Foreign Service Despatch, American Embassy in London to the Department of State, Washington, DC, October 25, 1951, RG 59, Decimal File No. 262.0041/10-2551, NARA. Hereafter cited as the O'Sullivan Report.
126. Memorandum from the United Jewish Survivors of Nazi Persecution to Senator Herbert J. Lehman, "Implementation of the Indemnification Law with regard to the former displaced persons now in the United States," July 15, 1950, RG 59, Records of the State Department 262.0041/4-951, 1950-1954, Box 1044, NARA, p. 4. The four major Jewish groups engaged on the issue of German restitution and compensation requested a meeting with Secretary of State Acheson, who was unavailable. In the Secretary's place, James Webb, met with the groups and they discussed the issues of most concern to them, including the Equalization of Burdens tax in Germany, and the exchange controls on German currency, both requirements in the way of indem-

nification of survivors from the FRG. See Memorandum of Henry A. Byroade to James Webb, "Request from Jewish Groups to Meet with the Secretary," April 16, 1951, RG 59, Records of the State Department 262.0041/4-1251, 1950-1954, Box 1046, NARA; Nahum Goldman, for the Jewish Agency for Palestine, Edward Warburg for the American Jewish Joint Distribution Committee, Inc., Nehemiah Robinson for the World Jewish Congress, and Jacob Blaustein for the American Jewish Congress, "Memorandum on Restitution and Compensation — Germany," April 27, 1951; "Various Problems in Germany in Which the Jewish Groups are Interested," Memorandum of Conversation, United States Department of State, April 27, 1951, RG 59, Records of the State Department 262.0041/4-2751, 1950-1954, Box 1046, NARA.

127. See Letter of Isadore H.Y. Muchnick to Congressman John F. Kennedy, January 7, 1950, RG 59, Records of the State Department, Decimal File 261.0041/2-2850, 1950-1954, Box 1041, NARA.
128. Letter of the American Embassy in Tel Aviv to the Israeli Foreign Ministry, October 24, 1950, RG 84, Records of the American Embassy in Tel Aviv, Classified General Records, 1950-1952, 321.9, Box 5, NARA.
129. Letter of Richard Ford, Charge d'Affaires to the Department, October 27, 1950, RG 84, Records of the American Embassy in Tel Aviv, Classified General Records, 1950-1952, 321.9, Box 5, NARA.
130. Memorandum of E.P. Keeler to The Ambassador, "Israel Protests Termination of War with Germany," July 10, 1951, RG 84, Records of the American Embassy in Tel Aviv, Classified General Records, 1950-1952, 321.9, Box 5, NARA.
131. Goldmann, p. 254.
132. Written Interview with Ambassador Uri Lubrani, Jerusalem, January 30, 2003.
133. Memorandum on the Israeli position regarding reparations, as an appendix to the Letter of M.S. Comay, for the Director, U.S. Division of the Foreign Ministry to Raleigh A. Gibson, Counsellor, American Embassy, RG 84, Records of the American Embassy in Tel Aviv, Classified General Records, 1950-1952, 321.9, Box 5, NARA, p. 6.
134. Ibid, p. 7.
135. Memorandum of Conversation, "Israeli Reparation Claim Against Germany," April 10, 1951, RG 84, Records of the American Embassy in Tel Aviv, Classified General Records, 1950-1952, 321.9, Box 5, NARA, p. 3..
136. Ibid.
137. Memorandum of Conversation, "Israeli Note on Reparation [sic] from Germany," June 7, 1951, RG 84, Records of the American Embassy in Tel Aviv, Classified General Records, 1950-1952, 321.9, Box 5, NARA, p. 2.
138. Reply of the Department of State to the Israeli Diplomatic Note of March 12, 1951, June 29, 1951, RG 84, Records of the American Embassy in Tel Aviv, Classified General Records, 1950-1952, 321.9, Box 5, NARA, p.5.
139. Memorandum of Conversation, "Israeli Claims Against Germany," June 29, 1950, RG 84, Records of the American Embassy in Tel Aviv, Classified General Records, 1950-1952, 321.9, Box 5, NARA, pp. 1-2.
140. Goldmann, p. 254.
141. Howard Sachar, *A History of Israel, From the Rise of Zionism to Our Time* (New York: Alfred A. Knopf, 1986), p. 464.
142. Goldmann, p. 255.
143. Telegram of Secretary of State Acheson to Frankfurt, London, Paris, and Tel Aviv, July 3, 1951, RG 84, Records of the American Embassy in Tel Aviv, Classified General Records, 1950-1952, 321.9, Box 5, NARA, pp. 1-2.

144. Chancellor Adenauer's September 27, 1951 speech to the Bundestag proclaiming that Germany would undertake to complete restitution to the Jewish people. *See, The O'Sullivan Report*, p. 33.
145. Ibid.
146. Nicholas Balabkins, *West German Reparations to Israel* (New Brunswick, New Jersey: Rutgers University Press, 1971), p. 85.
147. Telegram of Congressman Jacob Javits to Chancellor Adenauer, October 1, 1951, RG 59, Records of the Department of State, 1950-1954, 262.0041/10/251, NARA.
148. Sagi, p. 66.
149. Schwartz, p. 179.
150. Ibid, p. 74.
151. Zweig, p. 18; Balabkins, p. 94.
152. *Five Years Later, Activities of the Conference on Jewish Material Claims Against Germany, 1954-1958* (New York: Conference on Jewish Material Claims Against Germany, Inc., 1959), p. 1. Samuel Bronfman had been the President of the Canadian Jewish Congress. His son Edgar, who would succeed him at Seagram's, would also succeed Nahum Goldmann as President of the World Jewish Congress in 1981. Barnett Janner's son, Greville, who like his father, became a member of the House of Lords. Both Edgar Bronfman and Greville Janner would play leading roles in the restitution efforts of the 1990s. For more on Samuel Bronfman, see Peter C. Newman, *Bronfman Dynasty, the Rothschilds of the New World* (Toronto: McClelland and Stewart, Ltd., 1978), pp. 46-50; and Edgar M. Bronfman, *The Making of a Jew* (New York: G.P. Putnam's Sons, 1996), pp. 35, 51.
153. Telegram from E.W. Holmes, U.S. Embassy in Tel Aviv to the Secretary of State, December 26, 1951, RG 84, Records of the American Embassy in Tel Aviv, Classified General Records, 1950-1952, 321.9, Box 5, NARA.
154. Balabkins, p. 143.
155. "History of the Claims Conference, 1951-2001," The Conference on Jewish Material Claims Against Germany, July 2001, p. 9.
156. Interview with Ambassador Rozanne L. Ridgeway, Washington, DC, January 23, 2003. On August 15, 1953, the Soviet Union declared in a note to the Western powers that: "Germany had already fulfilled most of its financial and economic obligations to the U.S.S.R., France, Great Britain and the U.S." and proposed that Germany (not just East Germany) be released from all further reparation obligations effective January 1, 1954. On August 22, 1953, the Soviet Union and the German Democratic Republic (East Germany) signed the protocol previously referred to above in which the Soviet Union agreed that: "The German Democratic Republic is, therefore, released from her obligation to effect payment of reparation, outstanding after January 1, 1954."
157. See Letter of Senator Thomas J. Dodd to Douglas MacArthur II, Asst. Sec. for Congressional Affairs, Department of State, April 18, 1966; RG 59, Records of the Department of State, Office of the Legal Advisor, Office of Educational, Cultural, and Public Affairs, Subject Files, 1945-1997, Lot File 96D244, Box 41, NARA.
158. Summary of the Statement by Dr. Nahum Goldmann at the Conference of Minister Presidents called by the Federal Chancellor on June 26, 1959, Translated by the Department of State, RG 59, Records of the Department of State, Office of the Legal Advisor, Office of Educational, Cultural, and Public Affairs, Subject Files, 1945-1997, Lot File 96D244, Box 41, NARA.
159. Kurt R. Grossmann, "The Individual Claims Against Germany," unpublished, n.d., Papers of Kurt Richard Grossmann, Accession No. 75026 8.29, Box 25. Hoover Institution Archives, Palo Alto, California.

160. Anatole Shub, "Nazi Victims Shortchanged In $300 Million Bonn Error," *Washington Post*, March 11, 1966; Airgram from the American Embassy in Bonn to the Secretary of State, "Nahum Goldmann on Federal Compensation Legislation," August 8, 1966, RG 59, Records of the Department of State, Office of the Legal Advisor, Office of Educational, Cultural, and Public Affairs, Subject Files, 1945-1997, Lot File 96D244, Box 41, NARA.
161. Goldmann, p. 279.
162. Joint Four-Nation Declaration, Declaration on Austria, Moscow Conference, October 1943, The Avalon Project, Yale University, available online at .
163. "Conditions in Austria, An Interview with an Austrian Trade-Unionist and an Austrian Business Man," Information dated May 1943, Date of Report June 20, 1943, RG 226, OSS, Records of the Office of Strategic Services, Entry A1-170, Box 287, NARA, p. 3.
164. "Austrian Restitution Laws," United States Department of State, Released on April 4, 1947, RG 59, Records of the Department of State, General Records, Records of the Fine Arts and Monuments Adviser, Ardelia Hall Collection, Box 18, NARA.
165. Robert Knight, "Restitution and Legitimacy in Post-War Austria, 1945-1953," *Leo Baeck Institute Year Book XXXVI*, 1991, p. 421.
166 Gustav Jellinek, "A History of Austrian Restitution," edited by Kurt Grossman, 1964, Papers of Kurt Richard Grossmann, Accession No. 75026 8.29, Box 25, Hoover Institution, Palo
167. Knight, p. 432.
168. Ibid, p. 438.
169. Goldmann, p. 281.
170. Memorandum of Conversation, "Restitution in Austria," February 8, 1952, Department of State, RG 59, Records of the Department of State, General Records, Subject Files, Austrian Occupation and Peace Treaty, 1949-1955, Lot 58D 223, Box 8, NARA, p. 2.
171. Knight, p. 422.
172. Memorandum of Conversation, "Austrian Reparations to Israel," August 13, 1953, Department of State, RG 59, Records of the Department of State, General Records, Subject Files, Austrian Occupation and Peace Treaty, 1949-1955, Lot 58D 223, Box 8, NARA. Three weeks later, the Department hurriedly amended the report when challenged by the fear of exposure. The Near Eastern Bureau issued an amendment with the cooperation of the German Affairs Bureau. See note of Smith, Land, and Appling, September 3, 1953, Department of State, RG 59, Records of the Department of State, General Records, Subject Files, Austrian Occupation and Peace Treaty, 1949-1955, Lot 58D 223, Box 8, NARA.
173. Telegram from E.W. Holmes.
174. Jellinek, p. 18.
175. James K. Penfield, Deputy Chief of Mission, American Embassy Vienna to the Department of State, March 14, 1955, "Recent Developments of Possible Effect on the Restitution Negotiations Between the Austrian Government and the Committee for Jewish Claims on Austria," RG 59, Records of the Department of State, Central Decimal File, 263.0015/7-357, Entry 205 M, Box 1098, NARA.
176. Translation of a Radio Broadcast of Chancellor Ing. Raab, broadcast on March 6, 1955, translated by the Department of State, an inclusion in Penfield, March 14, 1955.
177. Jellinek, p. 18.
178. "Resolutions and Decisions," Fourth Plenary Assembly, World Jewish Congress, Stockholm, Sweden, August 1959, Archives of the World Jewish Congress, Series

A, Central Files, Box A9, File 05, p. 8, Jacob Rader Marcus Center of the American Jewish Archives, Cincinnati, OH.

179. Report of the Committee on Jewish Claims on Austria, "Memorandum, Summary of Meeting with Austrian Government Representatives, Wednesday, September 30, 1953, "Austrian-Jewish Negotiations," accompanying the Letter of Seymour J. Rubin to Livingston T. Merchant, Assistant Secretary of State, November 20, 1953, RG 59, Records of the Department of State, Miscellaneous Files, Files Relating to the Austrian Occupation and Peach Treaty, 1949-1955, Lot File 58D223, Box 8, NARA.
180. James K. Penfield, Deputy Chief of Mission, American Embassy Vienna to the Department of State, February 25, 1955, "Recent Developments of Possible Effect on the Restitution Negotiations Between the Austrian Authorities and the Committee for Jewish Claims on Austria," RG 59, Records of the Department of State, Central Decimal File, 263.0015/7-357, Entry 205 M, Box 1098, NARA.
181. Ibid.
182. Penfield, March 14, 1955.
183. Knight, p. 433.
184. Any attempt at the State Treaty while Stalin was alive, was according to Gordon Brook-Shepherd, an impossibility. Soon after Stalin's death, however, there were contingency plans undertaken for a Soviet withdrawal. See Gordon Brook-Shepherd, *The Austrians, A Thousand-Year Odyssey* (New York: Carroll & Graf Publishers, Inc., 1996), pp. 400-402.
185. Memorandum of Conversation, "Negotiations with Austrian Government on Restitution Questions," December 31, 1953, State Department, RG 59, Records of the Department of State, General Records, Subject Files, Austrian Occupation and Peace Treaty, 1949-1955, Lot 58D 223, Box 8, NARA, p. 2.
186. Letter of the Department of State, Office of German Affairs from Siegfried Geyerhahn of the American Association of Former Austrian Jurists, Inc., January 5, 1955, RG 59, Department of State, General Records, Central Decimal Files, 263.0015/7-1056 to 263.0041/12-2357, Entry 205M, Box 1098, NARA.
187. Letter of Ambassador Llewellyn E. Thompson, to the Department of State, March 31, 1955, RG 59, Department of State, General Records, Central Decimal Files, 263.0015/7-1056 to 263.0041/12-2357, Entry 205M, Box 1098, NARA.
188. Telegram from Ambassador Thompson in Vienna to the Secretary of State, December 18, 1953, State Department, RG 59, Records of the Department of State, General Records, Subject Files, Austrian Occupation and Peace Treaty, 1949-1955, Lot 58D 223, Box 8, NARA; and Memorandum of Conversation, from Robert L. Burns to Mr. Dorsey, "Possible Israel Intervention in Austrian Restitution Negotiations with Jewish Organizations," December 22, 1953, Department of State, State Department, RG 59, Records of the Department of State, General Records, Subject Files, Austrian Occupation and Peace Treaty, 1949-1955, Lot 58D 223, Box 8, NARA.
189. "State Treaty for the Re-establishment of an Independent and Democratic Austria (Vienna, 15 May 1955)" Australian Treaty Series 1961 No 14, Department of External Affairs, Canberra, Australian Treaty Series, 1961 No. 14, Australian Government Publishing Service Canberra, Commonwealth of Australia, 1996, available online at au/other/dfat/treaties/1961/14.html.
190. At that time, 1954, the conversion rate was $1 million for every 25 million shillings, therefore placing the settlement at $22 million. See Letter of Ambassador Llewellyn Thompson to the Department of State, May 18, 1956, RG 59, Department of State, General Records, Central Decimal Files, 263.0015/7-1056 to 263.0041/12-2357, Entry 205M, Box 1098, NARA.

191. Memorandum of Conversation, "Article 26 Claims," Department of State, May 19, 1958, RG 59, Department of State, General Records, Central Decimal Files, 263.0015/7-1056 to 263.0041/12-2357, Entry 205M, Box 1099, NARA.
192. Jellinek, p. 31.
193. Telegram of Wainhouse, from Vienna, to the Secretary of State, February 17, 1959, Department of State, RG 59, Department of State, General Records, Central Decimal Files, 263.0015/7-1056 to 263.0041/12-2357, Entry 205M, Box 1099, NARA.
194. Knight, p. 440.
195. Goldmann, p. 282.
196. Letter of Assicurazioni Generali S.p.A. Insurance Company to Mrs. Regina Schwartz, April 2, 1998.
197. Prof. Vojtech Mastny, "The Impact of Post-World War II Nationalizations and Expropriations in East Central Europe on Holocaust-Related Assets," in *The Proceedings of the Washington Conference on Holocaust-Era Assets*, p. 655.
198. Letter of Riunione Adriatica Di Sicurta to Zikmund Schmerler, June 9, 1956.
199. Testimony of Mart Druckerova Cornell before the National Association of Insurance Commissioners Seminar, "Insurance Claims of Holocaust Survivors and Their Heirs," Washington, D.C., September 22, 1997; Letter of Riunione Adriatica Sicurta to Victor Cornell, October 26, 1964; Martin Stern, telephone discussions, June 2002; Letter of Helen S. Weiss to Senator Alfonse M. D'Amato, May 4, 1998.
200. Letter of Mrs. Martha Saraffian to Gregg Rickman, March 26, 1998.
201. Letter of Assicurazioni Generali to George Goldberg, December 7, 1965; E-Mail of John C.L. Szekeres to Senator Alfonse D'Amato, March 2, 1998; Letter of Riunione Adriatica Di Sicurta to Mrs. Judith T. Karmi, November 14, 1990; Letter of Riunione Adriatica Di Sicurta to United States Senator Peter G. Fitzgerald, March 29, 1999.
202. "Generali In Post-War Eastern and Central Europe," in Assicurazioni Generali Source Materials on Communist Expropriations of Generali and Insurance Claims Paid to Holocaust Victims, Prepared for the National Association of Insurance Commissioners, Washington, D.C. January 15, 1998.
203. According to Generali alone, they lost all their major businesses, including all its offices, as well as 184 buildings and 14 companies controlled by Generali. Ibid.
204. Claim of Ilona Plaskin, Claim No. HUNG-2-222, Decision No. HUNG-2-1060, Foreign Claims Settlement Commission of the United States, November 1, 1976. Judith Karmi was the daughter and heir of Ilona Plaskin. The Foreign Claims Settlement Commission is a "quasi-judicial" agency of the United States Government. The Commission according to its 1995 annual report, "is to determine the validity and valuation of claims of United States nationals for loss of property in foreign countries, as authorized by Congress of following government-to-government claims settlement agreements." The Commission was created in 1954 by Congress. See 1995 Yearbook, Foreign Claims Settlement Commission of the United States, U.S. Department of Justice.
205. Letter of Charles Sonabend to Senator Alfonse D'Amato, July 18, 1996; Tom Bower, "The Extraordinary Story of One Jewish Family's Fight to Recover a Fortune From Secret Swiss Bank Accounts," *Daily Mail*, July 13, 1996, pp. 32-33.
206. "In re: Request dated 1.2.1963 originating from the Federal Justice and Police Department, Bern police division, regarding the valuables left at Bienne in 1942 at the time of the illegal entry into Switzerland of SONABEND-Goczalk husband and wife, Simon and Lili, born in 1899 and 1904 respectively, Belgian citizens," Canton Police, Bern, February 9, 1963, translated by Brian Hufker, courtesy of Charles Sonabend.
207. Rickman, p. 31.

208. See "Swiss Compensate Son, Daughter, of Jews Deported to Auschwitz," *Agence France Presse*, May 19, 2000.
209. Letter of Miklos Griesz to B.J. Moravek, Office of Senator Alfonse D'Amato, April 28, 1997.
210. Letters of Miklos Griesz to Dr. A. Preisig, Union Bank of Switzerland, Zurich, August 6 and 12, 1949 – UNDER DURESS. Letters and translation, courtesy of Miklos Griesz.
211. Brook-Shepherd, p. 417.
212. Letter of Dr. U. Roth and Dr. D. Heini to Miklos Griesz, September 26, 1997.
213. Ibid.
214. Discussion with Miklos Griesz, February 11, 2003.
215. Memorandum of Conversation" between Gottlieb Duttweiler and Members of the State Department's Western European Bureau, 4 January 1951, Records of the Department of State, RG 59, Box 1013, 254.0041/1-451, NARA.
216. Letter of Dr. H.E. Fabian to Kurt R. Grossman, April 22, 1958, Accession No. 75026 8.29, Box 4, Hoover Institution on War Revolution and Peace, Stanford University, Palo Alto, CA, p. 1.
217. Rickman, p. 18.
218. Ibid, p. 281.
219. Letter of Samuel J. Roberts, Attorney for Anny and Kurt Kadisch to Albert Marti, Swiss Bank Corporation, Zurich, May 23, 1939; and Letter of Swiss Bank Corporation to Samuel J. Roberts, June 2, 1939, RG 59, Records of the Department of State, Decimal File 1930-1939, 354.113T to 354.117/162, Box 1529, NARA.
220. Letter of Alfred Selden to United States Senator Alfonse D'Amato, December 2, 1996; Conversation with Alfred Selden, December 11, 1996; Letter of Senator Alfonse M. D'Amato to Christopher Roberts, Member of the Executive Board, Credit Suisse, December 12, 1996; Letter of Alfred Selden to Credit Suisse, Zurich, June 12, 1997, courtesy of Alfred Selden.
221. Letter of Andrea Steiner, Legal Department, Credit Suisse, Zurich, to Alfred Selden, June 6, 1997, courtesy of Alfred Selden.
222. Rickman, p. 22.
223. Peter Hug, "Haggling at the Conference Table Over Dormant Assets, Swiss-Polish correspondence not an isolated case," *Neue Zúrcher Zeitung*, No. 247, October 23, 1996, translated by David Skelly, CRS.
224. Rickman, p. 22.
225. London Debt Treaty, Signed February 27, 1953, In Force September 16, 1953, Westlaw, 1953 WL 9792 (TIA).
226. Michael Pinto-Duschinsky, *Nazi Slave Labour: The Unfinished Campaign for Compensation, A Preliminary Account* (London, United Kingdom: The Holocaust Educational Trust, December 1998), p. 18.
227. While not a subject of this work, a similar case occurred in 1951 with the signing of the San Francisco Peace Treaty with Japan. Japan as well as the United States Department of State argue that the United States waived its right to reparations in the treaty, while others, particularly former U.S. Prisoners of War in a lawsuit filed in 1999 contending that the treaty does not. In fact, Chapter V, Article 14 of the treaty, entitled "Claims and Property," specifically suggests that Japan should pay reparations to the United States but suggests, "...it is also recognized that the resources of Japan are not presently sufficient, if it is to maintain a viable economy, to make complete reparation for all such damage and suffering and at the same time meet its other obligations." See "Multilateral Treaty of Peace with Japan," 136 UNTS 45 TIAS: TIAS 2490 UST: 3 UST 3169. In July and September 2001, both Houses of

the United States Congress passed legislation affirming the right of former Prisoners of War to sue Japanese companies that held them as slave laborers in World War II. See "POWs' Right to Sue Affirmed by Senate," *The Washington Post*, September 11, 2001, Sec. A, p. 6.

228. Ibid.
229. Neima Barzel, "Dignity, Hatred and Memory - Reparations from Germany: The Debates in the 1950s," *Yad Vashem Studies*, Vol. XXIV, 1994, pp. 251-252.
230. Lubrani Interview, p. 2.
231. Goldmann, p. 256.
232. Tom Segev, *The Seventh Million, The Israelis and the Holocaust*, translated by Haim Watzman (New York: Hill and Wang, 1993), p. 214.
233. Barzel, p. 264.
234. Ibid, p. 266-274.
235. Krakowsky, p. 24.
236. Mayer Waxman, "Traumatic Hand-Me-Downs: The Holocaust, Where Does It End?," *Families in Society: The Journal of Contemporary Human Services*, No. 1, Vol. 81 (January 1, 2000).
237. Potter, p. 7.
238. Letter of Kenneth Merlo to Abigail Schirmann, Office of Senator Alfonse D'Amato, January 14, 1998.
239. Letter of Stephen Baer to Joseph A. Jiampietro, United States Senate Committee on Banking, Housing and Urban Affairs, June 13, 1996.
240. Report of the Paris Office to the Foreign Affairs Department, American Jewish Committee, November 10, 1952, American Jewish Committee Records, RG 347, Gen. 10, Folder #1, Box 295.

4

Coalitions and Accountability: U.S. Policy on Restitution, the Post-Cold War World

"In recent years, we have learned many unpleasant things about ourselves and have had to revise our attitudes to a whole range of issues.[1]—Former Soviet Academician Georgi Arbatov, 1990

The year 1985 brought the fortieth anniversary of the end of World War II and the Holocaust. It would prove to be a momentous year for this reason and many more. From the very start, although the participants did not yet know it, 1985 and the confluence of four events would, in that year, signal the beginning of the reckoning for those who had successfully evaded the issue of restitution for so many decades.

The first of these events occurred on January 28, 1985, when Edgar Bronfman, the Chairman of Seagram's, whose father, Sam, prominent in Canadian Jewry and a founding member of the Claims Conference, had been formally invited to visit Moscow—the first such visit by a head of the World Jewish Congress. He carried with him a message from Israeli Prime Minister Shimon Peres, advocating the reinstatement of diplomatic relations between the two nations.[2]

Three days later, in the second event occurring on January 31, 1985, Judge Pamela Ann Rymer of the United States District Court for the Central District of California, ruled against a group of slave laborers in a lawsuit filed by several attorneys, including Washington, DC attorneys Michael Hausfeld and Martin Mendelsohn, against Andrija Artukovic of Croatia.[3] The case was dismissed, wrote Rymer, because of "the prospect of innumerable private suits at the end of a war might be an obstacle to the negotiation of peace and the resumption of normal relations between nations."[4] Had Judge Rymer only known how true her reasoning would come to be.

Third, and the most momentous of all three of these events occurred on March 12, 1985, when Mikhail Gorbachev became General Secretary of the Communist Party of the Soviet Union and set that nation and Eastern Europe on the road to *Glasnost* and *Perestroika*, leading to the end of Communism in Europe and later in the Soviet Union itself as well.

Finally, the simple advance of time brought the fortieth anniversary of the end of World War II in May 1985. With this landmark event came a recognition that it was not only a moment to mark the vast undertaking and sacrifice that had saved the world from tyranny, but that it was also a time to revisit some of those issues that had been left unresolved since that era.

These four occurrences marked a spectacular turn of events in the long and arduous restitution story. Each, in its own way, provided an explanation of why restitution, after so many years of first tortuous and painful, but marginally successful, negotiations, and then the near stasis of this topic, would now suddenly burst forth with new vigor and life, turning the tables on the silencers and deniers responsible for this long unresolved issue.

The trip to Moscow by Edgar Bronfman would mark the beginning of the real rise of the World Jewish Congress (WJC) to prominence among Jewish organizations forty years after the end of the Holocaust. The filing of slave labor claims against an individual held as liable for the suffering of thousands marked a new and more assertive tact in the effort to redeem memory and justice for Holocaust survivors. These two events, arriving as they did in the year of the fortieth anniversary of the end of the Holocaust, brought a commemorative angle to the story, which aided in the understanding of why restitution could be, and was, sparked, even if in so small a manner at this late date in time. Finally, Gorbachev's momentous rise to power, and his historic dismantling of the Soviet Empire, would complete the process necessary to start the effort toward achieving justice for the survivors. A strong leader in this new effort, Edgar Bronfman, emboldened by the anniversary of the end of the Holocaust, and the beginning of the end of the Cold War of which Gorbachev would bring about, and further aided by new and bold initiatives, would achieve an accumulative level of justice not yet seen for survivors.

A Transformation of Social Relations

"Who is the real Gorbachev?" asked Serge Schmemann, in the *New York Times Magazine* on March 3, 1985, nine days before the former First Secretary from Stavrapol ascended to the "throne" in Moscow upon Konstantine Chernenko's death.[5] Schmemann wrote of a Gorbachev speech delivered in December 1984, in which he called for "a transformation of social relations in the Soviet system ..."[6] While Gorbachev was a leading agent for social change, Schmemann, or few others, could have known how much of a lead he would provide and how far and fast that lead would take him, the Soviet Union, and the world.

The socialization processes that Gorbachev began moved too fast for him, or for that matter, anyone, to control. "There was great pressure on me when I was President, to move faster and faster," and "we moved too fast," he later said. "Society wasn't ready."[7] As Gorbachev suggested, "we began with *Perestroika* a few years ago by saying, "We want to be understood."[8]

In seeking to be understood, Gorbachev undertook to bring the Soviet Union into line with the other nations of the world, and in doing so was forced to change the way the country was to operate. "Returning from false ideas and idols," in Arbatov's words, the Soviet Union under Gorbachev passed new laws on religious tolerance, with Gorbachev even referring to a call of "God on High."[9] The practice of internal exile was dropped, and foreigners were allowed to see the once isolated and forbidden labor camps. Budgets were disclosed, speech was opened, and history was challenged, for both good and bad. Once sacred features of the state, even the borders, were renounced, the genie, now released from the bottle, was impossible to force back in.

The End of the Cold War

With this widespread change, the Soviet Union evolved, waking from its slumber. Dreams of democracy, nascent and distant as it was, proliferated. As this occurred within the Soviet Union, so did it spread throughout the rest of the Soviet Empire, a development that was likewise far from discouraged. "Of course," Arbatov proudly declared:

> we are not imposing our *Perestroika* on others. But I do think that the very fact of *Perestroika* in our country, while giving others an example, also introduces a palpable element of normalization into the international situation.[10]

Former Soviet Foreign Minister Eduard Shevardnadze, elaborated on the conundrum Gorbachev and his advisers faced when it came to those "others," their erstwhile Eastern Europe satellite "allies."

> ... [w]e clearly saw that in almost all the countries of Eastern Europe the political leadership was rapidly losing control over the situation and was not finding adequate responses to demands for democratic changes. In some instances, stubbornly rejecting reform, conservatives employed methods and measures that, against their intention, solidified the unorganized opposition, facilitating its formation into a broad, nationwide democratic movement.[11]

These movements, both of people and ideas, brought Gorbachev's socialization to a fever pitch. With Communist control evaporating in Poland and Hungary, the Soviet Bloc was unraveling. On September 10, 1989, the Hungarian government announced that East Germans seeking to leave and go to the West via Hungary, were free to do so. Soviet Bloc embassies in East Berlin were serving as shelters for East Germans following the Hungarian removal of its border fortifications from Austria in May. By August, thousands, using the excuse of their summer vacations to travel, holed themselves up in the embassies, hoping the Hungarian route would expand. On August 13, the twenty-eighth, and last, anniversary of the construction of the Berlin Wall, there were demonstrations all over Berlin, with protesters lying in the streets and East German *Volkspolitzei* warily watching for further trouble.[12]

On the night of October 9, massive pro-democracy demonstrations that occurred in Leipzig on the fortieth anniversary of the establishment of the GDR. One month later, there were massive demonstrations at the "Anti-Fascist Protective Rampart," otherwise known as the Berlin Wall, all around that divided city. The East German leadership, in a panic, decided to open its borders with the FRG.[13] The Berlin Wall had fallen, and with it came the Cold War.

While Gorbachev had encouraged an openness and a rethinking of outdated policies, this now seemed "blasé" as former President George H.W. Bush would later write. With the fall of the Berlin Wall, however, he became apprehensive as to the extent which history had suddenly overtaken him. He expressed real concern over the events in Berlin, yet was, for all practical purposes, able to do little more than serve as a spectator in the unfolding drama.[14] Like the Domino Theory of the Cold War in reverse, the "remaining Communist regimes toppled with numbing speed, but it was almost anticlimactic after the shock produced by the fall of the Berlin Wall," wrote Bush and his National Security Advisor, Brent Scowcroft.[15]

German Reunification

East Germany

In East Germany too, there seemed to be the suggestion that improving the nation's lot could be achieved by discussion, like in the Soviet Union, if not commitment to indemnification. In the period of 1973-1974, leading up to the establishment of diplomatic relations between the GDR and the United States, East German leader Erich Honecker expressed the need to make progress on Jewish reparations claims against the GDR as it was adjudged by the West to hold a one-third financial portion of the blame for these costs. This judgment was determined by the establishment of reparations payments by the FRG. "Honecker's statement," wrote a U.S. diplomat in Berlin:

> made in [the] context of discussion of establishment of US-GDR relations, Honecker reportedly said that [the] GDR would make some kind of token payment to Jewish victims of Nazism, but added that [the] GDR would not attempt to match FRG in this regard, nor would it be so foolish as FRG in admitting to being a successor state to German Reich.[16]

Despite the offer of token aid, East German leaders steadfastly maintained their collective innocence, denying responsibility for reparations due, in their estimation, to their having already paid reparations to the Soviet Union, pursuant to the Potsdam Agreement.[17] As such, East German leaders refused to even meet with representatives of the Claims Conference, despite Jewish and U.S. demands to the contrary.

When the United States stated its position that there would be no diplomatic representation until claims were paid, GDR leaders retreated, promising to reconsider the matter, prolonging it even further, and in the estimation of the *Economist* in 1975, "So they will haggle and protest, but probably pay up something in the end."[18] If only this was to be the case.

In January 1983, Rozanne L. Ridgeway took up her post in East Berlin as U.S. Ambassador. By this time, the Claims Conference had proceeded, to its satisfaction, with the various restitution programs in the FRG, to now turn its attention to the GDR. Secretary of State George P. Shultz had assigned her to reexamine the GDR's restitution process and, working with Congressmen Ben Gilman and Lee Hamilton on Capitol Hill, Ambassador Ridgeway got down to business concerning this most difficult of tasks in her time in East Berlin.[19]

"There were things we wanted," Ridgeway explained about dealing with the East Germans, "and we had to scratch around to find a way to get things in return." The problem, however, she continued, was whether there was something that could be offered to them that "didn't disgust you to get a deal done." They were tough, unbending, and difficult, if not impossible, to negotiate with. East German officials wanted respect, she believed. They wanted to act separate from Moscow, a fact that Secretary Shultz supported and admired in her recognition of that fact.[20] That strive for independence, however, did not make negotiations any easier.

As per Shultz's instructions, and cognizance of the difficulties involved with negotiating with the GDR, Ridgeway presented the Chairman of the Council of Ministers, Willi Stoph, with three requests: work for the reunion of split German families, the return of stolen artwork, and fulfill outstanding claims. Keeping with the pitfalls of negotiating with the GDR, she warily presented these requests to Stoph who asked simply, "If I do all of those things, what are you prepared to do for me?" Her answer was simple: "nothing." Whatever attempts she did, or could have, made to arrive at any kind of arrangement with the East Germans, owing to their long and hostile record and string of broken promises, would surely, as she continues to believe even today, have come to nothing. She could place demands, as she did for over two years during her tenure there, but to achieve East German acquiescence was another thing entirely.[21]

Two Plus Four

With the Berlin Wall breached, effectively becoming a relic of history, it also became only a matter of time before the GDR would likewise fade into history as well. By spring 1990, talks were already underway to achieve a unification of East and West Germany. After debates over the sensitivities of the Soviet Union concerning a unified Germany, it was agreed upon that the Allies, as well as the Soviets and both Germanies, would participate in the negotiations. As such, the treaty would come to be known as the "Two Plus Four Treaty." As Ambassador Robert Zoelick described, "The U.S. intention was to unify Europe in peace and freedom, while seeking to avoid a 'Versailles victory' that invited its own destruction."[22]

After a series of ministerial meetings throughout the spring and summer of 1990, the countries met in Moscow on September 12 to sign the treaty reunifying Germany. In Article 7 of the treaty, the allies foreswore any further control over the now united Germany.

The French Republic, the Union of Soviet Socialist Republics, the United Kingdom of Great Britain and Northern Ireland the United States of America hereby terminate their rights and responsibilities relating to Berlin and to Germany as a whole. As a result, the corresponding, related quadripartite agreements, decisions, and practices are terminated and all related Four Power institutions are dissolved.[23]

With the unification came, in Brent Scowcroft's words, "the end of the Cold War."[24] For the fate of restitution for Holocaust survivors, however, the treaty meant much more. By surrendering their responsibilities over Germany, the Allies set in motion an important stipulation of the *London Debt Treaty of 1953.* In Article 5, Section 2 of that Treaty, again, it was stated and the Allies agreed to the

> Consideration of claims arising out of the second World War by countries which were at war with or were occupied by Germany during that war, and by nationals of such countries, against the Reich and agencies of the Reich, including costs of German occupation, credits acquired during occupation on clearing accounts and claims against the Reichskreditkassen shall be deferred until *the final settlement* of the problem of reparation.[25]

Both Germanies, now responsible for all of its affairs, domestic and foreign, took on all the obligations for what was rightfully placed in its now joint past. With this in mind, the period of deferral, called for in 1953, ended.[26] Now Germany, would be subject to outstanding claims, like those for slave labor. With unity came vulnerability.

"You cannot bring history back after sixty years"[27]

Another salient event of 1985 was the fortieth anniversary of the end of World War II and the Holocaust. Around the world, thousands marked the numerous aspects of the era with solemn remembrances and commemorations of victory and of loss, human and material. In state gatherings, the victors and vanquished alike met to assess their progress, both good and bad, forty years after the fact. In Zurich, at the time, in the newspaper *Tages Anzeiger*, University of Lausanne Professor Hans Ulrich Jost, pondered a key question:

> Actually, the bells tolling on May 8, 1945, also rang in the tough question of whether Switzerland, despite escaping physically undamaged, survived the war and the time of fascism morally unscathed.[28]

Jost could not have known the extent of his observation.

In Germany, the Bundestag commemorated the time as one of repentance for itself and liberation from tyranny for the victims. Yet at the same time, Chancellor Helmut Kohl, feeling politically vulnerable and stung by his exclusion from the previous year's commemoration of the landings at Normandy on D-Day, sought and obtained a commitment from President Ronald Reagan to visit to Germany and, after much consideration, a trip to Bitburg Cemetery.[29] Over the objections of several White House advisors, and revelations of the burial there of SS veterans who committed one of World War II's worst massacres, Reagan stubbornly stuck by Kohl and went ahead with the visit adding, though, a visit to the Bergen-Belsen concentration camp as a parallel event.[30]

Despite his loyalty to Kohl in carrying through with this event, it sullied his fine record with the Jewish community. It was, in retrospect, unnecessary and a categorical error. Reagan's comparison of those buried in the cemetery to Jews, in that they were both victims of Hitler, namely the German soldiers forced to fight for an evil cause, was disastrous for him and for the cause of memory, both in Germany and in the United States. As George Shultz wrote, "The Bitburg episode made me and countless others ponder against the profound and agonizing issues involved: 'the German question' and 'the Jewish question' ..."[31] Most importantly though, like the numerous other events of 1985, it had an enduring impact on restitution, simply through the revival of the memory of the loss. " ... [I]t gave rise to a fresh consideration of the Holocaust," wrote Shultz eight years after the fact, "the furor it caused showed that just such a fresh consideration was needed."[32]

"Are you here to take back the property?"

On a private trip to Poland in 1994 with my father-in-law, this author traveled to Warsaw. After walking about the city, we took a taxi to the outskirts of the capital, looking for his old family dacha. To our surprise, after a short while, and a few false hopes, we came upon a medium sized, two-story building immediately off the road. The home, capable of housing several people for a summer respite, had reverted to the Polish government after the war.

Having approached the house, we were greeted by the wife of one of three owners of the home. Her immediate question to two unknown Westerners was,

"Are you here to take back the property?" Astonished as we were, we later found that this was quite a common occurrence in Poland. Mariusz Gryckowski, a resident of Radzilow, Poland was interviewed in the *New York Times* about Polish-Jewish relations in the wake of the revelations in 2001 of the 1941 Jedwabne massacre. Steven Erlanger of the *New York Times* described Gryckowski as nervous, explaining, "He lives in a formerly Jewish house his father bought after the war from the state, he said. He worries about his title to it."[33] This suggestion, it seems, belies any assumption of innocence by the latter-day owners of property either in Poland or elsewhere. If Mr. Gryckowski worried about his title to his property, as did the owner of my father-in-law's parents' home, did they believe, like the Swiss bankers before them, that one day survivors would resurface to reclaim their property?

The time for silencing, the time for forgetting, would eventually be over. Now, with the Cold War ended, the reasons for withholding, or not pursuing, restitution were also over. As then Israeli Prime Minister Shimon Peres wrote in a letter to Avraham Burg, Chairman of the Jewish Agency for Israel in 1996, in advance of the first Senate Banking Committee hearing into the role of the Swiss banks, "In these trying days which will lead Israel into a better future, we remember our obligation from the past. We will not remain silent and we will not rest until the account is settled."[34]

"The road to the West can lead through Jerusalem"

In December 1985, Edgar Bronfman again traveled to Moscow as a follow-up to his first trip. He spent three days there and then proceeded on to Warsaw where he met with Polish leader General Wojciech Jaruzelski. WJC Executive Director Elan Steinberg traveled with Bronfman and was quoted as saying "We wanted to emphasize to the General that the road to the West can lead through Jerusalem." Steinberg added that "the fact that Rumania and Hungary have most favored nations status in the U.S. is not just accidentally linked to the fact that those Governments have relatively good records in their treatment of Jews and Jewish issues."[35] Bronfman, active in the effort to free Soviet Jewry, had achieved a position of international prominence and was accepted in Moscow and in Europe at the highest levels due not only to his role with the WJC, but with Seagram's as well.

Elan Steinberg's suggestion, however, that bettering a nation's relationship with Israel, and through that connection bettering its treatment of its Jewish population as well, was a shrewd tactic to use in the emerging post-Cold War atmosphere in Europe. While not a new invention, as a long-standing U.S. policy with regard to human rights in the Soviet Union, known as the Jackson-Vanik amendment, trade policy with a nation is predicated on that nation's treatment of its minorities, Jews included.[36] The suggestion that a country could better its economic, and even its political, position by improving the lot of its native Jewish population, was a tactic that was used in both directions, such as with East Germany in the early 1970s. In the case of Bronfman's trip to Moscow, the suggestion would dovetail quite nicely with the emerging plans for *Perestroika* in the Soviet Union.

With the fall of Communism in Eastern Europe, and the need to start anew, the newly independent governments of Eastern Europe, no less then their Communist predecessors, saw the wisdom of improving their relationships with their own, and the international, Jewish community. Altruistic or not, these states needed help and they consulted with Israelis, with whom they had recently begun to negotiate on the reestablishment of diplomatic relations, on the methods they could use to approach the U.S. for economic and political support.[37] At the same time, Israel Singer, the General Secretary of the World Jewish Congress, had surmised that, with some knowledge of the amount of Jewish property each former Eastern Bloc country had, there was perhaps a way they could work toward the betterment of the two goals at once. Help for the new democracies, in return for the restitution of Jewish property, would be a cornerstone of post-Cold War Eastern Bloc policy. "Privatization," explained Elan Steinberg, "was the buzzword. But we said there would be no privatizing to Aryanizers."[38] It was, nevertheless, in the words of Doug Bloomfield, then the Washington representative of the WJC, a "convergence of opportunity" that revived the issue of restitution and reparations in the post-Cold War world.[39]

For Steinberg and the WJC, privatization was to include returning not only state property, but Aryanized property as well. Long-standing WJC policy dictated that this principle be viewed in human rights parameters. While Steinberg stressed that an improvement in relations with Israel would help in Washington, DC, Eastern European leaders took this to mean an improvement with international Jewish groups as well. "They did not differentiate between Jewish groups and Israel." Steinberg explained. "They would tell us, I spoke with your Ambassador today ..."[40] David Singer, of the American Jewish Committee, explained that they were also approached for help in getting Western aid. "They think Jews in this country controlled the banks and government, and if they can win us over, the money will flow ..."[41] As Steinberg elaborated, "for their own propaganda, the U.S. was the main benefactor of Israel. Israel controlled the U.S. and the more they denied it the more they believed it and the more they were willing to abide by this line ..."[42] This duality, however confused, served the purposes of the WJC and helped propel the cause of restitution.

The World Jewish Congress and the Last Chapter of the Holocaust

"... [W]e are all writing the last chapter of the Second World War, and the investigation must go on until we have all the facts,"—Edgar Bronfman in 1996 to U.S. Senator Alfonse M. D'Amato.[43]

Bronfman had taken the WJC a long way since he had become the president of the organization in 1981, following Phillip Klutznik and, before him, Nahum Goldmann.[44] Like Gorbachev at the same time, Bronfman, too, became the leader of a new idea, setting new practices between states. Moreover, he transformed the WJC, a private non-Governmental Organization (NGO), into a body with international standing capable of swaying the policies of nations and people on a level rarely seen before. Bronfman's jet-setting trips to Eastern Europe and the Soviet Union, bringing the WJC into international prominence.

Bronfman, the son of "Mr. Sam," as he was known, took over the reigns of Seagram's, and handled himself quite well in the business sense. He liked to effect policy for the WJC on a personal model, by traveling and meeting with world leaders. Wealth, of course, beyond making this accessibility possible, brought him a sense of commitment to return something, as a sense of duty, as his father had wished him to become active in the WJC.

Before Bronfman, and especially at its inception, the WJC, however, was not the bold and provocative organization that the world had seen in the 1980s and 1990s. Interestingly, the WJC came to its height of power from the same cause that instigated its creation. The WJC was conceived out of the need to counter the rise of the Nazis and fate of the Jews in Europe. In 1933, it became obvious, in the words of the Committee on the World Jewish Congress, as formed out of the American Jewish Congress (AJC) that:

> The solution of Jewish problems in their world ramifications and the struggle for Jewish rights and for a normal existence cannot be undertaken by individual groups or parties representing certain trends of opinion. This must become the task of a parliament of the Jewish people, democratically elected by the Jews of various countries and devised for the purpose of solving the problems of the Jews as a national entity and the specific problems of the Jews in various countries.[45]

The idea for the WJC, sprung from the mind of Rabbi Stephen Wise, who had founded the AJC. Wise, a towering figure in American Jewry, was a family friend of the Morgenthaus. It was of his synagogue in New York that Henry Morgenthau Sr. was president, and to Henry Mogenthau Jr., as Secretary of the Treasury, that he would go to persuade to take action on behalf of the Jews of Europe by creating the War Refugee Board in 1943.[46] Wise had conceived of the idea of the WJC in 1932, and the planning for the implementation began soon thereafter. After meeting in Geneva in 1932, it would not be until four years later that the WJC would make its debut.[47] During the war, it had been the WJC's Geneva representative, Gerhard Reigner who had first brought news of the concentration camps to Wise who then brought the shocking news to Morgenthau and others in the Roosevelt Administration.

With Bronfman at the helm, there were two other prime components of the WJC that helped form this new triumvirate to pursue restitution. Together with Bronfman, Israel Singer and Elan Steinberg would drive the WJC to new heights of prestige and form the institutional framework necessary to write the "Final Chapter of the Holocaust," that Bronfman was so fond of ascribing to his mission.

Israel Singer

Having known Israel Singer since 1995, I can say that were it not for him, his energy, his commitment, his enveloping charm, the WJC, even with Edgar Bronfman, according to his own testimony, would not have become what it is. Israel Singer came to the WJC as a natural extension of all of his numerous abilities as a scholar and activist. Having tutored Bronfman in a reawakening of his religious belief and practice, Singer is akin to an evangelical bent on a mission. One cannot help but be taken in by his charm. Indeed, Bronfman was. " ... I was entranced by this man," he wrote, "one of the brightest I had ever met, as well as the most hardworking, driven, and at the same time, nicest."[48]

Singer, an ordained Orthodox rabbi, professor, 1960s activist, and child of Austrian refugees, and at the time, the General Secretary of the WJC, is quite different from Bronfman.[49] In one respect however, he is quite similar. As Bronfman liked the idea of access, meeting with royalty and presidents, so to did Singer. He likes to travel and in that sense, too, he likes the receptivity to which he is granted.

Elan Steinberg

The third member of the WJC triumvirate, was Elan Steinberg. Steinberg, at the time, had been the Executive Director and the planning and strategic force in the hierarchy of the organization. His deep abilities were such that they allowed him to compliment Singer. Singer would be the public face and conduct the diplomacy, and he would perform the role of sitting back as he liked to do "in the office all day and strategize."[50] Singer did not like the press so much, as he performed the official, call it diplomatic, duties of the WJC. Steinberg, however, thrilled in the daily conduct of relations with the press. As a driving force in the effort to achieve restitution in the post-Cold War world, each of these three men played an important role. Each in his own way was a leading force who, through as much as sheer force of will as anything else, brought about real change in U.S.'s, and even the world's, policy on restitution. Each drove policy on this issue ending the silencing of the post-World War II era. Most importantly, they changed the notion that the burden of proof for the loss of Jewish property rested not with the Jews, but more rightly with those who took it.

The World Jewish Restitution Organization

With the fall of the East German government and the unification of the two Germanies, Eastern Europe, as has been mentioned, began to fall one nation after the other. Soon these nations, realizing they needed a "ticket to respectability," began to liberalize their relationships with their own Jewish communities, the WJC, and Israel.[51] Soon all had re-established diplomatic relationships with Israel and, as such, the ideas of reconciliation meant returning property from the Holocaust, and, as Noach Flug of the Comité International D'Auschwitz in Israel quipped, "it began to have some worth."[52] The natural recipient for that property, at the time, was the Claims Conference. With operations in Germany, Israel, and the United States, the infrastructure was present and the staff was knowledgeable about the processes and personalities in Germany and elsewhere to ostensibly affect the proper transfer of title to thousands of properties to their proper owners.

Following unification, Germany passed another restitution law to deal with the accession of East Germany. With the law and the attendant claims procedures put in place, claimants were given two years hence upon which they could claim their properties through the Claims Conference. On December 31, 1992, the claims period was to end and the legal title to all unclaimed properties were to revert to the Claims Conference. According to Netty Gross of *The Jerusalem Report*, the Conference worked feverishly to register claims to every Jewish property it could before the deadline expired. By the time the deadline had passed, the Conference held title to some 51,000 properties in the former East Germany.[53]

Soon afterward, accusations began to appear of favoritism on the part of the Conference when it came to selling off the properties. Favored brokers, it was said, were used to sell off the vast quantities the Conference had gained by default.[54] Soon, these accusations spread throughout the survivors' community as well. It was less the complaints about the selling off of the properties than it was the exclusion from filing further claims and the slow pace of processing claims once they were made. Once title to properties had reverted to the Conference, regaining title to them by people who were late in filing became a torturous hurdle to clear for survivors. "I take the liberty," wrote Arnon Rubin of Tel-Aviv, "to appeal to you in mine and my two sisters' personal plight, all holocaust survivals"[sic].

> This painful matter deals with a familiar to you question of restoring holocaust victims' property into the hands of the rightful heirs, with a 'small' difference. The difference is that this time the property is withdrawn from us not by the 'callous' gentiles, but by the 'sensitive' Jewish organization-the "Conference on Jewish Material Claims against Germany, Inc.' ... I am only one of those Jews who missed the final date of registration, of December 31, 1992, issued by the German authorities, in order to receive the property into their own hands. All those properties together with the other Jewish ownerless properties had passed into the hands of the JCC, which though, professedly, promising to compensate the rightful owners, within the frame of a 'Goodwill-Fund,' actually is evading that vow, by introducing hereditary rules of its own ... [sic].[55]

For its part, the Conference claimed that it had no duty to release a list of the properties, as many in Israel and the United States had requested. Potentially more lucrative for survivors was the recovery of looted paintings from Eastern Europe, which the Conference filed a global claim to, making counter claims all the more difficult once a painting was found.[56]

By this time, the complaints and the promise of even larger, more varied, and more valuable returns on claims made against Eastern European countries caused many in the WJC to consider the creation of a new institution dedicated toward this new endeavor. Already in 1991, only two months before the end of the Soviet Union and the formal end of the Cold War, the WJC met in London on October 17, 1991, to discuss rising anti-Semitism in the new countries of Eastern Europe so soon after the fall of Communism.[57] The WJC declared that it was going to begin a "global offensive to end anti-Semitism." The first phase, Steinberg announced, would begin in Budapest where the WJC would press for property restitution. Following that, the second phase would begin in Brussels in July 1992 (later changed to June) at a world conference. Feeling that it was not feasible, perhaps not even promising due to gathering problems, to work through the Claims Conference, it was at this conference that the World Jewish Restitution Organization (WJRO) was formed.[58] Representing eight American and international Jewish Groups, the WJRO also represented Israel's interests as per an agreement signed with Israeli Minister of Finance Avraham Shochat and Bronfman.[59] In reality, however, while the WJRO was a consortium of international Jewish organizations, it was an extension of the WJC. Its president was to be Edgar Bronfman and the majority of its work would be carried out by the network of the WJC, Israel Singer and Elan Steinberg included.

Nevertheless, the WJRO, according to Benjamin Meed, president of the American Gathering of Jewish Holocaust Survivors, had set upon the goal "to locate the unclaimed properties and belongings which were left over in Europe of millions of people ..." In August 1992, following the Brussels conference, Singer granted interviews declaring, "We demand restitution of property taken away from Jews by two sets of illegal regimes—the Nazis and then the Communists." Estimates of the amounts to be collected, at the time, were as high as $10 billion.[60]

Restitution Pursued

In late April 1992, Bronfman met with President George H.W. Bush at the White House. He asked Bush to speak at the upcoming WJC conference in Brussels, but Bush declined due to scheduling problems. Bush then suggested that First Lady Barbara Bush speak in his place. She later agreed but in the end her appearance never occurred.

Coalitions for Expediency

"Bill Clinton is a master politician," wrote a very unlikely observer. "He is smart, savvy, and hardworking," wrote former New York Senator Alfonse M. D'Amato.[62] Hardly recognizable words from the Senator who would go on to serve as one of that president's chief inquisitors over the Whitewater affair and Clinton's arch political nemesis. Yet, in as much as the two could not have been much more different, these two unlikely allies came together, or more correctly, were brought together in service to Edgar Bronfman's efforts towards restitution. When then-Governor Bill Clinton of Arkansas defeated President George H.W. Bush and businessman Ross Perot in the election for the presidency in November 1992, Bronfman had been afforded the opportunity to recruit another new player for his team. When the Republicans took control of both houses of the United States Congress two years later, he found yet another player in Senator Alfonse M. D'Amato.

In this sense, Bronfman was creating a new institution with its practice being to establish the restitution of the assets of Holocaust victims and their heirs by the uncooperative nations and institutions that had been unjustly harboring those assets since the end of World War II. He sought to rewrite the rules of restitution, as he said in 1991, "It will be a political and moral cry against what we thought had ended with the collapse of Hitler."[63]

In doing so, however, he needed an institution to effect this change. Within that need came the recognition that help would be necessary to establish the framework for achieving restitution. As such, he created coalitions of expediency.

Within the context of those coalitions, the various participants, chosen by Bronfman, acted on their own initiative and, for their own reasons, to gain restitution—nevertheless obliging Bronfman's needs. As such, there would be disputes and differences. Each would attempt to operate along different rules and establish their own rules, all for the same goal.

A Political "Odd Couple"

In 1992, when both D'Amato and Clinton were running for office, the two shared the commonality of facing political defeat if not oblivion. Both were, at the start, presumed to have had no chance for success. D'Amato, then a two-term Republican Senator from a decidedly Democratic state, and Clinton, an upstart Southern governor derided by his enemies and critics for his "political nine lives," but "slick" approach to politics and life in general. Immediately before the election, when prospects began to look up at least for Clinton, it seemed as if D'Amato would desperately need to attach his political future to him.

D'Amato almost needed Clinton in order to anchor himself to meek out what would, in the end, be a win by a nose. There were even "Clinton-D'Amato" campaign buttons distributed at the end of the campaign.[64] This linkage, in hindsight, would prove to be enduring—a political "Odd Couple"—sometimes fractious, sometimes productive, but always intriguing.

Together, Clinton and D'Amato would act in concert to help Bronfman in his quest, although much more out of a sense of morality and justice, perhaps even odd respect, than friendship. In this respect, Bronfman met with President Clinton on April 22, 1996 and sought his help in his efforts.[65] To Bronfman's request for him to work with D'Amato, the president was said to have asked, "Do I really have to really work with D'Amato on this?" Bronfman's answer was that D'Amato was the Chairman of the Senate Banking Committee and that there would be hearings held on the issue, and that, in reality, it would be important for the cause. To that, Clinton agreed to the issue's importance and consented to lend the hand of his Administration to D'Amato.[66]

While Clinton had agreed to help, the argument could be made that, in this effort, as would grow to be the charge, he saw clear political advantage. From the very moment of the declaration of his candidacy, Bill Clinton showed a willingness to adapt the programs and policies of his opponents, accepting the rules and assuming the practices of others, making them his own. This practice of adaptation, while politically advantageous to him, also appeared to others as making him malleable, perhaps even vulnerable to being swayed in a sort of race for headlines. In this sense, he could be co-opted.[67] While no one ever accused Bronfman of taking advantage of this aspect of Clinton's personality, Doug Bloomfield of the WJC suggested that Clinton was certainly more "amenable and accessible" and, in that sense, was a better choice to join Bronfman's effort.[68] Within time, as the battle for restitution spread, other politicians and statesmen from the state and local levels would join the coalition as well.

The "Sexiest" Target

In 1992, Singer read a novel entitled, *The Swiss Account*, by Paul Erdman. Erdman, who received his dissertation from the University of Basel in 1956 (on the subject, *Swiss-American Economic Relations, 1936-54*, Tuebingen, 1959), wrote a factual novel, with footnotes, about Swiss-German banking and economic relations during World War II.[69] For Singer, this novel served as a prelude to pursuing an effort against the Swiss banks to convince, if not force, them to return the long dormant and forgotten bank accounts of Holocaust victims and their heirs.[70]

That same year, on October 26, 1992, a young historian, Jacques Picard of Switzerland, was commissioned by Lawrence Lever, the financial editor of the *Mail on Sunday*, and the *BBC*, "to examine from a professional standpoint, a report which the latter's private lawyer had previously written on the subject. This report was a preliminary study on the subject of the administration of assets in Switzerland of Jewish Holocaust victims, and the use to which they had been put ..."[71] Picard later expanded this study into a full length book entitled, *Switzerland and the Jews, 1933-1945*. The European branch of the WJC saw Picard's early work on the Swiss and the promise it held. This information was conveyed back to Singer in New York. From that point, the issue of the Swiss banks, in Bloomfield's words, "moved to the front burner; being the sexiest issue."[72]

Countdown to Confrontation

1993

The year 1993 brought more developments to Bronfman's efforts to further recognize the emergence of the Holocaust as the singular event of the twentieth century and toward the goal of obtaining restitution for its victims. Both at home and in Europe, events shaping the drive and, importantly, the coherence and prominence toward restitution, began to take place. While Switzerland would soon move into Bronfman's sights, other steps were necessary to be achieved before Bronfman's coalition could be formed and unleashed against the Swiss banks.

In April 1993, the Holocaust Memorial Museum opened in Washington, DC. Planning for the building of the museum, had began in 1979 under the stewardship of Stuart Eizenstat, then President Jimmy Carter's Domestic Policy Advisor. The opening of the museum brought the subject of the Holocaust into the nation's capital. Some, however, criticized the construction of the museum with public funds suggesting that it was not vital or necessary to use this funding for the purpose of honoring the memory of the Holocaust.[73] Nevertheless, following the eloquent opening attended by President Clinton, the museum quickly became a leading tourist attraction and served to solidify the Holocaust in the public's memory.

Near the end of that year, the film *Schindler's List* opened to critical and financial acclaim and popularity, adding to the reopening of memories of the Holocaust—portraying the righteous acts of a man who began the story as an opportunist Nazi but ended up saving the lives of over a thousand Jews. The film showed that hope was possible even during the Holocaust. Moreover, for the sake of restitution, the cinematic representation of dispossessed and dispersed Jewish people, even with scenes of abandoned luggage and jewelers surveying plundered jewels, watches, and even gold fillings, graphically explained the robbery of the Holocaust like never before, and like the opening of the museum before the movie's premier, further explained the Holocaust to a mass audience consisting of new generations, in all its graphic detail.

Also in 1993, Singer traveled in the guise of the WJRO to the newly independent Eastern Europe. While there, he met with various leaders and sought the return of looted and Aryanized property. On November 4, 1993, due to his intervention, the Slovakian Parliament passed legislation mandating the return of public and communal Jewish properties to Jewish organizations and communities.

November 30, 1993, Singer traveled on to Prague to meet with President Vaclav Havel on restitution issues and to understand the Czech position. Czech Prime Minister Klaus would later, however, tell WJRO officials, that "we cannot undue justice for people to do justice for you."[74] Yet, in the next year, on April 29, 1994, the Czech Parliament passed a law allowing for the return of the property of Holocaust victims. Havel's understanding of persecution, having long been persecuted as a political prisoner of the Communist Czech regime, made him a willing participant in the effort. Nevertheless, despite Havel's support, the kind of disregard expressed by Klaus for the issue was an ominous sign, and one of more to come, as soon other countries would offer the same justification for denying the return of the assets of victims, or what would become known as Holocaust assets.

1994

In July 1994, Itamar Levin, a journalist with *Globes*, an Israeli business newspaper, was sent to Davos, Switzerland to write an article on orthodox Jews vacationing in the Alps. While there, he met with Professor Yehuda Blum, a former Israeli Ambassador to the U.N. and a Holocaust survivor, who informed him that the "real story of the Jews in Switzerland is the bank accounts left by Holocaust victims. Go check into it," he was told.[75] In October 1994, Levin applied to S.G.Warburg Bank for information on an account of a relative from Poland and was turned down for any information.[76] Within a year, Levin would begin publishing articles on Holocaust victims' assets in Swiss banks.

In the autumn of 1994, Istvan Szabo, the Hungarian Minister of Finance, told Naphtalie Lavie of the WJRO, that Russian President Boris Yeltsin had attempted to better relations with Hungary by returning two paintings of Hungarian origin from the Pushkin Museum as a gesture, but was advised not to because his aides had received an indication that the two had been looted from Jewish families during the war and taken from the Germans back to Russia after the war. The return of these two paintings would lead to further questions about what other pieces of artwork the Russians held.[77]

While anecdotal, these two incidents point to the nagging question of the continued silencing of the assets issue in Europe. As an outgrowth of the silencing of the issue during the Cold War, it became quite commonplace for people to have simply, and quietly, kept knowledge of the existence of the assets of others to themselves. For them, and those around them, it seemed almost common knowledge, yet not common enough to divulge too expressly. It seemed as if everyone took it for granted that assets were still being held. That assumption of knowledge, however, was about to end.

1995

The year 1995 would prove to be another moment for ceremonies and remembrances, but unlike 1985 when the Cold War was still on, the activities related to the anniversary of the end of World War II would prove different. As Robert Moeller wrote:

> ... the passing of the Cold War meant that 1995 would not be a repeat of 1985; President Bill Clinton's dilemma was not how to cram visits to Bergen-Belsen and Bitburg into a few hours but, rather, how to be at Arlington National Cemetery on the morning of one day and make it to Moscow by the next. The geopolitical politics of war and peace had shifted, and 1995 was a year for the United States to acknowledge other alliances, other pasts.[78]

With the end of the Cold War, now achieved, and the approach of the fiftieth anniversary of the end of World War II, the WJRO now sought to capitalize on the moment. In November 1994, Bronfman and Singer met with Richard Holbrooke, who had become Assistant Secretary of State for Western European Affairs, seeking his help for their efforts toward restitution.[79] Holbrooke had also previously been U.S. Ambassador to Germany. When he traveled there in March 1993, he brought his mother with him, the first visit for her back to Germany in sixty years. Her reaction to the visit, Holbrooke told Doug Bloomfield, greatly affected his outlook and added to his decision-making on the issue of restitution.[80]

Not only did Holbrooke agree to their request, but he suggested that Stuart Eizenstat, then U.S. Ambassador to the European Union in Brussels, be the person to head the effort, with himself asking Eizenstat to take up the issue.[81] Eizenstat had long and varied government experience going back to the Johnson Administration in which he served with the Postmaster General, the former Department of Health, Education, and Welfare, and in the White House as a speech writer.[82] Moreover, he held a long and rich resume of Jewish community activities and honors. With his location, not to mention his access to all of the European capitals, he was perfect for the job of providing a consistent message to each of the countries the WJRO was targeting. He was, however, not immediately taken with the job and at first reluctant to accept the position.[83] Yet, he was the one man Holbrooke most trusted with this type of assignment.[84] With Eizenstat already talking informally on these issues with several European nations on smaller personal and cultural property issues, the choice was actually simple for Holbrooke.[85]

In April 1995, Singer, Zvi Barak of the Jewish Agency, and Elan Steinberg, traveled to Washington, DC to gain bipartisan Congressional support for a letter to then Secretary of State Warren Christopher requesting administration support for the WJRO's mission of restitution in Europe.[86] The result, several days later on April 10, was a letter signed by the most senior Congressional leaders expressing their belief that it should be the policy of the United States to seek prompt restitution from the newly independent and formerly Communist states of Eastern and Central Europe.[87]

While Bronfman and Singer were lobbying in Washington, DC in support of restitution, Itamar Levin in Israel, on a separate but equal track, published the first results of his examination of the Swiss banks on April 27, 1995.[88] Levin's article was read by then Jewish Agency Chairman, Avraham Burg. Impressed and intrigued by what he read, Burg spoke with the late Israeli Prime Minister Yitzhak Rabin, who told him that it was the "privilege of his generation" to pursue the issue and to "invest in the memory of the Holocaust and the lessons learned" from it.[89] Soon Levin and Burg would join Bronfman in the overall effort against the Swiss Banks.

On May 8, 1995, Europe celebrated the fiftieth anniversary of the end of World War II in Europe. On the same day, Swiss President Kaspar Villiger, in a televised message to the Swiss people, admitted "unforgivable" guilt and apologized for the Swiss government's turning back of Jewish refugees at the Swiss border during World War II. Villager's very public apology, inadvertently fueled Bronfman's campaign and could be said to have, "softened Switzerland up" for the coming campaign.

By this time, the memory of dormant Jewish assets in Swiss banks, stirred by Picard's and then Levin's work, as well as Villiger's pronouncement, made it easier for the Swiss Federation of Jewish Communities (SFJC) to make an approach to the Swiss Bankers Association to begin a dialogue regarding the assets. Michael Kohn, Vice President of the European Jewish Congress, asked Rolf Bloch, Swiss chocolate magnate and leader of the Swiss Jewish Community, to contact Edgar Bronfman and Israel Singer to inform them of their progress.

On July 17, 1995, Kohn, wrote Edgar Bronfman informing him of their progress toward negotiations with the Swiss banks, suggesting that, in light of the commemorations of the fiftieth anniversary of the end of World War II, and in view of their increasing role in international commerce, they agree to form a commission within the Swiss Bankers Association to examine the possibility of unclaimed, heirless assets in Swiss banks. He also told Bronfman of the Swiss government's proposal to set up a commission against anti-Semitism.[90]

In advance of the WJC/WJRO discussions with the Swiss banks, Bronfman sought the help of the Israeli government for his actions. In this way, he reasoned, he would be acting on behalf of Jews around the world. On September 10, 1995, he received that assurance when Israeli Prime Minister Yitzhak Rabin wrote Bronfman wishing him well for the upcoming meeting of the World Jewish Restitution Organization in Brussels and reiterated his and Israel's support for the process and his leadership on the issue saying, " ... as President of the World Jewish Restitution Organization, you represent the Jewish people and the state of Israel."[91]

December 7, 1995

In my book *Swiss Banks and Jewish Souls*, I summarized my feelings about the opportunity to participate in a great undertaking such as the restitution effort against the Swiss banks, "It is rare in life that one is fortunate enough to be a participant in a great enterprise. Moreover, it is rarer still to see such an enterprise to a conclusion."[92] That this was a "great enterprise" is explained simply by the amount of success that came from it all. Michael J. Bazyler explained it best.

> I still conclude that the accomplishments of the Swiss campaign outweigh its faults. The campaign was an unqualified triumph on the legal and political fronts, showing the enormous power of both the American system of justice and the American political process...Even more startling was the ability of the Swiss campaign to set the stage for the settlements achieved with Germany and its industries, Austria and its industries, French banks, European insurance companies and also American corporations for their reprehensible wartime activities. ... The Swiss campaign—judging by how it is already being emulated by other movements seeking redress for historical wrongs—will serve as a model for a long time to come.[93]

When Edgar Bronfman and Israel Singer came to Washington, DC in their continuing search for allies in their efforts, they arrived on an ominous day in history, December 7— the day in history World War II, for the United States at least, began. So too, for what can be called a political war against the Swiss banks, will December 7, 1995 be remembered as the day the campaign to regain the property stolen from the Jewish people half-a-century before began.

Sitting across the table in the Senate Dining Room in the U.S. Capitol, these two men with a sure, but as of yet undefined, plan to recapture the stolen goods of the Jewish people, came to speak with Alfonse M. D'Amato, the new Chairman of the Senate Banking Committee. They brought stories of Swiss intransigence, historic and recent—they had been shabbily treated by arrogant and unapologetic Swiss bankers. In D'Amato they sought an ally in an effort to bring pressure on the Swiss toward an end to that attitude. They sought a simple process of encouraging the Swiss bankers to be forthright with him and to cooperate, rather than obfuscate, his goals. They told D'Amato that it was no longer acceptable for Jews to have to prove that their property had been stolen from them. The experience of Kurt Grossman, and doubtlessly countless others, of being forced to prove their losses, could not be repeated. Bronfman and Singer told D'Amato of their early experiences with the Swiss bankers and asked for his help which he quickly promised.

Amateurs Study the Past

The practice of examining the past took on an entirely new form with the formation of Bronfman's coalition. Following the Swiss Bankers' Association's reneging on its deal with Bronfman to keep private the findings of its survey of dormant Holocaust era accounts, Singer and Steinberg traveled to Washington, DC in February 1996, to meet with me as D'Amato's lead investigator in the coming Senate Banking Committee investigation of the Swiss banks.

From this point on, an investigation would begin comprised of Senate aides, ivy league college interns, Secret Service financial crimes analysts, and outside historical consultants, all of whom would conduct what Ludmilla Jordanova would call "public history." She also suggested, however, that those non-professional historians conducting the very public search for, in this case, restitution, were "amateurs studying the past."[94]

What is unmistakable, however, was that these non-professional historians found long-forgotten documents written by Morgenthau's Treasury men, OSS analysts, military intelligence officials, and State Department diplomats during World War II discussing the role of the Swiss banks, German industry, and European art dealers and insurance companies in contributing to the pillaging of Europe's Jews. Piecing together the documents as if they were a giant jigsaw puzzle, the process would contribute, in the words of Zurich History Professor Thomas Maissen, in 1997, to a "collective historical memory [which] always has to be re-constructed [sic] confronting new questions and exigencies." [95] Regardless of the composition, this unlikely team would put together the story of the period that had been silenced for more than half-a-century.

The Swiss Banks and the Lessons Learned

Rusting Paper Clips and Disintegrating Rubber Bands

Following a meeting with Singer and Steinberg in February 1996, we began to investigate what information was available in the United States, and we began by approaching the National Archives in College Park, Maryland.

We began with a few boxes of intelligence files from Morgenthau's Treasury men. These old files were in the original boxes as they were shipped over from the government departments. As we began to sift through the thousands of fading onion-skinned documents, we would have to remove rusting paper clips from the 1940s. Other stacks of files and papers were bound by rubber bands that disintegrated at the touch. The condition of these files, testifying to their age and lack of use, were all that we needed to see to understand that this issue had been abandoned, relegated to the back storage rooms, first of the various government agencies, and then to the vaults of the National Archives. Files containing memorandum of Morgenthau's men, pleading for help and support of their position, had been collecting dust for half-a-century. Emotionally vacant responses from the State Department accompanied them. The work product of an entire era, largely unsuccessful in its effort, lay before us. In what began as a four page "finding aid" from the archivists as to available resources in College Park, within two years would grow to over one thousand. The finding aid was non-existent and had to be created from scratch, like the investigation we pursued. In the intervening years, the files this finding aid detailed, explaining the U.S. government's work on the issue, were boxed up and sent into storage. As the years passed, the documents collected dust and their authors moved on to other positions and other challenges. As was the case in Europe, the fate of the assets of the Jewish people in Europe from the Holocaust era was forgotten, but fortunately the story was not. As Tom Bower wrote concerning the investigation and its results:

> Burning with anger, Sam Klaus and the original crusaders had fought a valiant but eventually losing battle to compel the Allied governments to fulfill their wartime pledges, honor the ultimate sacrifice of millions and exact justice from those who had sought to profit from evil. It was a testament to western civilization that even after the passage of half a century, the inheritors of Klaus's [sic] mantle had marshaled sufficient strength to peacefully persuade the stubborn Swiss of the moral bankruptcy of retaining blood money.[96]

The paper found in those long-forgotten files in College Park was the fuel that fired a three-year investigation into the Swiss banks' behavior as well as additional investigations, studies, and conferences into the behavior of other countries during that era. What began as an attempt to exact justice from Switzerland, spread across Europe and back to the United States.

Hearings, Accusations, and Anger

D'Amato held his first of an eventually five hearings into the Swiss banks' behavior on April 23, 1996. At its start there was great anticipation as to just what would be presented as evidence of Swiss wrongdoing. In essence, aside from a few witnesses, the hearing was really just to set the stage and call attention to the topic. D'Amato's gift was, in the words of one Congressman, "theater," and theater it would be.[97] This was a show, if nothing else, because for us, establishing a strong and clear setting for the issue, and an understanding of the seriousness for the Swiss banks, was paramount. In short, the goal was to put them on notice that they were in our gun sights and that we would not hesitate to pull the trigger.

Upon the conclusion of the first hearing, the Swiss banks, whose lawyer/representatives sat at the back of the room, scoffed at any suggestion that damage had been done to their clients. They thought that the worst was over and that this was a desperate attempt by D'Amato to salvage his political reputation following his unsuccessful Committee hearings on President Clinton's Whitewater transactions. They were very wrong.

The first hearing fortunately accomplished an understanding of the problem, but in line with the lawyer's wishes, failed to put any real dent into their reputation. An agreement between the Swiss Bankers Association and the WJC one week later on May 2, forming a commission to essentially audit the banks chaired by former Federal Reserve Chairman Paul Volcker, seemed, at the time, as well, only cosmetic.

We soon realized that while hearings were good, we would need more. We came upon the idea that only through a relentless political campaign, fought through the press, could we drive home the point. Drip by drip, cut by cut, accusation by accusation, within months, the Swiss banks began to feel the pain of a public relations campaign directed at them of unprecedented accusatory harshness (in their history), that would establish, beyond all doubt, not only D'Amato's, and by connection Bronfman's, prominence with the issue, but of the new burden of proof, the new reality about which Bronfman had sought. From now on, those nations holding Jewish assets would be called to account for their misdeeds. Failure to do so would bring harsh and lasting effects upon their governments and institutions. For the Swiss, unless they conceded the fight, it would be war.

Soon, fueled by increasingly dramatic documents found, first in the National Archives, and later in Britain, and even Switzerland, newspapers across the country, and in Europe, were filled with sensational stories linking the Swiss banks with the laundering of Nazi-looted gold from national treasuries across Europe, victims' gold from teeth extracted in the concentration camps, tearful stories of deprived Holocaust survivors, and heart-wrenching tales of Swiss business depravity. With each revelation, the coherence of the issue increased, begging additional questions.

With the conclusion of D'Amato's second hearing, this time in New York in October of the same year, the Swiss were reeling. D'Amato had publicly accused the Swiss government of carrying out the exchange of assets with Communist Poland and Hungary in order to compensate their own businessmen in

1949 and 1950 respectively. These accusations, first denied, admitted, retracted, and fully admitted again, caused a tidal wave of revulsion toward Switzerland at home and abroad. Soon governments were condemning them for such perfidy, and Swiss citizens began to question the sincerity of their government, the ability of its representatives to at once defend them against the "outrages coming from America," and the incompetence of its handling of the entire affair.

Despite the appointment of Thomas Borer as a central coordinating figure with Ambassadorial rank to serve as the point person defending the government, and in essence the banks as well, the country would soon be rocked again by three events which sealed the nations', and its banks', fates. Toward the end of December, as his term was expiring, outgoing President Jean Pascal Delamuraz suggested in an interview that the Jews were trying to bring down the Swiss financial system with their outrageous demands for restitution. Fulfilling the very role of which we were accusing them, Delamuraz' statement was said to only be "representative of the feelings" pervading Switzerland. True or not, the statement only further isolated the country in the eyes of the world.

Only days before, in secret, the Swiss Ambassador to the United States Carlo Jagmetti, sent a memorandum explaining the country's political position at the time. On December 19, Jagmetti sent the classified fax to Borer in Bern. In this memo, Jagmetti outlined his views of how the campaign against Switzerland was carrying on and how it should be countered. "This is a war that must be fought and won by Switzerland on the inside and on the outside," ostensibly written by Jagmetti's trusted aide David Vogelsanger, under his name. Most of the enemies cannot be trusted."[98] The enemies to whom Jagmetti referred were, as explained earlier in his memo, "Jewish circles as well as senator [sic] D'Amato." Yet, the real enemies were in his own Foreign Ministry.

This embarrassing strategy memo was classified and addressed to Borer and it was to him that many addressed the blame for its leakage. Some in the Swiss Embassy in Washington, DC would later state, off the record, to a Swiss reporter, that this leak was no mistake, but a deliberate action against Jagmetti through a prominent Swiss newspaper.[99] Regardless of the source of the leak, Jagmetti, to his credit, resigned his post soon after the memo's disclosure in January 1997.[100]

As if this episode was not enough, the Swiss banks would face what could be called their final and fatal blow at the hands of a Swiss bank guard in Zurich by the name of Christoph Meili. A mild-mannered young bank guard, Meili was on duty on January 8, 1997 at the UBS branch in Zurich when he stumbled upon several carts of shredded documents in the basement of the bank. Upon closer examination, Meili, a born-again Christian who had spent time on a kibbutz in Israel and had followed the ongoing campaign against his country, found several bank ledgers detailing Holocaust-era default purchases by a long extinct Swiss bank later bought by UBS. The purchases were by the Eidgenossiche Bank when Jewish owners in Berlin were forced into default by the increasingly stringent policies of the Nazis regarding Jewish ownership of property.

When Meili disclosed the results of his find, the Swiss authorities reacted with dispatch and immediately opened an investigation into his alleged violation of bank secrecy by disclosing the shredding of bank documents, an action which was expressly forbidden by legislation at the time, recently passed by the Swiss Parliament creating an historical commission to examine, in the broadest sense, Swiss history during that era. The bank archivist who ordered the shredding was said to have not been notified of the new regulation, and simply suspended without pay. Meili was soon fired by the contracting security firm that was responsible for guarding the bank.

Following interviews with the international press, Meilli's life, and that of his children, were threatened by unnamed Swiss parties on multiple occasions. Fearing for his life, he sought D'Amato's help. D'Amato responded by quickly proposing and passing a private relief bill through Congress enabling Meili and his family to receive "Green Cards" to immigrate to the United States, making them eligible for citizenship.

Meili's discovery of document shredding, and Delamuraz' and Jagmetti's inopportune remarks, were certainly more than what was needed to convince the Swiss that they had to do something to assuage the mounting attacks upon them. By February 1997, the major three banks, Credit Suisse, Union Bank of Switzerland, and the Swiss Bank Corporation, together, along with the help of the Swiss government, agreed to the plan first formulated by then British Parliamentarian Greville Janner, to provide for a $200 million "interim fund" for those needy survivors waiting for their account claims with Swiss banks to be fulfilled.

The *Special Fund for Needy Victims of the Holocaust/Shoah* was created for this purpose, but was immediately challenged by Christoph Blocher, an industrialist and nationalist member of the Swiss Parliament who announced that he would move to block any attempt of the Swiss government to contribute taxpayer's money to it. In his mind, if the banks were the ones responsible for getting Switzerland into all of this trouble, why should the Swiss people be the ones to pay their way out of it for them? To add grist to the mill, Blocher made it clear as well that his country was under no obligation to apologize for its role in the war.[101] With a populist and inflammatory campaign, replete with nationalist-baiting remarks, Blocher helped whip up public opinion, if not only for opposition to the plan, then to promote himself too in the Swiss body politic.

With the Fund established, D'Amato issued a short public statement reacting to the news. The result of that statement would demonize him in the eyes of the Swiss people, more than anything else he said or done previously in this investigation and after.

"The Swiss Were Guilty"

"The world has already rendered its verdict," D'Amato's press statement read. "The Swiss were guilty. We're now debating the penalty, and the penalty should fit the crime."[102] This statement, quite honestly, was never intended to inflame, despite its content, much less affect any outcome. It was merely a statement intended to fill space in newspaper stories about the Fund's creation and to add the Senator's reaction to the establishment of an entity which he believed in and worked hard to establish. There was never the slightest notion that it would cause the public outrage in Switzerland that it did. Nevertheless, the quote, with a bit of help from a Swiss journalist, became a nationalistic insult on the grandest of scales.

In the conservative Swiss daily tabloid *Blick*, George Wuthrich, took D'Amato's statement and exclaimed, in a front page headline, "D'Amato, That's Enough!" Wuthrich complained "he's going too far: D'Amato insults the Swiss as being criminals." *Blick*, editorializing, asked "what is the man really after?" Wuthrich claimed that D'Amato had gone overboard and to justify this assertion, he quoted the Swiss Jewish leader, Rolf Bloch as saying "it was too much." Swiss Holocaust Assets Envoy, Thomas Borer, expressed the belief that statements like this "were hurting Switzerland at home."[103] Wuthrich managed to turn D'Amato's statement into nationalistic dishonor.

Concluding his story, Wuthrich wrote, "Dear *BLICK* reader: If you want to write your opinion to D'Amato, here is his address ..." *Blick* readers were encouraged to write D'Amato and complain. Wuthrich, added, "please provide a copy to *BLICK*."[104]

This was all that an enraged Swiss people needed to begin a letter writing campaign, leaving D'Amato's Washington, DC office with scores of letters, mostly in German and French, as well as a number in English. Letters, threats, pornographic insults, scholarly, and some laudatory comments poured in. While the languages of these letters certainly varied, all had one thing in common: they vilified D'Amato.

Under the weight of this "political and historical assault," came a collective Swiss anger, and enough resentment to go around. As descendants of the "heroes" of the generation that defied Hitler and saved their homeland, they fervently believed that courage, coupled with the wisdom of their leaders, spared their land and people from war. They felt great pride in that version of history. Now they were told that it was not true, that it was not their brave ancestors, but their nation's bankers, that not only bought their nation out of war, but did so on the backs, and even with the teeth, of Holocaust victims. As their national identity came under attack, so, too, did their personal identity. Their idea of themselves as noble and honorable people was destroyed.

D'Amato would hold three additional hearings. One hearing would feature Meili testifying to what he found and in a poignant moment, he pleaded for the help and protection of the Committee in the face of death threats in Switzerland.[105] Another featured Eizenstat providing the details of the findings of the Interagency team he led,[106] and finally, a hearing in July 1998 featured Swiss legislator Jean Zeigler who feared for his standing in Switzerland for his outspoken criticism of the banks, as well as of New York City and state officials regarding their actions with Swiss banks.[107]

At all these hearings, what was increasingly made clear was the growing shift in the rule toward restitution that Bronfman had sought to achieve. With each hearing, each press release, and each document disclosed, the understanding of the idea that no longer would survivors be forced to prove their losses, was confirmed in the minds of people. The banks' willingness to create the *Special Fund for Needy Victims of the Holocaust/Shoah* showed that restitution, as it existed in the immediate postwar and Cold War world, had changed. This new pursuit for restitution had begun to succeed.

Beyond D'Amato, Congress Joins the Fray

While D'Amato was an overwhelming presence in the Swiss banks investigation, there were others, however, that would join Bronfman's efforts, independently or recruited. First among them was Congressman Jim Leach of Iowa. Leach, a more moderate Republican, chaired the House Banking Committee and was known for a softer tone and for pursuing a straight line. His first hearing on December 11, 1996, featured all the players in the drama, including D'Amato, Borer, Eizenstat, Singer and Steinberg from the WJC, and other Swiss officials. He would go on to hold four more hearings, continuing them after D'Amato's electoral defeat in 1998, holding two additional hearings until his term limit on the chairmanship of the Committee expired.

Leach's hearings, while covering much of the same ground with the Swiss, also covered additional issues such as looted art and insurance, used many of the same witnesses, and, most importantly, served another purpose. Now with him leading hearings, it could not be said that it was only D'Amato who was the one "persecuting" the Swiss. Leach led a larger committee with several members with varying agendas. Having to run for reelection every two years, instead of the six as in the Senate, members approached the issue from a stance similar to that of D'Amato. Many saw no need to withhold their attacks. While they did not doggedly pursue the issue daily, they took their opportunity during hearings to tear into the Swiss on an emotional level that certainly had its effects back home in their districts, and sent the message that instead of only one critic in the personage of D'Amato, there were quite a few more.

"Over the years I have noticed," suggested Congressman Richard Baker of Louisiana:

> that a number of International, high profile, corrupt government officials and businesspeople [sic] have found sanctuary for their substantial wealth in Swiss banks. My question is: is the Swiss banking system accommodating this generation's thugs, and the countries they represent, in some of the same or different ways that sanctuary was given to the Nazi regime fifty-five years ago?[108]

Baker's pointed question showed that others in Congress were willing to take the Swiss on in ways they had probably not imagined. In itself, this type of closing remark by a Congressman, in the casual preparation for a hearing, showed that Bronfman's drive for reparations could, and would, have unintended consequences—namely that the investigation would grow beyond all estimated proportions, with additional self-directed agents joining the fray advocating actions that Bronfman or the others could have guessed.[109]

"If you can't make it in New York..."

Israel Singer had joked once during later negotiations that "if you can't make it in New York, you can't make it anywhere."[110] Singer, while joking, had, nevertheless, been profoundly right. Once the states, and even cities, had become involved in the campaign against the Swiss, the banks' position would steadily worsen.

As such, Bronfman's coalition was enlarged by a self-directed group of officials willing to add their say and their power to the campaign directed against the Swiss. In addition to those in the federal government, there were others in the individual states and cities as well. Some like Alan Hevesi, then the Comptroller of the City of New York, sought to engage the Swiss on his own initiative. Hevesi, the son of Eugene Hevesi, who as a representative of the American Jewish Committee during the 1950s, fought a losing battle to force the Swiss to return the deposits of Holocaust survivors, was influenced by the results of D'Amato's October 1996 hearing and sought to use his position as Comptroller to pressure the Swiss to come forward first with information and then with the accounts.[111] After a meeting with D'Amato in Queens in the spring of 1997, he took the opportunity to further engage himself in the effort and traveled to Switzerland to look into the matter further.[112] Within a short time, Hevesi was initiating overnight investment boycotts of City funds in the New York branches of the Swiss banks,[113] and organizing a December 1997 conference of public finance officers to publicly discuss the disinvestment option against Swiss banks. This conference would grow in the following year to a nation-wide collaboration of more than 800 public finance officers who held the public investment portfolios of hundreds of millions of dollars in

Swiss banks. Hevesi's campaign formed a powerful tool against the Swiss banks and, ultimately, was a major cause for their capitulation.[114]

Others, like then California State Treasurer Matt Fong, taking his cue from Hevesi, imposed a state moratorium on the investment of $32 billion in state funds in Swiss banks. Fong's move caused great consternation at the State Department and mainly for Eizenstat in his role as lead U.S. negotiator with the Swiss toward a settlement.[115] Hevesi, despite his large role, showed restraint when pushed to do so.[116]

Like the spread of Nazi-inspired laws against the Jews throughout Europe during the Holocaust, now, sixty years later, the spread of action suddenly swept across the U.S. against those who had deprived the Jews of their assets. Now the notion of disinvestment in retaliation for these crimes became the practice. Soon Vermont, Rhode Island, Kentucky, New Jersey, New York State, Pennsylvania, Illinois, Chicago, Massachusetts, California, Maryland, and Kansas City were all considering or actually implementing these same acts against the Swiss.[117]

Plaintiff's Diplomacy

It was a novel idea: "to go after the guy who sells the barbed wire," said New York University Law Professor Burt Neuborne.[118] Instead of filing a lawsuit against the actual perpetrator, the idea was to file a suit, in the words of Michael Hausfeld, that was "... one step removed from active participation in the crime itself."[119] These lawsuits would go on to shape the foreign policy of several nations, especially the United States, Switzerland, and later other European countries. This new notion was now called "plaintiff's diplomacy" by Anne-Marie Slaughter and David Bosco.[120] In 1996, lawsuits were initiated against the Swiss banks, first by a self-directed source, an attorney from New York by the name of Edward Fagan, and secondly, and more importantly, by a Washington, DC attorney Michael Hausfeld.

Fagan's lawsuit was a short, quickly prepared version of a suit against the banks for the deprivation of assets to the survivor-claimants. It was initiated by Fagan in response to an encounter with Holocaust survivor Gizella Weisshaus of New York.[121] Before the filing of his case, Fagan had tried desperately to gain D'Amato's attention, most especially at the October 1996 hearing. There, Fagan could not compete with the crowd. Following the filing of his suit, however, his reception was better.

Fagan had established an inauspicious career as a personal-injury attorney who had a checkered legal history. Fagan, in our experience, had proven to be more of a nuisance than an asset. As his role in the legal cases would grow, so would the controversies. His tactics were theatrical, bombastic, and loaded with exaggeration, all intended to inflame public opinion against the Swiss banks and in favor of the survivors.[122] Yet, when all was done, Fagan came under criticism from his own clients, including Weisshaus who later sued him for racketeering, as well as his receiving an admonishment from the New York Supreme Court for past unpaid penalties in a personal injury case.[123]

Yet, the filing of his suit did not prevent others from moving forward with their efforts. Michael Hausfeld's lawsuit was vastly different, and an improvement in both content and impact, over Fagan's. While Fagan had to work on getting D'Amato's attention, Hausfeld had been the recipient of such attention. In pursuing all avenues against the Swiss banks, I had enlisted the support of another Washington, DC attorney, Martin Mendelsohn, to obtain an experienced attorney to provide "open another front against the Swiss" to increase the pressure. Mendelsohn produced his friend, Hausfeld. The two had worked a decade earlier on a landmark slave labor lawsuit against the Croatian war criminal Andrija Artukovic of Croatia. As it turned out, Hausfeld had arrived at the same idea I had.

Hausfeld had a more prolific and solid background, especially in the area of class-action lawsuits. Aside from his work with Mendelsohn against Artukovic, Hausfeld had successfully sued Texaco for racial discrimination, Exxon for the spill of the *Exxon Valdez*, CD manufacturers for price-fixing, and many others.

There would soon be other lawyers as well, including Mel Weiss, known for decades for leading shareholder lawsuits against companies, who would lend his class-action expertise and collection of national offices and attorneys to the case.[124] Weiss would be aligned, for the most part, with Hausfeld, but would, at times, clash with him on policy on this case and as well in others. Bob Swift, who successfully sued the estate of Ferdinand Marcos for $2 billion, aligned himself with Fagan, but had less of a flair for the "theater" that Fagan so loved.[125] Swift had successfully used the Alien Tort Claims Act (ATCA) in this case and was seen as being one of the leading agents in instituting its use in this realm. William Marks, a Washington, DC-area attorney who in 1993 had made his fame representing Hugo Princz, an American civilian who was caught behind the lines in World War II and persecuted in a concentration camp, forcing the creation of another category of recipients of German reparation payments, became another Fagan ally. Additionally, there would be attorneys in Europe that became allies of both "warring parties" of attorneys.

The only historical precedent for what the lawyers were attempting was Swift's use of the ACTA. As such, the Alien Tort Claims Act of 1789 would prove quite valuable as a basis for action on behalf of survivors seeking restitution from the Swiss banks. This Act, "permits an alien to sue in federal court for a 'tort' committed 'in violation of the law of nations.'"[126] As Rudolf Dolzer wrote, in the normal acceptance of international law, the rules of war were assumed to have applied to relations between states not, as implied, by the charges placed upon the banks as involving individuals, not to mention corporations, either willing or unwilling, as participants in a war.[127] There were always very real concerns that the claims made by the lawsuits, in the long run, would not hold up through the various courts either for evidentiary reasons or due to the expiration of the statute of limitations.

More importantly, the use of the Alien Tort Claims Act (ATCA) was, in practice, rare if ever. When put into practice, however, the ATCA created an extraterritorial reach for American courts, only also making the Swiss feel as if the rules were being unfairly used against them. Primarily, it was Americans with claims against foreign states that used the Act. With the rise of the rule of seeking redress for human rights violations, the ATCA came into use as a practice in opposition to national and corporate levels.[128] The lawsuits then, served many purposes, the least of which was to impress upon the Swiss the notion that there would not be an easy way out of this drama for them and that, unlike the previous fight with the Allies over this issue, the fight would not be abandoned.

In all, the contribution by the lawyers, regardless of the differences between them, in the view of Stuart Eizenstat, "were the prod and the platform for all the pressure that was applied in the court of public opinion. Had they not existed, that pressure would not have been there, even with the U.S. Government involved."[129] The problem, however, was that the Swiss, as author Tom Bower had once told me, were thinking on a different plane; they didn't think like us and they believed they were right. More importantly, for legal purposes, as Eizenstat wrote, they "did not understand the breadth of the issues that class actions could raise."[130] These two factors would make them both ignorant of, and stubbornly resistant toward, ending their own predicament.

Settlement

By 1998, the pressure building on the Swiss banks and the Swiss government was incredible. Numerous state officials were either threatening, or actually applying, sanctions on the banks and there were suggestions, in one case by D'Amato himself, to impose them directly against the Swiss Government.[131] Pressure had built to such a point that a real diplomatic crisis had developed and talk of a trade war between the two countries was surfacing. Eizenstat had repeatedly expressed a very real disdain for the use of sanctions in any form, and coming in such a heated and emotional atmosphere the effects for U.S. foreign policy in Switzerland, and in Europe overall, could have been disastrous.[132]

Eizenstat, who had tried in vain since his assignment in 1996 to mediate and moderate the burgeoning political war between the WJC, D'Amato, Hevesi and the other public finance officers, the lawyers on the one side, and the Swiss on the other, found his job to be difficult and straining. He had to go at it in "an extremely objective fashion as a U.S. Government representative," he explained. His impartiality, in his eyes was paramount. " ... I had to be perceived as from the outside world, and view myself as purely objective ... in order to preserve our economic, diplomatic, and political relations with the other governments."[133]

Yet, with the flow of emotion, coupled with increased threats—Hevesi and New York State Comptroller Carl McCall had threatened serious and harmful state-wide sanctions by September if settlement was not achieved—fears of outright economic war over the issue seemed unavoidable. All the while, though, settlement talks had continued, sputtering on and off, with proposed numbers being discussed and shot down by one side or the other as inadequate or overwhelming. With Hevesi's threat, it became all too apparent for the banks, somewhat pressured by the Swiss Government and Eizenstat for political reasons, that this three-year long battle had to end.

Finally, on August 12, D'Amato, joined by Estelle Sapir, who had already settled with Credit Suisse in May for $500,000[134]; all the class action and defense attorneys, minus Eizenstat, however, for reasons of pride at having been excluded in the final crucial days of negotiations, appeared on the steps of the Federal Courthouse in Brooklyn to announce the long-sought after settlement of $1.25 billion between the banks and the claimants.[135] In later settlement allocation talks, the Swiss additionally agreed to allow compensation for Jews turned back at the border during the war. The agreement, effective in December 2001, allowed for payments of $3,625 for those expelled, $725 for those admitted into Switzerland but detained.[136]

For Bronfman, the settlement brought the first real victory in his drive for restitution. For D'Amato, it was a clear cut win and one he would use in his reelection effort over the next three months. For the lawyers, particularly Hausfeld, it was the partial conclusion to finishing the work of the Nuremberg war crimes trials.[137] For us, the researchers, it was, as Tom Bower had alluded in his book, the successful conclusion to the unsuccessful effort of Morgenthau's Treasury men's trials fighting the Swiss. For the survivors, it was justice—perhaps justice overdue, but justice nonetheless.

Taxing the Victory

Following the creation of the Swiss Interim Fund, we sought information on precedents for making the receipt of these and other funds sure to be on their way, tax-free. After research, we found that in 1994, Congress had passed legislation mandating that "payments made to individuals because of their status as victims of Nazi persecution shall be disregarded in determining eligibility" for programs of federal assistance.[138] In other words, Holocaust survivors receiving funds from Germany as reparations payments could not be denied essential social services in the United States because of income limits established or increased due to those reparations. Additionally, there were federal rulings from the Internal Revenue service—rulings made in an administrative form, assuming an assertive state, yet acting with the full force of directive law. These rulings, called Revenue rulings, excluded reparations payments from consideration for income tax purposes, considering their receipt as "reimbursement for deprivation of civil or personal rights."[139]

With this in mind, D'Amato sought to further harden the definition and to codify the exemption for this and future recipients and settlements. On October 5, 1998, following the Swiss settlement, he introduced the *Holocaust Assets Tax Exclusion Act* for this purpose.[140] The bill did not pass Congress as the session ran out soon after the bill's introduction.

The bill, however, was introduced the following year by Senators Peter G. Fitzgerald of Illinois, Spencer Abraham of Michigan, and the late Daniel Patrick Moynihan of New York.[141] The bill passed Congress four months later and included exclusions for the receipt of the proceeds from returned paintings and other properties included in the bill at the request of several attorneys from New York. The exclusion also extended to future settlements. Unfortunately, the bill, in the form of an amendment, was attached to a tax bill that was vetoed by President Clinton for unrelated reasons. The legislation, however, was again revived in 2001, by Fitzgerald, and approved by Congress in May 2001 and signed into law by President George W. Bush.[142] The bill was to last for ten years, but was extended indefinitely by a subsequent bill the next year by Fitzgerald and Representative E. Clay Shaw, Jr. of Florida.[143] Due to the exemption, the amount of money available to survivors under the Swiss bank settlement rose by $52 million.[144]

While the Federal effort was being undertaken, numerous states including Ohio, Missouri, Rhode Island, Massachusetts, California, Illinois, and Maryland passed legislation making the payment of state taxes from the receipt of reparations exempt. In Europe, too, in the United Kingdom, money recovered was ruled to be exempt from taxes as well.

Vindicated

For all that D'Amato had been attacked for, both for motive and on matters of fact, Eizenstat's first report had shown him to be right, but his was an American report. True vindication came, however, with the release of the long-awaited Volcker Committee Report, otherwise known as *Independent Commission of Eminent Persons Report on Dormant Accounts of Victims of Nazi Persecution in Swiss Banks*, on December 6, 1999. Three years in the making, the report detailed much of what we found while researching the illicit and indecent behavior of the Swiss banks during the Holocaust. The only difference, however, was that the magnitude of their findings was much greater than any of us had ever imagined.

While it is gratifying to have been proven right, this time by over 650 forensic auditors who, for the first time in Swiss history, were granted access to the banks' records, reviewing 4.1 million accounts,[145] it was very disturbing to find that there were 54,000 dormant accounts of Holocaust victims, when we were originally told by the bankers there were only 755. Of this new, higher number, nearly 39,000 were closed by the banks in the years following the lack of any response from their owners. More disturbingly, 2,305 were closed due to the excessive application of fees by the banks and the proceeds merged into the banks' general assets. Some accounts, in fact, were continuously drained and emptied by fees for a period of fifty years or more, even though it was quite evident that the account holders were dead. Additionally, 417 were paid out to Nazi authorities who gained access to the accounts, and there were 1,622 accounts found to have been held in the names of high-ranking Nazi or Fascist officials throughout Europe. Information was also found to show that safe deposit boxes were drilled open, which coincided with information we discovered as well. According to the report, the proceeds were sold off to pay the box fees, retroactively and prospectively. Who had access to the boxes once opened is anyone's guess. How much other information, such as that hidden by Johannes Rohony, is still another question. Documents, as in the case of Meili, had also been found to have been destroyed.[146] Unfortunately, there was great difficulty in obtaining exact matches for accounts. In some cases, there were, on average, four name matches to accounts. Moreover, there were many accounts with substantial amounts of money that had yet to be claimed.[147]

Europe: The Search Expands

Within a very short time, other nations in Europe were either coming under the microscope of researchers, or were, themselves, examining their past history. Delving into their own archives, European countries were finding that the Swiss were not alone in their crimes. There were other countries' crimes by omission and commission. During a war that consumed a continent, nations implemented laws to pillage the Jews. Others sought the opportunity to protect themselves and look the other way as the robbery progressed by the Nazis. In other situations, individuals equally looked the other way as opportunities presented opportunities to their less bashful fellow citizens to commit the robbery themselves. Now, however, these situations of greed and abandonment were being investigated and disclosed. More importantly, questions were being asked, and the inquisitors were not going away without answers.

The United Kingdom

One of the first nations that came under examination was the United Kingdom. Greville Janner, the son of Barnett Janner, one of the organizers of the

Claims Conference which led negotiations for reparations from West Germany, sought help from then British Foreign Secretary Malcolm Rifkin and Minister of Defense Michael Portillo, for an investigation into their respective archives in June 1996 as to fate of Holocaust victims' assets in Swiss Banks. The result, dubbed the "Rifkind Report" of September 10, 1996 explained that the Allies "did their best to gather in the maximum amount of Nazi gold, in Germany or abroad."[148] While the findings of Swiss-Nazi complicity were an important, early contribution to the issue, it was less important to explain the laundering of Nazi-looted gold then it was to ascertain the fate of victims' bank deposits. Yet, as it has been explained, the British at the end of the war, were thinking about the future, not the past, when it came to the Swiss banks. "The assistance for Holocaust survivors Switzerland had promised," Tom Bower wrote, "was, with British encouragement, cynically withheld in a successful ploy to protect German and Swiss fortunes."[149] Bank deposits in Switzerland, and as Janner's Holocaust Educational Trust disclosed first in September 1997, in the U.K., as well, were ignored. But, as Alasdair Palmer in the *London Sunday Telegraph* explained, " ... ignorance is no longer an excuse, because it is no longer possible."[150] As the Trust discovered:

> Money from Germany, Hungary, Bulgaria and Romania was kept by the British as reparations. In Germany's case this was sanctioned by international agreement. In the case of the other three countries, reparations were apparently taken unilaterally by Britain. The seized enemy money was used to repay British creditors of the four countries, such as oil companies who had lost money in Romania.[151]

Janner, it turns out, had hit upon an important, and unknown aspect, of the British story during the Holocaust. This discovery had hit hard in London, putting the British Government on par with the Swiss for perfidy in dealing with victims' assets as the Swiss had done with Polish and Hungarian Jewish victims' assets. The discovery poked a hole into Allied innocence, of sorts, when it came to the persistent lobbing of accusations on the Swiss. As they had felt besieged, seeing the U.K. hit with the very accusations which rocked their country, much less by a prominent British Jewish Member of the British Parliament, this discovery played very well in Switzerland, releasing some of the pressure, as it were, on them.

As the accusations became officially acknowledged by the British government, official inquiries were undertaken by that government and the British Bankers' Association (BBA) to locate and list the accounts. In all cases, the BBA sought to explain that it had followed all laws at the time and that its actions were based on government instruction.[152] Greatly embarrassed by the disclosure, the British banks and the government were taken to task in the British press, but actions taken immediately afterward distinguished them from the Swiss who were less than forthcoming for so long. The accounts were later published on the Internet. More importantly, the British Foreign Office began a process to examine all the records in a much deeper and comprehensive manner than done under the Rifkind Report, this time to answer the initial findings of the Trust. The result was a 144-page study released in April 1998.[153]

Once the British were exposed, for Bronfman, the battlefield had been widened and new avenues for the campaign had been found. Now the rest of Europe was open for examination.

France

"The youngest amongst us, I am glad to say," declared French President Jacques Chirac on the fiftieth anniversary of the roundup of French Jewry, "are receptive to all that concerns the Shoah. They want to know. And with them, an increasing number of French people are now prepared to stare their past in the face."[154] This speech, like Swiss President Villager's of a decade earlier, foreshadowed, to a lesser extent, the same examination of wartime behavior. Two years later, Prime Minister Lionel Jospin addressed the issue further. Before an audience of the Representative Council of Jewish Institutions in France, Jospin admitted that when it came to discussions of the confiscation of Jewish property in France, "I want all this cleared up."[155] Jospin continued:

> I am in a position to announce today that with the agreement of President Chirac, I intend to set up a task force as early as possible, to be headed by a prominent personality, to evaluate the extent of the confiscations, the subsequent fate of the confiscated property, the present location of such property and the legal position on it.[156]

France, undertaking a self-directed examination, nevertheless would not only be subjected to its own search, but that of others as well.

On April 27, Jospin appointed M. Jean Matteoli, Chairman of the Economic and Social Council and a former French Resistance leader, as the Chairman of that task force which soon became known as the Matteoli Commission.[157] Immediately, the new commission began work in the scattered French archives looking for confiscated Jewish apartments and other properties taken, examining over 62,000 case files.[158] Yet, in the climate exposing the inequities of the looting of the Holocaust, the formation of the Matteoli Commission set in motion many actions. Jospin's claim of wanting to see the history of the confiscations "cleared up" was taken seriously, and as such many self-directed agents took it upon themselves to dig for the truth. As D'Amato said at the time:

> We know that Swiss banks facilitated the looting of gold from all over Europe. We know that the accounts of great numbers of Holocaust victims were never returned by Swiss banks to their heirs. But we also know that our Nation had similar problems. Other nations had similar problems and participated. France was one of them.[159]

Only three days after Jospin announced the creation of the Commission, the Paris daily newspaper *Le Monde* disclosed a 1995 confidential report from the Court of Auditors in which it was admitted that French museums of the Louvre, Orsay, Georges, Pompidou, Sévres, and the Château de Versailles had held, ostensibly as trustee, 1,955 works of art from the war, largely of Jewish ownership. The museums, the report explained, were less than interested in returning the artwork, much less advertising their custody. Many were more concerned with holding the works as their own, fearing their return as a detraction from the museums' collections' integrity.[160] The 1,955 paintings were part of a total collection of nearly 100,000 paintings recovered after the war, 61,257 of which were returned after the war.[161]

In January 1998, the Commission presented its findings, which while numerous and complicated in nature, nevertheless showed 62,460 case files concerning some 90,000 people. Of those people, 23,000 of them experienced Aryanization and liquidation of their properties. The forced sales of securities and the seizure of bank deposits were also researched. Finally, the composition of, and contributions toward, the payment of the one billion franc fine were also examined.[162] The Commission also found widespread destruction and dislocation of files which resulted in the need to resort to sampling.

Following the publication of the findings of the Matteoli Commission, Prime Minister Jospin created a second commission, the "Commission for the Compensation of Victims of Spoilation Resulting from Anti-Semitic Legislation in Force During the Occupation," to be known as the Drai Commission, named after Pierre Drai, an Algerian Jew and chief judge on France's highest court of appeals. The Drai Commission was charged with calculating the damages for claimants based on the Matteoli Commission's findings.

French Banks

During the course of the campaign against the Swiss banks, Singer and Steinberg made it very clear to numerous European countries that the effort to gain restitution for Holocaust victims would not be restricted to Switzerland. By 1997, they were releasing documents from the U.S. National Archives that detailed the cooperation of American, British, and French banks in the plundering of Jewish assets in France. Soon afterward, these banks feared similar treatment as the Swiss banks received.[163] They would not be disappointed.

The banks were charged in the documents with turning over Jewish accounts to the Nazis. For this, the French banks of Paribas, Societe Generale, Credit Lyonnais, DDF, Natexis, Credit Agricole, The Bank of Worms, the American bank J.P. Morgan, and the British bank Barclays, openly feared retribution through lawsuits. On December 18, 1997, New York attorney Kenneth

McCallion filed suit against these banks and three others charging assets were wrongfully taken from their clients, asking for a full accounting and return of all seized assets.[164] With the filing of an amended complaint on March 12, 1998, McCallion included Hausfeld, Mel Weiss, and the famed Harvard law professor Arthur Miller, among several other attorneys.[165] Now Hausfeld and Weiss were engaged in another lawsuit against European banks, while the suit against the Swiss banks was also entering its critical stages. The banks attorneys, on behalf of their clients, expressed the belief that the filing of the lawsuit against the banks was unnecessary because the suits came a year after the formation of the Matteoli Commission and their cooperation, as such, obviated such legal action.[166] In truth, in comparison to the Swiss banks, the French banks, while difficult to deal with, were more forthcoming and willing to accommodate the negotiations. According to Eizenstat, who negotiated this lawsuit as well, their lawyers, understanding that the lawsuit would not be dismissed, were less belligerent by circumstance.[167] The French Government, despite the more accommodating banks' attorneys, were, in Eizenstat's view, however, the hardest with which to work, according to Phil Bechtel, an attorney for the French banks.[168]

The French banks' more compliant attitude was reflected in their suggestion, in February 1999, that they would be open to creating a fund to compensate victims. The fund, according to the French Bankers' Association (FBA), would have to be administered by the French Jewish community.[169] One month later, the WJC disclosed that the FBA was, in fact, negotiating for the creation of a fund.[170] This willingness put the French banks in a much more positive light in comparison to the Swiss banks.

Shortly after the announcement, the FBA also expressed its willingness to formally admit its moral debt to the victims of the Holocaust as well, and to work with claimants worldwide, abiding by the decisions of the Drai Commission in fulfilling claim awards.[171] While the French seemed to be moving in the right direction, the WJC was not entirely satisfied with the progress they were making. Serge Klarsfeld, husband of Beate Klarsfeld, the French Nazi hunter and a member of the Matteoli Commission, suggested that the banks should also pay pensions to French Holocaust orphans.[172] The WJC immediately jumped at this idea, adding more recipients to the list. This situation was similar to that of the Swiss as calls for the Swiss Interim Fund grew and spread among the various agents investigating and advocating for justice.

Unlike the Swiss case, the French acted much quicker. On November 13, 1999, the French Government took the step to announce its intention to issue a decree authorizing the payment of pensions for orphans of either a one-time payment of 18,000 French francs, or a monthly indemnity of 3,000 French francs.[173]

By September 2000, when U.S. District Judge Sterling Johnson refused to dismiss the lawsuit against the banks, as Eizenstat had predicted, the case seemed destined to reach settlement. While difficulties remained, according to both Phil Bechtel and Eizenstat, the French Government presented continuing arguments as to how the eventual settlement would be formed, including how a list of accounts would be published.[174]

Finally, however, the French could stall no longer, working up against a deadline imposed by the end of the Clinton Administration's term on January 20, 2001. Eizenstat frantically trying to successfully close negotiations with the French, signed a $475 million settlement. That sum, according to the total number and value of claims, could rise to over a billion dollars, as the established foundation, to have been chaired by the Austrian Nazi hunter Simon Wiesenthal,[175]

In return for the settlement, the attorneys agreed to drop the lawsuits and Eizenstat agreed, on behalf of the U.S. government, to provide the banks with a promise to file a "statement of interest" to counter any future claims against the banks. This promise stipulated that in case of another lawsuit filed against them, the United States government would file a statement declaring that the suit was counter to the national security interests of the country.[177] The plaintiffs' attorneys, while not happy with this aspect of the settlement, concluded that it would not carry the force of law, in as much as it was not a definitive legal block on any future legal actions, only a promissory expression by the government against any future filing.[178]

As of April 2003, there were 14,400 claims filed and 5,600 claims recommendations made.[179] The total sum of the claims to the government was $91 million in additional claims based upon the settlement.[180]

Despite the successful conclusion of the negotiations, the plaintiffs' attorneys have since complained that the French banks are not doing their part to fulfill their end of the settlement.[181] According to one of the attorneys, Harriet Tamen in New York, the banks have proven to be overly legalistic and have not attempted to reach all the appropriate claimants.[182] According to Tamen, there are even thoughts of trying to re-open the settlement. The chance for success on this proposal would presumably be difficult.

Sweden

"Sweden's trade policy dealings with Nazi Germany," wrote Ambassador Sven Fredrik Hedin and Göran Elgemyr:

> have been written into the history books, along with the concessions made on the political policy level. The Swedish Central Bank's gold transactions with the Third Reich, however, have scarcely been touched upon by Swedish historians. Abroad, considerably more interest is being shown in Sweden's role.[183]

Sweden, like Switzerland, was officially neutral during World War II, but like Switzerland as well, it was not innocent. Hedin, a retired diplomat, and Elgemyr, a reporter and historian for Swedish broadcasting, together acted out of an interest to correct the story of Sweden's not so neutral past. Together with disclosures by the WJC, and to a lesser extent by D'Amato and Eizenstat, they reopened up a confusing chapter in Swedish history.

Their articles, published in Stockholm's largest newspaper, exposed the illicit gold dealings of the Swedish central bank. The publication of the articles in January 1997, brought about a government-sponsored investigation. "Three days after the first article was published," Ambassador Hedin wrote:

> the Government decided to appoint a State Commission to look into all kinds of looted gold and other property, including that of Jews, that still might be around in dormant accounts, safe deposits, etc. in our country.[184]

After meeting with Israel Singer, Swedish Prime Minister Goran Persson agreed to a full-scale investigation into Sweden's wartime history that would later be entitled, *The Commission on Jewish Assets in Sweden at the Time of the Second World War*.[185] Hedin and Elgemyr's work had the unintended consequence of the creation of national self-doubt and introspection that began to set in about the country's neutrality at the time, and, more importantly, adding to this self-doubt, was an examination of the role of one of that nation's most prestigious families, the Wallenbergs.[186] It was, of course, the family of Raoul Wallenberg who disappeared in January 1945 in Soviet custody after his heroically saving thousands of Hungarian Jews came under scrutiny.[187] Yet, it was not Raoul, but his uncles Marcus, helpful to the Allies during the war, and Jacob, a scion of the family Enskilda bank that worked to aid the Nazis, laundering looted gold as well as performing other activities for them, that came under examination.

Within a year, the government reported that the Swedish Riksbank had acquired 59.7 tons of gold from the Nazis, including looted Dutch gold.[188] The possibility that some of that gold comprised victim's gold was not certain. The Commission was also tasked with finding dormant accounts. On March 4, 1998, the Commission announced the release of a list of 649 accounts left dormant following the war.[189]

Later, revelations revealed that hundreds of Swedes had joined the Waffen-SS, and that the Wallenbergs had traded in stolen Jewish securities. These unintended consequences resulted in a serious rethinking of the country's history, but compared with the similar attempt in Switzerland, it involved more soul-searching and had a lasting effect on the country and its people. In 2000, Sweden played host to an international conference on Holocaust remembrance and education. There was even a book printed for use by Swedish school children and translated into English for the same purpose.[190]

The campaign against Switzerland, in the end, it seems, had another unintended consequence, namely that their refusal to cooperate, and their subsequent punishment in a harsh public relations backlash, showed other countries, specifically Sweden, that it was easier, and more honest, to cooperate than fight.

Like Sweden, Norway encountered the same examination, and under the same circumstances. Begun by a journalist, Bjorn Westlie, in May 1995 in response to the remembrances of the fiftieth anniversary of the end of World War II, the investigation into Norway's past began, similarly after the publication of Westlie's article, when a government-sponsored commission was established.[191]

Austria: The First Victim

As Austria has always claimed, Austria was the Nazis' first victim. It was an appellation that was so prevalent in Austria that it became the standard retort of Austrian officials to avoid restitution. While Austria's experience in the 1950s was one of abject reluctance to even confront its role during the Holocaust, by the 1980s, it was Bronfman's intention to change this attitude. The WJC's coordinated assault on the historical record of Kurt Waldheim in 1986 was part of this effort. Waldheim, found to have been knowledgeable, if not responsible, for atrocities of Jews in Salonika, was exposed; furthering the false notion of an Austrian renaissance in thinking about the Holocaust. The Austrian people rallied around Waldheim who was seen as a victim of Jewish attack politics.

Yet, by 1991, with the effects of the end the Cold War reeling all over Europe, came a more enlightened view. The Austrian Chancellor Franz Vranitzky had gone farther, perhaps, than any of his predecessors in showing the new thinking that came as a result of the new Europe. Speaking before the National Council on July 8, Vranitzky suggested a new and surprising Austrian tone.

> And precisely because we want to bring our own painful experiences with us into this new Europe, precisely because we have in these past days been reminded so profoundly and emphatically of what independence and sovereignty, freedom and human rights mean to minorities, for precisely these reasons must we also admit the other side of our history. ... Many Austrians participated in the measure of oppression and persecution of the Third Reich, in some cases even in prominent offices.
>
> Even today we cannot ignore a moral complicity for the acts of our citizens.[192]

Indeed, it was under Vranitzky's Chancellorship that the idea of repairing Austria's past took hold. In February 1990, even before his historic speech, his government agreed to provide nearly $200 million in restitution for social benefit payments to Austrian survivors in the form of social insurance benefits. Of this sum, $30 million went toward elderly care in homes in Austria for survivors.[193] Moreover, in 1996, Austria created the *Mauerbach Fund for Jewish Survivors of the Holocaust in Need.* The Fund was created out of the proceeds of an auction by Christie's of some 8,000 works of art, books, coins, and medals confiscated from Jews during the Holocaust that raised $14.5 million. The artwork was authorized for sale by the Austrian Jewish community, with the proceeds again going to the needs of elderly survivors.[194]

Vranitzky's strong condemnation of his nation's past silencing of complicity and responsibility for the crimes of the Nazis was breathtaking and opened the door to additional compensation for Holocaust survivors and their families. It also opened the door for further attack by Bronfman's coalition.

While Ed Fagan had been considered a gadfly in the Swiss banks case, in Austria he found his calling. On October 5, 1998, Fagan, at the suggestion of Charles Moerdler who was an attorney for Bank Austria and Creditanstalt, filed a lawsuit in New York against the two affiliated banks.[195] Fagan's action added the two banks to his June 1998 lawsuit against Deutsche and Dresdner banks, two German banks. Arguing that while the two German banks had subsumed the two Austrian ones in the *Anschluss*, there was a very real liability due to the extent of Austrian complicity with the Nazis. For the Austrians, the liability lay with the German banks and not them, owing, as many before and after them would believe, that they were victims of the Nazis and that the blame was not there's.

With Moerdler's agreement with Fagan to create the situation whereby the banks were first sued, then expressed a need to review their past, they logically proceeded to publicly express a willingness to settle the case out of court. Throughout the following months, negotiations continued under the auspices of D'Amato, now a private citizen following his election loss in November 1998, as a Special Master. Both sides carried on in an effort to arrive at a figure which was agreeable to both sides. The fight, as it was, turned out to be more between the attorneys allied against the Austrian banks, including Fagan, Hausfeld, and Weiss, than with the Austrian banks' attorneys.

Moerdler, sensing these disagreements, arranged what was termed a negative auction whereby the various plaintiffs' lawyers were approached with requests for the lowest settlement terms they were willing to accept on behalf of the entire settlement class. In March 1999, Fagan emerged as the one willing to settle for the lowest amount, $40 million. Simply willing to settle almost for the act of settlement itself, Fagan undercut his co-counsel adding great agitation to an already exasperated relationship.[196] In the end, there were approximately 1,000 qualifying Austrian bank account claimants out of 58,000 applicants who were given payments averaging $5,000 each. Furthermore, in an effort to make the $40 million cash payment acceptable to the very disappointed co-counsels and the survivor community, the Austrian banks agreed to forgo their claims against the German banks for losses experienced during the war.[197]

Fagan had been handed a victory. The Austrians had essentially escaped the public criticism the Swiss banks brought upon themselves more than anything else, and they found an easy way out of what could have been a disastrous affair for them. In Fagan, Moerdler had found an acceptable target to both deliver a success for his client and play to his desire to bring the case to a conclusion, regardless of its acceptability to its own claimants.

Soon after the settlement, claimants voiced very vocal opposition to its low settlement amount. Survivors accused the attorneys of settling for much too small an amount of money and also turned on D'Amato for having once nominated Moerdler, a Republican, for a judgeship. D'Amato and his "proteges," its was declared, were trying to force an unjust settlement on the survivors.[198]

The WJC opposed the settlement, as did the Claims Conference. The WJC felt the settlement should have been at least ten times as high.[199] Both sought to have Alan Hevesi begin boycott proceedings against the banks and to institute legal moves to oppose the settlement. In the end, however, the survivors and the WJC agreed to drop their demands for a larger settlement. In return, Moerdler suggested that the banks were willing to open their archives to researchers in an effort to broaden and help substantiate the case against the German banks and to verify its use of slave labor during the war. While documents from the banks would prove to be of no use, Fagan's other cases would keep going.

Fagan's other proceedings against the Austrians for insurance and slave labor were later subsumed by others and wrapped into other settlements by which Austrian industry, in relation to slave labor, obtained "legal peace," just as the French banks had. By October 2000, the Austrian government had agreed to settle the slave labor cases, with Eizenstat's mediation, for a capped amount of $410 million.

Nevertheless, Fagan, despite the dramatics and antagonism bred between himself and his fellow attorneys and others as well, served a vital purpose. His place among the other negotiators served as a valued tool for Eizenstat in his role as U.S. negotiator. In each of the cases in which he became involved, Eizenstat could point Fagan out to the various negotiating parties, especially his statements as to what he would do next, as an assertive claim as to what could happen if they did not settle with him. Fagan, whether he understood this or not, was the "bad cop" to Eizenstat's "good cop."[200]

"I see no soul searching going on in the United States ... "[201]

In London, from December 2-4, 1997, nearly forty countries attended the London Conference on Nazi Gold. The purpose of the conference was to coordinate action on the issue of Nazi-looted gold and to arrange for the eventual disposition of the gold that had been held since the end of the war by the Tripartite Gold Commission, headquartered in Brussels and administered jointly by the United States, the United Kingdom, and France. Following the final disbursement of the remaining gold to satisfy a few outstanding claims, the remainder of the gold would be liquidated and the proceeds would be put into a new fund called the "Nazi Persecutees Relief Fund."[202]

I attended this conference as a member of the United States delegation led by Eizenstat. In addition to the issue of gold, there were many side discussions. In one case, Eizenstat had tried to make the case that it was in the United States' best interest to examine its own role in the issue of assets.[203] Eizenstat had come upon this notion for a number of reasons. Diplomatic pressure from the Swiss was no doubt heavy, and the manner in which the Swiss, and even other countries, were being so vigorously questioned, caused concerns in the State Department. As the investigations expanded, the pace and vehemence of the questions meted out to various countries by not only D'Amato and the WJC, but by Representative Leach's staff, Greville Janner's, and others, was clearly beginning to take its toll on the recipients and the State Department was hearing about it loudly in return. Furthermore, people in the United States were beginning to ask what all the Europeans were asking: what role did the United States play at this time? Their question, as it turned out, was not out of bounds to ask. As Seymour Rubin suggested in March 1997, "anyone early in the war would have put his money further than Switzerland and where they hoped to go after the war."[204]

In fact, it was Rubin, one of the lead negotiators with the Swiss in 1946 and other European governments in the 1950s, who had questioned how much victims' money was held in the United States. Rubin first made this suggestion in an oral history interview with the United States Holocaust Memorial Museum in January 1997.[205] More importantly however, Rubin wrote a letter to Eizenstat addressing these issues on March 11, 1997. Rubin had expressed his hope that Eizenstat's soon-to-be-released investigative report would delve into the problem.[206] It did not.

The letter, however, which soon received wide exposure in the press and the attendant whispers about the possibilities presented by the suggestion, was not wasted on Eizenstat, who, at the time, was still the Under Secretary of Commerce. As such, a proposal was drawn up by Eizenstat's staff at Commerce, among them Judith Barnett, the Acting Deputy Assistant Secretary of Commerce for Africa and the Near East. The Commerce draft called for the creation of a congressionally sponsored Commission to examine U.S. government attempts to restitute the assets that came under its control from before and during the war, as well as an examination of potential bank accounts of victims and survivors that might have escheated to the state governments after the war.[207] Europeans pressed for this from the United States as the London Conference was about to convene.[208]

In November, shortly before the conference convened, Eli Rosenbaum, Director of the Office of Special Investigations at the U.S. Department of Justice, put his hand to a second draft and sent it to Bennett Freeman, Eizenstat's State Department aid on the issue, and Stan Turesky, then of the Holocaust Museum.[209] The idea now seemed to have substantial input from several parts of the U.S. government.

On December 10, a follow-up meeting to the London Conference was held at the State Department with another conference to be held, this time in Washington, DC, in the following year on other outstanding issues not covered in London. Included in this meeting was an explicit effort to create a U.S. commission.[210]

With this meeting, there began weekly meetings in which I suggested that D'Amato would be amenable to drafting and introducing a bill to create such a commission. Between December 1997 and April 1998, there were half-a-dozen additional drafts negotiated between us and the State Department Legal Advisor's Office and the White House Legislative Affairs staff before the bill was ready for introduction on April 1, 1998.

The bill to create The President's Advisory Commission on Holocaust Assets in the United States was introduced on April 1. All the participants and supporters commented on the same basic theme: that it was long overdue to be examining this issue, and in Eizenstat's words, "Now the time has come to look more closely at assets here at home ... "[211] On the same day, the State Department announced that the Washington, DC conference on Holocaust-Era Assets would convene in November 1998. The State Department had clearly wanted to tie the two events together and to ensure that the bill would have enough time to clear the Congress in order that by the time the conference was held, the U.S. would not look hypocritical while questioning others.

There was never any real doubt as to the fate of the legislation creating the Commission and on June 11, Congress passed the legislation unanimously. President Clinton signed the bill on June 23, 1998.[212] The bill authorized the appropriation of $3.5 million for the Commission's operations, $1 million of which was appropriated by Congress.

From a hopeful beginning, the Commission became bogged down in an attempt to organize a research plan. Moreover, the scholars necessary to put this plan together were not yet hired and the job was left to the political appointees who were not experienced in the issue, and according to members of the Commission staff, later deliberately held back important information that the scholars found.[213] The planning for the research became utterly mired by political considerations, a lack of expertise, and simple bureaucratic considerations. On December 9, 1999, only three weeks before the original Commission was authorized to expire, Congress passed, and President Clinton signed into law, the *U.S. Holocaust Assets Commission Extension Act of 1999*.[214] The Commission, now extended for another year, had yet to begin any real work towards its original mandate.

When the Commission's final report had been filed, it was, to be kind, inadequate to the mandate put before it, oversimplified, and in some cases, duplicative of work done before the Commission's creation. Moreover, the report was a work replete with willful and gaping omissions, and an over-dependence on secondary sources that ignored the very access which the commission had available to it. The most important items from the originally mandated areas of study were missing, or were discussed with such short shrift as to make the report an unfulfilling contribution to the growing literature on subject.[215] According to the *New York Times* which commented on it two years later:

> The experts, historians and economists who worked from 1998 to 2000 on the panel, the Presidential Advisory Commission on Holocaust Assets in the United States, say that as a result it came up with a report that broke little new ground and failed to come to grips with the question of how much stolen art passed through American controls.[216]

The Commission recommended that the issue be renewed through a private-Congressionally mandated foundation. U.S. Senators Gordon Smith (OR) and Hillary Clinton (NY) proposed legislation creating such a foundation in 2001, and yet the bill, *The Holocaust Victims Asset, Restitution Policy, and Remembrance Act of 2001*, was not passed by the close of the 107th Congress.[217]

America's foray into investigating the actions of other nations proved to be a success. When it came to investigating itself, success was elusive. While planning for the Commission's mandate, there was talk of investing the role of U.S. companies. While it was ruled out due to political considerations, had this area of research been included, and honestly reported, there would have been much more to be found and a completely new angle on Holocaust restitution might well have been discovered.[218]

Whereas before the end of the Cold War, they had no one to forcefully speak for them, now they had more than they could handle. Bronfman and his partners had successfully handled the issues of the bank accounts and dormant financial assets. While not reaching a perfect conclusion, their success had been greater than anticipated. Many of the main issues were concluded, but there were, however, additional issues left to be discussed. With these issues, the unfinished business of the Holocaust would now get even more complicated.

The Forgotten Issues

Property Restitution

Stories of Leon Vlodinger's twenty-room villa in Constanta, Romania, confiscated by local officials in July 1941, stuck with his daughter Jacqueline

Waldman for more than fifty years. In 1996, with stories of lost bank accounts and other properties in the news, Jacqueline was pushed by friends to try and reclaim her father's villa.[219] Thus began a five-year battle with the post-Communist Romanian government for the property. Despite winning three consecutive court trials against the government, as well as an appeal before the nation's Supreme Court, the government continued to defy the judgments against it. Finally, only through the personal intervention of Representative Benjamin L. Cardin of Baltimore, her Congressman, and the help of the American Ambassador Jim Rosapepe, was the villa returned.[220]

Jacqueline Waldman's case, while successful, was nevertheless symptomatic of what every claimant to confiscated property had to endure when trying to work within the legal systems in Europe, both East and West. Governments, in the mid-1990s and beyond, despite the climate of hostility to those denying survivors their property, still retained the ability to resist those seeking to enforce their claims, doing so through complex legal maneuvering that involved costly procedures. As Laura A. Clerici, the Consul General in the American Embassy in Warsaw warned:

> The Embassy cautions individuals to recognize that the process of invalidating property-seizure decisions is long and may be expensive, and moreover that in cases where property has been returned, it is often impossible to legally remove the present tenants. Often the new owner may simply incur more in costs than she will ever gain in benefits.[221]

"... [P]rivate property restitution," Eizenstat reported in January 1996 when still the U.S. Ambassador to the European Union, "remains generally more difficult." Eizenstat continued:

> Citizenship and/or residency requirements for claimants are the major stumbling blocks in most—but not all—countries visited. Particularly affected are U.S. citizens (of all religions) whose relatives had property confiscated by either the Nazis or the communists and Jews who live in Israel or elsewhere. For both communal and private property claims, I frequently heard that the claims process is, at best, tedious and time consuming—sometimes due to exhaustive bureaucratic requirements and sometimes due simply to overburdened and inexperienced judiciaries.[222]

Obtaining property then, involved the retention of a local attorney, who knew the language of the country and the personnel in the courts as well as the archival systems in use both in the present as well as the past.[223] Citizenship requirements, coupled at times even with residency requirements, were a significant block put forward by governments, just as the Austrians proposed in the 1950s. People, who had fled under terrible circumstances were never going to move back to the country in order to acquire their inherited property, yet this requirement was retained.

For others, claiming property, while difficult, produced the improbable, and certainly unintended, consequence of acquiring property that they, in fact, could not utilize and more importantly, did not want. Zypora Frank inherited land upon which her grandfather's factory sat. As it turned out, that property formed a section of the Auschwitz death camp.[224]

In Germany, the problem of property restitution, intended to be resolved in the years following the war, was not conclusive. In succeeding years, claims to property surfaced that had lain in the hands of corporations none too willing to surrender profits to pay for the crimes—to which they might not have been remotely connected—of the past. In the years following the war, restitution was made of smaller properties being returned to their owners. In the larger cases, however, there was essentially too much at stake to challenge the status quo and only partial restitution was accomplished. In the case of Barbara Principe and her nephew Martin Wortham, direct descendants of the Wertheim department store fortune, restitution was not achieved. In their case, they found out only in 2000 that as heirs, they stood to claim property in the center of Berlin valued at more than $250 million.[225]

Claiming property in the most historic districts of Berlin, the Wertheim claim encompasses land central to the history of the Third Reich. As Gary M. Osen, their New Jersey attorney, explained in their 2001 lawsuit against defendant Karstadtquelle and Hertie Warenhaus und Kaufhaus GmbH, two of the largest retailers in Germany:

> Starting in 1934, several individual properties were sold by Wertheim Corp. to the Nazi government, such as Voßstraße 33, which was sold for the below market price of RM 1.6 million to the Administration of the Reichs-Autobahnen. ... Once World War II began, the Nazi government began construction of the elaborate bunker system below these properties which served as the focal point for the drama surrounding the last days of Hitler and his regime. Part of the above-ground Reichskanzlei was destroyed by Allied bombing and the rest was bulldozed by the Soviets after the war, in part, to prevent the site from becoming a Nazi shrine.[226]

Principe and Wortham had a case that stirred a legal dispute, not only between themselves and the two companies, but also between the German government and the United States. Because of Eizenstat's negotiations with other German companies, lawsuits against the companies following the successful settlement of the slave labor lawsuits, were to be, by agreement, assertively intervened against, by the United States government. This arrangement was achieved in the Austrian industries case, and was put to the test by this one. Germany argued that the case, stemming from Holocaust-era Aryanizations, placed it under the stipulations of Eizenstat's commitment.

Osen complained of the German Foreign Ministry's active lobbying of the State Department in favor of intervention. According to Osen, Michael Geier of the German Foreign Ministry wrote to the State Department, "A non-intervention by the US-Government [sic] would be taken by plaintiffs' lawyers as an invitation to reopen all major restitution cases under the allegation that plaintiffs were misled about the real value of the claims."[227] Principe and Wortham argued that the lawsuit did not because the land and buildings in question were, in the 1950s, considered worthless. They argued that a woefully inadequate settlement price, some $9,000, was offered and accepted by Principe's father. They considered the case to be one originating in the Holocaust-era but ripening into a fraudulent action in the post-war era.[228]

In October 2002, Eizenstat, though out of office, nevertheless sided with Principe and Wortham in a letter to their attorney. He agreed with the argument that the U.S. government should not be obligated to intervene on the side of the German government.[229]

In other countries in Europe, governments struggled to maintain relations with the various communities claiming the return of properties. Accusations passed back and forth between the communities claiming favoritism for one side or the other in the return of properties, making the process more difficult even than in the manner Eizenstat first had reported the problem. Many passed laws permitting the return of properties to citizens only, and others made actual properties, or similarly situated properties, available. Cumulative restitution funds were established to compensate survivors in numerous countries.

The U.S. role in these evolving changes is limited. Aside from Eizenstat's beginning role, the dynamic changed since the issue came to the fore. While the claims issue was a prominent topic internationally, settlements like Jacqueline Waldman's were, with patience, achievable. In others it was more difficult. As Randolph M. Bell, one of Eizenstat's successors as the Special Envoy for Holocaust issues advanced:

> There are of course limitations on what the United States can properly do. Under accepted international law and practice, we can formally espouse individual claims—that is present a claim to a government—only under very specific circumstances. We therefore concentrate our efforts on urging countries to put in place fair, transparent, nondiscriminatory restitution processes that will cover broad categories of cases.[230]

In Poland, this could not have been truer. The return of property there proved to be painfully unattainable. According to Naphtalie Lavie of the WJRO, 100,000 Jewish-owned homes, shops and other properties were taken during the war. As David Holley, of *The Los Angeles Times* wrote of Poland and its restitution problems, "The other democratic states of the former East Bloc, such as the Czech Republic and Hungary, have done much more than Poland to return real estate to pre-Communist owners."[231]

Following the war and the accession to power of the Soviet-installed Communist Party, these properties, would, by and large, be returned to native Poles.[232] Nationalization of property in Poland was asserted as a Marxist principle, and therefore an accepted practice for the new Communist state, $50 billion according to a Polish Treasury Department calculation in 2000.[233] While nationalization was enshrined in the new constitution of 1952, the nationalization of private land became too expensive for successive Polish Communist governments to deprive the peasants of their own land.[234]

In Poland, survivors would find a country that had fought its way out of communism and, while appreciative of that heritage, it was still hostage to its history of less than amiable relations with its Jewish population. With fears that "everyone will come," Lavie explained regarding the comment of Polish Prime Minister Leszek Miller, Polish officials resented Jewish claims, suggesting that history has passed and that being a new era, it cannot and should not be undone.[235]

When I went to Poland with my father-in-law, I saw the look on the faces of the people in the small town of Mirzaschin when we traveled about the town square looking for old property. We were seen as interlopers, returning long after the fact for property that had long since passed into the hands of others. Fearful of large payouts it cannot afford, Poland has had great difficulty in dealing with the influx of claims from survivors like my father-in-law and others. Claims for property in Poland number at 6,000 in the WJRO database as of 2002, alone.[236]

With the success of the Swiss banking investigation and the attendant publicity that it had gained, survivors, feeling emboldened, sought help in the area of property restitution as well. Soon letters began to come into Congressional offices seeking help and information on who to contact in Poland to regain title to their property. "Since I am one of your constituents," wrote Simona Frajndlich to Representative Steven C. LaTourette:

> I am writing to you asking whether you are able to help me in reclaiming my mother's property in Piotnkow Ttyb, POLAND [sic]. I am the youngest of eight siblings and the only one who is still alive. My parents and some of my siblings perished in Treblinka. I myself survived concentration camps. I thought I will try to reclaim the property again since Poland is now becoming a democracy and joining NATO.[237] (Letter of Simona Frajndlich to Representative Steven C. LaTorurette, March 18, 1998).

By 1999, the situation came to the point that diplomacy was of questionable effect in persuading the Polish government to ease the procedures for survivors to reclaim their land and property. As in the past, the vehicle for greater pressure through the application of the law and the use of the press was successful, Mel Urbach, who had participated in the lawsuits against the Swiss banks, tried this tactic when he filed a lawsuit in the U.S. District Court of the Eastern District of New York, on June 18, 1999, on behalf of eleven plaintiffs all seeking to reclaim their property from Poland.[239] Soon another suit would be filed in Chicago.

The Polish government angrily rejected the lawsuits, objecting to their filing in the U.S. as well as the potential costs. It was estimated that claims against Poland would bankrupt the country costing it over $29 billion, equal to the annual Polish budget.[240]

At the same time as the lawsuits began, the Polish Parliament began working on legislation to create a more efficient way for claimants to re-acquire their property. The legislation, however, caused great controversy when it passed the Parliament with stipulations in it requiring claimants to not only be citizens of the country, but residents as well, a proposition that did not sit well with the thousands who had long before fled the country and now sought their property. Additionally, the bill would have only provided for compensation for up to 50 percent of the properties value. On March 22, 2001, Polish President Aleksander Kwasniewski vetoed the bill on grounds of the overwhelming costs of the restitution involved.[241]

Claimants to property also received another blow on June 24, 2002, when Judge Edward Korman, the judge who mediated the Swiss banks settlement, dismissed Urbach's lawsuit on grounds that there was no jurisdiction. Urbach promised to appeal.[242] Despite promises that the issue of restitution in Poland has not died, neither legislation nor lawsuits have pushed the issue further. Property restitution in Poland seems very far off.

Artwork: The Never-Ending Search

> As you can see, wrote Dutch Foreign Minister Hans van Mierlo, after the war, Jacques Goudstikker's widow, Mrs. Goudstikker-Von Halban, chose consciously, and on the basis of expert legal and other advice, not to reclaim title to the paintings sold to Goering by her late husbands's art dealership. Instead, she chose to keep the money she had received for them, but at the same time, elected to reclaim title to real estate and other property sold to Mr. Miedl ... [243]

As the tragedy of Jacques Goudstikker had so greatly affected the family and the situation in which he was forced to part with his art gallery and collection, his family was hard pressed to make a conscious decision regarding its disposition based on its true value. In other words, the sale was under duress. After the war, the decision to seek compensation was made, though lacking all the necessary documents, in the flurry of their efforts to rebuild their lives. Nevertheless, the family, now led by the widow of Jacques Goudstikker's son Edward, Marie von Saher, sought restitution for the paintings sold and confiscated from her father-in-law.

Ms. von Saher's dispute with the Dutch government was typical of that which nearly all claimants to artwork have faced. Like the Wertheim case in Berlin, Ms. von Saher, had to contend with a government argument that a settlement, inadequate or not, or even a refusal to initially seek restitution, should be considered valid. Legalistic arguments, albeit not as stubbornly put forth as did the Swiss, still carry the day in this category of asset restitution. Those retaining artwork obtained during or after the war cling to the assertion that acquisition is not dependent upon motivation of the seller. What takes precedence over the restitution of a particular piece of artwork is the constitution of the holder's collection as a whole, and that of a particular item's role within that collection. Breaking up a collection for the purpose of restitution is unfortunately a hostile notion and one reason among many to deny a claim. This was the alibi of the French museums for withholding the paintings of Holocaust victims for more than fifty years.[244]

Worse yet is the argument, held mum by most art museum directors, but voiced in 2001 by Ian Lumsden, the Executive Director of the Beaverbrook Art Gallery in Fredericton, Canada, that the Nazis actually served mankind in looting these paintings, and protecting them from the ravages of war. "[I]t's not the worst thing in the world," that the artwork was stolen. "I don't really believe that people have right to ownership of a major work of art."[245] Insensitive as it might seem, this attitude was expressed with sincerity and conveyed the sense of artwork as eternal and its owners only transitory. This could not be truer when it comes to antiquities, like the Elgin Marbles, the likes of which museums strongly affirmed the right to keep and protect regardless of its national patrimony.[246]

Ms. von Saher, perhaps aided by high-level intervention by D'Amato with the Dutch officials and other interventions, finally received a painting from the Goudstikker collection in May 2001, *The Temptation of St. Anthony*, by J.W. de Cock. The painting, valued at $15,000 was discovered when it was offered up for auction at Christie's from the estate of the collection of Hertha Katz.[247] This painting, having been the first of the collection to be returned, Ms. von Saher, said, "will have the most value in my heart."[248] On February 6, 2006, the Dutch government announced that it would return 200 more paintings of the Goudstikker collection.

While other forms of property and assets were in some ways easier to obtain, due either to their tangibility, like money or gold, or their permanence and restriction on movability, like homes or land, artwork is highly movable and easily shipped, sold, and even hidden from public display for long periods of time.

The Goudstikker-owned *The Temptation of St. Anthony*, was owned by the Katz family for fifty years and only surfaced when offered for sale. Thus, the problems of discovering looted artwork are numerous. Provenance or the ownership history of artwork is a complicated and easily obfuscated part of a piece of artwork. To hide a painting or sculpture's history is easily done due to a lack of central record keeping. In essence, if a collector or museum wishes to hide a piece, it can and will do it with little chance of detection.

By 1998, like the issue of property in Europe, the volume of art claims rose as people became more attuned to the overall subject. As the claims rose, so, too, did the discovery of artwork in museums around the world and in the United States. As such the Association of Art Museum Directors (AAMD) came under fire for these accusations. "This demonization of museums," declared Philippe de Montebello, the director of New York's Metropolitan Museum, "may make good copy, but it really has no basis in fact. It puts museums unfairly on the defensive, whereas in fact we are eager to solve the problem."[249] The point Montebello expressly missed was the fact that now, as Bronfman had sought to do all along, was, in fact, to put those holding looted assets on the defensive. Paintings in museums around the world were found to have been looted precisely because until this time, no one ever posed the question to them: where did you get that painting? Like the past where no one dared challenge other holders of assets, so, too, it was the case with the world's museums.

The negligence of the museums in searching the provenance of their collections came back to haunt them, soon survivors were finding paintings hanging in collections that had once hung over the fireplaces of their homes in Europe.[250]

In June 1998, responding to pressure, the AAMD formulated a series of guidelines for museums to follow with respect to their own collections and those that were bequeathed, loaned, or bought by them. The guidelines were written suggesting that museums "should" commence provenance research and do so in order to ascertain the true ownership record of their collections. While suggestions were made as to how the collections should be examined and what to do should looted pieces be found, only proposals were made as to the dispensation of the piece in question. It was a highly suggestive set of guidelines, devoid of a real legal commitment for action.[251]

This set of guidelines failed to adequately achieve a solution to the problem. In the near future, the AAMD would accept similar guidelines under Eizenstat's initiative from the thirty-eight nations gathered at the *Washington Conference on Holocaust-Era Assets*, and the Presidential Commission on Holocaust Era Assets.[252] A productive process did, however, come out of the PCHA agreement with the AAMD, and that was only a statement to publish the findings of their provenance research. Websites on the Internet were promised that would hold this information. In some cases the museum sites have been assembled. In far too many others, however, they were and are lacking.[253]

Although not admitted, the requirement to conduct the research has been difficult to enforce owing to the cost and reluctance to actually search out the truth of the provenance of respective pieces of artwork. Fear of finding the true provenance of a piece, and finding that that piece was in fact looted, causes fear of adverse publicity, lawsuits, loss of prestige, and everything that goes along with the operation and maintenance of a prominent museum. Once some lists of provenance were posted to the Internet, immediately gaps in the timelines caused questions and the inevitable flurry of press releases to deny any wrongs by the museums.[254]

Auction houses, too, were put on alert fearing that once a painting was denounced as having been looted, they would also be tainted by the adverse publicity as well as perhaps legal responsibility for having sold the artwork.[255] This fear was a result of a long-simmering case evolving out of a loaned collection from the Leopold Collection in Austria. The Leopold loaned an exhibit of paintings by the expressionist Egon Schiele (1890-1918) to New York's Museum of Modern Art (MoMA), from the beginning of December 1997 through January 4, 1998.

Once the catalogue for the exhibit was released, there were two claims filed on two separate paintings in the Leopold exhibition. Henry S. Bondi, a nephew of the late Lea Bondi wrote to Glenn Lowry, Director of the MoMA explaining his family's claim to "Portrait of Wally," which was part of the exhibit.

> The painting was taken from Lea Bondi's collection—it was hanging in her apartment, where I saw it often as a boy—without her consent by Nazi agents or collaborators. Lea Bondi died at the age of ninety-three in London, in 1969, having three years earlier attempted to regain this painting. At no time had she or the Bondi family ever consented to any sale or transfer of the painting. Accordingly, the heirs of Lea Bondi are the true and lawful owners of the painting.[sic][256]

Immediately thereafter, with the publicity from this first claim, came a second by Kathleen and Rita Reif who also wrote seeking the return of a painting, when they wrote to Lowry five days later concerning their claim to "Dead City III."

> Accordingly, we call upon the Museum to live up fully to its moral responsibility, as well as its legal commitments, as a leading curator and guardian of works of art by addressing the issue raised by this case. In particular, we call upon the Museum to reach agreement with the Leopold Foundation voluntarily to leave the paintings in New York—with the Museum or with an independent, third-party fiduciary acceptable to all parties that have an ongoing interest in the painting - pending the resolution of this dispute.[257]

The MoMA came under attack. The museum's directors dug in their heels and refused to give in. Soon the Manhattan District Attorney Robert Morgenthau, Henry Morgenthau's grandson, issued a restraining order on the picture's move from the museum and the two paintings were eventually seized by Morgenthau's office. The Leopold Gallery equally became defensive and the resulting legal fight sent chills down the backs of museum and gallery directors fearing the consequences of either loaning, or receiving on loan, a painting later found or claimed to have been looted. After a prolonged legal fight, the State Department was obliged to come down on the side of the Austrian gallery for reasons of its role not only in diplomacy, but the regulation of the international loan of artwork between countries. Morgenthau pursued the case for some time until the New York State Supreme Court denied his ability to hold the paintings any longer.

With inconclusive histories and more claims, museums continued to find looted art. Three Albrecht Dürer drawings were found in the Cleveland Museum of Art in April 1998.[258] In August 1998, the Art Institute of Chicago settled a long simmering dispute over a Degas painting, *Landscape With Smokestacks* and its owner Daniel Searle, with claimants Nick and Simon Goodman.[259] The settlement was an eleventh hour deal in a case based on a lawsuit and intense public relations exercises by the Goodmans and the art provenance researcher Willi Korte. Princeton University's art museum came to an agreement with the heirs of a painting it found in its collection in 2001.[260] Finally, in the Menil Collection in Houston, the Minneapolis Institute of Arts, and the Museum of Modern Art in New York, it is thought that paintings were held all belonging to the collection of Alphonse Kahn, whose collection was plundered by the Nazis.[261]

Internationally, museums were checking their collections as well. Museums in Montreal, London, Scotland, Berlin, Augsburg, Prague, Sydney and Canberra, Australia have committed to find, and indeed have found, looted art works in their collections. Efforts are also under way to create a central Internet website to house all the provenance pages. This effort is still in its infancy, but the museums are working to make it a reality.[262]

There have been research groups that joined a small group of existing provenance researching organizations. The Art Loss Registry, which helped find and return *The Temptation of St. Anthony* to Marei von Saher, is one such group.

In all, the restitution of artwork has proven to be the most difficult. Eizenstat's vision for unified principles designed to streamline and advance the cause of provenance research were admirable, and an effort that gained international acceptance. On the whole, though, restitution for art work is done painstakingly, usually on an individual basis. Owing to the vast numbers of pieces it is thought were looted, a number well into the hundreds of thousands, not to mention the possible cost of each work based on the record-setting auction rewards for some pieces, the problems are infinitely difficult.

For each claim, the chain of custody must be established from the claimant's proverbial fireplace mantle, through the Nazi auction process, to the ostensibly but not universally "clean" buyer, to the series of owners, museums, or galleries and auction houses. This is an extremely difficult process which costs both time and money and involves travel, usually across Europe, to identify that chain of custody. In the cases where that chain is established, that process is soon proved to be easier compared to that which goes into forcing the surrender or negotiating for the transfer of the piece. Depending on how the piece was obtained, when, and where, all must be factored into the decision-making process for the strategies behind the entire effort. Many times, the present owner truly does not know the work's history. Moreover, as events have shown, it is an ironic a fact that a Jewish owner is found to have been in legal possession of a looted work, thereby making the claim morally difficult.

Looted art restitution then, is by most accounts the most difficult to achieve and the least affected by governmental or diplomatic intervention. It is for this reason that it is the most unlikely category of assets to ever be fully and successfully completed and will remain the true unfinished business of the World War II.

Another category of forgotten issues is that of life insurance. Nearly as difficult, the amounts of money involved, like that of artwork, also suggests great difficulty to solve.

Insurance: The Poor Man's Swiss Bank Account

In 1942, F.W. McCombe, the British Economic Warfare Officer based at the time in Washington, DC, and later a strong advocate for restitution from Spain and Portugal, described the problem of two particular claims for insurance polices with the Basle Life Insurance Company. The company had funds held by the Swiss Bank Corporation subject to legal attachment on behalf of the insurance claims. McCombe wrote John Pehle, who, at the time, was in Foreign Funds Control, concerning the claims.

> ... I know no general principle that a debtor who has a claim upon a corporate entity cannot pursue that claim either where he finds the entity or where he can attach its property, so that unless by express term of the insurance policy any claims are not only ascertainable according to the lax locus contractus but sold jurisdiction was centered there, I would be disposed to doubt that the arguments of the Basle Insurance Company are necessarily conclusive.[263]

Just as the United States Foreign Claims Settlement Commission wrote concerning the legitimacy of Judith Karmi's claims, above, against the government of Hungary in 1976 and her clear right to institute legal proceedings against any branch of a withholding institution,[264] claims against insurance companies, while just, at the time were hard to document.

Indeed, writing in 1961 about that proof, the dean of Holocaust historians, Raul Hilberg, wrote concerning this notion when he commented that the issue of private insurance was "an interesting problem ... which we have no documentation."[265] Today, Hilberg's observation is no longer true. There is documentation and it provides even greater insight into how the Nazis stole the assets of Holocaust victims.

As the *Economist* explained at the time, "Controversies over forgotten Swiss bank accounts and property once owned by Jews in Eastern Europe have jolted people into asking about other assets missing since the Second World War. Insurance policies are high on the list.[266] Once again, the experience of the Swiss banks was visited upon another industry found to be complicit in the hoarding of Holocaust victims' assets.

In 1996, Assicurazioni Generali Insurance of Italy, sought to increase its control of the Migdal Insurance Company in Israel. Soon afterward, questions were asked of Generali in the Israeli Knesset with a request by Yad Vashem, Generali asking for its files concerning the policies it sold in Eastern Europe and their fate during the Holocaust. At the same time, Allianz Insurance, one of Germany's companies also came under accusations from survivors in the United States. Criticism and the attendant press of each dispute complimented the claims against the other and amplified each.

Knesset members Avraham Hirschson and Michael Kleiner threatened to block Generali's $320 million purchase of Migdal, questioning whether that purchase would have been made with victims' money.[267] Soon they increased their pressure on Generali, threatening penalties and sanctions on their business in Israel, and by June 1999, Generali saw the need to alleviate its takeover plans and agreed to set up a $12 million restitution plan.[268]

Generali announced that it would donate money from the fund to survivor's medical and psychological care and to organizations perpetuating Holocaust memory.[269] Yet, despite this commitment, in newspaper advertisements in around the world, the company stuck to the explanation of its role as a victim.

> The cold-war Communist regimes in Eastern Europe nationalized and expropriated all major businesses, seizing all of Generali's insurance businesses there, including its offices, 1,184 buildings and fourteen companies controlled by Generali. As a result, Generali today has very little information and few records regarding policies issued by its former branches in Central and Eastern Europe.[270]

Generali had previously made one-time payments to needy survivors of $400 as well as fulfilling some claims to policy holders.[271]

Three months earlier, in March, the European Life Insurance companies got a feeling of what the Swiss banks had been going through when Ed Fagan filed a lawsuit on behalf of nine claimants. Each of the eight companies was sued for $1 billion each.[272] Soon the number of companies involved in the lawsuit rose to sixteen.

With the lawsuits came complaints of unfair criticism by the insurance companies. They felt they were being ganged up on by first the attorneys, and then by the individual State Insurance Commissioners who now joined the effort on behalf of the claimants. They began formal investigations under the rubric institutional structure of the National Association for Insurance Commissioners (NAIC). Now, Bronfman's coalition had grown to such proportions that entire institutions had been directed toward this ever-growing effort. Hearings were held in the larger U.S. cities, preferably where there were numerous survivors, as well as a robust press, waiting to be fed stories of illicit corporate dealings with the Nazis and against Holocaust victims. In one respect, the insurance companies were right. While they were doing their own fair share of work in contributing to their own poor reception in the press, Bronfman's goal of changing the rule of assumption facing survivors claiming assets was overwhelmingly successful in its practice.

In the press environment of the 1990s, with the accusations, it was readily assumed that companies faced with charges of stealing from victims and survivors, were guilty. The coverage received by the Swiss banks case proved that. With every passing day, readers around the world were fed with more and more stories that the idea of complicity in the Holocaust was now the rule. With that established, it was a short leap in logic to accept the rule that the survivors did not have to prove their claims concretely, but only repeatedly, in order to be proven right.

With the NAIC holding hearings, the individual Commissioners took a leading role in the effort. In New York, Neil Levin, first the State's Banking Commissioner and later the Insurance Commissioner, rose to the head of the New York-New Jersey Port Authority. Levin, a former D'Amato assistant, could be credited with much of the state's efforts to investigate the banks, insurance companies, and individuals associated with the withholding of assets, including the creation of the state's Holocaust Claims Office, which still exists to this day helping numerous claimants re-acquire their assets. Levin, tragically, in his last capacity as the Director of the Port Authority, died in the bombing of the World Trade Center on September 11, 2001.

In Florida, Bill Nelson, a former Congressman, and Space Shuttle astronaut, had gone back to Florida after his time in the House of Representatives, where he served as the state's Insurance Commissioner and Treasurer. He held hearings and launched websites on the Internet. Soon, his dogged work paid off, not only for Florida claimants, but for himself, as he ran for and won election to replace the retiring U.S. Senator Connie Mack in 2000.

In California, Chuck Quackenbush, had risen high on the list of elected Republicans. He, along with Levin, had done dedicated work to achieve restitution for claimants, not only in California, but nationwide as well. Quackenbush had held out against many in the state who said that withholding the right of the companies to do business there was unjust. Quackenbush, however, became embroiled in scandal and was forced to resign and subsequently left the state for Hawaii.[273]

As Fagan, who must actually be credited with bringing the insurance aspect to the fore, wrote to D'Amato in January 1998:

> ... from what I am observing, the issue of Holocaust Insurance Victims' claims against certain of Europe's largest insurance companies is gaining enormous political momen-

> tum with the National Association of Insurance Commissioners (who have held hearings in DC, Florida, California, Chicago, Washington [State], and have hearings scheduled for NY and Pennsylvania), at the individual state level (certain states principally NY state [sic] and national politicians are looking to enact legislation to benefit these Holocaust Victims claimants) ... [274]

Following the refusal of U.S. District Judge Michael Mukasey to dismiss Fagan's, and nearly a dozen other cases against them in September 1997, the companies realized they were in a serious predicament.[275]

Allianz, too, committed to resolving cases, delving into research among its various files for claimants calling a help line set up by the company. They also committed to commissioning a history of their company and its activities during the war. They hired University of California at Berkeley historian Gerald Feldman to write that history. But like Generali, they denied that any further claims were possible because " ... we can say that no assets of funds were left with the insurance companies."[276]

Allianz, however, like Generali, learned from the experience of the Swiss banks. The Swiss were obstinate, not only in the negotiating room, but out in public as well. In fact, they overwhelmingly objected to their treatment and fate at the hands of their enemies. Companies and other nations as well saw the effect it had on survivors, attorneys, Jewish groups, and U.S. government and congressional investigators and negotiators. Swiss behavior only bred further antagonism, the insurance companies saw this and vowed to not position themselves so prominently in the sites of their accusers. Allianz, despite the deep criticism it took for its lack of cooperation on policy-holders' information, nevertheless saw the wisdom of at least saying the right things. "We want to settle unpaid life insurance claims without delay," testified Christopher Worthley speaking on behalf of the company at one of Quackenbush's California conferences on the subject in January 1998. "Elderly people cannot be kept waiting for the outcome of lengthy court proceedings. We have made much progress over the past few months, and I am here today to tell you abut what we are doing and the legitimate claims we have uncovered."[277]

Insurance regulators and the survivors were not all that trusting of the various companies' level of cooperation. With insurance, being described as the "poor man's Swiss bank account," it was readily accepted that insurance policies were much more prevalent and widespread across Europe than were bank accounts with any particular country's banks. Since the insurance salesmen, like those of Generali, traveled all over Eastern Europe selling policies, even in the smallest of towns and Jewish communities and shtetls, their reach and the number of policies was presumed to be far greater. With this in mind, there needed to be another procedure created whereby research could be done, but by trusted parties other than by those of the companies themselves.

Since September 1997, Levin had been discussing with Singer and Steinberg, ways to achieve this. Using the creation of the Volcker Commission as a model, they proposed the creation of a similar institution comprised of all the interested parties, to research, audit, and document the problem and to establish a unified claims procedure for survivors.[278] On the day before D'Amato was to testify before Representative Jim Leach's Banking Committee on the progress of the Senate Banking Committee's investigation, Levin spoke with D'Amato and proposed that he use that opportunity to present this plan, and do so as his own. On February 12, 1998, D'Amato did just that, suggesting that the insurance companies would not "want to be in the same situation the Swiss banks have placed themselves in," he formally proposed the idea.[279]

Generali's Counsel Scott Vayer, testifying at the same hearing, wholeheartedly agreed with the D'Amato proposal, a fact confirmed before the hearing began, and proudly announced before the Committee.[280] Vayer came with numerous documents attesting to Generali's victimization of both the Nazis during the war and the Communists afterward. He went to great lengths to show how and why there were so few documents available to prove claims. He was, however, far from confrontational and went to great lengths to explain how Generali would cooperate in the future.[281]

Allianz was not as forthcoming as Vayer explained Generali was. Herbert Hansmeyer, Allianz Board Member, was polite yet defensive. "To be perfectly frank," he confessed:

> the last year has been very difficult for Allianz AG, especially for its European subsidiaries which over the past fifty years have successfully reemerged from the devastation of World War II. ... Let me stress a fact which is crucial to an understanding of our company's position. There is a clear distinction between the insurance companies' situation and that of the Swiss banks. Given the chaotic conditions that existed in central Europe after the War, there probably are some life insurance policies for which beneficiaries never received payment. At the same time, it should be stressed that, unlike the Swiss banks, Allianz AG subsidiaries are not holding onto dormant assets representing the residual value of those unsettled policies.[282]

The Commission's creation would enhance the power and authority of the NAIC to regulate the companies and to gain information and cooperation from them.[283] This new-found power would increase, in many ways, the antagonism between the companies and the various regulators who would later seek to punish the businesses for their foot-dragging on the release of information. For now, however, the commission idea was the perfect path out of trouble for the companies, not only for the fact that they were the targets of Fagan's lawsuit, but because any sign of cooperation with the commission would mitigate trouble on the legal end of the dispute. In this way, they could be seen to be working on the issue and thereby assert that a lawsuit would be an obstacle to an orderly process going on with the Commission.

Within weeks of the proposal, Generali had agreed to allow Quackenbush's investigators into the company's files.[284] As would prove to be the case, once access was granted with one company, requests would be made of others. Allianz, the other major company to which investigators sought access, was still not so quick to provide it. "I have spoken with Rabbi Singer last week," Hansmeyer wrote D'Amato, "and hope that we will soon have an agreement on a statement of principles that will guide our activities."[285]

Hansmeyer's cooperation was announced, along with that of three other companies, on April 8, 1998, when the companies signed a Memorandum of Intent committing them to the principles of the Commission of which D'Amato had outlined nearly two months earlier. Zurich Group, Generali, and the Equitable Life Insurance Company or AXA, joined Allianz, Singer on behalf of the WJC and WJRO, Saul Kagan on behalf of the Claims Conference and the WJRO, Levin, and Quackenbush. [286]

The creation of the Commission was both a blessing and a curse to Fagan who had initially refused to accede to its creation, sensing that it was aimed at him to undercut his effort. When promised a seat on the Tribunal, he relented and the commission became a reality.[287]

By August, the Memorandum of Intent, as an expression of the companies' accession to the idea of creating a commission, gave way to a Memorandum of Understanding (MOU). On August 13, 1998, one day after the Swiss bank settlement, Zurich Life signed the MOU.[288]

Six days later, Generali, through D'Amato's mediation, agreed to a fund of $100 million , some 15 percent of which would go for charities, and the rest to satisfy claims. There was also a provision that a list of some 300,000 names of policy-holders would be provided to Yad Vashem.[289] Roughly a month later, however, the deal fell apart with Fagan and attorneys in Florida objecting strongly to the settlement on grounds that the amount provided by Generali was woefully inadequate.[290] While Fagan had been reported to have agreed to drop his lawsuit against Generali, he denied this and pressed on with his opposition through the continuance of the lawsuit. Claiming to represent thousands of survivors with claims against Generali, Fagan opposed the settlement, feeling the amount was too low.[291] According to published reports, Fagan sought fees as high as 20 percent from the settlement.[292] He later denied such a number following a huge outcry from the WJC and Israeli lawmakers.[293]

During the settlement, D'Amato had sought to initiate a merger of the lawsuits with the MOU for the Commission. There were clear benefits to this proposal for the claimant/plaintiffs, mainly that the process would have insured a clear and enforceable claims procedure tied to the regulatory powers of the NAIC as well as a chance to obtain documents to substantiate their claims. For the companies, it would have taken the pressure off of them by putting a control on Fagan and the other attorneys. The companies, however, would not be able to reverse auction any settlement offers, such as that which occurred in the Austrian bank settlement and Fagan's accession to a lower settlement number.[294]

The merger proposition, however, was aimed directly at the lawsuits and engendered vocal dissent and opposition from the attorneys, especially Fagan. "The survivor claimants," he plead to D'Amato in a letter at the end of September:

> are furious at the WJC, the WJRO, the NAIC, and particularly Neil Levin. I am trying to hold them back, but all they see are the regulators and organizations *killing* their Generali settlement and interfering in their rights in the class action and with the claims against all the other companies.(underline in the author's original)[295]

In reality, Fagan had very adeptly fought against, and defeated, this first effort at establishing the settlement in the hope that it would be higher. He believed that while the amount most likely should have been higher, there was more to be gotten for all concerned.

In mid-October, Fagan injected the notion of campaign pressure on D'Amato to reverse course and oppose the Commission idea which, by that time, was gaining acceptance with the other insurance companies he had included in his lawsuit.[296] Fagan felt his legal battle slipping away.

> But the survivors—your voters—are getting really angry. They are beginning to ask "Why hasn't Sen. D'Amato done anything to help us and why is he choosing big organizations over US!...This could be another opportunity for you to "Save the Day" and keep your promises to survivors. It could be a good PR piece for your campaign at this time. I have to believe that the concept of actual survivors (including prominent and "poster child type" survivors who the Media love to photograph and interview) publicly expressing their gratitude at this key time and would help combat Chuck Schumer's relentless ads against you.[297]

While the Generali deal had, for the time being, fallen apart, the Commission proceeded as planned with former Secretary of State Lawrence Eagleburger accepting the Chairmanship of the Commission which was now being called the International Commission on Holocaust Era Insurance Claims (ICHEIC). Under Eagleburger, the ICHEIC agreed to evaluation formulas for future claims at nearly ten times the pre-war value of the policies, a rate arrived at in the earlier Eizenstat reports.[298]

With the settling in of the claims process, the companies, now dealing through ICHEIC, were subjected to searching for claims, an extremely complicated and time-consuming procedure that was found to be very legalistic, overly strict in its standards of proof, and simply very difficult to overcome. According to the companies, as of May 2000, only 124 of 909 claims were positively settled and 393 claims rejected. The others had been pending for months.[299] As Peter Lefkin, of the Fireman's Fund, an Allianz-owned company testified in Skokie, Illinois in October 2000, "I would be less than candid were

I to say that the problem of resolving unclaimed insurance policies is an easy one."[300]

By January 2002, the process had not improved. Soon Congress became reinvigorated in the matter. In a letter to Eagleburger, Senators Peter G. Fitzgerald and Bill Nelson wrote of less than 1 percent of 77,800 claims being filled. The two Senators asked for, and later received, an extension of the then February 2002 deadline for claims.[301]

Two weeks after the Senators' letter, Eagleburger publicly threatened to resign over the total lack of cooperation by the companies. According to a participant in the ongoing negotiations, Eagleburger was particularly upset with the total lack of cooperation from Allianz and AXA. The companies were dragging their feet on the claims issue, the provision of policy-holders' lists, and refused, particularly Allianz, to accede to the evaluation issue for policies.[302]

Eagleburger had also complained that the companies were not paying, as they had agreed, for the administrative upkeep of ICHEIC.[303] In all, Eagleburger, according to those close to the Commission, felt betrayed. When lawyers for the German companies suggested that Eizenstat, then in private legal practice, intercede as a moderator, Eagleburger was said to again become enraged.[304]

There were other problems as well for ICHEIC. Neal Sher, the Executive Director of the Commission, was forced to resign in July 2002, due, according to one story, to an impending divorce which would have tied up his finances as well as time for the job. According to others, however, there were allegations of airline travel reimbursement problems.[305]

Despite the ostensible unraveling of the ICHEIC process, on September 19, 2002, the Commission announced a $275 million agreement with the companies to provide for compensation and humanitarian funding. The deal which had been in negotiation for two years, helped alleviate many concerns as far as funding, but critics remained as to the amount being adequate for the real number of possible claims.[306] Nevertheless, in June 2003, the Claims Conference announced that there would be $15 million available for distribution in Israel and the United States from the Humanitarian Fund. Survivors in thirty-one countries would eventually become recipients.[307]

The fight would extend back to the states, as California passed a state law in 1999, enabling the Insurance Commissioner to withhold the right of the companies to sell insurance in the state if they refused to disclose their policyholders from the Holocaust-era. This state law, similar to laws passed in New York, Florida, Maryland, Minnesota, and Washington, was challenged in the courts and upheld by the Ninth Circuit Court of Appeals.[308] The companies then appealed the case to the Supreme Court for review. On March 26, 2003, 52 members of Congress signed an Amicus, or "Friend of the Court" Brief in support of the state's position.[309] On June 23, 2003, the Supreme Court reversed the decision of the Appeals Court, saying "The basis fact is that California seeks to use an iron fist where the President has consistently chosen kid gloves," the court ruled that California usurped the foreign policy prerogatives of the president in subjecting insurance companies to this law.[310]

The U.S. Congress continued to exhibit its anger at the companies, despite the publication of more than 50,000 policy-holders' names on the Internet. In bills introduced before in the 108th Congress, Representative Mark Foley and Senator Norm Coleman, would allow the stipulations imposed in California to be imposed nationally, thus increasing the risk for companies all over the country.[311]

The insurance aspect of the pursuit for assets remains one of a few rare settlements, and more than anything, an exercise in futility for many claimants.[312] This aspect of restitution initially followed successful processes from other categories. The establishment of a commission was expected to work alongside the class action attorneys and together create joint action. In this case, however, the commission overtook the lawsuits, which later fell apart within the legal system itself. Once the attorneys were excluded from the process of ICHEIC, there was no way to keep a constant and probative pressure on the companies which, left to their own to handle claims, by the stipulations of the agreements, whittled away the time and to this day, are simply waiting the survivors out. In short, the process was short-circuited by attempts to alter the successful model first established with the Swiss banks. Moreover, the lack of strong political pressure, such as that engendered in the other cases, seemed to doom the chance for success. Once the high-level hearings and the attendant publicity ended, so, too, did the progress.

The practice set by the various bank cases created an institution that worked well for them. For the banks the process was simple: first impose a legal process upon the target, then agree to a complimentary investigative authority, and, finally, agree to supplement the entire process with an over-riding governmental mediation effort to bring a negotiated settlement supplemented by the findings from the commission. In the insurance cases, important steps in this process were skipped, thus leading to the essential failure of the entire effort.[313] Attempts to alter the practice doomed the effort, and the survivors paid the ultimate price.

For the final category of the forgotten issues, compensation for Slave Labor, the case would be different. The model was followed and results, while probably inadequate for the numbers of potential claimants, were successfully achieved.

Slave Labor: ... "Jewish Survivors Must be Grateful" ...

Of all the categories of the "forgotten issues," historically, reparations for slave labor had been the most difficult to achieve. At least with the banks, art, and property issues, there had been some settlements over time. With slave labor, there had been only the rare token payments given during the post-war period, and even then to a limited number of survivors. In 1958, I.G. Farben compensated some of its slave laborers roughly $1,200 each.[314] In 1962, Siemens Industries agreed to provide DM 7.2 million for slave laborers.[315] In May 1966, Rheinmetall, agreed to provide DM 2.5 million for slave laborers.[316] Krupp, Flick, and Daimler-Benz had made similar donations as well.[317] Nevertheless, these were small settlements affecting small numbers of survivors.

The reason that survivors were denied reparations was, first, the deferral of claims enshrined in the London Debt Agreement of 1953. Secondly, and more importantly, in 1963, the German Supreme Court ruled that private German companies were entitled to the same deferral of claims as the German government.[318] Together, these two facts precluded survivors from even filing claims for reparations for slave labor.

With the reunification of Germany came the "Two Plus Four" Treaty which removed the obstacle of the ability of survivors to sue the German overnment. As such, with the flurry of Holocaust assets lawsuits, the same attorneys who were successful in suing European institutions, turned their sights to Germany for yet another legal battle.

In 1998, only two weeks after the Swiss banks settlement, Fagan filed a lawsuit against the German companies Siemens, Krupp, Henkel, BMW, Daimler-Benz, Volkswagen, Audi, Leica, and others on charges of slave labor.[319]

Soon Fagan's lawsuits were joined by suits filed by Hausfeld, Mendelsohn, and Weiss in another lawsuit against Volkswagen, Deutsche Bank, Dresdner Bank, and Commerzbank.[320] Suits were also filed against Bayer, BMW, Bosch, Degussa, DaimlerChrysler, GM, Krupp, Rheinmetall Group, and Siemens.[321] In May 1999, Hausfeld filed a series of further slave labor suits against Opel, BASF, Hugo Boss, Leica, Thysssen, and numerous others.[322] Finally, a few weeks later, Hausfeld added a suit against Ford Motor Company.[323]

Now, in a matter of a few short months, some of Germany's largest companies were being targeted by multi-billion dollar lawsuits over slave labor. The legal peace they were afforded for over forty years had gone the way of the Berlin Wall and the Cold War. In many ways, even more than with the various banks cases, they were being overwhelmed by the attorneys who were filing multiple lawsuits against the companies. More importantly, the level of evidence formed a chilling story of murder, abuse, and a total lack of respect for human life. As the documents and the survivors' testimonies were being circulated in the world's press, the number and quality of their excuses for avoiding the charges against them evaporated.

Immediately, the companies saw their vulnerabilities and with the experience of the Swiss behind them, they saw a need to find a speedy solution.

Siemens immediately began negotiations toward a compensation fund. By September 23, the company announced the creation of a $5.3 million Humanitarian fund for slave laborers. Within a year, the company had made payments to nearly 1,000 people.[324]

Before Siemens, however, Volkswagen, one of the subjects of Fagan's and Hausfeld's suits, had been threatened with a lawsuit by a University of Bremen lecturer Klaus von Muenchhausen, for its use of slave labor. In July, Volkswagen agreed to create a $12 million humanitarian fund. Volkswagen's liabilities at this time, however, were not what they would be once Hausfeld had launched his lawsuit against the company.

Hausfeld's researchers had found files in the National Archives among the unprosecuted war crimes cases detailing the starvation deaths of 350 to 400 Polish and Russian infants born to mothers performing slave labor in Volkswagen factories. The babies were kept in entirely inadequate sanitary conditions, left to the infestation of insects, and abandoned. The infants were buried in milk cartons in a mass grave. The documents were backed up by documents found in London by *CBS News* and, together with the American documents, they paint a horrific picture of the story of slave labor during the Holocaust.[325]

The creation of the two funds, independent of one another, put pressure on the other named companies and, by February 1999, it seemed quite obvious that they would have to do the same. On February 16, then German Chancellor Schröder announced the creation of a "Foundation Initiative of German Industry: Memory, Responsibility, and Future." The Fund comprised donations from Allianz, BASF, Bayer, BMW, DaimlerChrysler, Deutsche Bank, Degussa-Hülls, Dresdner Bank, Krupp, Hoechst, Siemans, and Volkswagen. According to the German Chancellery:

> The companies want to set a material sign of solidarity, justice, and self-esteem at the end of the century. This initiative is an immediate social supplement to the federal government's "making good again" policies. The state "making good again" policies were implemented with public tax funds, so that German industry has always participated in compensatory payments. Moreover, the companies have made direct payments to victims of Nazi persecution in past decades.[326]

Schröder, in making the announcement, however, declared that the Fund was to end "the campaign being led against German industry and our country."[327] While it was laudatory that the German government and companies, as a whole, had formally arrived at the notion of responsibility for their actions as practitioners of slave labor more than fifty years after the fact, the notion of ending the "campaign" against Germany was not the idea that the attorneys, and especially the slave labor survivors, had in mind. Moreover, suggestions that the Fund would perhaps not move forward if the lawsuits were not dropped, did all the more damage to the emerging negotiations over a future settlement that Eizenstat was encouraged to join by the German government.[328]

For the attorneys, the Fund was only a diversion from the negotiations over their legal efforts. The announcement of the Fund angered Hausfeld, who felt that its creation and "leak" was a sign of bad faith. Moreover, a refusal of the companies to seek legal closure not through the American courts, but through bilateral German-American negotiations, infuriated him.[329]

From this point, however, the negotiations seemed to turn more on the idea of the size of the fund, and variation and size of the payments, than anything else. As the negotiations developed, they did so on these points. Back and forth they went, all with the goal of, simply put, reaching the appropriate numbers necessary to satisfy all concerned.

In June, at about the same time as the announcement of the initial funding proposal for the German Foundation, Professor Lutz Neithammer, a historian at Jena University and an advisor to the German Government for the negotiations over the lawsuits, agreed to be interviewed by *Die Welt* on the creation of the Foundation. Speaking about proposed distinctions between the size of payments to survivors based upon their treatment, Niethammer explained:

> Those who were treated the worst and are today worst off will be helped which is understandable. Worst treated (by industry) were concentration camp prisoners. One has to point out that in many cases Jewish survivors must be grateful that their lives were saved by having been slave laborers.[330]

Niethammer's remarks, insensitive and illogical as they were, only worsened the attorneys' attitude toward their views of the government. Together with Schröder's blithe remark as to the need to end the campaign against Germany, and quips that the performance of the slave laborers was substandard at any rate, the attorneys were outraged at official German behavior.[331] Two years later, in Washington, DC, Wolfgang Gibowski, Spokesman for the Foundation, openly declared that without the forced and slave laborers, " ... it would have been impossible to maintain every day life in Germany."[332]

They lashed out, complaining that differentiating the classes of payments to slave laborers based on their suffering, was unfair and unjust and "unacceptable to the victims." They accused the German companies of stalling progress towards a resolution of the claims.[333]

In July, when the Federal Court in Newark, New Jersey began considerations of one of the lawsuits against the German chemical company Degussa, the lawyers for the company disclosed that the government had sent an amicus curiae brief seeking a dismissal of the suit. The government denied anything was wrong with its actions. It was, however, an important action, in that the government had put its trust in Eizenstat to settle the negotiations based upon the parameters of the Foundation and not through the courts. This much was clear in talking with many of the attorneys, the government felt that any court decision might well prove to be more harmful than anything on which they would have agreed.

In September, Judge Dickinson R. Debevoise of the Federal District Court in Newark dismissed the case against Degussa. At the same time, Judge Joseph A. Greenaway Jr., of the same court, dismissed the case against Ford. In both instances, the attorneys had been incensed at the actions of the judges. Their cases, and their procedural and public relations advantage, was falling apart before them.

Worse yet, attorneys at the Justice Department had expressed a strong desire to intervene on behalf of the plaintiffs.[334] They wanted to intervene on the appeal feeling that the judges had misinterpreted the German-U.S. agreements following the war, foreclosing reparations or claims, arguing that even the London Debt Treaty did not prevent a claim. In one respect, Eizenstat agreed with them,[335] explaining that the State Department believed the plaintiffs were right as well. The intervention, however, did not come. As Eizenstat explained:

> This came at a very delicate time in the negotiations and came at a time when we had just begun to talk about money. If we had intervened in favor of the plaintiff[s] it would wreck my capacity to be a neutral arbiter that had gained the confidence of the German Government. It would show, in German eyes, that we had taken sides in the legal dispute. Justice felt very, very strongly that we couldn't let a bad decision go, and I said look, there's always the Supreme Court if this is necessary. We cannot do this now. It would wreck my credibility.[336]

As Eizenstat had suggested, the sticky subject of a number had begun to surface. At the time, there were negotiations sputtering on and off. By October, German companies were offering $3.3 billion in terms of a settlement through the Foundation, an amount thought of as insufficient by the attorneys. Talks stalled. On November 16, the German Government raised the offer by $555 million based upon the entrance of new companies. This amount was still viewed as too small.

Again, the talks were canceled and then restarted. As with the Swiss banks case, there was a number from which the attorneys could not retreat. Demanding, at a bare minimum, they clung to $5.2 billion or higher for a settlement price. Germany had narrowed the difference and by December 15, the two sides had agreed to settle all claims in return for $5.2 billion to be split evenly between the German government and German industry. The negotiations had been very difficult and stagnated for a long period of time.

The final number, while seemingly high, would, in reality, work out to some $5,000 to $7,000 per surviving slave laborer, much less than they deserved, and according even to prevailing wages at the time, severely inadequate even if a price could be put to such involuntary servitude. The attorneys, despite winning a historic victory that no one before them had been able to achieve, were still bitter. Fagan felt that Jewish slave laborers were discriminated against in the settlement due to the inclusion of non-Jewish survivors, a point of very serious contention between Hausfeld and Weiss as well.[337] According to attorney Martin Mendelsohn, the German Ambassador to the United States, Thomas Matussek, had told him that the "Germans would have been willing to pay DM 20 billion over time for the Slave Labor cases to conclude them. Moreover, Mendelsohn claimed that Eizenstat had become too fixed on the larger number and not the per capita number, which, in reality, was much more important to the survivors.[338]

While there was relief at news of the settlement, disputes continued over the size of the payments, including those who had already received payments from Germany as part of previous reparations plans. Had Germany not dropped this plan, nearly 250,000 survivors would have been denied funds from the settlement.[339]

Other disputes also arose, especially concerning the composition of recipients: Jewish vs. non-Jewish recipients; survivors with claims against German banks; claims against German insurance companies; and personal injury claims, including claims for medical experimentation. Additionally, the percentage split between funds for survivors and educational and remembrance purposes also clouded the after-settlement allocation negotiations.

For the German government and companies as well, there was one overriding concern, and one which was, for months, a major sticking point for the consummation and approval of the plan by the Bundestag. That point, was termed "legal peace." As described above, the assumption of protection offered to the Germans, as it was to the French and the Austrians, was predicated upon the actions of not only the present administration, but of any future one as well.

Here, in the settlement with Germany and its companies, the rule of "legal peace" was proposed, accepted, and set upon future settlements as a practice to achieve legal closure for future claims. As former National Security Advisor to President Clinton, Samuel Berger, explained:

> Let us reiterate on behalf of the President, that the President and the Administration are committed, as provided for in the proposed executive agreement, to enduring and all-embracing legal peace for German companies, for present and for future cases, for consensual and non-consensual cases. We agreed to commit in the agreement to file U.S. statements of interest in U.S. courts, stating, among other things, the U.S. foreign policy interests in dismissal. This was in the President's December 13 letter to the Chancellor. The Chancellor accepted the President's letter as the basis for legal closure, stating that "I greatly welcome the commitment of the U.S. Administration to state that the dismissal of all ongoing and future lawsuits would be in its foreign-policy interest."[340]

In response, the German Chancellor's National Security Advisor Michael Steiner, wrote:

> The Chancellor regards the personal commitment of the President of the United States as crucial to the establishment of the Federal Foundation. The agreement now reached has removed the most important obstacle to the completion of the Foundation Act which will most likely be adopted by the German Bundestag on July 6.[341]

The agreement between both countries was achieved and ensured for success through these understandings. As such, the President of the United States committed himself and his successors to formally and legally object to any future legal cases brought against Germany or German companies, and later the French and Austrian Governments and companies. While only promissory in nature, these statements assumed a commitment akin to an Executive Agreement, generally recognized in United States institutional practice to only have the force of presidential authority for that president who authored it.

In the Supreme Court decision reversing the California law seeking policy names from insurance companies wishing to sell insurance in the state, the court concluded:

> Making executive agreements to settle claims of American nationals against foreign governments is a particularly longstanding practice, the first example being as early as 1799, when the Washington Administration settled demands against the Dutch Government by American citizens ... [342]

As such, the provision of "legal peace," allowed the final settlement to the issue of German compensation for slave labor on July 17, 2000. With the passage of the agreement by the German Bundestag on July 5, the plan was set to be implemented.

There were three categories of recipients receiving reparations. In the first category, imprisoned slave laborers in camps, ghettos, or prisons would receive a one-time payment of roughly $7,500. Those in the second category were those slave laborers deported from their country, working in the same conditions, except in industry, agriculture, or with local authorities, receive roughly $2,900. Finally, those in the third category were those whose assets had been looted and had not been previously compensated for those losses.[343]

The attorneys, cautious and fearful of even suggesting fees in the Swiss banks and similar cases, were equally so in this case. They did, however, make a case, and in a separate agreement concluded on the same day as the main agreement, July 17, it was agreed by Eizenstat, Otto Graf Lambsdorff and Mandred Gentz, the Chief Financial Officer of DaimlerChrysler and a representative of the Foundation, to set aside as much as $65 million for attorneys fees.[344] In the formal, published agreement, however, the amount was not specified and left open to a Foundation arbitrator.[345]

As earlier disputes regarding the final number for the settlement had arisen, with attorneys complaining of its inadequacies, the final settlement had proceeded. On March 7, 2001, however, U.S. District Judge for the Southern District of New York Judge Shirley Wohl Kram had refused to dismiss the plaintiffs' lawsuits, at their request, as called for in the settlement. She feared that the Foundation was, at that time, not fully funded, and more honestly, not providing enough money for the individual slave laborers. For their part, the companies, lacking the dismissal of the suits, withheld the money for the payments.[346]

Survivors, expecting their payments upon the conclusion of the agreement between the United States and Germany, were livid. The attorneys too, eager to finish the cases, were upset. The United States government filed a motion in support of the attorneys to appeal Judge Kram's action with the U.S. Second Circuit Court of Appeals. Kram hired David Boies, former Vice President Al Gore's attorney during the 2000 Florida Presidential ballot legal dispute, to represent her in the appeal.[347]

On May 10, 2001, the court ordered Kram to dismiss the cases. She did so with conditions, further infuriating both sides. Another appeal was made, and on May 15 she finally, unconditionally dismissed the lawsuits.[348] By the end of June, payments to slave laborers finally began.

Since this time, payments totaling almost $2.1 billion have been paid to over 1,217,000 former slave laborers, as of June 2002. Funds were distributed to affiliated foundations in Poland, Belarus, Russia, Ukraine, the Czech Republic, the Claims Conference, and the International Organization for Migration for non-Jewish claimants.[349]

Thus, more than a half-century later, the last major case of claims for assets and/or damages had been concluded. The fight for the solution to payments for slave labor was one of fits and starts and a difficult one even beyond the settlement. Beyond this, there would be other lesser-known cases that would arise, all equally important to the claimants, but not as wide-spread as the class participating in the slave labor payments. For these claims of the former, their fight for justice would be the result of what would come to be termed, "Holocaust accountability."

Spreading the Blame

On February 14, 1996, at a conference hosted by the WJRO at the Seagram's offices in Manhattan, Alfred Defago, then the incoming Swiss Ambassador following Jagmetti's abrupt departure, defensively explained to me that, we should realize that they, the Swiss " ... weren't the only ones."[350]

When the Swiss found that the Swedes had accepted looted gold from the Nazis as well, they quickly issued press statements explaining that they were not alone in the illicit gold trade. They were all too happy to find others to blame for the same misdeeds. Indeed, one could not deny the truth of disclosures like this. As much as it hurt to accept at the time, Defago was right.

Holocaust Accountability

"Throughout Europe," wrote Christopher Winner in USA Today, "contemporary views regarding Holocaust accountability are in constant flux."[351] The use of the term "accountability" in reference to the Holocaust was an application unthought of before Bronfman's assumption to self-acclaimed leadership of the new movement for restitution. The fact is that before his efforts began, the survivors were expected to justify their need for restitution. Afterward, this notion was reversed. For Bronfman, success meant more than restitution. It meant changing the way survivors were seen in history and in institutional discourse and practice.

So pertinent was this concept that Representative Mark Foley of Florida named his 1998 bill on the responsibilities of European insurance companies, "The Comprehensive Holocaust Accountability in Insurance Measure," CHAIM, Hebrew for "life."[352] Edwin Black, too, ascribed the responsibility of corporate behavior in the Holocaust-era, as "Holocaust accountability."[353]

For the concept of achieving restitution for Holocaust-era assets, the major issues of bank accounts, insurance, artwork, and property, had been addressed in the form of multi-national class-action lawsuits. Congressional hearings, world-wide press coverage, and high-level diplomatic settings , in cases which did not garner high-level press or political attention, were still pursued.

Accountability was the direct consequence, although not unintended, of the larger issues being addressed. As the larger issues were brought to light, the smaller ones surfaced not only because they were not yet addressed, but because the success of solving the larger ones simply made it possible to address the smaller ones as well. Success bred success and emboldened people from all parts of the world to begin to think that they, too, could bring conclusion to an issue that had been dormant for over half-a-century.

French Railways

On September 5, 2000, a dozen survivors sued the French national railroad company Société Nationale des Chemins de Fer Français (SNCF) for the transport of French Jews from France to Auschwitz.[354] The attorneys for the plaintiffs provided evidence that SNCF not only transported victims, but submitted bills and charged interest as well for late payments.[355] Because of the fact that SNCF was a private corporation, wholly owned by the French government, the railroad was able to escape damages pleading immunity due to its ownership under the U.S. law of *Foreign Sovereignty Immunity*. Under this law, a foreign government or government entity can evade prosecution in U.S. courts under reciprocal procedures in other national courts. The plaintiffs have appealed and have sought the help of the U.S. Congress in their fight.[356] On June 17, 2003, the U.S. Second Circuit Court reversed the decision of Judge David E. Trager of the Eastern District of New York, reinstating the case.[357]

IBM

"To facilitate persecution and genocide." On February 10, 2001, Hausfeld filed a lawsuit on behalf of five plaintiffs against IBM for its ostensible role in helping the Nazis use and manipulate data accumulated before and during the Holocaust for the purpose of carrying it out.[358] Based on archival work by his researchers, as well as the book *IBM and the Holocaust, The Strategic Alliance Between Nazi Germany and America's Most Powerful Corporation*, by Edwin Black, Hausfeld launched his lawsuit. The allegations were immediately denied by IBM as well as Franciszek Piper, the Auschwitz Museum's historian.[359] Black, maintained that IBM's purposeful cooperation with the Nazis enabled a coordinated and systematic use of data to carry out the Holocaust, yet denied any link of the release of his book with the filing of the lawsuit, although the timing was more than coincidental.[360]

Upon the filing of the lawsuit, the State Department issued a statement reiterating its intention to fulfilling its obligation with regard to the "Statement of Interest" for Legal Peace between the United States and Germany.

On March 29, Hausfeld, fearing that the case would unduly interfere with the ongoing implementation of the slave labor settlement money or provide the German companies with any excuse halting or suspending their agreed-upon payments, withdrew the lawsuit.

A Corporate Logo

Long before Hausfeld's war crimes cases against Volkswagen and IBM as well as the other cases, there evolved the defense that while their companies were seen to have been complicit in ghastly crimes, these were occurrences of the past. "Just as the Confederate States of America practiced slavery," wrote Eric Peters concerning Volkswagen:

> just as the U.S. government repeatedly abrogated lawful treaties made with sovereign American Indian tribes and stole their land. But that was a long time ago—and the principals are all dead. What happened was indeed tragic, cruel, and grossly maliciously iniquitous. But what has that to do with people born years after the fact—or companies whose only connection to their predecessors of half a century ago is a name on a corporate logo?[361]

In response to Peters, a letter to the editor a week later succinctly answered this defense. Neal H. Weinfield explained Volkswagen's ongoing problem by explaining that the new leaders of the company " ... selected the old VW name and business enterprise because of its reputation and so now they have a moral obligation to pay the individuals who helped to develop it."[362]

While Volkswagen was volunteering its complicity in light of accusations, other did so as well. Kodak confessed, following research at the National Archives, disclosing that its German plants used slave labor. ExxonMobil did the same. Kodak later contributed to the German Fund.[363]

"Victims of the American Holocaust"

Indeed, the question was being answered, not only was it us that committed these acts as well as others, but in this respect, it was "you, too, America" that committed these similarly evil acts. It was in this respect Seymour Rubin's accusations of misdeeds by the United States were taken with such credulity. These accusations were far more serious to those Swiss who saw their country the subject of daily attack and accusation. "We expect you to do your utmost following your re-election," wrote Jean-Marc Pochon of Bern, Switzerland to D'Amato in 1997, "to get reparations and compensations for the victims of the American holocaust [sic]." Pochon continued.

The Americans drove the Indians off their land, killing their wives and their children so that they could no longer reproduce. Those were the heroic deeds of the American cavalry. The Americans then went on to procure slaves in Africa, who they treated like animals and put to work for them. Moreover, they were sexually abused and half-breeds, who were not given the same rights as the whites, were conceived.[364]

Pochon, like dozens of others who wrote to D'Amato complaining of unequal treatment, suggested that we clean up our own house before we look after others'. In all, both the behavior of countries and companies, in the estimation of those targeted, was upheld to be relative according to the norms of the era. We looked at these issues through the prism of today's rules and practices, they looked at it through the prism of yesterday's.

The Vatican

"When certain principles, views, or institutional practices produce outcomes that either contradict other foundational principles or that are undeniably catastrophic," wrote Daniel Goldhagen, " ... it should lead a person of good faith to want to revisit, reconsider, and possibly recast or jettison altogether those principles, views, or practices."[365] In writing about the Catholic Church's moral responsibilities during the Holocaust, Goldhagen called for a moral reckoning and an effort to repair the damage from its role in the abandonment of the Jews and its accountability, or lack thereof, for that abandonment. As such, Goldhagen challenged the notion of the relativity of immorality.

Throughout the past decade, there have been a number of books and articles castigating the Vatican for its indifference during the Holocaust.[366] They center on the abject disregard for the plight of the Jews and offer numerous reasons for the actions of Pope Pius XII. "The vatican [sic] always responds," wrote an American diplomat in 1942, "that the Pope has come out already against barbarity in general and that a special protest at this point would not help any."[367] Most works on this issue center on the indifference of the Pope expressed in this cable. That same American diplomat wrote a little more than one month earlier that an important officer of the Holy See told him that " ... the Holy Father, has now changed his line and ... that he didn't think our side could triumph on the Continent ..."[368] For these reasons and others, there has been deep distrust, especially among Jews, of the Vatican's role in making amends for its indifference at that time.[369]

When in 1997, it was disclosed through documents from the U.S. National Archives that Vatican officials, and even Argentinean Catholic priests, were helping Nazis and Croatian war criminals escape Europe, and that they carried with them millions of Swiss Francs in victims' gold, there was a public outcry.[370]

Despite denials to the contrary, again, attorneys saw the need and the chance to file a lawsuit. In November 1999, Jonathan Levy of Cincinnati, Ohio filed a lawsuit against the Vatican, Croatian authorities, Swiss, German, Italian, Spanish, Portuguese, Argentine, and Brazilian banks, on behalf of twenty-two claimants in the United States District Court in San Francisco.[371] In June 2003, however, the case was dismissed. While this case was unsuccessful, the Roman Catholic Church in Germany voluntarily agreed to pay one-time payments separate from the German Fund, to some 1,000 slave laborers in Germany.[372]

Regardless of the lawsuits and the public castigation by numerous Jewish groups for this indifference, as well as its deep reluctance, to open the Vatican archives, Pope John Paul II, went to some length to lessen the chasm in Catholic-Jewish relations. In *We Remember: A Reflection on the Shoah*, the Vatican, while stopping short on some points toward accepting accountability for the Holocaust, went to greater lengths to accede to that accountability with the Jewish people when it declared " ... the Church draws sustenance from the root of that good olive tree on to which have been grafted the wild olive branches of the Gentiles ... that the Jews are our dearly beloved brothers, indeed in a certain sense they are 'our elder brothers.'"[373]

Pope John Paul II's call for Catholic repentance, in the introduction to this important statement, called upon the Church to encourage " ... her sons and daughters to purify their hearts, through repentance of past errors and infidelities. She calls them to place themselves humbly before the Lord and examine themselves on the responsibility which they too have for the evils of our time."

Holocaust accountability then, as Bronfman sought to promote, belongs, and now resides, back where it first was born, with the perpetrators of that tragic calamity of mankind.

Susceptibility to Attack

While accountability was achieved, there were factors beyond the various leading actors that influenced their ability to act. Companies that were subject to lawsuits were large, multinational corporations with ambitions for expansion. That expansion was seen as extending into the United States. In that choice of location, the Swiss, French, and German banks, German car companies, and European insurance companies, were seeking to enhance their opportunities at the expense of their flexibility to deal with claims by survivors.

Banks, in particular, were vulnerable because of the wave of bank mergers going on in the late 1990s. When the Swiss banks Union Bank of Switzerland and the Swiss Bank Corporation tried to merge, they were threatened with a block of that effort by D'Amato, Levin, and the New York State Banking Department.[374] While threatened, the banks were eventually allowed to merge by both the Federal Reserve and New York State. The dispute, however, created an opening that exposed vulnerability, one of many, in the Swiss banks' ability to counter the investigations, claims, and lawsuits against them.

In December 1998, Deutsche Bank and Bankers Trust merged. Both banks were being viewed for their record with respect to dormant or expropriated accounts. Deutsche Bank Chairman Rolf Breuer feared that the merger would fall through unless the German Foundation Fund gained acceptability in Germany.[375] Breuer understood his bank's position. Soon after Deutsche Bank tried to merge with Dresdner Bank, both banks subject to lawsuits for their roles in Aryanization in Germany. The WJC protested loudly over the proposition of the two banks, so heavily exposed for their wartime roles, to receive the advantage of a merger in the United States. Dresdner Bank called off the merger plan.

When Allianz bought Dresdner, and also tried, but failed, to buy Deutsche Bank, the company faced the same scrutiny, both from the WJC and, in California, from Quackenbush.[376] The same was true for Allianz when it tried to buy Pimco Advisors Holdings LP in 1999.[377]

In March 1999, Societe Generale, Bank Paribas, and Banque Nationale de Paris, became embroiled in merger and takeover efforts with one another. At the same time, they were facing the lawsuits by survivors. Like with the Swiss banks merger before them, their efforts made them vulnerable to threats by the WJC and Hevesi to block the mergers in the United States where they most wanted to do business.

German car makers were also put in the position of balancing their efforts toward growth in the international market with their critics over their progress toward restitution. Volkswagen, seeking to re-introduce the Beetle into the U.S. market, was all too aware of its liabilities when it announced its $12 million fund in July 1998.[378] It had also recently acquired Rolls-Royce Motor Cars and was trying to buy the Lambourghini car company.[379]

In May 1998, Daimler and Chrysler joined the rash of mergers when they agreed to join together, forming an immense industrial merger.[380] With a huge market share, the resulting company, just as Deutsche before it, was all too willing to join the Foundation Fund to ensure the success of its new company.

Shame: The Unintended Consequence

Walter Stucki, the Swiss negotiator with the United States in 1948, told State and Treasury Department officials that "the Swiss did not care to have history brand them as thieves."[381] After three years of political war with Bronfman, D'Amato, the attorneys, and all the others allied against them, Stucki's fears came true, the Swiss have, in fact, been branded as thieves. Along with the branding, however, came an element of shame as well.

An *Economist* story of December 1999 entitled, "Swiss shame, and solace," said a great deal about the Swiss experience of this time.[382] When the Bergier Commission had just finished its work, publishing a twenty-six volume study on Switzerland's wartime experience, legitimizing what first D'Amato, then Eizenstat, then the attorneys had all said: the Swiss Government and the Swiss banks had been callous, unforgiving, and had taken advantage of victims and survivors alike. The story, just as we had painted it, was not a pretty one.

While likely based more upon monetary concerns, shame was also a motivating factor that led the Swiss Parliament to approve an $8 million program to finance a public relations program intended to better its image after the beating the country took.[383] Swiss efforts at image restoration were a necessity. After three years of failing to understand how and why they achieved the branding they did, they would have to pay in order to restore that which was lost. Seeking to bring about "sympathy for Switzerland," the effort will be long and no set program will do.[384]

Shame also brought an apology from Roman Catholic Bishops in the country for the treatment of the Jews.[385] It also led the Parliament to back a proposal to overturn wartime convictions of Swiss citizens who broke laws aiding Jewish refugees seeking to enter the country.[386] In Poland, shame brought the government to officially apologize for the massacre of Jews at Jedwabne in 1941.[387] In Germany, shame brought a pediatricians organization to express regret for not defending its colleagues and participating in Aryanizations.[388] Shame also led the Bertelsmann Media Group to admit its role in the publishing and profiting from Nazi publications.[389]

The Swiss banks as a whole, the European insurers, together, and the art galleries, museums, and collectors, all accepted this notion and obeyed the idea that to expose one would be akin to exposing all, and therefore accepted the practice of silencing. Silencing of the honor of having held their secrets for so long was a practice accepted around the world, wherever there were assets of Holocaust victims held in the wrongful place.

Bankers, insurance company executives, art gallery owners, museum directors, as well as the owner of the dacha in Warsaw my father-in-law encountered in 1994, all lived by the practice of silencing. Keeping the honor among them, they observed, was alright, as long as they were not caught. As James Bowman wrote, "Honor ... could be and quite often was consistent with quite despicable behavior which never got out."[390] In other words, their deeds took the form of acceptability, as long as only they knew it. Once exposed, however, the socially imposed concept of shame set in. That shame, based on the rule of the public non-acceptance of their deeds by the wider group of agents, was in essence, punishment[391]—punishment meted out to the targets of Bronfman and his partners.

The shame endured by companies and governments was alleviated by monetary settlement. Considered appropriate by the companies, possibly perceived as a token sum by some of the survivors, the award was nevertheless a recognition of their shame much more than the damages they inflicted. In the case of what amount for which the German companies were willing to settle, as Mendelsohn testified, they could have waited for more, but in the end, the amount was that which was achievable to the circumstances prevailing at the time.

In the end, the various companies, governments, and individuals' settlements reflected a desire to rid themselves of the problem and as Sarah Schafer writing in *The Washington Post* explained, to "help improve relations with employées, consumers or the public ..."[392]

The Cost for These Services

On August 13, 1998, the Swiss people awoke to find that the three-year "war" over the Holocaust assets had ended. The daily barrage of accusations, mudslinging, and counter-accusations, not to mention the wounded prides of so many, was now over. The Swiss people, perhaps inured already to the charges, were, nonetheless, happy that it was over. The Swiss banks, reactionary and stubborn over the entire course of the "battle," were also relieved that they could now go about their way in the world, wounded, but largely intact, minus the $1.25 billion they had agreed to finally pay the day before to thousands of Holocaust survivors and their heirs, after more than fifty years of stonewalling them over the fate of their assets. Everyone in Switzerland seemed relieved.

In a variety of law offices in the United States however, the joy of settlement with the Swiss quickly turned to angst over how the money would be distributed and what the costs would be to them. "[O]ne can only fear the ugly pain, not to speak of the shame," wrote Teddy Preuss in the Israeli newspaper *Ha'aretz* shortly after, "that might be bared when the distribution of the Swiss money is discussed."[393] Settling with the Swiss was great, sorting out who got paid and how much, most particularly the touchy matter of lawyers' fees, was a different matter entirely.

While many of the attorneys representing clients in the Swiss banks' cases, worked pro bono, or only for expenses, others sought compensation beyond this. After the settlement, the fee structure was arrived at by Judge Edward Korman, fees were capped at 1.8 percent of the settlement figure, which amounted to $2.5 million. According to wire reports, nine lawyers asked Korman for a total of $13.5 million in fees, with New York attorney Ed Fagan seeking $4 million and Mel Urbach, representing the World Council of Orthodox Jewish Communities in a similar case against the Swiss banks, merged his fee request with that of the others.[394]

Fagan, in particular, never denied he would seek fees in this case. He declared this much to Gabe Kahn writing then for *The Forward*, that it was "precisely because his team had a financial stake in the outcome of the case, they will do a better job.[395]

On several occasions, he led sit-ins against the Swiss banks, traveled to Berlin to view property found to have been Aryanized and later purchased by the Union Bank of Switzerland, and represented the Swiss bank guard Christoph Meili in his emotional case against UBS and the security firm for which he worked for his dismissal for his discovery of the bank's shredding of historical documents. These "lawyerly duties," however, came with a price, and Fagan did not have the resources of Hausfeld or Weiss to enable him to simply waive his costs.

Moreover, Fagan had operated with an eye toward publicity throughout the time, and in the view of the other lawyers, in a way contrary to the best interests of his clients. By July 1998, his conduct, and that of Bob Swift, so riled another of the plaintiff's attorneys, Mel Weiss, that Weiss wrote to the other attorneys on the case that:

* * *

> The conduct of [Bob] Swift and Fagar is the most outrageous flaunting of a Court appointed Executive Committee mandate that I have ever encountered. ... The Judge has now called for a court conference and I think we should make a motion to remove both Swift and Fagan from the Executive Committee. I think we should also consider the imposition of sanctions.[396]

It was, of course, merely days following the settlement of the Swiss banks case that the lawsuits against the car companies and others were filed. Yet, with the tortured history of the lawyers' intense conflicts and disagreements, especially over fees, there was a growing cry against the taking of fees in any of the Holocaust cases. This battle would rage on into the other settlements as well. With the slave labor case settlement, the outcry was only multiplied. This drive for profiting from the very cases that, in and of themselves, were built on the very denunciation of profit-taking from such heinous crimes, smacked of hypocrisy for many. For the attorneys too, it was difficult to request, but they could only work for free for so long. It would be on this precise point that the battle lines for the next phase of Holocaust-era assets would be drawn.

The imposition and assumption of shame brought about one final, but vitally important, unintended consequence: accusations of mistreatment of the recipient of that shame. "Still, where shame 'works," wrote Stephen P. Garvey, "it may impose hardships no one thinks the shamed offender really deserves."[397] That mistreatment, critics began to suggest, was rooted in deeper meanings and causes, ultimately they believed, in ulterior motives on the part of the accusers. Those motives, the critics suggested, form the basis of the final part of this story.

Following the settlement of billions of dollars in restitution for Holocaust survivors, critics suggested that the real motive behind it all was all to more sinister ends. The tactics and consequences of the politicians, attorneys, and Jewish groups all came under suspicion as a symptom of those ends. As those critics charged, they were forming a new institution of practices not for the sake of restitution, but for the creation of a "Holocaust Industry."

Notes

1. Georgi Arbatov, "Perestroika, Glasnost and Soviet-American Relations," Paper delivered at a University of Miami Conference, Coral Gables, Florida, May 26, 1990, p. 2.
2. "Jewish Congress Leader Gets Invitation to Visit Moscow," *Chicago Tribune*, January 28, 1985, p. 2.
3. Decision of the United States District Court for the Central District of Calfornia, Leo Handel, Leon and Shari Kabiljo, and Isaac and Hanna Handy on behalf of themselves and all other situated persons v. Andrija Artukovic, No. 84-1411 PAR (Kx), 601 F. Supp. 1421; 1985 U.S. Dist. LEXIS 22932.
4. Ibid.
5. Serge Schmemann, "The Emergence of Gorbachev," *New York Times Magazine*, March 3, 1985, p. 44.
6. Ibid, p. 45.
7. Remarks of Mikhail S. Gorbachev at the National Republican Senatorial Committee Question & Answer Session, November 5, 1993, Washington, DC.
8. Remarks of Mikhail S. Gorbachev.
9. Arbatov; "Call to 'God on High' Is Made by Gorbachev," *New York Times*, September 2, 1985, p. 3.

10. Arbatov.
11. Eduard Shevardnadze, *The Future Belongs to Freedom*, trans. by Catherine A. Fitzpatrick (New York: The Free Press, 1991), p. 116.
12. The author was present in East Berlin on that day. There were loud and persistent protests that day and the Volkspolitzei were very much on guard against further disturbances or escapes by their fellow countrymen.
13. Tina Rosenberg, *The Haunted Land, Facing Europe's Ghosts After Communism* (New York: Vintage Books, 1995), p. 269; George Bush and Brent Scowcroft, *A World Transformed* (New York: Alfred A. Knopf, 1998), pp. 145-147; Joseph Held, ed. *The Columbia History of Eastern Europe in the Twentieth Century* (New York: Columbia University Press, 1992), p. lx.
14. Bush and Scowcroft, p. 150.
15. Ibid, p. 152.
16. Klein to the Department of State Telegram, "GDR Position on Claims," September 2, 1974, RG 59, Office of the Legal Adviser, Office of Educational, Cultural & Public Affairs, Subject Files 1945-1997, Lot File 96D244.
17. Klein to the Department of State Telegram, "GDR Recognition Issues: Claims," February 23, 1973, RG 59, Office of the Legal Adviser, Office of Educational, Cultural & Public Affairs, Subject Files 1945-1997, Lot File 96D244.
18. "East Germany: Better Late," *The Economist*, March 1, 1975, p. 46.
19. George P. Shultz, *Turmoil and Triumph, My Years as Secretary of State* (New York: Charles Scribner's Sons, 1993), p. 572; Interview with Ambassador Ridgeway.
20. Interview with Ambassador Ridgeway; Shultz, fn. 3, p. 572.
21. Interview with Ambassador Ridgeway. The paintings Ambassador Ridgeway managed to negotiate an East German surrender of were a collection of paintings by the American-born painter Lyonel Feininger which were abandoned in Nazi Germany when Feininger fled the country. See "48 Feininger Oils Reach U.S.," *New York Times*, March 15, 1984, p. 17.
22. Robert B. Zoellick, "Two Plus Four, The Lessons of German Unification," *The National Interest* (No. 61) Fall 2000, p. 19. Zoelick is now the Deputy Secretary of State in the Bush Administration.
23. The Treaty Establishing a Monetary, Economic and Social Union between the Federal Republic of Germany and the German Democratic Republic, September 12, 1990, American Society of International Law, Washington, DC. (Vol. 29, No. 5).
24. Bush and Scowcroft, p. 299.
25. London Debt Treaty. Italics are those of the author.
26. See Joseph D. Ament, "Presentation at Northwestern University Law School Conference on Holocaust Litigation," May 26, 1999, p. 3. Courtesy of Joseph D. Ament.
27. Former Polish Prime Minister Tadeusz Mazowieski to Noach Flug, as told by Noach Flug, Interview with Noach Flug, Director, Comité International D'Auschwitz, Jerusalem, Israel, April 10, 2002.
28. Cited in "Even for the Swiss, It's Time For Another Look at the War," *New York Times*, May 12, 1985, p. 6.
29. Deborah E. Lipstadt, "The Bitburg Controversy," *American Jewish Year Book, 1987*, Vol. 87, p. 21; Shultz, pp. 543-560.
30. James M. Markham, "SS Unit's History Overlooked in U.S. Plan on German Visit," *New York Times*, April 28, 1985, p. 1.
31. Shultz, p. 560.
32. Ibid.
33. Steven Erlanger, "Soul-Searching at Another Polish Massacre Site," *New York Times*, April 19, 2001, p. 3.

34. Letter of Prime Minister Shimon Peres to Avraham Burg, Chairman of the Jewish Agency for Israel, April 21, 1996. Courtesy of Avraham Burg.
35. "Jews are Cautious After Soviet Visit," *New York Times*, December 14, 1985, p. 6.
36. Tommy Daniels, The Jackson-Vanik Amendment, Excerpts from The Congressional Research Service, The Library of Congress. The Jackson-Vanik Amendment is a key element in the normalization of US commercial relations with communist countries. The amendment establishes the requirements for a country to meet, first to access US Government financial facilities and subsequently to receive Most Favored Nation (MFN) trade status. The requirements are based upon the country's emigration policies and prohibit the US from establishing such relations with a country that does not allow their citizens to freely emigrate. A country's compliance with the amendment's requirements must either exist, or if not, under specific conditions the President may waive the requirements. Available online at .
37. Interview with Doug Bloomfield, Washington Representative of the World Jewish Congress, February 5, 2001.
38. Interview with Elan Steinberg, Executive Director, World Jewish Congress, February 15, 2001.
39. Interview with Doug Bloomfield, Washington Representative of the World Jewish Congress, February 13, 2001.
40. Interview with Steinberg.
41. Diana Jean Schemo, "Good Germans: Ignoring the Heroes. Hiding the Holocaust," *New York Times*, June 12, 1994, Sec. 4, p. 1.
42. Interview with Steinberg.
43. Letter of Edgar Bronfman to U.S. Senator Alfonse M. D'Amato, May 1, 1996.
44. Edgar M. Bronfman, *The Making of a Jew* (New York: G.P. Putnam's Sons, 1996), pp. 43-44.
45. "Aims and Principles of the World Jewish Congress," Committee on World Jewish Congress, Office of the Secretary, American Jewish Congress, World Jewish Congress Collection, Series A, Central Files, 1919-1975, Subseries 3, Plenary Assemblies, Pre-1936, Conferences & Special Conferences, 1932-1975, Box A40, File 4, The Jacob Rader Center of the American Jewish Archives, Cincinnati, OH.
46. Blum, *From the Morgenthau Diaries, Years of War*, pp. 209-221; Beschloss, pp. 38-45.
47. Goldmann, pp. 125-132.
48. Bronfman, p. 44.
49. Jeanette Friedman, "Israel Singer, Meeting Mr. Right," *Lifestyles* (January 1997), Vol. 26, No. 147, pp. 16, 17.
50. Telephone discussion with Doug Bloomfield, Washington Representative of the World Jewish Congress, June 14, 2002.
51. Charles Hoffman, "Czechs Want a Boost from Bronfman," *Jerusalem Post*, October 24, 1989.
52. Interview with Noach Flug.
53. Netty Gross, "The Old Boys Club," *The Jerusalem Report*, May 15, 1997, p. 30; Netty Gross, "The Outrage Grows," *Jerusalem Report*, May 29, 1997, p. 30.
54. Ibid.
55. Letter of Arnon Rubin to Senator Alfonse M. D'Amato, March 22, 1998.
56. Interview with Willi Korte, Washington, DC, October 4, 2000.
57. Michael Simmons, "Jewish Congress Begins Global Offensive on Anti-Semitism," *The Guardian*, October 18, 1991.
58. Interview with Steinberg.

59. The members of the WJRO are: The Claims Conference, the WJC, the American Gathering of Jewish Holocaust Survivors, the American Jewish Joint Distribution Committee, B'nai B'rith International, the Jewish Agency, the Center of Organizations of Holocaust Survivors in Israel, and the World Zionist Organization, in Susan Birnbaum, "New Group Filing Material Claims Against East European Countries," *Jewish Telegraphic Agency*, August 7, 1992; Bronfman, p. 141.
60. "Jewish Group to Seek Restitution for Nazi and Communist Thievery," *Los Angeles Times*, August 4, 1992.
61. Bronfman, p.207.
62. Alfonse M. D'Amato, *Power, Pasta, and Politics, The World According to Senator Al D'Amato* (New York: Hyperion, 1995), p. 287.
63. Michael Simmons, "Jewish congress begins global offensive on anti-Semitism," *The Guardian*, October 18, 1991.
64. Then New York State Assemblyman Dov Hikind, a Democrat stalwart ally of D'Amato had the buttons created for this purpose.
65. Speech of Edgar Bronfman, Meeting of the World Jewish Congress, New York, New York, October 23, 1996.
66. Interview with Eizenstat.
67. Interestingly, while a competition evolved with a number of Republican lawmakers, D'Amato, for one, seemed to create a special case for Clinton. In one instance, regarding legislation that D'Amato was pushing to impose economic sanctions on Iran in 1995, shortly before the Swiss banks investigation began, Clinton aides were quoted in the *Wall Street Journal* as saying they would not be outflanked by him, declaring "Nobody gets to the right of us on Iran." See Washington Wire, "Clinton Scrambles to say ahead of Congress on pressuring Iran," *Wall Street Journal*, March 24, 1995, p. 1.
68. Discussion with Bloomfield, February 5, 2001.
69. Helen B. Junz, "Holocaust Era Assets - Globalisation [sic] of the Issue, Draft article for Lessons and Legacies VI," Northwestern University, November 17-20, 2000, pp. 2, 3 (fn.3)
70. Discussion with World Jewish Congress Secretary General Israel Singer, in Washington, February 14, 1996. Singer presented a copy of the book to this author at this time.
71. Jacques Picard, *Switzerland and the Assets of the Missing Victims of the Nazis, Assets in Switzerland belonging to victims of political persecution and their disposition between 1946 and 1973*, 1993.
72. Discussion with Bloomfield, February 2, 2001.
73. As a Congressional staffer working for Senator D'Amato, this author was in receipt of numerous telephone calls from New York constituents asking why federal dollars were being used to fund the construction of the Holocaust Museum. In truth, however, many of the calls were from those not supportive of the issue in general and quite possibly hostile to Jews in the abstract.
74. Interview with Naphtalie Lavie.
75. Itamar Levin, *The Last Deposit, Swiss Banks and Holocaust Victims' Accounts*, translated by Natasha Dornberg (Connecticut: Praeger, 1999), p. xiii.
76. Itamar Levin, *The Last Chapter of the Holocaust? The Struggle over the Restitution of Jewish property in Europe*, Jewish Agency for Israel, 1997, p. 22.
77. Interview with Naphtalie Lavie.
78. Robert G. Moeller, "War Stories: The Search for a Usable Past in the Federal Republic of Germany, The American Historical Review, Vol. 101, No. 4 (October 1996), p. 1045.

79. Doug Bloomfield, "The Swiss Don't Get It," *Washington Jewish Week*, May 15, 2003.
80. Discussion with Bloomfield, February 5, 2001.
81. Interview with Stuart Eizenstat, Washington, DC, December 3, 2002; Discussion with Bloomfield, February 5, 2001.
82. *Nomination of Stuart E. Eizenstat to be Under Secretary of Commerce*, Hearing Before the Committee on Banking, Housing, and Urban Affairs, United States Senate, One Hundred Fourth Congress, Second Session, March 19, 1996 (Washington, DC: United States Government Printing Office, 1996), p. 37.
83. Interview with Eizenstat; Stuart E. Eizenstat, *Imperfect Justice, Looted Assets, Slave Labor, and the Unfinished Business of World War II* (New York: Public Affairs, 2003), p. 25.
84. Discussion with Bloomfield, February 5, 2001.
85. Interview with Stuart Eizenstat.
86. Bronfman, p. 142; Interview with Bloomfield, February 5, 2001.
87. Letter of Speaker of the House Newt Gingrich, House Minority Leader Richard Gephardt, Rep. Benjamin Gilman, Chairman of the House International Relations Committee, Rep. Lee Hamilton Ranking Member of the House International Relations Committee, Senate Majority Leader Bob Dole, Senate Minority Leader Tom Daschle, Senator Jesse Helms, Chairman, Senate Foreign Relations Committee, and Senator Claiborne Pell, Ranking Member of the Senate Foreign Relations Committee to Secretary of State Warren Christopher, April 10, 1995.
88. Levin, *The Last Chapter of the Holocaust? The Struggle over the restitution of Jewish property in Europe*, p. 25.
89. Talk of Avraham Burg at the United Jewish Appeal Young Leadership Conference, held at the Washington Hilton Hotel, Washington, DC, March 23, 1998.
90. Letter of Michael Kohn, Vice-President of the European Jewish Congress, to Edgar Bronfman, President of the World Jewish Congress, July 17, 1995.
91. Letter of Israeli Prime Minister Yitzhak Rabin to Edgar Bronfman, September 10, 1995, courtesy of the World Jewish Congress.
92. Rickman, p. 285.
93. Michael J. Bazyler, *Holocaust Justice, The Battle for Restitution in America's Courts* (New York: New York University Press, 2003), p. 51.
94. Ludmilla Jordanova, "Public History, Amateurs Study the Past,"*History Today*, May 1, 2000 (No. 5, Vol. 50).
95. Thomas Maissen, Presentation before a Panel Discussion at the Swiss Embassy in Washington, D.C., December 8,1997, p. 1.
96. Bower, p. 329.
97. Discussion with Congressman Chris Smith (R-NJ), Washington, DC. March 25, 2003.
98. Memorandum of a letter from Swiss Ambassador to the United States Carlo Jagmetti to Ambassador Thomas Borer, Task Force of the Swiss Foreign Ministry, 19 December 1996, as it appeared in the 27 January 1997 edition of *Tages-Anzeiger*, translated by Brian Hufker.
99. Thomas Rust, "Victim of a Conspiracy," *Tages Anzeiger*, 28 January 1997, translated by Brian Hufker.
100. Letter of Resignation of Swiss Ambassador to the United States Carlo Jagmetti to Swiss President Arnold Koller, 27 January 1997, translation from the Swiss Embassy in a facsimile letter to United States Senator Alfonse M. D'Amato, 27 January 1997.
101. Rickman, p. 147.

102. Press Statement of United States Senator Alfonse M. D'Amato, 26 February 1997.
103. Rickman, p. 148.
104. George Wuthrich, "D'Amato, That's Enough!," *Blick*, 28 February 1997, p. 1, translated by Brian Hufker, office of Senator Alfonse D'Amato.
105. *Swiss Banks and the Shredding of Holocaust-Era Documents*, Senate Banking Committee Hearing Transcript, Mary 6, 1997.
106. *Swiss Banks and Attempts to Recover Assets Belonging to the Victims of the Holocaust*, Senate Banking Committee Hearing Transcript, May 15, 1997.
107. *Current Developments in Holocaust Assets Restitution*, Senate Banking Committee Hearing Transcript, July 22, 1998.
108. Opening Statement of Congressman Richard Baker, Full Committee Hearing on the Disposition of Assets Deposited in Swiss Banks By Missing Nazi Holdings, December 11, 1996, p. 2.
109. There were additional hearings in both Houses of Congress. Congressman Leach would hold four additional hearings:

    The Eizenstat Report and Related Issues Concerning United States and Allied Efforts to Restore Gold and Other Assets Looted by the Nazis During WWII, House Banking Committee Hearing Transcript, July 25, 1997.

    The Restitution of Art Objects Seized by the Nazis from Holocaust Victims and Insurance Claims of Certain Holocaust Victims and Heirs, House Banking Committee Hearing Transcript, February 12, 1998.

    World War II Assets of Holocaust Victims, House Banking Committee Hearing Transcript, September 14, 1999.

    Restitution of Holocaust Assets, House Banking Committee Hearing Transcript, February 9-10, 2000.

    Congressman Benjamin Gilman, as Chairman, held a hearing in the House International Relations Committee:

    Heirless Property Issues of the Holocaust, House International Relations Committee Hearing Transcript, August 6, 1998.

    Senator Gordon Smith, as Chairman of the European Affairs Subcommittee of the Senate Foreign Relations Committee held a hearing:

    Legacies of the Holocaust, Senate Foreign Relations Committee Hearing Transcript, April 5, 2000.

    The House Government Reform Committee led by Congressman Dan Burton and Congressman Henry Waxman held a hearing at Waxman's urging:

    The Status of Insurance Restitution for Holocaust Victims and Their Heirs, House Committee on Government Reform Hearing Transcript, November 8, 2001.

    Finally, the bicameral Congressional Commission on Security and Cooperation in Europe held a hearing:

    The Long Road Home: Struggling for Property Rights in Post-Communist Europe, Commission on Security and Cooperation in Europe Hearing Transcript, March 25, 1999.
110. Eizenstat Interview.
111. Rickman, p. 190.
112. John Authers and Richard Wolffe, *The Victim's Fortune* (New York: HarperCollins Publishers, 2002), p. 65.
113. This action amounted to a loss of $300,000, Ibid, p. 66. Further investments along these lines amounted to a total loss of $1.3 million Rickman, p. 200.
114. Rickman, pp. 204-229.
115. "Fong Halts Deals with Swiss Bankers; U.S. Subsidiaries Also Barred From State Contracts," *The San Francisco Examiner*, July 2, 1998, p. A-16.

116. Ibid, pp. 210-213.
117. Eizenstat, *Imperfect Justice*, pp. 160-161; Rickman, pp. 196-203; On First Reading, "States Act on Jewish Assets in Swiss Banks," *State Legislatures Magazine*, July 1, 1997; Metro Digest, "Holocaust Restitution," *Kansas City Star*, August 7, 1998.
118. Michael D. Goldhaber, "Runners-Up: Holocaust Attorneys," *National Law Journal*, December 20, 2000.
119. Francine Parnes, "Fighting On: Legal Actions by Nazi Victims Seeking Compensation Meet with Mixed Results," *American Bar Association, ABA Journal*, March 2002.
120. Anne-Marie Slaughter and David Bosco, "Plaintiff's Diplomacy," *Foreign Affairs*, September-October 2000.
121. Rickman, pp. 177-180.
122. For example, when it came to the actual number of clients in the Swiss bank case, he admitted to me that in fact, the number was not as high as he publicly claimed and used to substantiate the legitimacy of his claim.
123. Telephone Discussion with Jeanette Bernstein (niece of survivor-claimant Estelle Sapir), September 15, 2000; "Holocaust Survivors Blast Own Attorneys," *New York Post*, March 23, 1999, p. 5; Barry Meir, "Judge Warns Lawyer to Pay Past Penalties," *New York Times*, September 13, 2000, p. A15; Barry Meir, "Lawyer in Holocaust Case Faces Litany of Complaints," *New York Times*, September 8, 2000, p. A1. Fagan understood one thing however, the attention he received for these cases brought him a form of notoriety that no amount of money could buy. In the United States, his connection in the Swiss banks case and others as a secondary figure. In Europe, however, he was seen as the leading attorney—interview with Hannah Lessing. He would continue to clash with Hausfeld on the other cases in which they both became entangled, including a $100 billion case against thirty-four corporations, including the Swiss banks from the Holocaust case, for their roles in allegedly propping up the South African Government's program of Apartheid. See Nicol Degli Innocenti and John Reed, "The defendants are thirty-four of the world's biggest companies and banks, accused of having supported apartheid," *Financial Times*, May 19, 2003, p. 11.
124. Lingling Wei, "Class-Action Lawyer Weiss Aims to 'Undo" Corporate Harm," *Wall Street Journal*, October 29, 2002; Rickman, pp. 217-231.
125. Letter of Bob Swift to Gregg Rickman, November 5, 1996.
126. Anita Ramasastry, "Secrets and Lies? Swiss Banks and International Human Rights, *Vanderbilt Journal of Transnational Law*, (Vol. 31, Number 2), March 1998, pp. 387-388.
127. Rudolf Dolzer, "The Settlement of War-Related Claims: Does International Law Recognize a Victim's Private Right of Action? Lessons after 1945, Stefan A. Riesenfeld Symposium 2001, "Fifty Years in the Making: World War II Reparation and Restitution Claims," *Berkeley Journal of International Law*, Boalt Hall School of Law, University of California, Berkeley, Vol. 20, No. 1, 2002, p. 297.
128. Nicol Degli Innocenti and John Reed, "Civil Rights Statute Was Dormant for 200 Years," *Financial Times*, May 19, 2003, p. 11.
129. Interview with Eizenstat.
130. Eizenstat, *Imperfect Justice*, p. 76.
131. *Swiss Banks and Attempts to Recover Assets Belonging to the Victims of the Holocaust*, Senate Banking Committee Hearing Transcript, May 15, 1997.
132. Eizenstat had also dealt with the issue of sanctions against foreign states in the Helms-Burton Law and the Iran-Libya Sanctions Act. He steadfastly fought against the use of sanctions, feeling they unduly harmed relations between the United States

and our allies. Having worked on the Iran-Libya Sanctions Act, this author can attest to his strong opposition to their use. So prevalent was his time spent dealing with the issue, he was, according to his own testimony, referred to as the "Sanctionsmeister," of the Clinton Administration. See Eizenstat interview.

133. Interview with Eizenstat.
134. Sapir did not want to settle. She feared the affect on the other claimants. D'Amato had to force her to accept the award. Interview with D'Amato, Washington, DC, February 28, 2001.
135. On July 30, 2001, the U.S. Second Circuit Court of Appeals upheld the settlement after a group of survivors sued over the stipulations of the allocation plan. See Daniel Wise,"Holocaust Survivors $1.25 Billion settlement upheld by 2nd Circuit," *New York Law Journal*, July 30, 2001.
136. "Former Refugees to Switzerland Paid More than $2.2 Million," Email of the Claims Conference to the author, June 19, 2003.
137. "Suing for Reparations," *Baltimore Sun*, January 17, 1999, p. 1D.
138. Public Law 103-286, 108 Stat. 1450, August 1, 1994.
139. Revenue Ruling 56-518, Internal Revenue Service, 1956-2 C.B.25; Letter of Jody J. Brewster, Assistant Chief Counsel, Income Tax & Accounting, Office of Chief Counsel, United States Department of Treasury, Internal Revenue Service to United States Senator Alfonse M. D'Amato, June 22, 1998.
140. S.2549, United States Senate bill, referred to the Senate Finance Committee.
141. S.779, *The Holocaust Era Assets Tax Exclusion Act of 1999*, United States Senate bill, referred to the Senate Finance Committee.
142. S.749, *The Holocaust Victims Tax Fairness Act of 2001*, United States Senate bill.
143. H.R.4823, *The Holocaust Restitution Tax Fairness Act of 2002*, United States House of Representatives bill.
144. "Holocaust Survivors To Get Another $52 M From Swiss Banks," *Wall Street Journal*, October 30, 2002.
145. Interview with Michael Bradfield, Paul Volcker's Deputy on the Commission, April 30, 2002.
146. *Independent Commission of Eminent Persons Report on Dormant Accounts of Victims of Nazi Persecution in Swiss Banks*, Final Report, December 6, 1999, pp. 84-114.
147. Interview with Bradfield.
148. "Rifkind Report," "Nazi Gold" Information from the British Archives," Foreign & Commonwealth Office, September 1996, p. 16. In May 1997, Part II of the Rifkind Report had been released.
149. Tom Bower, "Blame Britain, Not Truman," *New York Times*, May 12, 1997, p. A23.
150. Alasdair Palmer, "Comment: Let's get ethical about our debts to Holocaust victims Alasdair Palmer on the British theft of millions of pounds from those who fled the Nazis," London Sunday Telegraph, November 30, 1997.
151. Stephen Ward and Ian Locke, "Ex-Enemy Jews"—The Fate of the Assets in Britain of Holocaust Victims and Survivors, Second Edition, (London: The Holocaust Educational Trust, March 1998), p. 5.
152. BBA Press Release, "British Banks Support Moves to Remedy Post-War Injustice," September 8, 1997, available online at http://www.bba.org.uk/public /newsroom/ pressreleases/ 44589/610?version=1.
153. History Notes, "British policy towards enemy property during and after the Second World War," No. 13, (London: Foreign & Commonwealth Office, General Services Command, April 1998.)
154. Speech of French President Jacques Chirac, July 16, 1995.

155. Speech of Prime Minister Lionel Jospin before the Representative Council of Jewish Institutions in France, January 25, 1997.
156. Ibid.
157. The members of the Commission were the following: Adolphe Steg, Jean Favier, Jean Kahn, Serge Klarsfeld, Alain Pierret, Annette Wieviorka, and François Furet who died soon afterward.
158. Shmuel Trigano, "France Faces its Past, French Jews Face an Uncertain Future," Institute of the World Jewish Congress, Policy Forum No. 17, p. 22.
159. Floor Statement of U.S. Senator Alfonse M. D'Amato, United States Senate, Congressional Record, S3890, May 1, 1997.
160. "Museums holding 1955 works of art taken from Jews during the Occupation, In 1995, a confidential report from the Court of Auditors has assessed the extent of the thievery," *Le Monde*, January 28, 1997, translated by David Skelly, Congressional Research Service.
161. See letter for Ambassador François Bujon' de l'Estang to United States Senator Alfonse M. D'Amato, April 30, 1997.
162. *The Commission for the Study of the Spoilation of Jews in France*, (the "Matteoli Commission") *Interim Report*, April - December 1997, pp. 58-69.
163. "French banks fear Jewish Holocaust claim paper," *Reuters*, August 26, 1998.
164. Bodner, et al.. v. Banque Paribas, et al., Case No. 97 Civ. 7433 (SJ) (E.D.N.Y.), amended complaint filed March 12, 1998.
165. "Notice of Appearance of Additional Counsel for Plaintiffs," Letter of Karen J. Mandel, Lieff, Cabrasser, Heimann & Bernstein, LLP to the Clerk of the Court of the United States District Court, Eastern District of New York, November 25, 1998.
166. Letter of Frederick T. Davis, Shearman & Sterling to Gregg Rickman, August 20, 1998.
167. Eizenstat, *Imperfect Justice*, p. 326.
168. Discussion with Philip Bechtel, November 29, 2000.
169. Irwin Arieff, "French banks, Jews say Holocaust fund an option," *Reuters*, February 17, 1999.
170. Joan Gralla, "French banks negotiating a Holocaust fund—WJC," *Reuters*, March 15, 1999.
171. "French Banks Announce Comprehensive Measures of Restitution and Reparation for Holocaust victims," *PR Newswire*, New York, March 24, 1999.
172. Joan Gralla, "Holocaust orphans deserve French bank pensions—WJC," *Reuters*, April 5, 1999.
173. Press Release, "France Compensates Deportation Victims' Descendants," Embassy of France in the US, August 23, 2001, available at .
174. Interview with Bechtel; Interview with Eizenstat; and "French banks, NY officials differ on publishing list of WWII Jewish accounts," *AFX News*, September 17, 1999.
175. On September 20, 2005, Wiesenthal died at the age of ninety-six.
176. Interview with Bechtel; "French Banks Make Out-of -Court Holocaust Agreement, Lawyers Say," *Bloomberg*, January 9, 2001.
177. The subject of a "statement of interest" is being dealt with in respect to the French banks settlement first, and below, with the settlement of the Austrian industries case, only out of topical order. Chronologically, the idea first came to the fore with the settlement, described below, of the Slave Labor cases against German companies. This case established the ideational precedent for the settlement that was later applied to the settlement of the others.
178. Interview with Bechtel.

179. Philip Carmel, "Compensation claims in France continue to climb, new report says," *Jewish Telegraphic Agency*, April 22, 2003.
180. "Panel: France owes WWII Jews millions," *Jerusalem Post*, April 18, 2003.
181. Discussion with Harriet Tamen, June 2, 2003.
182. Letter of Harriet Tamen and Richard Weisberg to Ambassador J.D. Bindenagel, January 31, 2002; Letter of Kenneth McCallion, Harriet Tamen, and Richard Weisberg to Special Envoy Randolph Bell and Ambassador Francis Lott, August 1, 2002.
183. Ambassador Fredrik Hedin and Göran Elgemyr, "Stolen goods in the Central Bank: Sweden swapped iron for looted gold," *Dagens Nyheter*, January 21, 1997, translated by Ambassador Fredrik Hedin, courtesy of the author.
184. Letter of Ambassador Fredrik Hedin to U.S. Senator Alfonse M. D'Amato, February 5, 1997.
185. Andy Soltis, "Swedes agree to join hunt for Nazi victims' 'lost' cash," *New York Post*, March 12, 1997; Press Release of The Commission on Jewish Assets in Sweden at the Time of the Second World War, March 4, 1998.
186. Jon Henley, "War papers cast shadow over Swedish dynasty Family of Jews' savior traded with Nazis," *The Guardian*, February 24, 1997; Walter V. Robinson, "Sweden probes a dark secret, Family long viewed as heroic profited from Nazi deals," *Boston Globe*, July 6, 1997, p. A1.
187. In September 1991, the *Swedish-Russian Working Group* was formed following the conclusion of the Cold War to examine documents in the former Soviet archives on the fate of Raoul Wallenberg. The report issued in 2000 commented that the "case cannot be finally closed." To this day, there are still claims and counter claims coming out about his fate. See *Raoul Wallenberg, Report of the Swedish-Russian Working Group*, (Stockholm, 2000), p. 9.
188. *Sweden's Gold Transactions With Nazi Germany*, The Government of Sweden, February 1998; available online at .
189. Press Release of The Commission on Jewish Assets in Sweden at the Time of the Second World War, March 4, 1998.
190. See Stéphane Bruchfeld and Paul A. Levine, *Tell ye your children...A book about the Holocaust in Europe 1933-1945*, (Stockholm: Regerinskansliet, Lavande Historia, 1998).
191. "Norway: The Courage of a Small Jewish Community; Holocaust Restitution and Anti-Semitism, and Interview with Bjarte Bruland and Irene Levin," Jerusalem Center for Public Affairs, Post-Holocaust and Anti-Semitism, No. 10, July 1, 2003. See, *The Reisel/Bruland Report on the Confiscation of Jewish Property in Norway During WWII, The Official Norwegian Report*, June 1997.
192. Günther E. Sturm, ed., "Speech by Chancellor Franz Vranitzky, Excerpt from the speech to the National Council on July 8th, 1991," *National Fund, National Fund of the Republic of Austria for Victims of National Socialism*, May 2003, p. 6.
193. Ari Goldman, "Upheaval in the East: Austria; Vienna to Extend Social Benefits To Jewish Victims of the Nazi Era," *New York Times*, February 14, 1990.
194. Douglas C. McGill, "Austria Sets Up System To Yield Nazi-Held Art," *New York Times*, December 3, 1985; "Mauerbach Fund for Jewish Survivors of the Holocaust in Need - in Austria and Internationally, Stipulations for Eligibility for Grants.
195. Authers and Wolffe, p. 328.
196. Burt Neuborne, Presentation before the 2002 Institute for Law and Economic Policy Litigation Conference: Litigation in a Free Society: preliminary Reflections on Aspects of Holocaust-era Litigation in American Courts, *Washington University Law Quarterly*, Fall 2002; Authers and Wolffe, p. 328.
197. Neuborne.

198. Greg B. Smith, "Holocaust Survivors Bash D'Amato," *Daily News*, September 27, 1999.
199. Joan Gralla, "Jewish groups say shun BankAustria over Holocaust," *Reuters*, July 14, 1999.
200. Eizenstat Interview; Interview with Hannah Lessing, Secretary General, National Found of the Republic of Austria for Victims of National Socialism, General Settlement Fund, Washington, D.C., May 8, 2003.
201. Letter to the Editor of Herman Pedergnana, Winterthur, Switzerland, *International Herald Tribune*, April 21, 1998.
202. See "Account Agreement between the Federal Reserve Bank of New York and the Government of the United Kingdom of Great Britain and Northern Ireland," London Conference on Nazi Gold, December 2-4, 1997, author's personal papers. Eighteen countries pledged nearly $60 million to the fund. Of this total, the United States pledged and Congress appropriated $25 million. The appropriation for this funding was authorized by an act of Congress, S.1564, *The Holocaust Victims Redress Act*, P.L.105-158, authored by Senator D'Amato. This author worked on the passage of this legislation. As such, the funds for this pledge were appropriated during Fiscal Years 1998-2000. Of the total sum of $25 million, $23.068 million was allocated to organizations that were able to use pre-existing contacts with local aid networks to apply direct assistance to needy Holocaust survivors. These funds were allocated to the Claims Conference, the Foundation for Polish-German Reconciliation, and the International Gay and Lesbian Human Rights Commission. A further $1.9 million was supplied to a number of organizations to fund education and research projects, social assistance programs, and conferences to promote tolerance and human rights. See "U.S. Contribution to the Nazi Persecutee Relief Fund," United States Department of State, Bureau of European Affairs, courtesy of Michael Bazyler.
203. Discussions between the author and Eizenstat.
204. Interview with Seymour Rubin, March 21, 1997.
205. Interview with Seymour Rubin, United States Holocaust Memorial Museum, January 6, 1997.
206. Letter of Seymour J. Rubin to Stuart Eizenstat, March 11, 1997, courtesy of the author.
207. "Proposal on a Congressional Commission Concerning the Assets of Holocaust Victims in the United States," April 24, 1997, in the author's files.
208. Roger Boyes, "U.S. role in Holocaust gold saga heralds fiery test of diplomacy," *Times of London*, September 2, 1997.
209. Eli Rosenbaum, "Proposed U.S. Commission on Assets Looted by Nazi Germany and its Allies and the Fate of Axis External Assets in the USA: Draft Outline," November 21, 1997, from the author's files.
210. Author's notes, December 10, 1997.
211. Statement of Under Secretary of State Stuart E. Eizenstat Proposing a U.S. Holocaust Assets Historical Commission," April 1, 1998.
212. See Statement by the President, on signing the "U.S. Holocaust Assets Commission Act of 1998, June 23, 1998. The bill became P.L.105-186.
213. Posting of Marc Masurvosky on the H-Net List for History of the Holocaust, July 13, 2001, available online at
214. "Statement on Signing the U.S. Holocaust Assets Commission Extension Act of 1999,"*Public Papers of the Presidents*, December 9, 1999.
215. Discussions with several of the researchers from the PCHA.
216. Ralph Blumenthal, "Panel on Nazi Art Theft Fell Short, Experts Say," *New York Times*, March 3, 2003, p. B1.

217. Press Release of U.S. Senator Gordon H. Smith, "Smith Introduces Holocaust Assets Bill," December 19, 2001.
218. From personal experience in the National Archives researching the issue, much information on this issue can be found in the files of the United States Treasury Department from the era. Morgenthau's men had investigated a large number of U.S. companies, foreign and domestically owned. The FBI as well had done the same.
219. Telephone discussion with Jacqueline Waldman, June 3, 2002.
220. Letter of Representative Benjamin L. Cardin to President Emil Constantinescu, July 1, 2000; Press Release of Ambassador Jim Rosapepe, American Ambassador to Romania, "U.S. Ambassador Rosapepe Joins U.S. Citizens as She Recovers Romanian Property Confiscated From Her Family, January 8, 2001.
221. Letter of Laura A. Clerici, Consul General, U.S. Embassy, Warsaw, Poland to The Honorable Steven C. LaTourette, n.d.
222. Report of Ambassador Stuart E. Eizenstat, Department of State Special Envoy for Property Claims in Central and Eastern Europe, January 22, 1996, enclosure to Letter of Wendy R. Sherman, Assistant Secretary of State for Legislative Affairs to United States Senator Alfonse M. D'Amato, February 22, 1996, p. 2.
223. The author's personal experience with attempting to file a claim for family members in Poland.
224. Serge Schmemann, "Jewish Family Heirloom: 15 Square Miles of Death," *New York Times*, July 10, 1998, p. A2.
225. Robert F. Worth, "Jewish Family Fights for Its Stolen Legacy," *New York Times*, May 24, 2002, p. A23. See also, Peter Finn, "U.S. Family Presses Complex Holocaust Claim," *The Washington Post*, December 14, 2003, p. A32.
226. Martin G. Wortham, and Barbara Principe v. Karstadtquelle Ag; Warenhaus Wertheim GmbH; and Estate of Arthur Lindgens, A.K.A. Johann Rudolf Arthur Lindgens, Civil Action No. 01 Cv 2741, United States District Court Southern District of New York, courtesy of Gary M. Osen.
227. Email from Gary M. Osen to Gregg Rickman, June 26, 2002.
228. Worth, "Jewish Family Fights for Its Stolen Legacy."
229. Brian Perkin, "Wertheim Heirs Win Support in Legal Fight with Karstadtquelle," *Bloomberg News*, October 1, 2002.
230. Testimony by Randolph M. Bell, Special Envoy for Holocaust Issues before the Helsinki Commission on Property Restitution in Central and Eastern Europe, July 16, 2002, p. 5.
231. David Holley, "Fight to Return Seized Property Gains Ground," *Los Angeles Times*, July 30, 1999, p. A2.
232. Interview with Lavie.
233. Peter Finn, "Poles May Bar Payments for Postwar Acts, Panel Narrows Definition of Who May Be Compensated," *Washington Post*, January 8, 2000, p. A13.
234. Graóyna Skapska, Jaroslaw Kadylo, Grzegorz Bryda, "Public Debate on Reprivatisation and Restitution of the Nationalised Property in Poland [sic]," Working Paper 2, *Property Restitution and the Post-1989 Transformation Process in Germany and Poland*, Joint Project of the University of Plymouth, the Humboldt-University of Berlin, and the Jagiellonian-University of Cracow, December 1999, p. 3.
235. Interview with Lavie; Skapsa, Kadylo, and Bryda, p. 5.
236. Ibid, p.7.
237. Theo Garb, et al., vs. The Republic of Poland, Ministry of the Treasury of Poland, Civil Action 99 Civ. 3487, courtesy of Mel Urbach.

238. "Andrzej Stylinski, "Poland Rejects US Holocaust Lawsuits," *Associated Press*, August 6, 1999.
239. "President Vetoes Property Restitution Bill," *Radio Free Europe/Radio Liberty Poland, Belarus, and Ukraine Report*, Vol. 3, No. 11, March 27, 2001.
240. Thomas J. Lueck, "Judge Dismisses Suit on Seizure of Polish Land," *New York Times*, June 25, 2002, p. A25.
241. Letter of Hans van Mierlo, Minister of Foreign Affairs of the Netherlands to United States Senator Alfonse M. D'Amato, March 25, 1998, p.2.
242. "Museums holding 1955 works of art taken from Jews during the Occupation, In 1995, a confidential report from the Court of Auditors has assessed the extent of the thievery."
243. Ian MacLeod, "Nazi looting saved art from bombings, gallery director says, Plunder of native works is of greater concern: Lumsden," *National Post*, January 4, 2001.
244. See, Celestine Bohlen, "Major Museums Affirm Right to Keep Long-Held Antiquities," *New York Times*, December 11, 2002.
245. "Heir to Vast Art Collection Recovers Old World Painting Looted by Nazis; First Painting from Famed Goudstikker Collection Returned to Family," *Business Wire*, May 24, 2001; Kathryn Shattuck, "Metro Briefing New York: Manhattan: Nazi-Looted Art Returned," *New York Times*, May 25, 2001, p. B4.
246. Telephone discussion with Marie von Saher, August 2, 2001.
247. Ronald Powers, "Head of Metropolitan says museums committed to returning looted art," *Associated Press*, July 14, 1998.
248. Wesley Fisher, formerly of the United States Holocaust Memorial Museum, had shown me just such a picture hanging over the fireplace mantle of his parents in Europe. The painting was later found in a museum exhibition catalogue.
249. "Report of the AAMD Task Force on the Spoilation of Art during the Nazi/World War II Era (1933-1945), Association of Art Museum Directors, June 4, 1998, courtesy of the Metropolitan Museum of Art in New York.
250. "Principles With Respect to Nazi-Confiscated Art," Washington Conference on Holocaust-Era Art, United States Department of State, December 3, 1998, from the author's files.
251. Some museums have in fact placed provenance information their websites: The Metropolitan Museum of Art in New York, the Museum of Fine Art in Boston, the J. Paul Getty Museum in Los Angeles, The Art Institute of Chicago, The Wadsworth Athenum Museum of Art in Connecticut, and Harvard University among others.
252. Barbara Ross, "Records Fuzzy on Nazi-Era Museum Art," *Daily News*, April 13, 2000; "New York City museum says Reubens is not Nazi loot," *Reuters*, March14, 2000.
253. Walter V. Robinson, "Sotheby's takes work tied to Nazis off block," *Boston Globe*, November 25, 1997; Colin Gleadell, "The Arts: Did the Nazis loot this? Colin Gleadell reports on Christie's worry over its star lot ... " *Daily Telegraph*, July 13, 1998.
254. Letter of Henry S. Bondi to Glenn D. Lowry, Director, The Museum of Modern Art, 30 December 1997.
255. Letter of Kathleen and Rita Reif to Glenn D. Lowry, Director, The Museum of Modern Art, 4 January 1998.
256. Steven Litt, "3rd Drawing Part of Nazi Hoard," *Cleveland Plain Dealer*, April 14, 1998.
257. Judith H. Dobrzynski, "Settlement in Dispute Over a Painting Looted by Nazis," *New York Times*, August 14, 1998; "Profile: The Search; 50-year family search for stolen painting by Nazis during World War II finally found in United States at the Art

Institute of Chicago, Transcript of the January 19, 1997 broadcast of *60 Minutes*; Nick Goodman, Simon Goodman, and Lili Vera Collas Gutmann vs. Daniel C. Searle, 96 Civ. 5316, United States District Court, Southern District of New York, courtesy of attorney Thomas R. Kline.

258. *JTA Global News*, June 14, 2001, available online at .
259. Michael Dobbs, "Suspicion Hangs in U.S. Museums, Search for Art Stolen by Nazis Spreads to America's Collections," *Washington Post*, May 5, 2000, p. A1.
260. Ralph Blumenthal, "New Efforts To Recover Nazi Plunder, But Pessimism Grows For Recoveries," *New York Times*, February 27, 2003, p. B1.
261. Letter of F.W. McCombe to John Pehle, November 21, 1942, RG 131, Foreign Funds Control, NARA.
262. Claim of Ilona Plaskin, Claim No. HUNG-2-222, Decision No. HUNG-2-1060, Foreign Claims Settlement Commission of the United States.
263. Hilberg, Raul, *The Destruction of the European Jews* (Chicago: Quadrangle Books, 1961), p. 302.
264. "Insurance and the Holocaust: Life insurance was a favourite investment of European Jews before the second world war. Where are those policies now?," *The Economist*, March 15, 1997.
265. Rickman, pp. 262-263; Interview with MK Michael Kleiner, Tel Aviv, April 10, 2002.
266. Letter of the Central Director, Assicurazioni Generali S.p.A. to Rabbi Abraham Ravitz MK, Michael Kleiner MK, and Abraham Hirchson [sic], June 16, 1999.
267. Assicurazioni Generali, Exhibits to Accompany Testimony before the House Committee on Banking, February 12, 1998, Washington, DC.
268. "An Open Letter to the Families of Holocaust Victims," Assicurazioni Generali S.p.A., *New York Times*, July 25, 1997, p. A18.
269. Netty C. Gross, "Who is Getting the Generali Fund's $12 Million?," *Jerusalem Report*, March 27, 2000.
270. Rickman, p. 263.
271. Dan Nakaso, "Politician looks for new life, new career in Hawaii," *Honolulu Advertiser*, April 15, 2003, p. A1.
272. Memorandum of Edward D. Fagan to Senator Alfonse D'Amato, January 21, 1998.
273. "Judge Won't Drop Holocaust Lawsuits," *Associated Press,* September 25, 1997.
274. "Questions and Answers Concerning Life Insurance Policies Issued Between 1920-1945," *Allianz AG, Progress Report*, Allianz Aktiengesellschaft, December 8, 1997, p. 3.
275. Statement of Christopher Worthley on Behalf of Allianz AG for California Department of Insurance Claims; and Restitution of Victims Assets Stolen by the Nazi Third Reich, Los Angeles, California, January 13, 1998, p. 2.
276. Memorandum of Neil D. Levin to Senator D'Amato, February 11, 1998, in the author's files.
277. Statement of Senator Alfonse M. D'Amato Before the House Banking Committee Hearing on European Insurance Companies, February 12, 1998.
278. "Generali Will Cooperate with Commission Established to Examine Holocaust Insurance Issue, Company Reiterates its Moral Commitment to Victims of the Holocaust," Press Release of Assicurazioni Generali, February 12, 1998. Vayer proudly handed copies of the press release out at the hearing.
279. Opening Statement of M. Scott Vayer, Representative of Assicurazioni Generali Before the U.S. House of Representatives Committee on Banking and Financial Services, February 12, 1998.

280. Statement of Herbert Hansmeyer on Behalf of Allianz AG, United States Congress Committee on Banking and Financial Services, February 12, 1998, p. 1.
281. Memorandum of Neil Levin.
282. Henry Weinstein, "State to Inspect Firms' Files in Holocaust Case," *Los Angeles Times*, March 18, 1998, p. B1.
283. Letter of Herbert Hansmeyer to Senator Alphonse [sic] M. D'Amato, March 25, 1998.
284. Memorandum of Intent, April 8, 1998, signed by Rolph Huppi, Chairman of the Zurich Group; Herbert Hansmeyer, Board of Directors of Allianz AG; Guido Pastori of Generali; Wendy Cooper, of the Equitable Life Insurance Company, or AXA; "NY & CA Insurance Regulators, Worldwide Jewish Groups and Major Insurers Agree to Establish and International Commission as a Means to Resolve Holocaust Claims, " News Release of the New York State Insurance Department, April 8, 1998.
285. David Cay Johnston, "Accord Signed to Name Tribunal ON Holocaust Insurance Claims," *New York Times*, May 7, 1998, p. A5.
286. Letter of R.F. Hüppi, Zurich Life to Superintendent Neil D. Levin, August 14, 1998; "Zurich Insurance Reaches Agreement with U.S. Insurance Commissioners on Joint Approach to Policies from the World War II Era," Press Release of the Zurich Group, August 14, 1998.
287. Interview with Wayne Berman, an attorney representing Generali, August 18, 1998.
288. In November 2000, Generali reinstituted the settlement.
289. Telephone conversation with Neil Levin, 13 August 1998. Fagan, according to Levin, who was the Commissioner for Insurance for the State of New York, engaged in screaming fights with D'Amato, who tried to replicate his role in bringing Generali and the claimants to a settlement, just as he had done a week before with the Swiss banks.
290. Alex Somekh and Shlomo Shamir, "Jewish groups furious at lawyer's demand for 20 percent of Generali funds," *Ha'aretz*, 27 August 1998.
291. Joe Ungaro, "Attorney for Holocaust survivors angry about report in Israeli paper, *Associated Press*, 29 August 1998.
292. "Merger of MOU and Class Action Procedures," courtesy of Ed Fagan.
293. Letter of Ed Fagan to Senator Alfonse D'Amato, September 22, 1998.
294. Winterthur, Allianz, AXA, Basler Leben soon joined the MOU process for the Commission.
295. Letter of Ed Fagan to Senator Alfonse D'Amato, October 16, 1998.
296. "Plan for Holocaust-Era Insurance Claims," *New York Times*, August 10, 1999, p. A4.
297. Henry Weinstein, "Insurers Reject Most Claims in Holocaust Cases," *Los Angeles Times*, May 9, 2000.
298. Statement of Mr. Peter A. Lefkin, Senior Vice President, Fireman's Fund Insurance Company, Government & Industry Affairs before the Illinois House of Representatives Committee on Judiciary and Civil Law, Skokie, Illinois, October 5, 2000, p. 3.
299. Letter of Senator Peter G. Fitzgerald and Bill Nelson to Lawrence Eagleburger, January 9, 2002.
300. Discussion with an unnamed official connected to ICHEIC.
301. Philip Shenon, "Holocaust Claims Commission Falling Into Turmoil Over Finances," *New York Times*, p. A 4.
302. "Envoy Cries Foul In Squabble Over Restitution Effort," *The Forward*, February 1, 2002, p. 1.
303. Nacha Cattan, "Restitution Exec Was Probed on Spending: Sher Resigned After Inquiry," *The Forward*, November 1, 2002.

304. This amount was arrived at in the agreement between the American and German governments to conclude the slave labor cases. The amounts earmarked for ICHEIC were as follows: $96.5 million for ICHEIC to compensate unpaid and not otherwise compensated insurance policies of German companies and $168.9 million for the humanitarian fund of ICHEIC. In that agreement, the amount of claims German insurance companies were held to be responsible was set at this latter amount, with legal responsibility capped. The WJC did not believe that this was necessarily prejudicial in that, despite the number of claimants, the actual number of successful claims is thought to be within that range. While the agreement amount was roughly $7 million short of the original amount, the Foundation raised it to $275,000,000. See Kai Hennig, Spokesman, Foundation, "Remembrance, Responsibility, and Future," "Meeting the Moral Challenge of Holocaust Restitution, A Progress Report, Konrad Adenauer Conference, United States Capitol, Washington, DC, June 14, 2002.
305. "Holocaust Survivors to Receive $15M," *Associated Press*, in *New York Times*, June 2, 2003.
306. "Dear Colleague Letter" of Representatives Henry Waxman, Eliot Engel, and Janice Schakowsky, March 12, 2003.
307. Brief of Rep. Henry A. Waxman and 51 Other Members of Congress as Amicis Curiae in Support of Respondent in American Insurance Association, American Re-Insurance Company Et. Al., v. John Garamendi in his capacity as Commissioner of Insurance for the State of California, No. 02-722, United States Supreme Court.
308. Ruling of the Supreme Court of the United States, American Insurance Association et al., v. Garamendi, Insurance Commissioner, State of California, No. 02-722, Majority Opinion, Justice David Souter, June 23, 2003, p. 28.
309. See the "Comprehensive Holocaust Accountability in Insurance Measure," in the House of Representatives, and S.972 in the Senate. H.R.1210, "The Holocaust Victims' Insurance Relief Act of 2003, by Representative Henry Waxman, would establish a Holocaust Insurance Registry by the Archivist of the United States and disclosure requirements by the companies to the U.S. Commerce Department.
310. An exception to the lack of insurance settlements was that of the Stern family who had filed a lawsuit against Generali in Los Angeles Superior Court on February 8, 1998. See Michael Kahn, "Holocaust suit against Italian insurer is settled," *Reuters*, November 24, 1999; Adolf Stern, et al., v. Assicurazioni Generali S.P.A., BC 185376, Los Angeles Superior Court, Los Angeles, California, February 5, 1998.
311. Bazyler, pp. 164-165; the author's personal experience with the operation and successful conclusion of the Swiss banks case.
312. Telegram of D.A. Wehmeyer to the Department of State, July 9, 1959, RG 59, Office of the Legal Adviser, Office of Educational, Cultrual & Public Affairs, Subject Files, 1945-97, Lot File 96D244, Box 40, NARA.
313. Ibid.
314. Pinto-Duschinsky, p. 19; McGhee to Department of State, Subject: Slave Labor Claims Against Rheinmetall, May 11, 1966, RG 59, Office of the Legal Adviser, Office of Educational, Cultural and Public Affairs, Subject Files, 1945-1997, Lot File 96D244, Box 40, NARA.
315. Eizenstat, *Imperfect Justice*, p. 209; James M. Markham, "Company Linked to Nazi Slave Labor Pays $2 Million," *New York Times*, January 9, 1986.
316. Ament, Written Presentation," p. 3.
317. Helene Pollack et al. v. Siemens, et al., filed August 30, 1998, United States District Court, Eastern District of New York.
318. Elly Gross, et al. vs. Volkswagten A.G., United States District Court, District of New Jersey, Filed August 31, 1998; Henry Duveen, et al. v. Deutsche Bank, et al. United States District Court, Southern District of New York, Filed May 14, 1999.

319. Marian Solarczyk, et al. v. Bayer, et al. United States District Court, District of New Jersey, Filed, January 28, 1999.
320. Felix Opatowski, et al. v. Adam Opel, et al. United States District Court, District Court of New Jersey, Filed May 13, 1999.
321. Simon Wiesenthal Center, Gray Davis, et al. v. Deutsche Bank A.G., et al. Civil Action 302420, Superior Court of the State of California in and for the Country of San Francisco, March 31, 1999.
322. George Boehmer, "Siemens to continue slave labor payments With US-Holocaust-Slave Labor," *Associated Press*, September 14, 1999.
323. Memorandum of Major George W. Haley to Deputy Theater Judge Advocate, War Crimes Branch, United States Forces, European Theater, September 28, 1945, RG 338, U.S. Army War Crimes Files , Box 486, NARA; Headquarters Seventh Army, Report of Investigation, Death of 350-400 Russian and Polish infants in the care of German authorities, FO 309/172, Public Records Office, London.
324. "Common Declaration," Foundation Initiative of German Industry: Memory, Responsibility, and Future, from the German Chancellery, February 16, 1999.
325. Roger Cohen, "German Companies Adopt Fund For Slave Laborers Under Nazis, Chancellor Sees 'Campaign' Against His Nation," *New York Times*, February 17, 1999, p. 1.
326. "German firms see end to suits as fund prerequisite," *Reuters,* March 10, 1999; Eizenstat, *Imperfect Justice,* pp. 213-214.
327. Letter of Michael Hausfeld et al. to Gerd Westdickenberg, Legal Advisor to the Ministry of Foreign Affairs, June 10, 1999.
328. "Interview with German Historian Lutz Niethammer," *Die Welt*, June 2, 1999, translated by the Law Office of Cohen, Milstein, Hausfeld & Toll.
329. Michael D. Hausfeld, Remarks at the Washington, DC Conference on Slave and Forced Labor, Washington, D.C., May 12, 1999, p. 1.
330. Remarks of Wolfgang G. Gibowski, Spokesman, German Industry Foundation Initiative, "Meeting the Moral Challenge of Holocaust Restitution: A Progress Report," a Konrad Adenauer Foundation Conference held at the United States Capitol, Washington, DC, June 14, 2002.
331. "Germans Stall Progress Toward Resolution of Slave Labor Claims," Press Release of Cohen, Milstein, Hausfeld & Toll, June 10, 1999.
332. In a series of answers to questions provided by United States Senator Orrin Hatch to Acting Assistant Attorney General David Ogden, Ogden denied taking any position on these treaties. See "Responses of the Department of Justice to Questions From Senator Hatch, June 28, 2000, available online at ; Justice Department Interview with unnamed Justice Department attorneys as well as Plaintiff's attorney Martin Mendelsohn. In fact, Mendelsohn and Hausfeld sought the paperwork from the Justice Department Attorneys explaining this opinion and they sought these documents first through means of a Freedom of Information Request and later through subpoena. See Letter of Michael D. Hausfeld to James M. Kovakas, Freedom of Information/Privacy Act Officer, United States Department of Justice, November 4, 1999; and Subpoena to Janet Reno, United States Attorney General, Case Number 99-C-472, United States District Court, District of Columbia, November 4, 1999.
333. Interview with Eizenstat.
334. Ibid.
335. Bert Herman, "Nazi-era Compensation Said Biased," *Associated Press*, December 16, 1999; "Russians' Lawyer Faults Holocaust Pact," *Reuters*, December 16, 1999; Several discussions with researcher and aide Miriam Kleiman, of Cohen, Milstein, Hausfeld & Toll.

336. Interview with Martin Mendelsohn, Washington, DC, January 29, 2003.
337. Michael Shapiro, "Germany drops proposal to limit payments to some former laborers," *JTA Online*, February 2, 2000; By the middle of 2006, the fund will have paid out benefits to about a million people, See Alissa J. Rubin and Elisabeth Penz, "Former Forced Laborers Laud Austrian Fund," *Los Angeles Times*, December 6, 2005.
338. Letter of Samuel Berger, Assistant to the President for National Security and Beth Nolan, Counsel to the President, to Michael Steiner, National Security Assistant to the Federal Chancellor, June 16, 2000.
339. Letter of Michael Steiner to Samuel Berger, July 5, 2000.
340. Ruling of the Supreme Court of the United States, American Insurance Association et al., v. Garamendi, Insurance Commissioner, State of California, p. 16.
341. Annex A of the Agreement between the Government of the United States of America and the Government of the Federal Republic of Germany concerning the Foundation "Remembrance, Responsibility and the Future," Berlin, Germany, July 17, 2000; "Nazi slave labour compensation fund: the details," *Agence France Presse*, July 17, 2000.
342. Open Letter, "To the plaintiffs' attorneys participating in the negotiations," signed by Stuart E. Eizenstat, Otto Graf Lambsdorff, and Manfred Gentz, July 17, 2000.
343. State Department Informal Translation prepared by the U.S. Embassy, Berlin on the Creation of a Foundation "Remembrance, Responsibility & Future," July 14, 2000.
344. Interview with Martin Mendelsohn, Plaintiffs' attorney, April 16, 2001.
345. "U.S. Judge Hires David Boies to Defend Holocaust Claims Ruling," Bloomberg News, April 9, 2001; Interview with Mendelsohn, April 16, 2001.
346. "All Sides Laud Ruling On Holocaust Case," *New York Times*, May 18, 2001, p. A20.
347. "Fact Sheet on the "Remembrance, Responsibility and the Future" Foundation, June 14, 2002; "Report on the German Foundation, "Remembrance, Responsibility, and the Future," as required by Section 704 of the Foreign Relations Authorization Act, FY 2003, P.L. 107-228, enclosure to letter of Paul V. Kelly, Assistant Secretary of State for Legislative Affairs, to Representative Henry J. Hyde, Chairman, Committee on International Relations, House of Representatives, March 31, 2003, p. 4.
348. Rickman, p. 146.
349. Christopher P. Winner, "Contemporary views of Holocaust are in constant flux," *USA Today*, February 17, 1997, p. A8.
350. Daniel Kurtzman, "U.S. Congress heightens role in Holocaust restitution issue," *JTA*, February 17, 1998, p. 6.
351. Bert Herman, "Author of book on IBM and Holocaust denies release was linked to lawsuits," *Associated Press*, February 23, 2001.
352. Raymonde Abrams et. al., v. Société Nationale des Chemins de Fer Français, CV 100 5326, September 5, 2000, United States District Court, Eastern District of New York.
353. Telephone interview with Harriet Tamen, attorney for the plaintiffs, May 26, 2003.
354. On July 25, 2003, U.S. Reps. Ileana Ros-Lehtinen (FL) and Carolyn Maloney (N.Y.) introduced a bill Friday that would allow survivors to sue the railway in U.S. court.
355. Hamblett.
356. Thomas Grossman, et. al., v. International Business Machines, Corporation, Filed February 10, 2001, United States District Court for the Eastern District of New York.
357. "Auschwitz Historian Rebuts Author's Claim," *Chicago Tribune*, February 13, 2001."

358. Herman, "Author of book on IBM and Holocaust denies release was linked to lawsuits."
359. Eric Peters, "Don't Blame VW for Nazi Crimes," *Wall Street Journal*, September 14, 1998.
360. Letter to the Editor of Neal H. Weinfeld, *Wall Street Journal*, September 22, 1998.
361. John S. Friedman, "Kodak's Nazi Connections," *The Nation*, March 26, 2001; Joan Gralla, "U.S. Kodak Says German Unit Used Nazi-Era Labor," *Reuters*, April 27, 2000.
362. Letter of Jean-Marc Pochon to Senator Alfonse D'Amato, March 12, 1997.
363. Daniel Jonah Goldhagen, *A Moral Reckoning, The Role of the Catholic Church in the Holocaust and Its Unfulfilled Duty of Repair* (New York: Alfred A. Knopf, 2002), pp. 183-184.
364. Among these works are *Constantine's Sword* by James Carroll, *A Moral Reckoning, The Role of the Catholic Church in the Holocaust and Its Unfulfilled Duty of Repair,* and *Hitler's Pope, The Secret History of Pius XII*, by John Cornwell.
365. Tittmann to Harrison, "Papal protest against Nazi atrocities," Bern, August 3, 1942, RG 226, Office of Special Services, Entry 4, R & A, 1941-42, NARA.
366. Tittmann to Harrison, Papal Talk of Negotiated Peace," Bern, June 29, 1942, RG 226, Office of Special Services , Entry 4, R & A, 1941-42, NARA.
367. Yair Sheleg and Zohar Blumenkrantz, "Rabbi Lau: 'Church hasn't done enough to confront Shoah'," *Ha'aretz English Edition*, March 3, 2000.
368. OSS Outgoing Message to Washington, February 8, 1945, RG 226, Records of the Office of Strategic Services, Entry 190, Field Station Files, Box 163, NARA; Letter of Emerson Bigelow to Harold Glasser, October 21, 1946, RG 226, Records of the Office of Strategic Services, Entry 1183, Box 29, NARA.
369. Alperin et al., v. The Vatican Bank, et al., No. C99-4941 MMC, filed November 1999, United States District Court, Northern District of California in San Francisco.
370. Victor Homola, "Germany: Church Payouts," *New York Times*, November 8, 2000, p. A6.
371. "We Remember: A Reflection on the Shoah," *Commission for Religious Relations with the Jews*, The Vatican, March 17, 1998.
372. Testimony of Acting Superintendent of Banks, Elizabeth McCaul, Before the Executive Monitoring Committee, Offices of New York City Comptroller Alan Hevesi, New York City, March 26, 1998; Rickman, pp. 206-209.
373. William Drozdiak, "German Banks Make Redress," *Washington Post*, February 17, 1999, p. A11.
374. "Allianz Says It Will Acquire Dresdner Bank for $20 Billion," *New York Times*, April 2, 2001, p. C2; Matthew Miller, "German Equity Preview: Allianz, Dresdner Bank, Siemens, Thysssen," Bloomberg News, April 6, 2000.
375. Stephen Cohen, "O.C. Business Plus: Firm's Interest in Pimco Scrutinized; Insurers: Quackenbush Seeks to Force Allianz AG to Increase Cooperation with Holocaust Investigation," *Los Angeles Times*, October 14, 1999.
376. Interview with Eizenstat; Michael Pinto-Duschinsky, "Can the Beetle Live Down its Terrible Past?" *The Times*, August 25, 1997.
377. Andrews, "Volkswagen, in Shift, Will Set Up Fund for Slave Workers."
378. "Daimler Benz and Chrysler in Talks," Canada Newswire, May 6, 1998; Form Letter of Robert J. Eaton and Jürgen E. Schrempp to Gregg Rickman, November 17, 1998.
379. Statement of Senator Alfonse M. D'Amato, Read by Gregg Rickman, Legislative Director, Senator D'Amato, Before New York City Comptroller Alan G. Hevesi and The Executive Monitoring Committee, March 26, 1998, p. 1.
380. "Swiss shame, and solace," *The Economist*, December 18, 1999, p. 17.

381. "Swiss OK Program To Improve Image," *Associated Press*, December 8, 1999.
382. E. Richard Mills, *Image Crisis Management,* an unpublished Masters Thesis, American University, 1999, pp. 54-55.
383. "Swiss Catholics admit failings during Nazi era," *Ha'aretz English Edition*, March 10, 2000.
384. "Swiss Back Reversal of War Convictions," *Washington Post*, December 10, 2002, p. A25.
385. "Poland, Facing Its Past, Apologizes for WWII Pogrom," *New York Times*, July 10, 2001.
386. "Doctors group sorry for Nazi-era deeds," *News and Observer*, Raleigh, North Carolina, October 4, 1998.
387. Roger Boyes, "Publisher admits Nazi past," *London Times*, January 25, 2000.
388. Ibid, p. 6.
389. Stephen P. Garvey, "Can shaming punishment educate?" *University of Chicago Law Review*, (Vol. 65, No. 3), Summer 1998.
390. Sarah Schafer, "Settling Lawsuits With a Gesture," *Washington Post*, February 11, 2001, p. H1.
391. Teddy Preuss, "Financial debts can be settled, but what about moral obligations?" *Ha'aretz*, 24 August 1998.
392. Joan Gralla, "Lawyers fees in Swiss bank case roil Jewish groups," *Reuters*, 17 November 1999.
393. Gabriel Kahn, "Federal Judge Could Represent Bellwether on Swiss Restitution," *The Forward*, 3 January 1997, p. 3.
394. Memorandum from Melvyn I. Weiss to the Swiss Banks Executive Committee, "Re: Swift-Fagan Press Conference," 15 July 1998.
395. Garvey, "Can shaming punishment educate?"

”

5

Unintended Consequences—The Holocaust Industry

"Great success often prompts a corresponding envy in others, and our occasional humbling is a rich and guilty pleasure often indulged in by friends and foes alike."[1]

"I've spoken to many who only loathe you and your crowd at the WJC," wrote Norman J. Finkelstein to this author.[2] Finkelstein, had gained a reputation attempting to refute widely accepted conceptions of the Arab-Israeli conflict. He took aim at the settlements, Bronfman, the tactics used by Bronfman's allies, and just about everything else associated with the entire effort in a controversial 2000 book, *The Holocaust Industry, Reflections on the Explanation of Jewish Suffering.*

Finkelstein, however, was not the first to take exception to Bronfman's methods regarding restitution or his overwhelming success. Years before Finkelstein's exposition on the ostensible deviance of Bronfman's effort, journalists and columnists were calling into question the tactics and motives of the Holocaust's presentation in general. Finkelstein was simply the shrillest of them.

"A little less unique, a little less guilty"

In 1997, soon after the Swiss agreed to establish the Interim Fund, Michael Hirsh wrote in *Newsweek*, on the possible reactions to Bronfman's efforts.

> As a moral issue, the case seems to clear-cut. On one side, the Nazis and their accomplices, the Swiss banks; on the other, Holocaust survivors whose money and property were stolen by the Germans and laundered through Switzerland, or whose bank accounts the Swiss may have plundered.[3]

Referring to the Fund's creation, however, Hirsh continued:

> At long last, a measure of justice, right? Don't count on it. A moral reckoning for the evils done in the 1940s may be no match for U.S. tort law in the 1990s. *Newsweek* has

learned that a feud has erupted between lawyers for the survivors—a fight over who gets the cash and how—that could tie up the fund for years to come.[4]

Lars- Erik Nelson, a syndicated columnist expanded on these fears suggesting, "If the result of this new furor over Switzerland":

is a fund to make life easier for the declining years of Holocaust victims, well and good. But the price may be high: A dilution of the reality of the Holocaust. If everyone was more or less complicit, the German Nazis and their henchmen become a little less unique, a little less guilty.[5]

There were others, too, less strident, less condemnatory, perhaps even cleverer and less blunt than Finkelstein, who expressed real misgivings about how the Holocaust was being used, and some argued, abused. Peter Novick, one of Finkelstein's critical and less shrill literary forerunners wrote of the effect of the Holocaust on American life, edging toward a subtle suggestion of ulterior motives. He described the Holocaust as:

a symbol well designed to confront increasing communal anxiety about 'Jewish continuity' in the face of declining religiosity, together with increasing assimilation and a sharp rise in intermarriage, all of which threatened demographic catastrophe.[6]

Tim Cole, a precursor to Finkelstein's progenitors, went further suggesting that the American fascination with the Holocaust had deeper implications, suggesting that " ... the contemporary fascination with the 'Holocaust' may in reality be less about a concern with the Holocaust than about other, more internal matters."[7]

Interestingly, enough, the later dissent from the process was most strongly voiced from Jews themselves. For Yossi Klein Halevi, the issue was less of the players, but more of the identity of the Holocaust as history, as an experience, and of survivors themselves. Klein believed that remembrance of the Holocaust should not be relegated to the subject of Jews pursuing money, reinforcing the very stereotypes used against them with such lethality by the Nazis.[8]

Former Israeli Ambassador to Switzerland Gabriel Padon, who was in the unenviable position of not only representing Israel in Switzerland, but in this role viewed by the Swiss as representative of all Jews, expressed the belief that the "Jewish negotiators and their American political supporters, should not be viewed as selfless knights righting a historic wrong." Their tactics, he believed, were aimed as much at the Swiss as at their own constituents.[9]

For the columnist Charles Krauthammer, the problems were many. His denunciation of the attorney's tactics cut deep and opened up the debate more broadly.

It is late, very late for this kind of restitution. The war ended fifty-three years ago. Instead, what is happening is that the lawyers and community bureaucrats will reap the

> power and the payoff that comes from collecting in the name of those whose names are forever lost. They risk causing, to borrow a phrase from Abe Foxman of the Anti-Defamation League, "an industry to be made on the memory of victims."[10]

For Krauthammer, the quest to reclaim assets devolved into stereotypes for all the parties concerned, bringing out the worst in the drama's players, instead of the best. He questioned whether the entire effort was worth dredging up anti-Jewish feeling in return "for blood money from the Holocaust ..."[11]

Indeed, it was Foxman who took exception to this new institution. Like Nelson before him, Foxman questioned the effect the pursuit of assets played on memory, on accountability, and on uniqueness.

> Certainly, individuals who had bank accounts, insurance policies or works of art that were stolen have a right to pursue their claims. But when these legitimate clams become the main focus of activity regarding the holocaust, rather than the unique horror of six million Jews, including 1.5 million children, being murdered simply because they were Jewish, then something has gone wrong. A new "industry" has sprung up, spearheaded by lawyers and institutions, in an effort to get what they call "justice" for Holocaust victims. As a Holocaust survivor, I question for whom they speak and how they define "justice." The focus must remain on discovering the truth, on revealing and owning up to the past.[12]

Foxman complained that the Swiss, against whom the campaign was so vigorously focused in the beginning, did not offer regrets or come to grips with the reality of their crimes. Yet, he argued, the distribution of the funds from the Swiss became a fight for control and prestige, souring the good that came of the battle with the Swiss. Like others, he complained about those claiming credit for the settlement, the lawyers, the politicians, or the Jewish organizations.[13]

While there were complaints, and loud ones, there were also defenders. Attorney Ronald Goldfarb countered, that it was not a sin for the "lawyers who did well by doing good ..."[14] Richard Cohen, the columnist, argued as well that while much of what Foxman and Krauthammer decried was correct, in fact it was wrong in interpretation. Yes, the stereotypes were perhaps brought all too much into the open, and, yes, the pursuit might have gotten out of hand. Yet, what are survivors to do when faced with this situation?

> Holocaust victims paid once for being Jewish. Now, in a way, they and their heirs are being asked to pay again—a virtual Jewish tax which obliges them not to act as others would in the same situation. But in avoiding one stereotype, they adopt a worse one—perpetual victim.[15]

Survivors found themselves caught between those that changed the rules for them, bringing them success, and the unintended consequences of that change. The success survivors now enjoy were the fruits of that change. No longer did they have to prove their losses. No longer did they have to chase after those holding their assets. Bronfman through all those that joined his effort, changed how Holocaust survivors were viewed, "deified" in the words of former Prime Minister Bobby Brown, Prime Minister Benjamin Netanyahu's advisor on the issue,[16] and, by connection, their right to restitution.

As Representative Henry Hyde wrote, "Great success often prompts a corresponding envy in others..." Bronfman had successfully changed the rules for restitution for survivors. But had he, as Goldfarb said of the attorneys, "done well," perhaps too well, "while doing good?"

The Perpetual Victim

The adoption of an identity as a survivor, by its very definition, necessitates a status as a victim. Failure in confronting the keepers of their assets, as they were trying to reclaim after the war, extended that status, that identity. It was not enough for them to have survived the Holocaust, having lost family and their assets, they were then devalued by their failure at retrieving them. Their identity as a victim was extended. They were the perpetual victim.

Hoping for success, survivors needed restitution for continuity and memory. Kristin Hass, in this vein, wrote of post-World War II memorialization in material terms versus post-World War I memorialization.

> ... this practical turn in the work of memorializing was an expression of genuine commitment to the material expectation of post-war nationalism in the US. The people who wanted memorials did not want to waste time and money on symbolic stone that did not advance the cause of the prosperity of the democratic nation for which they fought. Americans seemed to want to reap the benefits of this free world for which they felt they had sacrificed so much. So they built places for the experience of pleasure and places that symbolized somehow the future. They built football fields, playgrounds, highways, and called them war memorials. The whole country, in a sense, became a living memorial to the Second World War.[17]

In the same manner, reclaiming property and funds from their families, served as a living memorial not only to those families, but to their suffering and that of the victim. Indeed, as Elazar Barkan writing about the phenomenon of the rash of restitution explained, " ... victims hope to benefit from a new recognition of their suffering and to enjoy certain material gains."[18] Assets, then, served as something tangible to pass on to families and descendants. These few, many times token assets, were strong indelible links—and sometimes the only ones—to their families, their past, indeed the identity as a victim. As the decades passed beyond the end of the war, memorials were built to the victims as a whole. Individuals, however, had no such memorials. In so many instances, survivors had nothing more than memories of their loved ones. Restitution, while not the cure-all, provided a concrete remnant of their loved ones. Individual remnants, in the form of assets, were those individual memorials, but survivors were denied them.

Yet, Bronfman's efforts as well as the others', were also, and possibly unknowingly, designed to reverse that idea of perpetual victim. If Jews were weak for failing to reclaim their assets, reclaiming them, in this logic, could make them strong, no longer perpetual victims. If victims had to plead for their assets, they were weak. If they fought back and were successful, albeit with unorthodox tactics, they were strong. Cohen's argument, then, is true: in trying to avoid the stereotype of acting in pursuit of money, they need to let pass the opportunity to reclaim what is legally and rightfully theirs.

Indeed, others, if placed in the same situation as Jewish survivors were to actively seek that which was stolen from them, there would not have been such an outcry. Yet, when Jews, appear to fulfill the stereotype of seeking money, when in fact they seek restitution for what was legitimately theirs, there is an outcry. Is this a double standard? Are those making the argument that because of this Jews as a people must remain outside the mainstream and not do as others would and seek recompense?

By denying that Jewish survivors have the right to seek the return of their assets, this relegates them to their unique victim status—the very opposite of the status ostensibly so cherished by the very Jewish organizations that advocate daily for fair treatment for the Jewish people, and survivors as well, and, in part, feared backlash over the tactics used to achieve restitution. If Jews were to be denied a right of action in another realm, there would be an uproar. But when restitution is sought, Jews must remain unequal, and therefore unique, the logic proceeds.

If the pursuit of assets is seen as cheapening the meaning and memory of the Holocaust, then that pursuit erases that uniqueness and changes their identity from weak to strong. It is a purity that is seemingly being protected by suggesting that assets should not be sought for the mere equality of the effort. The lessons of the Holocaust—that Jews were separated out, denied opportunity, making them unequal, all as a precursor to their death, is seemingly forgotten. If survivors are denied or restricted in their ability to reclaim their assets, they remain separate. That the Nazis first took away those assets, seeking them with an utter lust through the passage of legions of laws and decrees—on the way toward devaluing the Jews a people—should be held as seminal to the Holocaust and part and parcel of Holocaust memory. If only that trying to get those assets back did not seem so inherently stereotypical, then it would not be so seemingly bad.

Moreover, as Cohen argued, there should be a complete understanding of the reasons behind the harsh treatment that attorneys, and one could add politicians and the Jewish groups as well, used against the various institutions that withheld the assets. In order to fight back, the effort could not be done softly. Hard-edged tactics had to be used. "Who, then," Cohen suggested:

> are better suited to taking on European insurance companies and banks which, smiling and always cordial, insisted on death certificates for the poor souls who went into the

> atmosphere as ash from the Nazi crematoriums? Who better to demand an accounting from companies whose management in the 1930s and 1940s did business as the Nazis wanted?[19]

In the simplest of terms then, the method used to regain assets had to be force—harsh words, threats, and accusations. In the 1950s diplomats offered niceties and pleasantries, and the result was niceties and pleasantries in return, accompanied by any number of excuses why the assets could not be returned. Yet, these tactics formed the heart of the complaints of those supporting the Holocaust Industry idea, and formed the unintended consequences of the rule.

The "Industry" as Denial

Indeed, these tactics did not sit well with everyone. In short, the assumption, on a personal level, of the practices used by those pursuing restitution, was not internalized by all. Although not the first, or the last, chief among those who failed to accept these new practices was Norman Finkelstein.

Finkelstein's leading argument explained that the Jewish organizations were not performing the task they claimed they were performing.

> The shakedown of Switzerland and Germany has been only a prelude to the grand finale: the shakedown of Eastern Europe. With the collapse of the Soviet bloc, alluring prospects opened up in the former heartland of European Jewry. Cloaking itself in the sanctimonious mantle of "needy Holocaust victims," the Holocaust industry has sought to extort billions of dollars from these already impoverished countries. Pursuing this end with reckless and ruthless abandon, it has become the main fomenter of anti-Semitism in Europe.[20]

Finkelstein continued:

> A vast, well-heeled bureaucracy has sprung up. Insurance companies, banks, art museums, private industry, tenants and farmers in nearly every European country are under the Holocaust industry gun.[21]

Finkelstein took the effort to reclaim assets as one of greed. He believed that that greed served to legitimize Israel and its actions, "conferring total license on Israel."[22] Furthermore, he argued that since his mother, a survivor, did not receive in all her years what "Kagan rings up in twelve days, Eagleburger in four days, and D'Amato in ten hours,"[23] an injustice occurred.

In this vein, what seems to have rankled Finkelstein, and perhaps other critics, is what Representative Hyde suggested, namely "the pathology of success." First, he acknowledged the success of Bronfman's rules by suggesting that an "industry," or more correctly an "institution," had, in fact, been created. Had it not been for the success of these efforts, the practices used would not have evolved into the institution he so reviled.

Second, that Bronfman's successful establishment of just such an institution was achieved, is a symbol of an end to survivors' status as perpetual victims which he seemed to resent. "[I]t is important to preserve," Finkelstein wrote, "—fight for—the integrity of the historical record."[24] Yet, for Finkelstein, the coherence of that record was being corrupted by its success and, therefore, changing the identity of survivors from victims to victors.

As victors, he believed, the survivors sought to profit from the successful fight. "Too many public and private resources have been invested in memorializing the Nazi genocide," he wrote. "Most of the output is worthless, a tribute not to Jewish suffering but to Jewish aggrandizement."[25] Curiously, though Finkelstein, having published this book, sought himself to publicize it and, by connection, to sell books—and dare say—profit just the same. Finkelstein even established a website to this effect, including as he wrote to me "some of the more provocative letters I've received."[26]

Moreover, Finkelstein explained his own victimhood and self-directed role as a leading, albeit protesting and competing source of authority on the issue, as a price to pay for his efforts at opposing the new restitution. "I'm being censured," he explained. "This is the Holocaust industry at work. Almost everyone I name is a beneficiary of the Holocaust industry. But I bet they feel like the ground beneath them is trembling."[27] In essence, then, he was attempting to establish his own prominence and coherence in order to contrast and compete with the new reality of restitution.

In the end, Finkelstein established a shrill and accusatorial dialogue with those he could engage to further his efforts at protest. He was viewed with disapproval by many, warmth by others. For the Holocaust scholar John K. Roth, "[h]is book is worrisome." The attention it is getting in Europe bears witness to that.[28] Roth further addressed Finkelstein's book in one of his own entitled *Holocaust Politics*. Roth wrote that Finkelstein's book "misstates and even falsifies history, fails to treat evidence fairly, refuses to recognize complexity, overgeneralizes, resorts to personal attacks, and displays other flaws that good teaching and sound inquiry about the Holocaust always guard against."[29]

In Europe his book was, on the whole, warmly received by Bronfman's critics there who saw a son of Jewish Holocaust survivors dissenting from the ostensibly monolithic view of Bronfman's "righteousness." "His words carried more weight," wrote Salomon Korn:

> with large segments of the non-Jewish public than did those of even the most renowned non-Jewish historians. In public opinion, this "Jewish bonus" continues to count for much more than the quality of the arguments. The previously unknown Finkelstein was in demand not as a political scientist, but as a prosecutor with Jewish credentials.[30]

The demand then, centered less on the public's interest in the issue then it did on the fact that Finkelstein, "as prosecutor," was lending further arguments to the cause European opponents of Bronfman's efforts espoused, "Holocaust denial." Critics labeled Finkelstein a "Holocaust denier," for not only his arguments, but the vehemence with which he presented them. While he denied this charge, it is not unimportant that this cause was enthusiastically embraced much earlier by him than others, deniers among them, and that they used identical terminology, echoed later by him and others after.

David Irving, who lost a libel trial in May 2000 to historian Deborah Lipstadt over charges on Holocaust denial and was then jailed in Austria for the same in February 2006, was quoted in a 1992 *Washington Post* article on his efforts to publish ostensible portions of Joseph Goebbels' diary, "one year from now the Holocaust will be discredited," he declared. For Irving, this would be the death knell for Israel, "because of the vested interests involved in the *Holocaust Industry*."[31]

A year before, Jerome Brentar, a Cleveland supporter of accused Nazi camp guard John Demjanjuk and Chairman of the Committee Against the Use of Soviet Evidence in U.S. Courts, wrote of his opposition to the efforts of the Justice Department's Nazi hunting bureau which, at the time, was active in trying to deport his friend Demjanjuk. Brentar wrote that "[i]n order to keep the multimillion-dollar *Holocaust 'big business' industry* flourishing, and due to the U.S. Department of Justice's Office of Special Investigation's inability to discover these so-called Nazi war criminals, its investigators have turned to the Soviet Union, to East European countries, and to Israel for assistance."[32] Internet websites have also popped up listing a variety of quotations enlisting opposition to the ostensible "industry."[33]

Historically, use of the term has not been restricted to opponents of Holocaust remembrance, but by supporters as well, with Abba Eban known to have bemoaned that "there's no business like Shoah business."[34] Paula Hyman, the author of "Dreyfus to Vichy," used the term in 1980 to point out the growing number of Holocaust centers in the United States.[35] Cole wrote of the subject forming a "tiny cottage industry before 1967," as Holocaust studies began to grow.[36]

With this in mind, it is obvious that the attempt to create a backlash to the new policies on restitution did, itself, have an unintended consequence, namely that the arguments lent themselves to use by deniers and minimizers of the Holocaust. Yet, it is not entirely supportable to say that all those proposing and supporting the notion of the Industry are, in fact, deniers themselves. While Finkelstein's lead argument is that the intent behind the Industry is different than Bronfman's, at no time does he deny the existence of the Holocaust. His argument, along with that of Foxman's, is that the "creation" of the industry serves, beyond arguments as to intent, to destroy the uniqueness of the phenomenon. The uniqueness, the pristineness of the Jews as weak Holocaust victims, is shattered when they ultimately deny their abusers and violators of the fruits of their victory by successfully reclaiming their assets. Without success in the restitution battles, victims remain victims and the effort to reclaim assets would have remained one more battle to be chalked up to the heritage of victimhood of the Jews. Success upset tradition, failure upheld it.

Although success came after a half-century of struggle, the victory achieved over the banks, insurance companies, art museums, property squatters, and the like defied predictions. It was the product of a great movement, with people all woven together in an effort to correct an historic wrong. That despite tactics which offended some and angered others, this movement, this coalition, was successful because, inherently, the agents within that coalition were pursuing the establishment of a new practice that, in part, corrected the iniquity of what was done to Holocaust victims, and that this new reality was accepted by the majority of people faced with it, for one reason or the other. Opposition to the attempt at restitution was simply a minority dissent that did not achieve the acceptance of a greater audience.

Unintended Consequences: Backlash

"Claims on property," wrote Avi Beker, "highlight the fact that Germany's horrible schemes could not have been realized without the enthusiastic collaboration or war criminals of other nationalities and greedy bystanders who took advantage of the distress of their Jewish neighbors." Beker continued, "Each nation created for itself a collective national memory, in which historical facts were mingled with myths, half-truths and self-denial."[37]

The pursuit of assets across Europe caused anguish and resentment. From the angry denials of the Swiss banks, to desperate questions as to how far back in history should the search go,[38] Europeans felt as if they were being ganged up upon.[39] Their reactions to these charges formed another unintended consequences.

When former German Chancellor Gerhard Schröder declared that the creation of the German Fund was to end "the campaign being led against German industry and our country" he was voicing a sense of exasperation. After the decades of restitution, with Germany being the one nation to truly acknowledge its historic responsibilities, Schröder's statement, while wrong, was a sign of how deep Germany's reaction truly was.

Schröder was not alone, as Irwin Cotler explained, there were numerous excuses Europeans assembled to explain away their behavior. Cotler listed nine excuses, and with some variation and alteration, these were all the common refrain: "We were victims not perpetrators"; "The crimes were committed by a foreign government, by the Nazis"; "We were not only 'victims,' 'but were the vanguard of the resistance, while protecting the Jews"; "We were victims, not only of the Nazis, but also the Communists"; "We were officially neutral"; "This is history, it's time to bury the past"; "We have already made restitution"; "The statute of limitations has already passed."[40] To these nine, I would add two more: "Restitution would bankrupt us, we can't pay"; and "Isn't it really ours to keep as war booty?"[41]

These claims on the part of Europeans epitomize the depth to which they went to avoid responsibility. Some have argued that everything would have been just perfect for the Europeans had they been allowed to get away with their misdeeds. As James Bowman had suggested, those accused would have been quite happier, and in their eyes more honorable, if only their " ... despicable behavior ... never got out."[42]

The backlash then, was mostly of resentment, avoidance, and arrogance, but sometimes, admittedly, basic necessity. As Barkan wrote, extending further Elan Steinberg's explanation for the new European willingness to address the issue:

> A comparative review of the policies of several of the new governments suggests that for all of them the justification for restitution may have been formulated to accommodate the rush to a market economy. Yet its specific implementation was shaped more by issues of each country's national identity than by market considerations.[43]

" ... the example of the WJRO case against Europe should be the same for the Palestinians ..."

"Yet despite its support for restitution of Jewish property in Europe," Issam Mufid Nashashibi, a Palestinian-American complained, "Israel refuses to return Palestinian property and insists that compensation for it must be paid on a government-to-government basis within an overall regional settlement."[44]

Such were the claims of Palestinians, upset that the WJRO, in Nashashibi's words, "an Israeli-endorsed" group, was successful in achieving restitution from Europe. Like Finkelstein, there was a resentment and assertions that:

> the WJRO case against Europe should be the same for the Palestinians towards Israel; even more so in view of the overwhelming support of the international community and the support of international law to the Palestinian cause.[45]

Seeing that Jewish survivors were successful created another backlash and, as such, like the construction of the Holocaust Industry idea, the Palestinian reaction was an unintended consequence of Bronfman's success. This success bred Palestinian calls for similar action for their own claims. "The Palestinians in the current context," wrote Naseer Aruri:

> have to look away from restitution from established governments and conventional means, and look toward building an international grassroots movement toward that

end. The structure of inequality is global, and thus reparations and restitution have emerged as central issues separating the affluent North from the poor South, with the United States leading the anti-reparations camp.[46]

With this in mind, as the negotiations in 2000 between Israel and the Palestinians picked up, there inevitably began talk about United Nations General Assembly Resolution 194 of 1948, calling for the return of Palestinian refugees to their homes in what became Israel. As such, the PLO began assembling files on Palestinian property they accuse Israel of taking in 1948 and after for use in final status negotiations.[47]

There was a hue and cry over the need to achieve the "right of return," and gathering property loss statistics was something the Palestinians hoped to use as leverage in the negotiations with Israel for compensation in case the full realization was not achieved. Interestingly though, despite the claims to the massive return of Palestinians, in a July 2003 poll of 4,500 Palestinians on the West Bank, Palestinian pollster Dr. Khalil Shikaki found that only 10 percent of those interviewed demanded permanent residence in Israel. That number dropped when asked if they would be required to adopt Israeli citizenship or if their homes were destroyed.[48]

Just as the Palestinian backlash formed another unintended consequence, this, in itself, formed yet another. Sephardi Jews, according to Lenny Ben-David, the former chargé d'affaires at the Israeli Embassy in Washington, DC from 1997-2000, began gathering information on lost assets in Arab communities only after hearing that the Palestinians were doing it as well.[49]

Itamar Levin, too, writing in 2001 on the seizure of Jewish properties by Arab countries following the establishment of the state of Israel, suggested "there is a good probability that the Palestinian authority [sic], as they resume within the framework of negotiations with Israel for a permanent settlement, will demand compensation for properties confiscated from Palestinian refugees."[50]

Yet, while it is argued that Jewish claims against Arab states in reaction to Arab claims of the same, the Jewish claims did have an earlier origin. From 1949-1950, and again in 1969, Jewish claims for property in Arab states were registered in Israel, but little else was done. In 1974, Israeli Knesset member Mordechai Ben-Porat sought to address the issue on a more comprehensive basis.[51] Despite this, again little else was heard of the effort. Following the settlement with the Swiss banks in 1998, the issue was revived.

"Now that you have won your case against the Swiss banks," wrote Heskel M. Haddad, President of the World Organization for Jews From Arab Countries, "we should tackle our demands for compensation from the Arab Countries especially the banks where our money has been frozen in Iraq, Syria, Egypt and all the Arab world. We deserve compensation from these countries too, not just the banks.[sic]"[52]

By the following year, the American Sephardi Federation had joined the fight and the WJC had agreed to help as well.[53] Yet, the pursuit of these assets would not be as easy, in as much as the entire question was wrapped up in the near intractable Arab-Israeli dispute. When the Palestinians and Israelis began negotiations at Camp David II under President Clinton, the issue of mutual compensation arose and then, finally, the Israeli government decided to address the issue.

While Camp David II collapsed and was followed by what has come to be called the Second Intifada, the Israeli government has not, however, let the issue drop. In the Prime Minister's Cabinet meeting on March 23, 2002, the Cabinet decided to expand the registration program formed in 1969, placing it in the Justice Ministry, under then Justice Minister Meir Sheetrit.[54] Sheetrit, would, along with the American Sephardi Federation, launch a new registration effort for claims and coordinate and accumulate them within his ministry.

The effort would, as with the case against European banks and other companies, be aided by lawsuits against first the Arab League, and later against the frozen assets of Saddam Hussein's regime, following its removal by American forces in spring 2003.[55] Billions of dollars are at stake and, tied up in the overall Middle East Peace Process, it is difficult to gauge the movement's success either politically or materially.

Unintended Consequences: The Breeding of Stereotypes

Jews and Money

Beyond the success of the pursuit of assets, the detractors of that success, and the counter claims, one unavoidable unintended consequence was that of the reinforcement of stereotypes. When the effort against the Swiss banks began, we knew all too well what the Swiss bankers and others would say about it. From Pasqal Delamuraz' remarks that the Jews were trying bring down the financial system of Switzerland to the charges of blackmail by Herbert Hansmeyer of Allianz,[56] the stereotype of the money-hungry Jew was a predictable counterclaim. "The struggle for justice, however," wrote Israel Singer, "was not about money, and those who chose to make it so, whether they were Jews or non-Jews, tried one more time to revise history and failed."[57]

In Switzerland, the idea of Jews pursuing money was rife among the population. "As in the past," wrote the authors of *Anti-Semitism in Switzerland*, the official report of the Swiss Federal Commission Against Racism:

> anti-Semitism serves to overcome a crisis situation at the expense of the Jewish minority. Holocaust victims become the offenders, transformed into "blackmailers" seeking money to which they are not entitled. In extreme cases they are demonized. Ultimately, taking up anti-Semitic stereotypes. Leads to a perception of oneself as the victim of Jewish intrigue.[58]

Indeed, Switzerland was rife with anti-Semitism. Editorial cartoons appeared with Jews, stereotypical hooked nose praying in front of a wall of gold ingots.[59] Letters and phone calls came into the offices of the Swiss Jewish community in Bern with threats[60] and letters to D'Amato suggesting Hitler " ... didn't do the gas chambers big enough to get rid of those parasites" [sic].[61]

In Switzerland then, as Stuart Eizenstat explained, "the Swiss felt a piling on with some of Bronfman's statements, D'Amato['s] ... with my report ... and their was great resentment which by the way remains today by every objective measurement."[62]

The Attorneys

In general, if there was anti-Semitism in the rest of Europe, it was certainly not as explicit there as it was in Switzerland following the overall campaign. In the various countries of Europe, each campaign took on a different angle of attack, while the tactics remained largely the same. In particular, the attorneys drew criticism. In Germany, Eizenstat suggested, "I would say that the German government did not feel that way," as to the question of feeling besieged, "but the German companies did. They felt that they had made a good faith gesture in creating the German Initiative and initially providing what they said would be about one-and-a half billion Deutschmarks and they felt that ... they were being unfairly pressured to do more," by the attorneys.[63]

The French, who had begun their wartime examination in 1995 "were angry at the class action lawyers and they did resent ... that [the attorneys] did not realize that the structures they had put into place ... were sufficient from their standpoint to handle the whole problem."[64]

In Austria, " ... the Austrians on the property case ... felt that their seven restitution laws after WWII had been adequate and had taken care of the problem—and they were not—and they were upset that they were being asked to go back to the well again" by the attorneys. In the end, in Eizenstat's estimation, "to varying degrees they were all upset about this and particularly about some of the tactics."[65]

In most respects, the backlash remained at these levels, with resentment restricted to the banking, insurance, and other business sectors. Yet, in the countries hardest hit, or more historically resentful, of their identity regarding the Holocaust, the pursuit of assets had the greatest, and perhaps harshest, lasting effects.

In Switzerland, in 1999, elections for the lower house of Parliament were shaken when the People's Party made a surprising showing in the October elections, capturing forty-four seats, making it the second largest party there. Analysts in Switzerland tied this outcome directly to the campaign against the banks.[66]

The attorneys in Europe were viewed derisively, and there was no difference in that description here in the United States. Survivors were indignant when they read of the fee fights between the attorneys. While they were happy that the attorneys had played a crucial role in the campaign, they resented the fact that they got paid first, and in some cases at all.[67] To this day, survivors believe that the initially slow pace of the settlement payouts was due to the attorneys and they believed that, once again, they were being taken advantage of by their supposed saviors.

The Jewish Groups

When the funds were initially stalled due to procedural disputes, there were immediate claims that the WJC was secretly arranging to keep the settlement money. Because the groups, including the WJRO sought funds from the Swiss settlement, survivors sued in court to block the move.[68] A Jewish leader declared privately that the WJC wanted to be the "judge, jury, and banker."[69] There was discord among the groups and the idea of the Holocaust Industry was emboldened.

When I attended a Holocaust assets restitution conference in Chicago in 1999, I heard numerous complaints over the composition of the leadership of the Jewish groups deciding on the distribution of the settlement funds. "Those Easterners," I heard Chicago area survivors complain, were making all the decisions. These survivors were not alone.

"What disturbs me," wrote a survivor Gabor Hirsh on the H-NET List for the History of the Holocaust:

> is that our Jewish leadership (Bronfman, I. Singer, E. Steinberg, A. Hevesi, Hungarian born or originated) are able the [sic] exercise every pressure for the restitution of the victims but are unable to raise any money to publish and keep the memories of the victims by publishing their names world-wide.[70]

Survivors were beginning to feel that the attorneys and the organizations were taking the funds which were rightfully theirs, and many in the journalistic community wasted no time in exploiting this notion for publication.[71] In the beginning this thought prevailed, largely because the groups, to whom were left the fruits of their own victory, had not been sufficiently ready for the massive task of identifying to whom the benefits should go, much less how much the survivors should receive.

Jewish federations across the country began discussions as to how the money should be split up. Funding formulas were addressed, sometimes heatedly, and the long-held views of the Claims Conference were being challenged. The Conference had an established figure of an 80 percent disbursement of funds for social services with the remaining 20 percent going to Holocaust education and memorialization.[72] Battles raged on.

Many survivors believed that beyond the actual claimants, the funds should go strictly the needy among the survivors. Survivors in a number of states claim precedence over those in other countries, claiming oversight by the distributing organizations and frustration over lack of heating and healthcare.[73] One person advocating such domestic provision of aid is a Jewish leader Menachem Rosensaft, who calls these aid categories as well as more for housing.[74] "[H]ow is it possible," wrote Jewish leaders:

> —given the dire need—that restitution funds are being used for anything but meeting the basic welfare needs of survivors: Can we really afford to use precious, one-time settlement funds to support educational, archival and memorial projects when survivors are lying sick without proper care, and dying alone?[75]

> A survivor in New York agreed, complaing, "it's stolen property that belonged to our murdered parents and brothers and sisters and not charity to be doled out."[76]

Others did not agree, explaining that they felt that some degree should go toward Holocaust memorialization and education. "The Nazis, it must be remembered," wrote Kalman Sultanik, "sought not only to annihilate the entire Jewish people physically, but also to eradicate Jewish history and Jewish culture."[77] This fight surfaced to an even larger extent with the suggestion of the creation of a "Fund for the Jewish People" in April 1998.

This suggestion, considered an informal proposal, was essentially a trial balloon and was simply talked about among Jewish leaders until the idea gained the support of then Deputy Foreign Minister Rabbi Michael Melchior in early 2000. In August 2000, then Israeli Prime Minister Ehud Barak lent further support to the idea in a letter to Edgar Bronfman. "This fund," Barak wrote:

> will be the platform for formulating a comprehensive plan to meet the serious challenges facing our people worldwide. We have a mutual interest to take advantage of the restitution funds and meet the educational opportunities that have been neglected for too long.[78]

About the Fund, Singer went quite a bit further, establishing the need for Jewish organizational leadership and control of the funds:

> Holocaust survivors are not the only persons charged with making decisions for the Jewish people about how to use monies that will not be needed after they die. While our first obligation is to take care of Holocaust survivors, the remainder of any monies should be spent to ensure the existence of the Jewish people—not necessarily the existence of Jewish organizations. These decisions, which are about the future rather than the past, affect the entire Jewish people. The entire Jewish people are the heirs of survivors...Survivors have tremendous institutional memory—without which the Jewish people couldn't understand their own existence in this time. However, survivors should not decide all questions about funds restored to the Jewish people from the Holocaust.[79]

Singer's forthright defense of the idea of a Fund, caused a great deal of discussion and its directness, moreover, showed that he and the Fund's other advocates were serious in their intention to pursue this idea. Yet, the idea was roundly criticized by other Jewish groups and survivors alike who viewed Singer's defense of the community's prerogative to retain overall control of the restitution funds as only one more suggestion that their money was not going to them. Some however, supported the idea, as long as the WJC did not end up with all the money.[80] In this regard, Professor Gil Kahn, of Kean University in New Jersey, suggested the creation of a fund, clearly prioritizing the recipients and directing the overall control of the money to non-Claims Conference groups and control.[81]

Inherently, the Fund had been thought about for a while. The amount of money that had been won by all these efforts almost necessitated this idea. Israel Singer had told me in New York in 1997, that the community, in the end, would not be able to absorb the amount of money he envisioned would eventually come. Owing to the ensuing settlements, he was probably right. Patterns of distribution, requirements of proof unfulfilled, and settlement numbers that were more arbitrary estimates than actual tallies of the losses, contributed to this belief. While so many unfulfilled claims remain, it seems entirely realistic that money won from those that denied it to the survivors will outlast them, as Singer wrote.

When I met him again in Jerusalem in April 2003, he seemed to confirm that there would be a large amount of money that would remain. At the time, Singer was about to assume the leadership of the Claims Conference. It was with this in mind, that he told me he "wanted to make sure the money went to the right places." These were vital decisions, and the "right places" would be important as the distribution of billions in restitution funds were a direct consequence of all of these efforts, while the unintended consequence of this victory was its size.

While larger than expected and more than they could handle, the settlements, nevertheless, accounted for a measure of justice. While Finkelstein and others could complain that because more money was realized than could be utilized, this was a sign of evil intentions, this claim is not supportable. Because of the scale of the Nazis' and their allies' robbery of the Jews, the case could be made that no amount could erase the damages done to so many. While there might not have been enough survivors remaining to claim the various settlement funds, there is no question that the amount received thus far still does not equal the amount taken, and is therefore justified.

The companies who did their part in relinquishing these funds to the Jewish groups and attorneys that fought them have been relieved of the effort that had been such a curse upon their business. Those seeking restitution now had, or would have, the money they so eagerly sought, but they had to find a place to which it could be dedicated. As time goes by and more and more survivors pass on, the money remains, and the purpose to which it is put is the new mission of the group that worked so hard to obtain it. The money, while back with the Jewish people, is now their burden.

The Purposes of Holocaust Remembrance

As important as the drive for restitution has been, and how hard it has been fought, the question over its place in the overall realm of Holocaust education should be considered. For those who advocate spending part of the funds won from companies and governments alike, the fear is that with the passing of the generation of survivors of the Holocaust, so will the memory as well. With the memory, they fear, will go the relevance of this most egregious act of violence upon the Jewish people. If today, survivors, in Bobby Brown's words, are deified, will they remain so with the passage of time? Will their experiences live on as a lesson for mankind?

Education and research arguably are what in part achieved the results to date. Research and the attendant time and cost cannot be dismissed. "There has to be education," declared Hannah Lessing, Secretary General of the National Fund of the Republic of Austria, "because we are the next generation and without education, there is no memory."[82] Lessing is correct, but there must be a balance struck. Funding must be put first and foremost into the care for elderly Holocaust survivors. Most are not well off, most need urgent medical care and funds on which to live. Only when the needs of survivors are met, should education and memorialization be considered, not for the perpetuation of victimhood, but for policy implementation and the protection of future minorities facing the same threat.

"Don't Use Bayer Aspirin!"

When I was young, I remember my mother always lecturing me not to buy Bayer aspirin or drive German cars. I never understood why the proscription against all things German. She never really responded further than explaining that these were German companies, and "you know what the Germans did in World War II." After participating in the effort to exact restitution from the Swiss banks and others, I now understand. For my mother, like countless other Jewish mothers, the same admonitions stood, as if perpetual. The blame lay eternally with Germany.

By passing down from generation to generation the need to avoid German products, the memory of what the Germans did is passed on as well, as is the memory of victimization. If we do not buy Bayer aspirin, we do not subsidize a company that gassed Jews. If we do not buy German-made cars, then we do not subsidize a company that used slave labor to build German war equipment used to kill Jews. Whether right or wrong, we are spreading the guilt of the Holocaust, not to other countries as the period of the 1990s did with the notion of Holocaust accountability, but to further generations—of Germans. Because these Germans, all present-day Germans, are somehow still Nazis, this logic dictates, we must not let them forget what their fathers and grandfathers did.

On the face of it, this appellation of eternal guilt originates not with the Jews, but with the Germans, for it was Hans Frank, the Nazi functionary who declared at Nuremburg in April 1946, " … A thousand years will pass and this guilt of Germany will still not be erased."[83] Yet, the argument could be made that the perpetuation of German guilt continues Jewish victimhood. To this, Elie Wiesel, wrote:

> Am I wrong to believe that to humiliate a German today just for having been born German and to boycott an evening for him is not what Jewish ethos is about? I would like to remind some of my fellow Jews that Hitler's Germany condemned all of us not for what we did or did not do, but solely for having been born Jewish.[84]

Wiesel, a Nobel Prize laureate, and one of the most renowned survivor/author/activists, despite his fair mindedness on the issue, is ridiculed and castigated by Finkelstein no less, for his role in perpetuating the Holocaust for personal gain. Cole even declared that "the Holocaust is a corporation headed by Elie Wiesel."[85]

Yet, Wiesel's argument is central to this issue. Germany, despite its clearest and deepest understanding of all those accused of war crimes, was, and still is, unable to wash itself of its sin. That sin has now been transferred to the next generation. Germans cringe at association with the Nazis, as shown by the national reaction to Italian Prime Minister Berlusconi's comparison of a German Minister to a concentration camp guard in July 2003. Now, through the concept of Holocaust accountability, the guilt of the Holocaust is extended, not merely from country to country, but from industry to industry.

Collective and endless guilt then is tied inextricably to identity with endless victimization. By personifying the guilt of the Germans and others, the perpetuation of the Holocaust is, in itself, kept. But to seek and accept restitution is to advance responsibility for the Holocaust, and is not an evil attempt to perpetuate victimhood, but an attempt to grant the victims equality with other victims seeking redress. Assets held by those complicit in the Holocaust, as well as the Nazis' enablers and opportunistic bystanders, should, therefore, consider themselves equally indebted and responsible to their accusers. It is possible for victims to forgive, thus avoiding eternal guilt, but they need not be held responsible for forgetting.

Is Property Restitution Worthy of Inclusion in Holocaust Studies?

Through the study of the Holocaust one sees many things and constructs his or her own individual interpretation. In this vein, "[t]hus does 'history proper'," wrote the historian Jacques Barzun, "intertwine with our speech, our beliefs, our passions, and our institutions."[86]

The robbery of the Jews, as a precursor to their murder, served as the primordial act of the disenfranchisement and dehumanization of the Jews. As the Holocaust historian Michael Berenbaum wrote, "[t]he Germans and their allies and collaborators sought to murder Jews, to eradicate all memory of their crime and to profit from the proceeds."[87] Moreover, as Elie Wiesel declared at a Senate Banking Committee hearing in New York in 1996, "Now we know that they didn't simply want to kill Jews, as horrible as this may sound; they wanted Jewish money. It came down to money."[88] Finally, as James Carroll wrote, "[T]hat the bank deposits and artworks of murdered Jews exist only in locked Swiss vaults and on unprovenanced museum walls and not also in a starkly untied rope of history ... suggests why accomplishing a true moral reckoning with the Shoah has proven so difficult ..."[89] The subject of the robbery and restitution of Holocaust-era assets then, is clearly a part of the record and a necessary to the study of the Holocaust in general. It is, therefore, an unavoidable part of the story of the Holocaust.

How the robbery was realized through the imposition of new rules, practices, and entire institutions, all directed toward the annihilation of the Jews, can serve as a model for others to both follow and likewise to predict the awful repetition through the observation thereof. In short, through the edification of the robbery of Holocaust as a memory of terrible inequity and a precursor to the violence, lessons can be learned to ensure, as the post-Holocaust motto suggests, "Never Again."

Because the disclosure of this new history shocked and exposed both the unknowing and unwilling accusations of theft by seeming bystanders, it was hard for many to believe, especially those accused. It was new and different view of what conventionally came to be an all too understood view of the Holocaust. For nearly all, it was Hitler, or his eager henchmen, who perpetrated this awful crime.

As I began this study, I explained that it was more important to understand not why, but *how* the Holocaust was perpetrated. With the robbery of the Jews coming first, that understanding is deepened. That people did not like how we have arrived at that understanding is a different matter. The pursuit of Holocaust-era assets took more than a half-century to evolve as an idea realized, and as a notion achieved. Its success drew criticism only because that success was achieved in a way different from the past. People did not expect the rule of operation for survivors to change. Once a victim, always a victim, it was thought. That Holocaust victims and their supporters—Bronfman and his coalition—actually changed the rule, shifting it against the victimizers, was new and strange. It made some angry, others nervous, but the effort was successful. For want of a better excuse, as the saying goes, "we had to break a few eggs to make the omelet." It was that breaking effort that bothered people. Myths were shattered, new identities were established, and cherished notions of an idyllic past were lost.

When new light is shed on history, people react with denial, with shame, with disbelief. When highly derogatory, and even thoughtless, anti-Semitic diary passages of President Harry S. Truman surfaced a few years ago in which he severely castigated Henry Morgenthau, Jr. for pleading with him to provide help for a Jewish ship on its way to Palestine, presumably the *Exodus*, and then proceeded to bitterly complain about Jewish behavior and practice, there was shock and dismay.[90] How could such statements have been written by such a staunch friend of the Jews, supporters exclaimed? Yet, it was true. These passages were authenticated and released by Truman's Presidential Library. The diary attests to highly unsavory views held by an otherwise previously held sanctified friend of the Jews.

Yet, thus is the makeup of history. It is based upon the previously unknown, the revealed. The constructs of our times and our political needs at any given time make it new and ever changing. It was the disbelief and denial of the methods used to uncover that history that made for the unintended consequences that made this story's end so uncomfortable.

In the end, the words of Emil Fackenheim, again comes to mind. "Yet the better the Holocaust historian succeeds in explaining the event," Fackenheim wrote, "the closer he comes to suspecting the inevitability of ultimate failure."[91] It does, therefore, not suffice then, to attempt to explain the Holocaust, but to understand it—to understand and accept the nuances, the new ideas, the new views.

Those advocating the idea of the "Holocaust Industry," are, in essence then, trying to understand the unanswerable—the "why" of the Holocaust, not the "*how*." The inclusion of the study of the robbery of the Jews in the Holocaust, and the effort to correct that robbery, answer the question of *how* by explaining the rules, practice, and institutions the Nazis created to exact that robbery.

If we better understand *how* the Holocaust happened at that time, we can better understand, and hopefully predict, the telltale signs of when it might happen again. Those harboring evil ideas have a model by which to pattern their intentions. We, too, can see how that model was used once before. It is our job to spot the reemergence of that model and prevent its reapplication.

Yet, we should not fool ourselves. As Barkan wrote, "[a]greements are reached voluntarily, if under pressure, and as part of a democratic process."[92] Not everyone is able to obtain restitution as a salve for past, albeit egregious, wrongs. Survivors and family from the 1921 Tulsa riots still seek reparations. African-Americans seek the same for centuries of slavery. Victims of Soviet genocidal acts, aboriginal and native descendants from Hawaii to America, Canada, Australia, and other lands have all sought reparations for their or their families' suffering. While a subject of further study, the success of Holocaust survivors has been singularly unique among groups seeking such relief. This success has not escaped others seeking an equal chance for recompense.

At the hands of the Nazis, Jews were the object of scorn not envy, and success was purposely denied them. Through the formation of a coalition designed to reverse that condition, as it became enshrined in the collective memory and unifying identity of the Jewish community, is a testament to will power, as much as dedication to the pursuit of justice. As Horace Walpole wrote, "Justice is rather the activity of truth, than a virtue in itself. Truth tells us what is due to others, and justice renders that due ..."[93]

Notes

1. Representative Henry J. Hyde, "Pathology of Success," Opening Remarks before a Hearing of the House International Relations Committee Hearing, February 11, 2003.
2. Email posting of Norman J. Finkelstein to Gregg Rickman on H-NET List for History of the Holocaust, August 17, 2000.
3. Michael Hirsh, "The Holocaust in the Dock, It once seemed so clear: Hitler's victims vs. greedy Swiss bankers. Then the lawyers got into the act," *Newsweek*, February 17, 1997.
4. Ibid.
5. Lars Erik-Nelson, "Swiss Gold Hunt Devalues Horror of Nazi Crimes," *New York Daily News*, May 12, 1997, p. 27.
6. Peter Novick, *The Holocaust in American Life* (Boston: Houghton Mifflin & Co., 1999, p. 7.
7. Tim Cole, *Selling the Holocaust: From Auschwitz to Schindler, How History is Bought Packaged and Sold,* (New York: Routledge, *1999)*, p. 15.
8. Yossi Klein Halevi, "Reducing the Holocaust to a Search for Assets," *Jerusalem Report*, March 6, 1997, p. 28.
9. "When the Yodel Turned Shrill," Interview with Dr. Gabriel Padon, *Jerusalem Post International Edition*, August 22, 1998, p. 9.
10. Charles Krauthammer, "The Holocaust Scandal," *Washington Post*, December 4, 1998, p. A29.
11. Ibid.
12. Abraham H. Foxman, "The Dangers of Holocaust Restitution," *Wall Street Journal Europe*, December 7, 1998.
13. Foxman; Hanan Sher, "Opening Salvos, Squabbling has now begun over the $1.25 billion Swiss Holocaust asset settlement," *The Jerusalem Post*, October 12, 1998.
14. Ronald Goldfarb, "Holocaust Lawyers," *The Washington Post*, December 8, 1998, p. A21.
15. Richard Cohen, "The Money Matters," *The Washington Post*, December 8, 1998, p. A21.
16. Interview with Bobby Brown, Jerusalem, April 10, 2002.
17. Kristin Hass, "Objects of Memory: Producing, Protecting a Shared Past," Research Libraries Group 1999 Annual Membership Meeting, p. 5, available online at .
18. Elazar Barkan, *The Guilt of Nations* (New York: Norton, 2000), p.321.
19. Cohen.
20. Norman Finkelstein, *The Holocaust Industry* (London: Vorso, 2000), p. 130.
21. Ibid, pp. 137-138.

22. Ibid, p. 50.
23. Ibid, p. 88.
24. Ibid, p. 8.
25. Ibid.
26. Email letter from Norman Finkelstein to Gregg Rickman, August 20, 2000.
27. Victor Frölke, "Shoah Business," Salon.com.
28. Email letter from John K. Roth to Gregg Rickman, August 17, 2000.
29. John K. Roth, *Holocaust Politics* (Louisville, Kentucky: Westminster John Knox Press, 2001), p. 277.
30. Salomon Korn, "Attacking the 'Holocaust Industry,' *Frankfurter Allegemeine Zeitung, English Edition*, August 23, 2000, available online at .
31. Glenn Frankel, "The Furor Over Goebbels's [sic] Diaries; Sunday Times Blasted for Deal With Neo-Nazi," *Washington Post*, July 11, 1992, p. C1; italics in the quotation are mine.
32. Letter of Jerome Brentar to *Washington Times*, September 23, 1991, p. E2; italics in the quotation are the author's.
33. One such site is a French-language site, "Quelques dénonciations du shoah-business," [Some denunciations of the Shoah Business], translated by Colleen Sanchez, available online at http://www.abbc.com/aaargh/fran/archFaur/1991-1994/RF930913.html; italics in the quotation are mine.
34. Michael Freedland, "Final Word on the Final Solution?" *London Times*, August 20, 1989.
35. Paula E. Hyman, "New Debate on the Holocaust," *New York Times*, September 14, 1980.
36. Cole, p. 11.
37. Avi Becker, Institute of the World Jewish Congress Policy Studies, Policy Study #9, *Unmasking National Myths, Europeans Challenge Their History,* p. 4.
38. Swiss envoy Thomas Borer reacted to a press question to this effect at the London Conference on Nazi Gold in December 1997, "how far back does one go in history—back to the American Indians," an obvious point to suggest that each nation had its historical vulnerabilities.
39. Despite the belief to the contrary of Stuart Eizenstat during the time of his negotiations.
40. Irwin Cotler, "The Holocaust, 'Thefticide' and Restitution: a Legal Perspective," in Avi Beker, editor, *The Plunder of Jewish Property during the Holocaust, Confronting European History*, Palgrave, 2001, pp. 66-71.
41. The first claim, regarding bankruptcy refers to Poland, where Andrzej Olechowski, a former Finance Minister and Foreign Affairs Minister claimed "Leaving reprivatization to the courts threatens to cause a catastrophe of state finances, not to speak of impairing Poland's image int eh international arena." See Aleksander Pinski and Jan Pinski, "The Bill for Kwasniewski," Warsaw Wprost in Polish, June 8, 2003, translated by FBIS, The Foreign Broadcast Information Service. The second claim comes from Christoph Bubb, a former Minister in the Swiss Embassy in Washington who made the statement to author Tom Bower.
42. Ibid, p. 6.
43. Barkan, p.114.
44. Issam Mufid Nashashibi, "Restitution of Palestinian Property," Information Brief No. 5, Palestine Center, available online .
45. Salman Abu-Sitta, "Restitution and Compensation," Compensations as Part of a Comprehensive Solution to the Palestinian Refugee Problem Workshop Papers, available online at .

46. Naseer Aruri, "Will Israel ever Atone? Will the Palestinians gain Restitution?" Trans-Arab Research Institute, available online at .
47. Isabel Kershner, "The Refugee Price Tag," *Jerusalem Report*, July 17, 2000.
48. James Bennet, "Palestinian Mob Attacks Pollster Over Finding on 'Right of Return," *New York Times*, July 14, 2003.
49. Interview with Lenny Ben-David, Washington, DC, October 9, 2002.
50. Itamar Levin, *Locked Doors, The Seizure of Jewish Property in Arab Countries*, translated by Rachel Neiman, (Westport, Connecticut: Praeger Publishers, 2001), p. xv.
51. Ibid, pp. 211-215.
52. Letter of Heskel M. Haddad to Senator Alfonse D'Amato, September 1, 1998.
53. Ira Stoll, "Billions of Dollars in Lost Property Sought by Sephardim," *The Forward*, May 21, 1999; Joan Gralla, "Jewish group aims at Arabs as new restitution target," *Reuters*, June 21, 1999.
54. Cabinet Communique, Israeli Government, March 3, 2002.
55. Rachel Pomerance, "Sephardi Jews to sue Arab League to counter Palestinian refugee claims," *JTA*, June 18, 2002; Ran Dagoni and Itamar Levin, "Iraqi Jews mulling compensation lawsuits against Iraq," *Globes*, July 2, 2003.
56. Cited by Stuart Eizenstat, Eizenstat Interview.
57. Israel Singer, "Transparency, Truth and Restitution," Shma.com, June 2002, available online at
58. Georg Kreis, Boél Samboc, and Doris Angst Yilmaz, *Anti-Semitism in Switzerland*, a report of the Federal Commission Against Racism, Switzerland, November 1998, p. 38.
59. Editorial cartoon, *Grand Quotidien Suisse*, January 8, 1997.
60. Discussion with Rolf Bloch, a leader of the Swiss Jewish Community, London, December 3, 1997.
61. Unidentified letter to Senator Alfonse M. D'Amato from Geneva, Switzerland, 1997.
62. Eizenstat interview.
63. Ibid.
64. Ibid.
65. Ibid.
66. Elizabeth Olson, "Swiss Voters, Tilting Right, Unsettle Traditions," *New York Times*, October 28, 1999, p. A14; and Alan Cowell, "Switzerland Is Odd Piece in the Continent's New Music, *New York Times*, December 4, 2003.
67. Steve Chambers, "Lawyers want millions as Cut of Holocaust settlement," *Cleveland Plain Dealer*, August 15, 2000, p. A8.
68. Marilyn Henry, "Survivors challenge WJRO's bid for special standing in Swiss bank settlement," *Jerusalem Post*, January 14, 1999, p. 5.
69. Comment of an unidentified Jewish leader, May 2002.
70. Email posting of Gabor Hirsh on the H-NET List for the History of the Holocaust, April 24, 2001.
71. Many in the press were very clearly pushing the story of where the funds were going and to the extent they were delayed in being distributed, their stories proliferated. Some examples were: Michael Hirsch, "What's Taking So Long?," *Newsweek*, April 13, 1998, p. 49; Marilyn Henry, "Survivors expected to have no say on Swiss funds," *New Jersey Metro West Jewish News*, February 27, 1997; and Marilyn Henry, "Half of Nazi victims aid funds not yet distributed," *The Jerusalem Post*, July 2, 2000.
72. See Stewart Ain, "Shoah Funding Split To Get Fresh Scrutiny," *New York Jewish Week*, March 7, 2003, p. 1; Eli Kintisch, "Policy Body: Shoah Funds All Must Go To Survivors," *The Forward*, March 3, 2003, p. A1. In a meeting on July 22, 2003, the

Claims Conference voted unanimously to keep the 80-20 funding split, despite widespread protests to the contrary. See Joe Gerkofsky, "After debate, Claims Conference votes to continue education funding," *JTA,* July 23, 2003.

73. Letter of Samuel Dubbin to Undersecretary of State Stuart Eizenstat, December 1, 1998; and Letter of Representative Ileana Ros-Lehtinen to Undersecretary of State Stuart Eizenstat, November 25, 1998.
74. See Brian Moss, "Seeking Fund for Survivors," *New York Daily News*, May 18, 1997, p. 38; Menachem Rosensaft, "For Aging Survivors, a Prescription for Disaster," *The Forward*, January 31, 2003, p. A11.
75. Letter to the Editor of Israel Aarbeiter, Yehuda Evron, Leo Rechter, David Mermelstein, Joseph Sachs, David Schaecter, Alex Moskovic, Leon Stabinsky, and Fred Taucher, Allocate All Restitution Monies to Survivors," *The Forward*, February 14, 2003, p. A8.
76. Joseph Berger, "After Pain beyond Price, Feeling Short-Changed: Holocaust Funds Should Go to Survivors, Not to Cultural Causes Many Say," *New York Times*, May 8, 2005, p. 25.
77. See Kalman Sultanik, "Carry the Legacy of Remembrance," *The Forward*, March 7, 2003, p.A8. Sultanik is the President of the Federation of Polish Jews in the United States, and a Vice President of the World Jewish Congress.
78. Letter of Prime Minister Ehud Barak to Edgar Bronfman, August 28, 2000.
79. Singer.
80. Discussion with unnamed Jewish leader, May 2002.
81. Gilbert N. Kahn, *A Proposal for the Restitution and Distribution of Newly Reclaimed European-Jewish Assets*, February 1999, pp. 16-19.
82. Interview with Lessing.
83. The Trial of German Major War Criminals, Sitting at Nuremberg, Germany, 16th July to 27th July 1946, One Hundred and Eighty-Seventh Day: Friday, 26th July, 1946, (Appendix Part 3 of 3) (Part 12, p. 109), available online at 19/ tgmwc19appendix03.shtml .
84. Elie Wiesel, "Only the Guilty Are Guilty, Not Their Sons," *New York Times*, May 5, 2001.
85. Cole, p. 4.
86. Jacques Barzun and Henry F. Graff, *The Modern Researcher*, Third Edition (San Diego: Harcourt Brace Jovanovich, Publishers, 1977), p. 9.
87. Michael Berenbaum, "Introduction: Questions of Values, Questions of Truth," the Introduction to Gilbert N. Kahn, *A Proposal for the Restitution and Distribution of Newly Reclaimed European-Jewish Assets*, February 1999, p. 2.
88. *Holocaust Victims Assets in Swiss Banks*, Senate Banking Committee New York City Field Hearing Transcript, October 16, 1996.
89. James Carroll, *Constantine's Sword, The Church and the Jews, A History*, Houghton Mifflin Company, 2001, p. 424.
90. President Harry S. Truman's 1947 Diary Book, transcribed by Raymond H. Geselbracht, Harry S. Truman Presidential Museum & Library, Entry for July 21, 1947.
91. Fackenheim, p. 230.
92. Barkan, p. 322.
93. Horace Walpole, Horace Walpole's Miscellany 1786-1795, p. 62, ed. Lars E. Troide, Yale University Press (1978), cited in *The Columbia World of Quotations*, 1996 available online at http://www.bartleby.com/66/86/63186.html.

Bibliography

Books

Aalders, Gerald, and Wiebes, Cees. *The Art of Cloaking Ownership: The Case of Sweden, The Secret Collaboration and Protection of the German War Industry by the Neutrals*. Amsterdam: Amsterdam University Press, 1996.

Acheson, Dean. *Present at the Creation, My Years in the State Department*. New York: W.W. Norton, 1969.

Arendt, Hannah. *Antisemitism*. San Diego, CA: Harcourt Brace Jovanovich, 1968.

_________ *Eichmann in Jerusalem, A Report on the Banality of Evil*. New York: Penguin Books, 1992.

Assicurazioni Generali, Source Materials on Communist Expropriations of Generali and Insurance Claims Paid to Holocaust Victims, Prepared for the National Association of Insurance Commissioners, January 15, 1998.

Authers, John and Wolffe, Richard. *The Victims Fortune, Inside the Epic Battle over The Debts of the Holocaust*. New York: HarperCollins, 2002.

Aycoberry, Pierre. *The Nazi Question, An Essay on The Interpretations of National Socialism, (1922-1975)*, Translated by Robert Hurley. New York: Pantheon Books, 1981.

Balabkins, Nicholas. *West German Reparations to Israel*. Rutger's Books, New Brunswick, New Jersey, 1971.

Bankier, David, ed. *Probing the Depths of German Antisemitism, German Society and the Persecution of the Jews, 1933-1941*. New York: Berghahn Books, 2000.

Barkan, Elazar. *The Guilt of Nations*. New York: W.W. Norton, 2000.

Barkai, Avraham. *From Boycott to Annihilation, The Economic Struggle of German Jews, 1933-1943*. translated by William Templer. Hanover, NH: Brandeis University Press, 1989.

Barnet, Richard J. *The Alliance, America, Europe, Japan, Makers of the Postwar World*. New York: Simon and Schuster, 1983.

Barraclough, Geoffrey. *The Origins of Modern Germany*. New York: Capricorn Books, 1963.

Bauman, Zygmunt. *Modernity and the Holocaust*. Ithaca, New York: Cornell University Press, 1991.

Bazyler, Michael J. *Holocaust Justice, The Battle for Restitution in America's Courts*. New York: New York University Press, 2003.

Beker, Avi. editor. *The Plunder of Jewish Property During the Holocaust, Confronting European History*. Houndmills, Hampshire, U.K.: Palgrave, 2001.

Beschloss, Michael. *The Conquerors, Roosevelt, Truman and the Destruction of Hitler's Germany, 1941-1945*. New York: Simon & Schuster, 2002.

Bird, Kai. *John J. McCloy. The Chairman, The Making of the Establishment*. New York: Simon & Schuster, 1992.

Black, Edwin. *IBM and the Holocaust, The Strategic Alliance Between Nazi Germany and America's Most Powerful Corporation*. New York: Crown Publishers, 2001.

Blum, John Morton. *The Morgenthau Diaries, Years of Crisis, 1928-1938*. Boston, MA: Houghton Mifflin Company, 1959.

__________The Morgenthau Diaries, Years of Urgency, 1938-1941, From the *Morgenthau Diaries*. Boston, MA: Houghton Mifflin Company, 1965.

__________*The Morgenthau Diaries, Years of War, 1941-1945, From the Morgenthau Diaries*. Boston, MA: Houghton Mifflin Company, 1967

Borkin, Joseph. *The Crime and Punishment of I.G. Farben*. New York: Pocket Books, 1978.

Bosmajian, Haig A. *The Language of Oppression*. Washington, DC: Public Affairs Press, 1974.

Bower, Tom. *Nazi Gold*. New York: HarperCollins, 1997.

__________ *The Paperclip Conspiracy, The Hunt for the Nazi Scientists*. Boston, MA: Little, Brown & Company, 1989.

Brook-Shepherd, Gordon. *The Austrians, A Thousand-Year Odyssey*. New York: Carroll & Graf Publishers, Inc., 1996.

Brooks, Roy L., ed. *When Sorry Isn't Enough, The Controversy over Apologies and Reparations for Human Injustices*. New York: New York University Press, 1999.

Bronfman, Edgar M. *The Making of a Jew*. New York: G. P. Putnam's Sons, 1996.

Brown, J.F. *Surge to Freedom, The End of Communist Rule in Eastern Europe*. Durham, NC: Duke University Press, 1991.

Browning, Christopher. *Nazi Policy, Jewish Workers, German Killers*. Cambridge, U.K.: Cambridge University, 2000.

___________ *Ordinary Men, Reserve Police Battalion 101 and the Final Solution in Poland*. New York: Harper Perrenial, 1998.

Bullock, Alan. *Hitler, A Study in Tyranny*. New York: Harper Row, 1964.

Burch, Kurt. *"Property" and the Making of the International System*. Boulder, CO: Lynne Reiner Publishers, 1998.

___________ "Toward a Constructivist Comparative Politics," in Daniel Green, editor, *Constructivism and Comparative Politics*. Armonk, New York: M.E. Sharpe, 2002.

Bush, George and Scowcroft, Brent. *A World Transformed*. New York: Alfred A. Knopf, 1998.

Carroll, James. *Constantine's Sword, The Church and the Jews, A History*. Boston, MA: Houghton Mifflin Company, 2001.

Childers, Thomas. *The Nazi Voter, The Social Foundations of Fascism in Germany, 1919-1933*. Chapel Hill, NC: University of North Carolina Press, 1983.

Clay, General Lucius D. *Decision in Germany*. New York: Doubleday & Company, Inc. 1950.

Clifford, Clark and Holbrooke, Richard. *Counsel to the President*. New York: Random House, 1991.

Cole, Tim. *Selling the Holocaust : From Auschwitz to Schindler, How History is Bought Packaged and Sold.* New York: Routledge, *1999.*

D'Amato, Alfonse M. *Power, Pasta, and Politics, The World According to Senator Al D'Amato*. New York: Hyperion, 1995.

Dawidowicz, Lucy. *The War Against the Jews, 1933-1945*. New York: Holt, Rinehart, Winston, 1975.

Eizenstat, Stuart E. *Imperfect Justice, Looted Assets, Slave Labor, and the Unfinished Business of World War II*. New York: Public Affairs, 2003.

Engelmann, Bernt. *In Hitler's Germany*. Translated by Krishna Winston, London, Meuthen Mandarin, 1986.

Epstein. Helen, *Children of the Holocaust, Conversations with Sons and Daughters of Survivors*. New York: Penguin Books, 1979.

Fackenheim, Emil. *To Mend The World, Foundations of Post-Holocaust Jewish Thought*. New York: Schocken Books, 1989.

Feingold, Henry L. *The Jewish People in America, A Time for Searching, Entering the Mainstream, 1920-1945*. Baltimore, MD: The Johns Hopkins University Press, 1992.

Feliciano, Hector. *The Lost Museum*. New York: Basic Books,1997.

Ferencz, Benjamin B. *Less Than Slaves, Jewish Forced Labor and the Quest for Compensation*. Cambridge, MA: Harvard University Press, 1979.

Fest, Joachim C. *Hitler*. Translated by Richard and Clara Winston. New York: Vintage Books, 1973.

__________ *The Face of the Third Reich, Portraits of the Nazi Leadership*. Translated by Michael·Bulluck. New York: Pantheon Books, 1970.

Fierke, Karin M. and Jørgensen, Knud Erik, eds. *Constructing International Relations, the next generation*. Armonk, NY: M. E. Sharpe, 2001.

Finkelstein, Norman. *The Holocaust Industry*. London: Vorso, 2000.

Friedländer, Saul. *Nazi Germany and the Jews, Volume I, The Years of Persecution, 1933-1939*. New York: HarperCollins Publishers, 1997.

Fritzsche, Peter. *Germans into Nazis*. Cambridge, MA: Cambridge, Harvard University Press, 1998.

Gellately, Robert. *Backing Hitler, Consent & Coercion in Nazi Germany*. Oxford University Press, 2001.

Gilbert, Martin. *The Holocaust, A History of the Jews of Europe During the Second World War*. New York: Henry Holt & Company, 1985.

Gillis, John R., ed., *Commemorations, The Politics of National Identity*. Princeton, NJ: Princeton University Press, 1994.

Goldmann, Nahum. *The Autobiography of Nahum Goldmann, Sixty Years of Jewish Life*, New York: Holt, Rinehart, Winston, 1969.

Goldhagen, Daniel Jonah. *Hitler's Willing Executioners: Ordinary Germans and the* New York: Knopf, 1996.

Grunberger, Richard. *The 12-Year Reich, A Social History of Nazi Germany, 1933-1945*. New York: Holt Rinehart Winston, 1971.

Heiden, Konrad. *Der Fuehrer*. Translated by Ralph Manheim. Boston, MA: Houghton Mifflin Co., 1944.

Held, Joseph. ed. *The Columbia History of Eastern Europe in the Twentieth Century*. New York: Columbia University Press, 1992 .

Herbert, Ulrich. *A History of Foreign Labor in Germany, 1880 - 1980*, Translated by William Templer. Ann Arbor, MI: The University of Michigan Press, 1986.

__________Ed., *National Socialist Extermination Policies: Contemporary German Perspectives and Controversies*. New York: Berghahn Books, 2000.

Herf, Jeffrey, *Divided Memory, The Nazi Past in the Two Germanys*. Cambridge, MA: Harvard University Press, 1997.

Hilberg, Raul. *The Destruction of the European Jews*, Three Volumes, Revised and Definitive Edition. New York: Holmes and Meier, 1985.

__________*The Destruction of the European Jews*. Chicago, IL: Quadrangle Books, 1961.

__________*Perpetrators, Victims, Bystanders, The Jewish Catastrophe 1933-1945*, Asheville, NC: Aaron Asher Books, 1991.

Hitler, Adolf, *Mein Kampf*, translated by Ralph Manheim. Boston, MA: Houghton Mifflin: 1971.

Homze, Edward L. *Foreign Labor in Nazi Germany*. Princeton, NJ: Princeton University Press, 1967.

Ioanid, Radu. *The Holocaust in Romania, The Destruction of the Jews and Gypsies Under the Antonescu Regime, 1940-1944*. Washington, DC: Ivan R. Dee and the United States Holocaust Memorial Museum, 2000.

Irey, Elmer L. as told to William J. Slocum, *The Tax Dodgers, The Inside Story of the T-Men's War with America's Political and Underworld Hoodlums*. New York: Greenberg Publisher, 1948.

Isaacson, Walter and Thomas, Evan. *The Wise Men, Six Friends and the World They Made*. New York: Simon & Schuster, 1986.

Johnson, Eric A. *Nazi Terror, The Gestapo, Jews, and Ordinary Germans*. New York: Basic Books, 2000.

Jordan, Ulrike, ed. *Conditions of Surrender, Britons and Germans Witness the End of the War*, I.B. London: Tauris Publishers, 1997.

Kahn, Arthur D. *Betrayal, Our Occupation of Germany*. Boston, MA: Beacon Service Co., 1950.

Kershaw, Ian. The Nazi Dictatorship, Problems & Perspectives, 4th Edition. London: Arnold, 2000.

Klee, Ernst, et al, editors. *"The Gold Old Days," The Holocaust as Seen by Its Perpetrators and Bystanders*, Translated by Deborah Burnstone. New York: Konecky & Konecky, 1988.

Klemperer, Victor. *I Will Bear Witness, A Diary of the Nazi Years, 1942-45*, translated by Martin Chalmers. New York: Random House, 1999.

__________Klemperer, Victor, translated by Martin Brady, *The Language of the Third Reich, LTI-Lingua Tertii Imperii, A Philologist's Notebook*. London: The Athlone Press, 2000.

Koestler, Arthur. *The Call Girls*. New York: Random House, 1973.

Kuklick, Bruce. *American Policy and the Division of Germany, The Clash with Russia Over Reparations*. Ithaca, NY: Cornell University Press, 1972.

Langer, Lawrence L. *Admitting the Holocaust*. Oxford, U.K.: Oxford University Press, 1995.

__________*Holocaust Testimonies, the Ruins of Memory*. New Haven, CT: Yale University Press, 1991.

__________*Preempting the Holocaust*. New Haven, CT: Yale University Press, 1998.

Lebor, Adam. *Hitler's Secret Bankers*. Secaucus, NJ: Birch Lane Press,1997.

Levi, Primo. *The Drowned and the Saved*, Translated by Ramond Rosenthal. New York: Vintage Books, 1988.

Levin, Itamar. *The Last Chapter of the Holocaust: The Struggle over Restitution of Jewish Property in Europe*. Jerusalem: Jewish Agency for Israel, 1997.

__________*The Last Chapter of the Holocaust: The Struggle over Restitution of Jewish Property in Europe*, Second Revised Edition. Jerusalem: Jewish Agency for Israel and the World Jewish Restitution Organization, 1997.

__________*The Last Deposit*. Boulder, CO: Westview, 1999.

Levin, Nora. *The Holocaust, The Destruction of European Jewry, 1933-1945*. New York: Thomas Y. Crowell Co., 1968.

__________*The Holocaust Years: The Nazi Destruction of European Jewry*. Malabar, FL: Robert Krieger Publishing Co., 1990.

Kubálková, Vendulka, Onuf, Nicholas, Kowert, Paul, eds. *International Relations in a Constructed World*. Armonk, NY: M.E. Sharpe, 1998.

Manchester, William. *The Arms of Krupp, 1587-1968*. Boston, MA: Little, Brown & Company, 1968.

Mann, Thomas. *This Peace*. New York: Alfred A. Knopf, 1938.

Marrus, Michael R. *The Holocaust in History*. New York: Meridian Books, 1987.

McCullough, David. *Truman*. New York: Simon & Schuster, 1992.

Moore, Bob. *Victims & Survivors, The Nazi Persecution of the Jews in the Netherlands, 1940-1945*. London: Arnold, 1997.

Moses, Siegfried. *Jewish Post-War Claims*. Tel Aviv: Irgun Olej Merkaz Europa, 1944.

Nicholas, Lynn. *The Rape of Europa*. New York: Vintage,1994.

Novick, Peter. *The Holocaust in American Life*. Boston: Houghton Mifflin & Co., 1999.

Onuf, Nicholas Greenwood. *World of Our Making: Rules and Rule in Social Theory and International Relations*. Columbia, SC: University of South Carolina Press, 1989.

Perlmutter, Amos. *FDR & Stalin, A Not So Grand Alliance, 1943-1945*. Columbia, MO: University of Missouri Press, 1993.

Read, Anthony and Fisher, David. *Kristallnacht, The Nazi Night of Terror.* New York: Random House, 1989.
Reich, Simon. *The Fruits of Fascism, the Postwar Prosperity in Historical Perspective.* Ithaca, NY: Cornell University Press, 1990.
Richarz, Monica, ed. *Jewish Life in Germany, Memoirs from Three Centuries*, translated by Stella P. Rosenfeld and Sidney Rosenfeld. Bloomingdale, IN: Indiana University Press, 1991.
Rickman, Gregg. *Swiss Banks and Jewish Souls.* New Brunswick, NJ: Transaction Books, 1999.
Rosenbaum, Ron. *Explaining Hitler.* New York: HarperPerennial, 1999.
Rosenberg, Tina. *The Haunted Land, Facing Europe's Ghosts After Communism.* New York: Vintage, 1995.
Ruppin, Arthur. *The Jewish Fate and Future*, translated by E.W. Dickes. Westport, CT: Greenwood Press Publishers, 1940.
__________ *The Jews in The Modern World.* London: Macmillan and Co., Ltd., 1934.
Sachar, Howard. *A History of Israel, From the Rise of Zionism to Our Time.* New York: Alfred A. Knopf, 1986.
Sagi, Nana. *German Reparations, A History of the Negotiations.* Jerusalem: Magnes Press, 1980.
Sayer, Ian and Botting. *Nazi Gold.* New York: Congdon & Weed, Inc. 1984.
Schapiro, Jane. *Inside a Class Action, The Holocaust and the Swiss Banks.* Madison, WI: University of Wisconsin, 2003.
Schwartz, Thomas Alan. *America's Germany, John J. McCloy and the Federal Republic of Germany.* Cambridge, MA: Harvard University Press, 1991.
Segev, Tom. *The Seventh Million, The Israelis and the Holocaust*, translated by Haim Watzman. New York: Hill & Wang, 1993.
Selig, Rabbi Harris L. *The Eternal Fount.* New York: Hebrew Publishing Company, 1941.
Shevardnadze, Eduard. *The Future Belongs to Freedom*, trans. by Catherine A. Fitzpatrick. New York: The Free Press, 1991.
Shirer, William L. *The Rise and Fall of the Third Reich.* New York: Simon and Schuster, 1960.
Shultz, George P. *Turmoil and Triumph, My Years as Secretary of State.* New York: Charles Scribner's Sons, 1993.
Simpson, Christopher. *The Splendid Blond Beast, Money, Law, and Genocide in the Twentieth Century.* New York: Grove Press, 1993.
Simpson, Elizabeth , ed. *The Spoils of War.* New York: Henry N. Abrams Inc. Publishers, 1997.
Smart, Ninian. *The Long Search.* Boston, MA: Little, Brown and Company, 1977.
__________ *The Religious Experience of Mankind.* New York: Charles Scribner's Sons, 1969.
Society for the History of Czechoslovak Jews. *The Jews of Czechoslovakia, Historical Studies and Surveys*, Vol. I.. Philadelphia: The Jewish Publication Society of America, 1968.

Sofsky, Wolfgang. *The Order of Terror, The Concentration Camp,* translated by William Templer. Princeton, NJ: Princeton University Press, 1993.

Sowell, Thomas. *Conquests and Cultures, An International History*. New York: Basic Books, 1998.

Speer, Albert. *Inside the Third Reich*, translated by Richard and Clara Winston. New York: Bonanza Books, 1982.

Stefan A. Riesenfeld Symposium 2001, "Fifty Years in the Making: World War II Reparation and Restitution Claims," *Berkeley Journal of International Law*, Boalt Hall School of Law. Berkeley, CA; University of California, Berkeley, Vol. 20, No. 1, 2002.

Steiner, George. *Language and Silence, Essays on Language, Literature, and the Inhuman*. New York: Atheneum, 1967.

___________*The Portage to San Cristobal of A.H.* New York: Simon and Schuster, 1981.

Steiner, Herbert and Kucsera, Recht als Unrecht, Quellen zur Wirtshaftlichen Entrechtung der Weiner Juden durch de NS-Vermögensverkehrstelle. Vienna, Austria: Österreichisches Staatsarchiv, 1993.

Steinlauf, Michael C. *Bondage to the Dead, Poland and the Memory of the Holocaust*. Syracuse, NY: Syracuse University Press, 1997.

Symposium, Holocaust Restitution: Reconciling Moral Imperatives With Legal Initiatives *and Diplomacy*, International Law Journal, November 1, 2001. New York: Fordham University.

Szulc, Tad. *The Secret Alliance, The Extraordinary Story of the Rescue of the Jews Since World War II*. New York: Farrar, Straus & Giroux, 1991.

Taylor, A.J.P. *The Origins of the Second World War*, Second Edition. Greenwich, CT: Fawcett Premire Books, 1961.

Taylor, Edmond. *The Fall of the Dynasties, The Collapse of the Old Order, 1905-1922*. New York: Doubleday & Co., 1963.

Teveth, Shabtai. *Ben-Gurion and the Holocaust*. New York: Harcourt Brace and Company, 1996

__________ *Ben-Gurion, The Burning Ground, 1886-1948*. Boston, MA: Houghton Mifflin Co., 1987.

Trevor-Roper, H.R. *The Last Days of Hitler*. London: The MacMillan Company, 1947.

__________ *Introduction and Preface, Hitler's Table Talk, 1941-1944*. New York: Enigma Books, 2000.

Tuchman, Barbara W. *Practicing History, Selected Essays*. New York: Ballantine Books, 1981.

Vernadsky, Vladimir I. The Biosphere, translated by David B. Langmuir. New York: Springer-Verlag, 1998.

Vincent, Isabel. *Hitler's Silent Partners*. New York: William Morrow & Co., 1997.

von Bernhardi, General Friedrich. *Germany and the Next War*. New York: Chas. A. Eron, 1914.

von Lang, Jochen, with Sybil, Claus eds. Translated by Ralph Manheim, *Eichmann Interrogated, Transcripts from the Archives of the Israeli Police*. New York: Da Capo Press, 1999.

Zeigler, Jean. *The Swiss, The Gold, and the Dead, How Swiss Bankers Helped Finance The Nazi War Machine*. New York: Harcourt, 1997.

Zeimke, Earl F. "Reckonings With the Past," in *The U.S. Army in the Occupation of Germany, 1944-1946*, Army Historical Series, Center of Military History, Washington, DC: United States Army, 1975.

Zuccotti, Susan. *The Holocaust, The French, and the Jews*. New York: Basic Books, 1993.

__________*The Italians and the Holocaust, Persecution, Rescue, Survival*. New York: Basic Books, 1987.

Zweig, Ronald W. *German Reparations and the Jewish World: A History of the Claims Conference*. Boulder, CO: Westview, 1987.

Articles

Adler, Emanuel. "Constructivism in International Relations: Sources, Contributions, Debates, and Future Directions," Chapter 5 of *Handbook of International Relations*, ed. By Walter Carlsmaes, Thomas Risse, and Beth A. Simmons, Sage, 2001.

Ancel, Jean, "Confiscation and Seizure of Jewish Property in Romania," *The United States Holocaust Memorial Museum Symposium, "Confiscation of Jewish property in Europe, 1933-1945: New Sources and Perspectives, March 22, 2001.*

Alk, Isadore G., and Moskovitz, Irving. "Removal of United States Controls Over Foreign-Owned Property," *Federal Bar Journal*, Vol. X, No. 1,October 1948.

AMCHA, *National Israeli Center for Psychosocial Support of Survivors of the Holocaust and the Second Generation*, May 2001.

Arad, Yitzhak, "The Holocaust of Soviet Jewry in the Occupied Territories of the Soviet Union, *Yad Vashem Studies*, Vol. XXI, 1991.

Bartov, Omer. "Defining Enemies, Making Victims: Germans, Jews, and the Holocaust," *American Historical Review* (June 1998).

__________"Did Punch Cards Fuel the Holocaust?" *New York Newsday*, March 25, 2001, p. B12.

Barzel, Neima. "Dignity, Hatred and Memory - Reparations from Germany: The Debates in the 1950s," *Yad Vashem Studies*, Vol. XXIV, 1994.

Bazyler, Michael J. "Litigating the Holocaust," *University of Richmond Law Review*, Vol. 33, No. 2, May 1999.

Bender, Daniel J., "In Re Application to Quash Grand Jury Subpoena Duces Tecum Served on the Museum of Modern Art, Case Commentary, Symposium Issue, Art Wars: International Art Disputes," *New York University Journal of International Law and Politics*, Vol. 31, No. 1, fall 1998.

Bernstein, Richard K., "Edited Presentations, Symposium Issue, Art Wars: International Art Disputes," *New York University Journal of International Law and Politics*, Vol. 31, No. 1, Fall 1998.

Binder, Sim C. "Practical Aspects of Foreign Property Control," *New York University Law Quarterly Review*, Vol XIX, No. 1, November 1941.

Bishop, Joseph W. "Judicial Construction of the Trading with the Enemy Act," *Harvard Law Review*, Vol. 62, No. 5, March 1949.

Booth, W. James, "Communities of Memory: On Identity, Memory, and Debt," *American Political Science Review*, Vol. 93, No. 2, June 1999.

Bopf, Britta, "Discrimination Against and Forced Transfer of Jewish Real Estate in the Third Reich,"*The United States Holocaust Memorial Museum Symposium, "Confiscation of Jewish Property in Europe, 1933-1945: New Sources and Perspectives, March 22, 2001.*

Boughton, James M."The Case against Harry Dexter White: Still Not Proven," *IMF Working Paper*, WP/00/149, August 2000.

Braiterman, Zachary, "Against Holocaust Sublime, Naive Reference and the Generation of Memory,"*History & Memory*, Vol. 12, No. 2, Fall/Winter 2000.

Browning, Christopher "The Final Solution in Serbia, The Semlin Judenlager—A Case Study,"*Yad Vashem Studies*, Vol. XV, 1983.

Bruzzese, Pamela, "Distributing the Past: Jewish Cultural Property in Lithuania, Symposium Issue, Art Wars: International Art Disputes," *New York University Journal of International Law and Politics*, Vol. 31, No. 1, Fall 1998.

Carlston, Kenneth S. "Foreign Funds Control and the Alien Property Custodian," *Cornell Law Quarterly*, Vol. XXXI, No. 1, September 1945.

Charney, Jonathan I., "The Impact of the International Legal System of the Growth of International Courts and Tribunals," *New York University Journal of International Law and Politics*, Vol. 31, No. 4, Summer 1999.

Checkel, Jeffrey T., "Norms, Institutions, and National Identity in Contemporary Europe," *International Studies Quarterly*, Vol. 43, No. 1, 1999.

__________"The Constructivist Turn in International Relations Theory," *World Politics*, Vol. 50, No. 2, January 1998.

Cohen, Frederick, "The Jews in the Channel Islands During the German Occupation, 1940-1945," *Institute of Contemporary History and Weiner Library*, United Kingdom, 1998, online at http://www.cihistory.org/jews/resident.html.

Cohn, Werner, " 'Bearers of a Common Fate?' The 'Non-Aryan Christian Fate-Comrades of the Paulus Bund, 1933-1939,' " *Leo Baeck Institute Yearbook*, Vol. XXXIII, 1988.

Confino, Alon, "Collective Memory and Cultural History: Problems of Method," *The American Historical Review*, Vol. 102, No. 5, December 1997.

Cooter, Robert, "Do Good Laws Make Good Citizens? An Economic Analysis of Internalized Norms," *Virginia Law Review*, Vol. 86, No. 8, November 2000.

Cotler, Irwin, "The Holocaust, Thefticide, and Restitution: A Legal Perspective, 20 *Cardozo Law Review*, 1998.

Crane, Susan A., "Writing the Individual Back into Collective Memory," *The American Historical Review*, Vol. 12, No. 5, December 1997.

Crettol, Vincent and Halbeisen, Patrick, *Monetary Policy Background to the Gold Transactions of the Swiss National Bank in the Second World War*, 1998.

Cruz, Consuelo, "Identity and Persuasion, How Nations Remember Their Pasts and Make Their Futures," *World Politics*, Vol. 52, No. 3, April 2000.

Dadrian, Vahakn, N., *The Historical and Legal Interconnections Between the Armenian Genocide and the Jewish Holocaust: From Impunity to Retributive Justice*, Yale Journal of International Law, 23, Number 2, summer 1998.

Dean, Martin, "The Expropriation of Jewish Property in *Reichskommissariat* Ostland, 1941-44," From the Author.

__________"The Finanzamt Moabit-West and the Development of the Property Infrastructure, 1933-45," *The United States Holocaust Memorial Museum Symposium, "Confiscation of Jewish property in Europe, 1933-1945: New Sources and Perspectives, March 22, 2001.*

__________"Jewish Property Seized in the Occupied Soviet Union in 1941 and 1942: The Records of the Reichshauptkasse Beutestelle, *Holocaust and Genocide Studies*, Vol. 14, No. 1, Spring 2000, pp. 83-101.

Denberg, Stephen, A. "Reclaiming Their Past: A Survey of Jewish Efforts to Restitute European Property, *Boston College Third World Law Journal*, spring 1998.

Dewey, Mary M. "Foreign Funds and Property Control - The Powers and Duties of the Alien Property Custodian," *George Washington Law Review*, Vol. 11, 1943.

Dikötter, Frank, "Race Culture: Recent Perspectives on the History of Eugenics," *American Historical Review*, Vol. 102, No. 2, April 1998.

Dingell, Jeanne, "The Haupttreuhandstelle Ost and its Sonderabteilung Altreich (1939-45) in the Context of Expropriations During the Third Reich," *The United States Holocaust Memorial Museum Symposium, "Confiscation of Jewish property in Europe, 1933-1945: New Sources and Perspectives, March 22, 2001.*

Downey, William Gerald, "Captured Enemy Property Booty of War and Seized Enemy Property," *American Journal of International Law* (July 1950), Vol. 44, No. 3.

"East Germany: Better Late," *The Economist*, March 1, 1975, p. 46.

Eisner, Frederick W. "Administrative Machinery and Steps for the Lawyer," *Law and Contemporary Problems*, Duke University School of Law, Vol. XI, No. 1, Winter-Spring 1945.

Feldman, Gerald D."Confiscation of Jewish Assets and the Holocaust," Unpublished paper delivered at the United States Holocaust Memorial Museum Conference, *Confiscation of Jewish Property in Europe, 1933-1945: New Sources and Perspectives*, March 22, 2001, courtesy of the author.

Feliciano, Hector, "Edited Presentations, Symposium Issue, Art Wars: International Art Disputes," *New York University Journal of International Law and Politics*, Vol. 31, No. 1, Fall 1998.

Foley, Edward H. Jr., "Freezing Control as a Weapon of Economic Defense," Address delivered before the Committee on Insurance Law, American Bar Association, September 29, 1941, reprinted in the New York Federal Reserve Bank, *Circular*, November 1941.

Finnemore, Martha and Sikkink, Kathryn, "International Norm Dynamics and Political Change," *International Organization*, Vol. 52, No. 4, autumn 1998.

Fitzpatrick, James, F., "Stealth UNIDROIT: Is USIA the Villain?, Symposium Issue, Art Wars: International Art Disputes," *New York University Journal of International Law and Politics*, Vol. 31, No. 1, Fall 1998.

Florini, Ann, "The Evolution of International Norms," *International Studies Quarterly*, Vol. 40, No.3, September 1996.

Friedman, Jeanette. "Israel Singer, Meeting Mr. Right," *Lifestyles* (January 1997), Vol. 26, No.147.

Garreau, Joel. "Hinges of Opportunity, When the World Moves, The Important Thing To Figure Out is What's Being Born," *Washington Post*, October 14, 2001.

Ganz, Jody Berlin, "Heirs Without Assets, and Assets Without Heirs: Recovering and Reclaiming Swiss Bank Accounts," *Fordham International Law Journal*, 1997.

Garvey, Stephen P. "Can shaming punishment educate?" *University of Chicago Law Review*, Vol. 65, No. 3, summer 1998.

Gay, Peter, "My German Question," *American Scholar* (Autumn 1998), Vol. 67, No.4.

Gerstenfeld, Manfred, "Europe's Moral Attitudes Toward the Holocaust in Light of the Current Defamation of Israel," *Jerusalem Viewpoints*, No. 475, April 1, 2002.

Glazer, Nathan, "Culture and Achievement," *Public Interest*, No. 140, summer 2000.

Goldhaber, Michael D. "Runners-Up: Holocaust Attorneys," *National Law Journal*, December 20, 2000.

Goldhagen, Daniel Jonah, "The Paradigm Challenged, Study of the Holocaust," *Tikkun*, Vol. 13, No. 3, May 15, 1998.

Gong, Gerrit W., "The Beginning of History: Remembering and Forgetting as Strategic Issues," *Washington Quarterly*, Spring 2001, Vol. 24, No. 2.

Netty Gross, "The Old Boys Club," *Jerusalem Report*, May 15, 1997.

__________"The Outrage Grows," *Jerusalem Report*, May 29, 1997.

Heilbrunn, Jacob, "A Disdain for the Past, Jörg Haider's Austria," *World Policy Journal*, Vol. XVII, No. 1, spring 2000.

__________"Germany's New Right," *Foreign Affairs*, Vol. 75, No. 6, November/December 1996.

Himmelfarb, Milton. "No Hitler, No Holocaust," *Commentary*, March 1984.

Hirschman, Albert O., "Exit, Voice, and the Fate of the German Democratic Republic,

An Essay in Conceptual History," *World Politics*, Vol. 45, No. 2, January 1993.

Hopf, Ted, "The Promise of Constructivism in International Relations Theory," *International Security*, Vol. 23, No. 1, summer 1998.

Charles Hoffman, "Czechs Want a Boost from Bronfman," *The Jerusalem Post*, October 24, 1989.

"Hungary and the Holocaust, Confrontation with the Past," Symposium Proceedings, United States Holocaust Memorial Museum, Center for Advanced Holocaust Studies, 2001.

Ignatieff, Michael, "The Danger of a world without enemies, Lemkin's World," *New Republic*, February 26, 2001, pp. 25-28.

Independent Commission of Eminent Persons Report on Dormant Accounts of Victims of *Nazi Persecution in Swiss Banks*, Final Report, December 6, 1999.

Institute of the World Jewish Congress Policy Studies and Forums: Policy Study #1, Weinbaum, Laurence, *Righting an Historic Wrong, Restitution of Jewish Property in Central and East Europe.*

Policy Study #8, Levin, Itamar, *The Fate of Stolen Jewish Properties, The Case of Austria and the Netherlands.*

Policy Study #9, Becker, Avi, *Unmasking National Myths, Europeans Challenge Their History.*

Policy Study #11, Hedin, Sven Fredrik and Elgemyr, Göran, *Sweden and the Shoah, The Untold Chapters.*

Policy Forum #13, *The Sinister Face of 'Neutrality,'the Role of Swiss Financial Institutions in the Plunder of European Jewry.*

Policy Forum #13, Zabludoff, Sidney, *'And it all but disappeared,' The Nazi Seizure of Jewish Assets.*

Policy Forum #15, Doobov, Arieh, *The Vatican and the Shoah: Purified Memory or Reincarnated Responsibility.*

Policy Forum #16, Feliciano, Hector, *The Great Culture Robbery, The Plunder of Jewish-Owned Art.*

Policy Forum #17, Trigano, Shmuel, *France Faces its Past, French Jews Face an Uncertain Future.*

International Conference: War Criminals and Nazism in Latin America: 50 Years Later, B'nai B'rith, United States Holocaust Memorial Museum, and the Washington College of Law, University of Maryland, October 20, 1996.

Jennings, M. Kent, "Political Responses to Pain and Loss, Presidential Address, American Political Science Association, 1998," *American Political Science Review*, Vol. 93, No. 1, March 1999.

Jick, Leon, "The Holocaust: its Use and Abuse within the American Public," *Yad Vashem Studies,* Vol. XIV, 1981.

Jordanova, Ludmilla. "Public History, Amateurs Study the Past,"*History Today*, May 1, 2000, No. 5, Vol. 50.

Jurgensmeyer, Mark, "The Worldwide Rise of Religious Nationalism," *Journal of International Affairs, School of International Affairs, Columbia University*, Vol. 50, No. 1, summer 1996.

Kahn, Gilbert N., *A Proposal for the Restitution and Distribution of Newly Reclaimed European-Jewish Assets*, February 1999.

Kaye, Lawrence M., "Art Wars: The Repatriation Battle, Symposium Issue, Art Wars: International Art Disputes," *New York University Journal of International Law and Politics*, Vol. 31, No. 1, fall 1998.

Karagueuzian, Hrayr S., "Unclaimed Life Insurance Policies in the Aftermath of the Armenian Genocide," *Armenian Forum*, 2, no. 2.

Kenkmann, Alfons, "The Supervision of Jews and the Plundering of Jewish Assets by the Regional Financial Administration: the Example of Westphalia," *The United States Holocaust Memorial Museum Symposium, "Confiscation of Jewish property in Europe, 1933-1945: New Sources and Perspectives, March 22, 2001.*

Kingsbury, Benedict, "Foreward: Is the Proliferation of International Courts and Tribunals a Systemic Problem?," *New York University Journal of International Law and Politics*, Vol. 31, No. 4, summer 1999.

Robert Knight, "Restitution and Legitimacy in Post-War Austria, 1945-1953," *Leo Baeck Institute Year Book XXXVI*, 1991, pp. 413-442.

Koschmann, J. Victor, The Nationalism of Cultural Uniqueness, *The American Historical Review*, Vol. 102, No. 3, June 1997.

Kouymjian, Dickran, "Confiscation and Destruction, A Manifestation of the Genocidal Process, *Armenian Forum*, 1, (autumn 1998), pp. 1-12.

Kubálková, Vendulka."Towards and International Political Theology," *Millennium: Journal of International Studies*, Vol. 29, No. 3, 2000.

Krah, Markus, "The Germans as Victims?" *Jerusalem Report*, June 17, 2002, pp. 31-33.

Kramer, Jane, "Annals of Accountability, Manna From Hell," *New Yorker*, April 28-May 5, 1997.

Kurz, Michael J. "Resolving A Dilema: The Inheritance of Jewish Property," *Cardozo Law Review*, Vol. 20, No. 2, December 1998.

Kunz, Diane B., "Remembering the Unexplainable, The Holocaust, Memory, and Public Policy," *World Policy Journal*, winter 1997-1998.

Laureys, Eric, "The Looting of Antwerp's Jewish Diamond Dealers," *The United States Holocaust Memorial Museum Symposium, "Confiscation of Jewish property in Europe, 1933-1945: New Sources and Perspectives, March 22, 2001.*

Lerner, Ralph E., "The Nazi Art Theft Problem and the Role of the Museum: A Proposed Solution to Disputes over Title, Symposium Issue, Art Wars: International Art Disputes," *New York University Journal of International Law and Politics*, Vol. 31, No. 1, fall 1998.

Lippman, Matthew, "Fifty Years After Auschwitz: Prosecutions of Nazi Death Camp Defendants," *Connecticut Journal of International Law*, Winter 1996.

__________"The Convention on the Prevention and Punishment of the Crime of Genocide, Fifty Years Later, *Arizona Journal of International and Comparative Law*, spring 1998.

__________"War Crimes Trials of German Industrialists: The Other Schindlers,"*Temple International and Comparative Law Journal*, V. 9, Fall 1995.

Lipstadt, Deborah E "The Bitburg Controversy,"*American Jewish Year Book, 1987*, Vol. 87.

Littauer, Rudolf M. "Confiscation of the Property of Technical Enemies," *Yale Law Journal*, Vol. 52, September 1943.

Lowenthal, Constance, "Edited Presentations, Symposium Issue, Art Wars: International Art Disputes," *New York University Journal of International Law and Politics*, Vol. 31, No. 1, fall 1998.

Lowenthal, David, "Fabricating Heritage," *History & Memory*, Vol. 10, No. 1, spring 1998.

Luebke, David Martin and Milton, Sybil. "Locating the Victim: An Overview of Census-Taking, Tabulation Technology, and Persecution in Nazi Germany," *IEEE Annals of the History of Computing,* (1994) Vol. 16, No. 3.

Mandelbaum, Michael, "The Future of Nationalism," *The National Interest*, No. 57, fall 1999.

Mann, Vivian B., "Special Issues Affecting Jewish Museums and Libraries, Symposium Issue, Art Wars: International Art Disputes," *New York University Journal of International Law and Politics*, Vol. 31, No. 1, fall 1998.

Mason, Malcolm S. "Relationship of Vested Assets to War Claims," *Law and Contemporary Problems*, Duke University School of Law, Vol. XVI, No. 3, Summer 1951.

Matkovski, Aleksandar, "The Destruction of Macedonian Jewry in 1943," *Yad Vashem Studies*, Vol, III, 1959.

"May 15th: Zionist Colonization of Palestine," *PFLP Bulletin* (May 1979) Nr. 27, p. 11.

May, Christopher, "Thinking, buying, selling: Intellectual property rights in political economy,"*New Political Economy* (Vol. 3, No. 1) March 1998, pp. 59-78.

Mauer, Ely, "Protection of Non-Enemy Interests in Enemy External Assets," *Law and Contemporary Problems*, Duke University School of Law, Vol. XVI, No. 3, Summer 1951.

Meinl, Susanne, "Confiscation of Jewish Property in Europe, 1933-1945 - New Perspectives," *The United States Holocaust Memorial Museum Symposium, "Confiscation of Jewish property in Europe, 1933-1945: New Sources and Perspectives, March 22, 2001.*

Merryman, John Henry, "The Free International Movement of Cultural Property, Symposium Issue, Art Wars: International Art Disputes," *New York University Journal of International Law and Politics*, Vol. 31, No. 1, fall 1998.

McKale, Donald. "A Case of Nazi 'Justice'—The Punishment of Party Members Involved in the Kristallnacht, 1938," Jewish Social Studies (July - October, 1973), Vol. XXXV, No. 3-4, p. 232.

Miller, Judith, "Erasing the Past, Europe's Amnesia About the Holocaust," *New York Times Magazine*, November 16, 1986.

Miller, Paul, "Imagined Enemies, Real Victims: Bartov's Transcendent Holocaust," *American Historical Review*, Vol. 13, No. 4, October 1998.

Moeller, Robert G., "War Stories: The Search for a Usable Past in the Federal Republic of Germany,"*The American Historical Review*, Vol., 101, No. 4, October 1996.

Mommsen, Hans. "Future Challenges to Holocaust Scholarship as an Integrated Part of the Study of Modern Dictatorship," J.B. and Maurice C. Shapiro Annual Lecture, December 13, 1999, *United States Holocaust Memorial Museum Center for Advanced Holocaust Studies*, 2000.

Monteath, Peter. "The Fuhrer's Decision; new evidence pinpoints Dec. 12, 1941 as date of decision to complete Holocaust," *History Today* (September 1998), Vol. 49, No. 9.

Myron, Paul V. "The Work of the Alien Property Custodian," *Law and Contemporary Problems*, Duke University School of Law, Vol. XI, No. 1, winter-spring 1945.

Nathan Associates, *Forced Labor Under the Third Reich*, Pts. I & II, August 20, 1999.

Neuborne, Burt. Presentation before the 2002 Institute for Law and Economic Policy Litigation Conference: Litigation in a Free Society: preliminary Reflections on Aspects of Holocaust-era Litigation in American Courts, *Washington University Law Quarterly*, Fall 2002.

Novack, David, "Law: Religious Or Secular?," *Virginia Law Review*, Vol. 86, No. 3, April 2000.

"Norway: The Courage of a Small Jewish Community; Holocaust Restitution and Anti-Semitism, and Interview with Bjarte Bruland and Irene Levin," Jerusalem Center for Public Affairs, Post-Holocaust and Anti-Semitism, No. 10, July 1, 2003.

O'Connor, Sandra Day, "Federalism of Free Nations," *New York University Journal of International Law and Politics*, Vol. 28, Nos. 1-2, summer 1999.

On First Reading, "States Act on Jewish Assets in Swiss Banks," *State Legislatures Magazine*, July 1, 1997.

Parnes, Francine. "Fighting On: Legal Actions by Nazi Victims Seeking Compensation Meet with Mixed Results," *American Bar Association, ABA Journal*, March 2002.

Philpott, Daniel, "The Religious Roots of Modern International Relations," *World Politics*, Vol. 52, No. 2, January 2000.

Polk, Judd, "Freezing Dollars Against the Axis," *Foreign Affairs*, October 1941.

Potter, Nancy. "Giving Uptake," *Social Theory and Practice* (September 22, 2000), No. 3, Vol. 26.

Ramasastry, Anita. "Secrets and Lies? Swiss Banks and International Human Rights, *Vanderbilt Journal of Transnational Law*, (Vol. 31, Number 2), March 1998.

Reevs, William Harvey. "The Control of Foreign Funds by the United States Treasury," *Law and Contemporary Problems*, Duke University School of Law, Vol. XI, No. 1, winter-spring 1945.

Reiter, Dan, "Learning, Realism, and Alliances, The Weight of the Shadow of the Past," *World Politics*, Vol. 46, No. 4, July 1994.

Response by Union Bank of Switzerland and Swiss Bank Corporation to the Letter of Senator Alfonse M. D'Amato of February 5, 1997 to Alan Greenspan of the Federal Reserve Bank, February 27, 1998.

Rickman, Gregg, "Anti-Semitism in Europe ... Again?" *Details*, Spring 2002, pp. 11-15.

Robinson, Nehemiah, *Indemnification and Jewish Reparations, Jewish Aspects*, Institute of Jewish Affairs of the World Jewish Congress, New York, 1944.

__________Spoilation and Remedial Action, The Material Damage Suffered by Jews *Under Persecution, Reparations, Restitution and* Compensation, Institute of Jewish Affairs of the World Jewish Congress, New York, 1962.

__________ "War Damage Compensation and Restitution in Foreign Countries,"*Law and Contemporary Problems*, Duke University School of Law, Vol. XVI, No. 3, summer 1951.

Rogers, Barbara."Auschwitz and the British; when the British knew about the concentration camps," *History Today* (October 1, 1999), Vol. 49, No. 10.

Rosenbaum, Eli M., "Edited Presentations, Symposium Issue, Art Wars: International Art Disputes," *New York University Journal of International Law and Politics*, Vol. 31, No. 1, fall 1998.

Rosenfeld, Alvin H. "The Assault on Holocaust Memory," in *The American Jewish Year Book, 2001*, pp. 3-20.

Rubin, Seymour J., and Schwartz, Abba. "Refugees and Reparations," *Law and Contemporary Problems*, Duke University School of Law, Vol. XVI, No. 3, summer 1951.

Ruggie, John Gerard, "What makes the world hang together? Neo-utilitarianism and the social constructivist challenge," *International Organization*, Vol. 52, No. 4, Autumn 1998, Lexis-Nexis version, downloaded December 9, 2003, p. 1.

Sargeant, Howland H, and Creamer, Henrietta L. "Enemy Patents," *Law and Contemporary Problems*, Duke University School of Law, Vol. XI, No. 1, winter-spring 1945.

Schmemann, Serge. "The Emergence of Gorbachev," *New York Times Magazine*, March 3, 1985.

Schemo, Diana Jean. Good Germans: Ignoring the Heroes. Hiding the Holocaust," *The New York Times*, June 12, 1994, Sec. 4, p. 1.

___________ "Us and Them, The Burden Of Tolerance In a World of Division," *New York Times*, December 29, 2002, Section 4, pp. 1,3.

Scott, Robert E., "The Limits of Behavioral Theories of Law and Social Order," *Virginia Law Review*, Vol. 86, No. 8, November 2000.

Shapiro, Daniel, "Repatriation: A Modest Proposal, Symposium Issue, Art Wars: International Art Disputes," *New York University Journal of International Law and Politics*, Vol. 31, No. 1, fall 1998.

Sherman, Daniel J., "Bodies and Names: The Emergence of Commemoration in Interwar France," *The American Historical Review,* Vol. 103, No. 2, April 1998.

Siemens, Rene L. "Claims on History: Holocaust Survivors are Asserting Their Rights in U.S. Courts to Insurance Benefits that European Carriers Have Long Denied," *Los Angeles Lawyer*, September 1998.

Skapska, Graóyna, Kadylo, Jaroslaw, and Bryda, Grzegorz. "Public Debate on Reprivatisation and Restitution of the Nationalised Property in Poland [sic]," Working Paper 2, *Property Restitution and the Post-1989 Transformation Process in Germany and Poland*, Joint Project of the University of Plymouth, the Humboldt-University of Berlin, and the Jagiellonian-University of Cracow, December 1999.

Slaughter, Anne-Marie and Bosco, David. "Plaintiff's Diplomacy," *Foreign Affairs*, September-October 2000.

Status Report by Credit Suisse, Union Bank of Switzerland, and Swiss Bank Corps to the *International Conference on the Return of Dormant Holocaust-Related Swiss Bank Accounts and Hidden Assets,* New York City, December 6, 1999.

Status Report from the Independent Committee of Eminent Persons, September 17, 1998.
Stern, Fritz, "The Goldhagen Controversy, One Nation, One People, One Theory?" *Foreign Affairs*, Vol. 75, No. 6, November/December 1996.
__________"The Importance of 'Why'," *World Policy Journal*, Vol. XVII, No. 1, spring 2000.
Sullivan, Andrew. "This is a Religious War," *The New York Times Magazine* (October 7, 2001).
The Conference on Jewish Material Claims Against Germany, *Fifty Years of Service to Holocaust Survivors, 1951-2001*, July 2001.
The Holocaust Educational Trust, *Nazi Gold, The British and Allied Attempt to Deal with Loot From the Second World War, and the Implications for the Tripartite Gold Commission*, March 1997.
__________*Ex-Enemy Jews - The Fate of the Assets in Britain of Holocaust Victim's and Survivors*, March 1998.
"The Restore UK Project: a Summary," The British Bankers' Association, May 8, 2000.
Tillman, Alderman Dorothy, "The Case for Reparations, Why?*How?*When?," *Ebony* August 2000.
Turlington, Edgar. "Vesting Orders Under the First War Powers Act, 1941," *American Journal of International Law*, Vol. 36, July 1943.
Van Bienia, David, "Poisoned Lives," *Washington Post Magazine*, April 24, 1988.
Vladimir I. Vernadsky, "The Biosphere and the Noösphere," *American Scientist*, January 1945, Vol. 33, No. 1.
Waite, Robert G. "Returning Jewish Cultural Property: The Handling of Books Looted by the Nazis in the American Zone of Occupation, 1945 to 1952," *Libraries and Culture,* Summer 2002, Vol. 37, No. 3, pp. 213-228.
Waxman, Mayer. "Traumatic Hand-Me-Downs: The Holocaust, Where Does It End?," *Families in Society: The Journal of Contemporary Human Services*, No. 1, Vol. 81 (January 1, 2000).
Wendt, Alexander, "Anarchy is what states make of it: the social construction of power politics," *International Organization* 46, 2, spring 1992.
__________"Constructing International Politics," International Security, Vol. 20, No. 1, September 1995.
Weinberg, Steven, "Five and a Half Utopias," *Atlantic Monthly,* January 2000.
Weinman, Martin, et al., *Das Nationalsozialistische Lagersystem*, 1990.
Weinschenk, Fritz, " 'Murderers Among Them'—German Justice and the Nazis," *3 Hofstra Law & Policy Symposium 137*, 1999.
Whitworth, Andrew. "Biosphere and Noösphere: Understanding Environmental Politics," 2001.
"Who Made Money out of WWII," *Dagens Nyheter*, October 21, 1997.
Wistrich, Robert S. "The Old-New Anti-Semitism," *The National Interest,* Number 72, summer 2003.
World War II Assets of Holocaust Victims, House Banking Committee Hearing Transcript, September 14, 1999.

Yavnai, Elisabeth M., "Nazi Seizure of Jewish Cultural Property and its Post-War Recovery: The Fate of Jewish Book Collections Found in Czechoslovakia," *The United States Holocaust Memorial Museum Symposium, "Confiscation of Jewish property in Europe, 1933-1945: New Sources and Perspectives, March 22, 2001.*

Zoellick, Robert B. "Two Plus Four, The Lessons of German Unification," *The National Interest*, No. 61, fall 2000.

Government Publications, Argentina

Commission Enquiry into the Activities of Nazism in Argentina (CEANA), Second Progress Report, July 1998.

Commission Enquiry into the Activities of Nazism in Argentina (CEANA), Final Report, 1999.

Government Publications, Austria

Günther E. Sturm, ed., "Speech by Chancellor Franz Vranitzky, Excerpt from the speech to the National Council on July 8th, 1991," *National Fund, National Fund of the Republic of Austria for Victims of National Socialism*, May 2003.

Government Publications, Czech Republic

"Jewish Gold and Other Precious Metals, Precious Stones, and Objects made of such Materials–Situation in the Czech Lands in the Years 1939 to 1945," Report by a Team of Experts Created by the Joint Task Force based on Decision No. 773 of the Czech Government, November 25, 1998.

Government Publications, France

Summary of the Work by the Study Commission on the Spoilation of Jews in France, The Matteoli Commission, Interim Report, April - December 1997.

Summary of the Work by the Study Commission on the Spoilation of Jews in France, The Matteoli Commission April 17, 2000.

Government Publications, Norway

The Reisel/Bruland Report on the Confiscation of Jewish Property in Norway During *WWII, The Official Norwegian Report*, June 1997.

Government Publications, Poland

Grela, Marek, et al. *Determinations of the Interministerial Fact-Finding Commission on the Negotiations and Implementation of the Polish-Swiss Agreements of 1949* (Polish Government, 1996).

Government Publications, Sweden

The Nazi Gold and The Swedish Riksbank, Interim Report, August 1998.

Sweden's Gold Transactions With Nazi Germany, The Government of Sweden, February 1998; available online at .

Government Publications, Switzerland

Bergier, Jean François, Director, Independent Commission of Experts (Bergier Commission), *Switzerland and Gold Transactions in WW2*, May 25, 1998.
__________*Switzerland and refugees in the Nazi era*, December 10, 1999.
__________*Gold Transactions in the Second World War: Statistical Review with Commentary*, December 1997.
__________*Switzerland, National Socialism and the Second World War, Final Report*, 2002.
Hug, Peter and Perrenoud, Marc, *Assets in Switzerland of Victims of Nazism and the Compensation Agreements with East Bloc Countries*, Translated by the Foreign Broadcast Information Service, January 23, 1997.

Government Publications, U.K.

British Policy Towards Enemy Property During and After the Second World War, April 1998.
Nazi Gold, Information from the British Archives, January 1997, Second Edition.
Papers from the London Conference on Nazi Gold, December 2-4, 1997.

Government Publications, U.S.

Administration of the Wartime Financial and Property Controls of the United States *Government*, United States Treasury Department, Foreign Funds Control, December 1942.
Brooks, James R., *Preliminary Study of Certain Financial Laws and Institutions: Decrees, France*, Treasury Department, Office of the General Counsel, June 1, 1944.
__________*Preliminary Study of Certain Financial Laws and Institutions: France*, Treasury Department, Office of the General Counsel, June 1, 1944.
Callis, Louis E., *Preliminary Study of Certain Financial Laws and Institutions: Greece*, Treasury Department, Office of the General Counsel, May 1944.
Census of American-Owned Assets in Foreign Countries, United States Department of the Treasury, Office of the Secretary, United States Government Printing Office, 1947.
Current Developments in Holocaust Assets Restitution, Senate Banking Committee Hearing Transcript, July 22, 1998.
Documents on German Foreign Policy 1918-1945, Series C, "The Third Reich: First *Phase," Vol. V, March-October 1936*, U.S. Government Printing Office, 1966.
Documents Pertaining to Foreign Funds Control, United States Treasury Department, June 15,1945.
Elimination of German Resources for War, Testimony of Russell A. Nixon, former Acting Director, Division of Investigation of Cartels and External Assets, Office of Military Government in Germany (United States), Hearing of the Subcommittee of the Committee on Military Affairs, United States

Senate, 79th Congress, February 25, 1946 (Washington, D.C.: United States Government Printing Office, 1946).

Eizenstat, Stuart ed., *Preliminary Study on U.S. and Allied Efforts To Recover and Restore Gold and Other Assets Stolen or Hidden by Germany During World War II*, May 1997.

__________*U.S. and Allied Wartime and Postwar Relations and Negotiations With Argentina, Portugal, Spain, Sweden, and Turkey on Looted Gold and German External Assets and U.S. Concerns About the Fate of the Wartime Ustasha Treasury*, June 1998.

Heirless Property Issues of the Holocaust, House International Relations Committee Hearing Transcript, August 6, 1998.

Holocaust Victims Assets in Swiss Banks, Senate Banking Committee New York City Field Hearing Transcript, October 16, 1996.

Hynning, Clifford J., *Preliminary Study of Certain Financial Laws and Institutions: Decrees, Germany*, Treasury Department, Office of the General Counsel, May 1944.

__________*Preliminary Study of Certain Financial Laws and Institutions: Germany*, Treasury Department, Office of the General Counsel, May 1944.

Lancione, Nelson, *Preliminary Study of Certain Financial Laws and Institutions: Denmark*, Treasury Department, Office of the General Counsel, September 1944.

Klepper, Sidney et al, *Report on the Investigation of the Deutsche Bank, Office of the Military Government for Germany*, November 1946.

Legacies of the Holocaust, Senate Foreign Relations Committee Hearing Transcript, April 5, 2000.

Locker, Melville E., *Preliminary Study of Certain Financial Laws and Institutions: Decrees, The Netherlands*, Treasury Department, Office of the General Counsel, May 1943.

__________*Preliminary Study of Certain Financial Laws and Institutions: The Netherlands*, Treasury Department, Office of the General Counsel, May 1943.

Mayer, Belle, *Preliminary Study of Certain Financial Laws and Institutions: Decrees, Hungary*, Treasury Department, Office of the General Counsel, September 1944.

__________*Preliminary Study of Certain Financial Laws and Institutions: Hungary*, Treasury Department, Office of the General Counsel, September 1944.

__________*Preliminary Study of Certain Financial Laws and Institutions: Decrees, Yugoslavia*, Treasury Department, Office of the General Counsel, September 1, 1943.

__________*Preliminary Study of Certain Financial Laws and Institutions: Yugoslavia*, Treasury Department, Office of the General Counsel, September 1, 1943.

Montgomery, Doris E., *Preliminary Study of Certain Financial Laws and Institutions: Decrees, Rumania*, Treasury Department, Office of the General

Counsel, November 1944.

_________*Preliminary Study of Certain Financial Laws and Institutions: Rumania,* Treasury Department, Office of the General Counsel, November 1944.

Nominations of: Stuart E. Eizenstat to be Under Secretary of Commerce, Hearing Before the Committee on Banking, Housing, and Urban Affairs, United States Senate, One Hundred Fourth Congress, Second Session, March 19, 1996 (Washington, D.C.: United States Government Printing Office, 1996)

Plunder and Restitution: The U.S. and Holocaust Victims' Assets, Findings and Recommendations of the Presidential Advisory Commission on Holocaust Assets in the United States and Staff Report, December 2000.

Private Bill Initiative for Christoph Meili, Senate Judiciary Committee Hearing Transcript, May 20, 1997.

Proceedings of the Washington Conference on Holocaust-Era Assets, November 30-December 4, 1998.

Property Transferred Under the Nazi Regime in Germany. Foreign Economic Administration, Liberated Areas Branch, United States Government. June 1944.

Restitution in the Four Zones, Office of Military Government for Germany (U.S.), November 1947.

Restitution of Holocaust Assets, House Banking Committee Hearing Transcript, February 9-10, 2000.

Scott, Robert D., *Preliminary Study of Certain Financial Laws and Institutions: Decrees, Austria*, Treasury Department, Office of the General Counsel, September 1944.

__________*Preliminary Study of Certain Financial Laws and Institutions: Austria*, Treasury Department, Office of the General Counsel, September 1944.

_________*Preliminary Study of Certain Financial Laws and Institutions: Norway*, Treasury Department, Office of the General Counsel, August 15, 1943.

_________*War Laws of Norway, A Study of the Laws of the Kingdom and the Occupied Territory*, United States Treasury Department, Office of the General Counsel, 1943.

Smith, Fred, B., *Preliminary Study of Certain Financial Laws and Institutions: Decrees, Czechoslovakia*, Treasury Department, Office of the General Counsel, October 1944.

_________Preliminary Study of Certain Financial Laws and Institutions: *Czechoslovakia*, Treasury Department, Office of the General Counsel, October 1944.

Swiss Banks and Attempts to Recover Assets Belonging to the Victims of the Holocaust, Senate Banking Committee Hearing Transcript, May 15, 1997.

Swiss Banks and the Shredding of Holocaust-Era Documents, Senate Banking Committee Hearing Transcript, Mary 6, 1997.

Swiss Banks and the Status of Assets of Holocaust Survivors or Heirs, Senate Banking Committee Hearing Transcript, April 23, 1996.

The Disposition of Assets Deposited in Swiss Banks by Missing Nazi Victims, House Banking Committee, December 11, 1996.

The Eizenstat Report and Related Issues Concerning United States and Allied Efforts to *Restore Gold and Other Assets Looted by the Nazis During WWII*, House Banking Committee Hearing Transcript, July 25, 1997.

The Long Road Home: Struggling for Property Rights in Post-Communist Europe, Commission on Security and Cooperation in Europe Hearing Transcript, March 25, 1999.

The Restitution of Art Objects Seized by the Nazis from Holocaust Victims and Insurance *Claims of Certain Holocaust Victims and Heirs*, House Banking Committee Hearing Transcript, February 12, 1998.

The Status of Insurance Restitution for Holocaust Victims and Their Heirs, House Committee on Government Reform Hearing Transcript, November 8, 2001.

Thompson, Emily, *Preliminary Study of Certain Financial Laws and Institutions: Decrees, Belgium*, Treasury Department, Office of the General Counsel, July 1944.

__________*Preliminary Study of Certain Financial Laws and Institutions: Belgium*, Treasury Department, Office of the General Counsel, July 1944.

World War II Assets of Holocaust Victims, House Banking Committee Hearing Transcript, September 14, 1999.

Government Publications, U.S., New York City and State

New York City Council Hearing on the Swiss Banks, Transcript, February 10, 1997.

Papers from the International Conference on the Return of Dormant Holocaust-Related *Swiss Bank Accounts and Hidden Assets,* New York City, December 6, 1999.

Oral History Interviews

Oral History Interview with Lucius D. Battle, Harry S. Truman Presidential Museum and Library, downloaded, May 27, 2001.

Oral History Interview with Nathan M. Becker, by Richard D. McKinzie, Harry S. Truman. Museum and Presidential Library, June 19, 1973, available online at downloaded August 13, 2002.

Oral History Interview with Bernard Bernstein, Harry S. Truman Presidential Museum and Library, available online at downloaded, May 27, 2001.

Oral History Interview with Lucius D. Clay, Harry S. Truman Presidential Museum and Library, downloaded, August 13, 2002.downloaded, May 27, 2001.

Oral History Interview with General William H. Draper, Harry S. Truman Presidential Museum and Library, downloaded, December 27, 2002.

Oral History Interview with Elbridge Durbrow, Harry S. Truman Presidential Museum and Library, downloaded, August 13, 2002.

Oral History Interview with W. Averill Harriman, Harry S. Truman Presidential Museum and Library, downloaded, August 13, 2002.

Oral History Interview with Ben Brown Hill, Harry S. Truman Presidential Museum and Library, downloaded, December 27, 2002.
Oral History Interview with Charles P. Kindleberger, Harry S. Truman Presidential Museum and Library, downloaded, May 27, 2001.
Oral History Interview with E. Allan Lightner, Jr., Harry S. Truman Presidential Museum and Library, downloaded, October 1, 2002.
Oral History Interview with Sir Roger Makins, Harry S. Truman Presidential Museum and Library, downloaded, October 1, 2002.
Oral History Interview with Paul Porter, Harry S. Truman Presidential Museum and Library, downloaded, October 1, 2002.
Oral History Interview with James W. Riddleburger, Harry S. Truman Presidential Museum and Library, downloaded, October 1, 2002.
Oral History Interview with Judge Samuel I. Rosenman, Harry S. Truman Presidential Museum and Library, downloaded, October 1, 2002.

Unpublished Works

Clarke, Margaret, *Safe Haven Project*, Foreign Economic Administration, 1945.
Gilbert, Abby L. U.S. Department of the Treasury, "Defrosting of Foreign Funds Control."
__________"Foreign Funds Control, Freezing of Assets."
__________ "Alien Property Custodian - Bureaucratic History."
Krakowski, Morris. *Memoir*, June 1995.
Maissen, Thomas Presentation before a Panel Discussion at the Swiss Embassy in Washington, DC, December 8,1997.
Mills, E. Richard. *Image Crisis Management*, an unpublished Masters Thesis, American University, 1999.

Theses/Dissertations

Grbovaz, Stanley J. "United States Foreign Funds Control," Masters Thesis, The George Washington University School of Government, June 3, 1942.
Harver, Jeffrey David, "The Cultural Production of Domination in Nazi Germany: Architecture as Propaganda, Masters Thesis, Simon Fraser University, 1990.
Masurovsky, Marc Jean *The Safehaven Program: The Allied Response to Nazi Post-Defeat Planning 1944-1948*, Masters' Thesis, American University, May 4, 1990.

Internet Sources

Armstrong, Cara and Nelson, Karen, "Ritual and Monument, *Architronic,* Vol. 2.05, Online at http://architronic.saed.kent.edu./v2n2/v2n2.05.html.
Boekle, Henning, Rittberger, Volker, Wagner, Wolfgang. "Norms and Foreign Policy: Constructivist Foreign Policy Theory," Center for International Relations/Peace and Conflict Studies, Institute for Political Science, University of Tübingen, 1999, available online at http://www.uni-tuebingen.de/uni/spi/taps/tap34a.htm.

Bowman, James. "What Happened to Honor?," *The Bradley Lecture*, American Enterprises Institute, June 10, 2002, available online at http://jamesbowman.net/artcle_print_version.asp?pibID=1169.

Breitman, Richard."What Chilean Diplomats Learned about the Holocaust," National Archives and Records Administration, Interagency Working Group on the Nazi War Crimes Disclosure Act, July 2, 2001, available online at http://www.nara.gov/iwg/papers/chile.html.

Bytwerk, Randall. *German Propaganda Archive*, on-line at http://www.clavin.edu.edu/acedemic/cas.

Cohen, Frederick. "The Jews in the Channel Islands During The German Occupation, 1940-1945," Jersey Heritage Trust and the Institute of Contemporary History and Weiner Library Limited, 2000, pp. 7-11, available online at http://www.chihistory.org/jews/resident.htm.

Cohen,Richard A. "The Holocaust is a Christian Issue," Paper presented on June 20, 2001, in Jerusalem at an international conference marking the 85th birthday of Professor Emil Fackenheim, available online at http://ghansel.free.fr/holocauste.html.

Goldberg, Jonah."Don Imus, Moral Philosopher," *National Review Online*, July 26, 2001, the website of the *National Review*, http://www.nationalreview.com/nr_commnent/nr_comment072601b.shtml.

Kater, Michael H."Order as a Premise for Destruction," *Simon Wiesenthal Center Annual 3*, available online at http://motlc.wiesenthal.com/resources/books/annual3/chap14.html.

Lowenthal, David. "Fabricating Heritage," *History & Memory*, Vol. 10, No. 1, available online at http://iupjournals.org/history/ham10-1.htm, p. 3 .

Patterson, Charles. Preface to *Eternal Treblinka, Our Treatment of Animals and the Holocaust,* Internet advertising for the book, http://www.powerfulbook.com/index.html.

Posting by Aliza Kolker, re: IBM and the Holocaust, February 14, 2001, H-Net List for History of the Holocaust, available online at http://www2.h-net.msu.edu/~holoweb/.

Schlampige Anklage, Der Amerikaner Edwin Black wirft IBM eine Mitverantwortung am Holocaust vor, doch sein schlect recherchiertes Buch bietet vor allem eins: Desinformation," ("Slipshod Charge, The American Edwin Black reproaches IBM for its joint responsibility in the Holocaust, but his badly researched book offers above all one thing: disinformation.) translated by Monkia Muggli, Berliner Morgenpost, February 18, 2001, in a posting of February 18, 2001 by Monika Muggli on the H-Net List for History of the Holocaust, available online at http://www2.h-net.msu.edu/~holoweb/ .

Scott, Shirley V. "International Lawyer: Handmaidens, Chefs, or Birth Attendants? A Response to Philip Alston," *European Journal of International Law* (Vol. 9, No. 4), 1998, available online at http://www.eji.org/jounral/Vol9/No4/art6.html.

"The Importance of Understanding the World's Worldviews," Extract from Ninian Smart, The World's Religions (London: Cambridge University Press,

1992) available online at http://www.mcauley.acu.edu.au/~yuri/vb/religions.htm..

Wright, Robert. "The Accidental Creationist, Why Stephen Jay Gould is Bad for Evolution," originally published in *The New Yorker* (December 13, 1999), available online from a website offering the author's book, *Nonzero: The Logic of Human Destiny*. New York: Pantheon Books, 2000, online at http://www.nonzero.org/newyorker.htm.

Index